From Sea to Shining Sea

To Glennis —
in Jesus' Love,
Peter Marshall
Feb. 1990

p. 18
p. 125 - causes of War of 1812
p. 228 - slavery
p. 249 - slaves, not married offically

p. 333 survived attack of grizzly bear
p. 333-4 Jedediah Smith - godly man
p. 338 Dr. Marcus Whitman

p. 394 Rev. Elijah P. Lovejoy

BY Peter Marshall and David Manuel:

The Light and the Glory

From Sea to Shining Sea

Peter Marshall/David Manuel

Fleming H. Revell Company
Old Tappan, New Jersey

Unless otherwise identified Scripture quotations are from the King James Version of the Bible.

Library of Congress Cataloging-in-Publication Data

Marshall, Peter, 1940–
From sea to shining sea.

Bibliography: p.
Includes index.
1. United States—History—1783–1865. 2. United States—Social conditions—To 1865. 3. United States—Church history—19th century. 4. History (Theology) 5. Providence and government of God. I. Manuel, David. II. Title.
E301.M35 1986 973 85-20428
ISBN 0-8007-1451-2

Published by Fleming H. Revell Company
Old Tappan, New Jersey 07675

Printed in the United States of America

TO

the memory of the unknown pioneer families
who braved unknown perils and suffering
as they headed west
and sometimes left unmarked graves.

Acknowledgements

As in our previous volume, *The Light and the Glory,* we would like to again thank Cay M. Andersen and Judy H. Sorensen, directors of the Community of Jesus, for their steadfast support and encouragement, and the rest of the members of the Community for their prayers. Once again, we owe deep appreciation to our wives, Barbara Manuel and Edith Marshall, who have given new definition to the word *long-suffering.* Finally, we acknowledge our complete dependence on the continuing grace and inspiration of our heavenly Father, without which this book could never have been written.

Contents

Seeds of Darkness

We began our previous book with a look at the condition of America today—or rather at America eight years ago, when that book was completed. We were concerned with the worsening state of moral decay, pointing to the national divorce rate, which had reached one marriage in three, and sexual permissiveness, which had allowed pornography to insinuate itself into the fabric of our daily life. As part of the antidote, and to restore to American Christians the spiritual heritage of which many were unaware, we undertook to examine the first three hundred years of our country's history and to discern, if possible, God's hand in the nation's affairs. *The Light and the Glory* did that, and it appeared that God did have a plan for America, just as the Pilgrims and Puritans maintained.

According to the journals, letters, and sermons of those First Comers, they sailed for the New World in response to God's call on their lives to be a covenanted people under Him, and proof to the rest of the world that it was possible for men to live with one another in harmony. Through great trials and perils, they held on to that vision, and the Lord sustained them. Finally with victory in the War for Independence, America had won her freedom to become "one nation under God."

But neither God's plan for America, nor His hand in preserving the possibility of that plan coming to pass, ended with the Treaty of Paris in 1783. Indeed, in many ways the real struggle had only just begun. For without the threat of being crushed under the heel of the mightiest military power on earth and indefinite years of cruel subjection, the United States of America were about as disunited as it was possible to be. Moreover, their shared Christian faith—the mortar that had held them together in so many crises—had lost its vitality. For a variety of reasons, the Church had lost its traditional role of spiritual leadership. Perhaps this resulted from the arrival of peace after so long and harrowing an ordeal, or the explosive prosperity of a young republic with no enemies and limitless natural resources, or the ministers who had once again made the conditions for conversion so impossible that even many churchgoers despaired of ever joining the ranks of the redeemed.

A profound change took place in America, and indeed throughout the western world, for the possibilities of democracy seized the imagination of idealists everywhere. In a few years, the French would trigger their own revolution, boasting that, unlike America, their new republic would achieve the Brotherhood of Man, without the Fatherhood of God as a prerequisite. Their version of republicanism, a heady brew, flattered man into believing that his own intellect reigned supreme. Its proponents made it a new secular religion, and its evangelists, among them American heroes like Tom Paine, brought their faith to our shores with missionary zeal. And because no strong, vital, appealing Christian faith opposed them, almost overnight their cynical, mocking Deism made astonishing inroads into the centers of our creative thinking.

An antispiritual invasion rolled over our land. But as He always had in the past, God raised up the men to stop it—men like Timothy Dwight and Lyman Beecher. And He had a cadre ready to lead the counterattack: Francis Asbury and his totally given soldiers of the Cross—the Methodist circuit riders who, like Whitefield and company before them, wanted nothing so much as to be "on the stretch for God." With these and other frontier Presbyterian and Baptist preachers acting as His vanguard, God shed His grace on America in a tremendous outpouring of His Spirit that came to be known as the Second Great Awakening. Indeed, though it subsided, it never ceased: wave upon wave of revival would break across the land, with new converts accepting their responsibility to love their neighbors, in addition to loving the Lord their God. In the wake of revival came a reform movement the likes of which the country had never seen. Foreign and home missionary societies were founded, along with innumerable charitable institutions for the deaf and the blind, the old and the destitute, the orphaned and the mentally ill. Reform politicians won office in landslide elections, and temperance leagues sprang up everywhere, to do battle with one of the most devastating social problems of the era: demon rum.

Yet all these inspired measures barely kept America on the rails as the concurrent tensions of sectional rivalry threatened to topple her into the gorge. The North was rapidly becoming an industrialized society, while the South, with its much greater heat and humidity, was destined to play an agricultural role, and the West beckoned small farmers from all other sections. Inevitably, the interests and desires of the different sections would clash, but there was one impediment in America's path that seemed certain to derail her, for at the bottom it was a spiritual matter, one in direct conflict with the vision that God had given the First Comers. As such, although flesh and blood would contest it, the ultimate battle was between principalities and powers. That impediment was slavery.

Ever since Christopher Columbus (whose first name meant "Christ bearer") sighted the New World, the struggle between the forces of light and darkness over the destiny of the North American continent had begun. For if, as the Pilgrims and Puritans believed, God had a special plan for America, then the dark prince of this planet was aware of that plan and would do everything in his power to thwart it. *The Light and the Glory* traced that struggle, and the victory of the Light, as the fledgling nation won her right to exist.

But the war was far from over. The enemy was content to watch and wait, confident that it would not be long before greed and jealousy, self-righteousness and self-reliance would reassert themselves and begin to undo all that had been accomplished. For long before, he had sown seeds of darkness. No one paid much attention to the tiny shoots at first, but they would grow into a fearsome jungle that would cover the sky and threaten to choke out the Light.

At the time of harvest, the weeds of slavery would be separated out from the wheat and destroyed by fire—but that time was not now. To attempt such a separation before harvest time would be to jeopardize the entire field. It appeared, therefore, that God's plan for America, during the first half century of her independence, was essentially to preserve the possibility of her fulfilling her call, while the enemy did all he could to divide her house against itself prematurely, with slavery his most effective wedge.

This book opens in Philadelphia, in the summer of 1787, when the seeds of darkness were planted and sealed in the Constitution, and closes exactly fifty years later, with the murder of antislavery editor Elijah Lovejoy, and with John C. Calhoun, who had assumed Jefferson's mantle as the South's leading thinker and spokesman, declaring before the Senate that the movement to abolish slavery and the Union itself could no longer coexist.

In the interim, we will come to know the pioneers and presidents, the missionaries and mountain men, the soldiers and circuit riders who kept the vision of America's destiny in their hearts, and the flame of freedom alive. By no means did all Americans share the vision, and more often than not, God was working His purpose out through men who did not have close personal relationships with Him. Their lack of faith could not impede His design, for God was God, the Lord of all history. But there needed to be enough committed Christians to get the job done and to make democracy work. For democracy is not a natural form of government; it is supernatural, relying on a dynamic Judeo-Christian ethos to provide the continual spiritual renewal needed to inspire naturally selfish men to selflessness. The framers of the Constitution understood the reality of man's fallen nature, which was why they created our unique system of checks and balances. It took a supernatural infusion of God's grace for man to love his neighbor as himself, and on that selfless love, democracy has always depended.

These are some of the things we will see in America's first half century, as her wagons roll and she stretches westward over plains and mountains. We need to see them, for the Scripture tells us that "without a vision, the people perish" (*see* Proverbs 29:18). If we are to recover our nation's God-given purpose, we must know our Christian heritage, and the many unsuspected ways in which God has blessed us . . . as He poured out His grace from sea to shining sea.

PETER MARSHALL
DAVID MANUEL
Cape Cod, Massachusetts

From Sea to Shining Sea

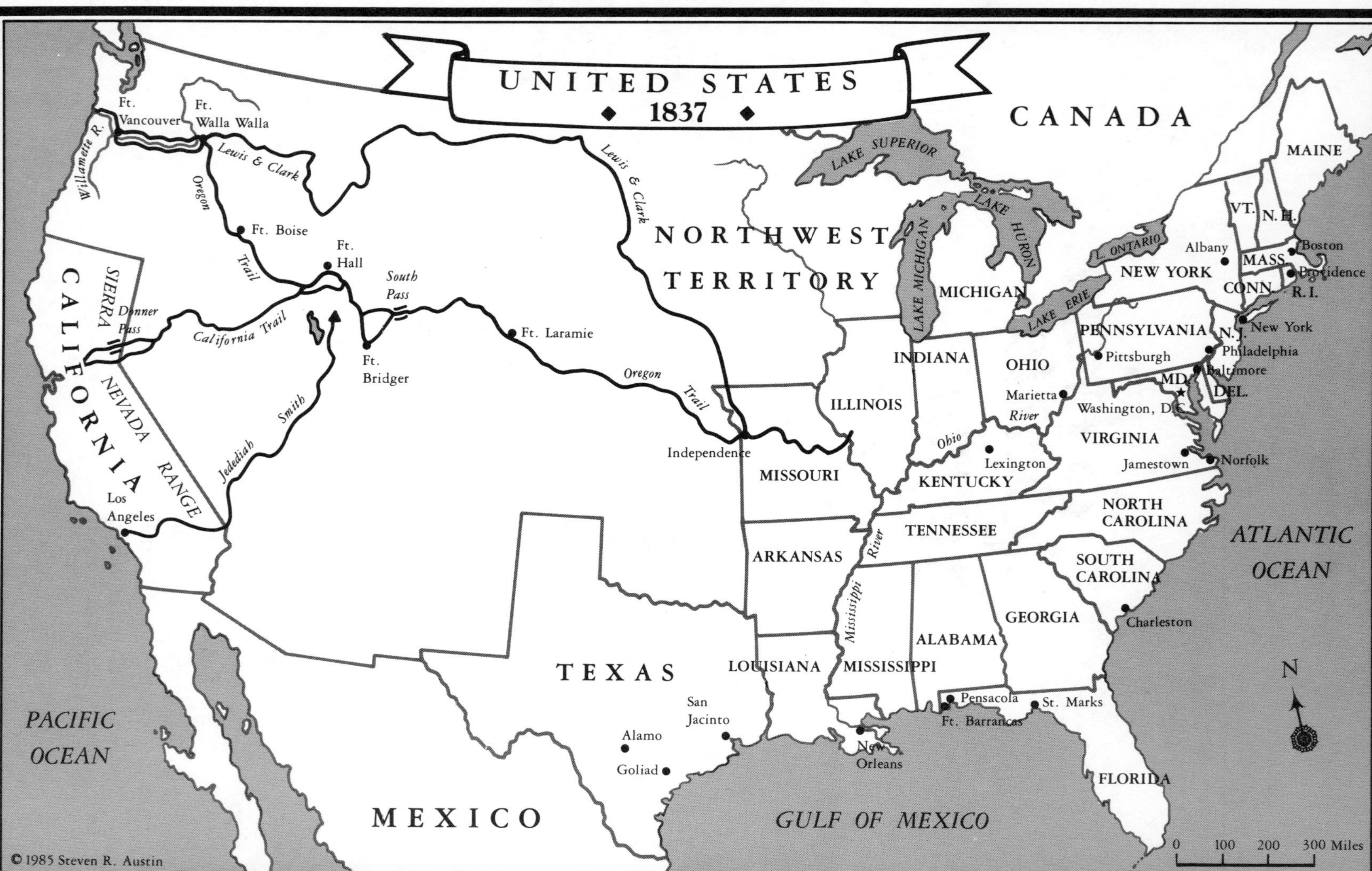
UNITED STATES
1837
CANADA
NORTHWEST
TERRITORY
LAKE SUPERIOR
LAKE MICHIGAN
LAKE HURON
L. ONTARIO
LAKE ERIE
MAINE
VT.
N.H.
MASS.
CONN.
R.I.
NEW YORK
N.J.
PENNSYLVANIA
MD.
DEL.
MICHIGAN
INDIANA
OHIO
ILLINOIS
MISSOURI
KENTUCKY
VIRGINIA
NORTH CAROLINA
SOUTH CAROLINA
TENNESSEE
ARKANSAS
GEORGIA
ALABAMA
MISSISSIPPI
LOUISIANA
FLORIDA
TEXAS
MEXICO
CALIFORNIA
SIERRA NEVADA RANGE
Donner Pass
PACIFIC OCEAN
ATLANTIC OCEAN
GULF OF MEXICO
Ft. Vancouver
Ft. Walla Walla
Willamette R.
Lewis & Clark
Oregon Trail
Ft. Boise
Ft. Hall
South Pass
Ft. Bridger
Ft. Laramie
California Trail
Jedediah Smith
Los Angeles
Independence
Albany
Boston
Providence
New York
Philadelphia
Baltimore
Pittsburgh
Washington, D.C.
Marietta
Ohio River
Lexington
Jamestown
Norfolk
Mississippi River
Charleston
Pensacola
Ft. Barrancas
St. Marks
New Orleans
San Jacinto
Alamo
Goliad
N
0 100 200 300 Miles
© 1985 Steven R. Austin

1

1787

The last rays of the setting sun streamed through the tall south windows, which were opened as wide as possible to admit any hint of a breeze. The midsummer humidity in Philadelphia could be brutal, and today it was unbearable. Behind desks covered with green felt and arranged in a semicircle facing the chairman's, the delegates slumped in various attitudes of indifference, some making an attempt to concentrate on what was being said, most not even bothering. Alexander Hamilton, the delegate from New York, had already gone home in disgust, and several other delegations were contemplating similar action. A delegate from one of the smaller states was on his feet, making yet another impassioned plea for equality in at least one of the two bodies that would represent the legislative arm of the republic whose constitution they had gathered to construct. He closed by insinuating that if the large states refused to grant it, they might well find the smaller states withdrawing and seeking succor from more receptive foreign powers. When he finished, a delegate from one of the larger states wearily got to his feet to offer the obligatory rebuttal, insinuating that the larger states might have to resort to force, to keep foreign powers out of the land whose freedom from these powers had been recently purchased with so much blood and treasure.

One can imagine Ben Franklin shaking his head in despair. Eleven years before, he and a number of those now present had met in this very room and reached a decision that would alter the course of history: they declared their independence from Great Britain and gave birth to a new nation. It was the most momentous occasion of their lives, and each of them knew it. How proudly Colonials had hailed the United States of America, and how valiantly they had followed the red, white, and blue banner into battle! Though vastly outgunned, outshipped, and outnumbered, they had stood toe to toe with the oppressor, and beaten the mightiest military power on earth to a standstill.

They had won their independence, and some preachers had even declared that the long-awaited arrival of the Kingdom of God on earth was now at hand. Let the Millennium begin!

Ben Franklin was not much for millenniums. He had seen preachers come and go, and precious few had lived their own lives with the selfless faith they expounded. There had been his evangelist friend, George Whitefield, of course; he had never known another man of God whose heart was so given to his Master. But not even Whitefield could persuade America's foremost scientist and philosopher to give his own heart to Christ. Yet as he approached the end of his days on this mortal coil, having now exceeded his allotted fourscore years, he might have found himself wondering. . . .

The next speaker droned on, and Franklin eased the watch out of his waistcoat pocket, dipped his head ever so slightly, so that he could see it through the spectacles perched on the end of his nose, and noted that there was still a half hour to go before they would be mercifully released, and he might enjoy a bit of cold roast beef and a glass of claret. Dutifully, he turned his attention to what the man from Connecticut was saying—something about deploring the tariffs the states were raising against one another, as if they were separate countries. As the earnest young man went into specifics, Franklin groaned and glanced at Washington, presiding over this travesty, noting in his face the sense of tragic loss that he himself felt.

Washington was all that was holding this convention together. Many of them had come in response to his personal, urgent appeal, and while as chairman he refused to enter into the wrangling debate, the strength of his character and the universal respect it commanded were all that kept this pot from boiling over and other states from following the lead of the now departed New York. Such was the magnitude of the General's dignity that a number of incidents were preserved in the diaries of his contemporaries. For example: in between sessions, James Madison and some friends were discussing Washington's demeanor, when Gouverneur Morris, the tall and peg-legged, flamboyant and brilliant—albeit as John Adams privately noted, erratic and *très légere*—delegate from Pennsylvania, denied that Washington was such a formidable figure. Certainly, Morris exclaimed, *he* did not stand in awe of him, or of any other man, for that matter. Very well, Madison replied, if Morris, on the next social occasion where Washington was present, would go up to him and give him a friendly clap on the back as he greeted him, Madison would buy their group dinner. Morris accepted the challenge. At the next opportunity, he did greet Washington in just such a familiar manner. The General's response to this liberty was so chilling that Morris withdrew, shaken and abashed. At Madison's dinner, he confessed that, while he had won the wager, he would never again repeat the experiment.[1]

Yet despite Washington's firm command of the convention, the bickering went on interminably, and Franklin was ready to give up hope. How far they had sunk, since that sunburst of light in '76! Then the states had supported one another totally and without thinking. But victory, a few years of peace, and a beckoning frontier had wrought appalling changes in the states' attitudes toward one another. Now they vied with each other for foreign trade, some of the larger states even sending ambassadors abroad, to gain a competitive edge. And now that they were out from under Britain's authority, men seemed to resent coming under *any* authority, even the feeble Confederation they themselves had constituted. In Massachusetts, the farmers were rebelling against having to pay usurious taxes, and James Warren, who had written to Ambassador John Adams, over in London, "Money is the only object attended to, and the only acquisition that commands respect. Patriotism is ridiculed; integrity and ability are of little consequence,"[2] now followed with another letter: "We are now in a state of anarchy and confusion bordering on civil war."[3] Indeed, the whiff of rebellion seemed to hang in the air, and in Paris, Ambassador Thomas Jefferson for one, was all for it. In a letter to his friend and fellow Virginian, James Madison, he briefly revealed his true colors: "I hold it that a little rebellion now and then is a good thing . . . a medicine necessary for the sound health of government."[4]

Small wonder, then, that in Philadelphia, the delegates eyed one another with suspicion, construing the worst possible motives behind every proposal, every seemingly innocuous compromise. Those who had been present in this room on July 4, 1776, and had affixed their signatures to the most significant document of their age were at the point of despair: the "United" States—it was almost a mockery, and soon it would be a tragedy, a noble experiment, sunk beneath the waves of jealousy and petty bickering. What possible good could come out of all this contention? Would they soon be reduced to thirteen satrapies, pathetically scrambling to see which could align itself with what European monarchy? It would take a miracle to bring anything out of this chaos. . . .

The speaker sat down, and another was about to take his turn when Franklin caught Washington's eye and indicated that he wished to speak. The General nodded and asked the next speaker if he would defer to the most senior delegate. Surprised, the would-be speaker acceded, and Franklin, leaning on his walking stick, stood erect. This would be one speech he would deliver himself, rather than asking his fellow delegate from Pennsylvania to read it for him. In that instant, boredom departed from the chamber, as all eyes turned to see what he would say.

"How has it happened, sir, that we have not hitherto once thought of humbly applying to the Father of lights to illuminate our understanding? In the beginning of the contest with Britain, when we were sensible of danger, we had daily prayers in this room for Divine protection. Our prayers, sir," he looked at Washington, "were heard, and they were graciously answered. All of us who were engaged in the struggle must have observed frequent instances of a superintending Providence in our favor. . . . And have we now forgotten this powerful friend? Or do we imagine we no longer need His assistance?"

There was dead silence in the room. Franklin, well-known for his Rationalist views, was hardly the person they would have expected to ask such a question. But he was not finished, and now he turned again to Washington. "I have lived, sir, a long time, and the longer I live, the more convincing proofs I see of this truth: 'that God governs in the affairs of man.' And if a sparrow cannot fall to the ground without His notice, is it probable that an empire can rise without His aid?"

Whitefield himself could not have put it better. Franklin seemed to gain strength as he continued. "We have been assured, sir, in the sacred writings that except the Lord build the house, they labor in vain that build it. I firmly believe this. I also believe that, without His concurring aid, we shall succeed in this political building no better than the builders of Babel; we shall be divided by our little, partial, local interests; our projects will be confounded; and we ourselves shall become a reproach and a byword down to future ages. And what is worse, mankind may hereafter, from this unfortunate instance, despair of establishing government by human wisdom and leave it to chance, war, or conquest."

Washington slowly nodded; the old statesman was expressing his own misgivings. Franklin shifted his weight and concluded. "I therefore beg leave to move that, henceforth, prayers imploring the assistance of Heaven and its blessing on our deliberations, be held in this assembly every morning before we proceed to business."[5]

He sat down, and in the ensuing silence no one moved to second his motion; no one moved at all. It was clearly the most extraordinary speech that had been delivered in the three months that they had been convening. And of all people to make such a motion! It was out of the question, of course; the French Enlightenment and the new Rationalism, personified by Tom Paine's *Age of Reason,* had rendered such public appeals to faith unfashionable. Indeed, the long era of church's influence on state was drawing to a close; this convention and the Constitution that would come out of it were the final products of the old order, which was rapidly giving way to its new secular, democratic replacement. In fact, so close was the timing that, had the convention taken place one year later, it is doubtful anything more than a continuation of the existing Confederation would have come of it—which would have held the republic together about as effectively as a rope of sand.

The delegates adjourned without taking action. But that evening, the spirit that Franklin's strange request reflected stirred the hearts of many delegates, calling to mind their original mission. Nearly all had arrived with high hopes, and a number had caught the vision that had galvanized Washington: what hung in the balance was far more than just national independence. Some would say God had a plan for America, that she was to be a people covenanted together in the freedom and fulfillment that comes with living for Him, instead of for self—a light for all men. All would agree that American democracy was the noblest social experiment ever devised. As Morris put it, speaking of himself: "He came here as a representative of America; he flattered himself he came here in some degree as a representative of the whole human race, for the whole human race will be affected by the proceedings of this convention."[6] Some felt that for that reason, this convention would be as momentous as the one that produced the Declaration of Independence. But as historian Page Smith has observed: "It was one thing to *declare* a nation; it was something vastly more complex to accomplish it."[7] For more than two months they had been hard at it, with precious little to show for their endeavors.

Yet Franklin's proposal, even though it would be ignored, seemed to have struck a responsive chord: things did go better afterwards. Too much hung in the balance. As the Marquis de Lafayette wrote to his former commanding general from Paris: "Upon the success of this convention depends perhaps the very existence of the United States . . . Good Lord! The American people, so enlightened, so wise, so noble, after having scaled the steep cliffs, now stumble on the easy path."[8]

So, thanks largely to a plan presented by Virginia, of which Madison was the chief architect, they were able to come up with a unique solution to the large-state–small-state dilemma: a bicameral legislature—*two* houses, one based on population per state, the other ignoring population per state. But now, with that preoccupying problem at last out of the way, a truly ominous one emerged as the delegates were wrestling with how slaves would be counted, when it came to determining the number of representatives a given state would send to Congress. That brought into question the institution of slavery itself—did it even belong in the new republic? Most of the slaves were on large plantations along the southern seacoast, from the Virginia Tidewater, where tobacco was the cash crop, down to Charleston and the sea islands of Georgia, which were growing rice and indigo and a small amount of long-staple, hand-combed cotton. The cotton gin, which would overnight make cotton a high-demand commodity, would not be invented for another six years. Once it was in place, the South would become increasingly locked into a slave economy. But right now, American slavery remained in its infancy.

However, this enormously profitable infant strongly appealed to man's two basest instincts, the love of power and the love of money. Those two desires were common enough, but the Pilgrims and Puritans in New England shared a powerful Christianity that called upon them to eschew such evils, while the Cavaliers who came to Virginia saw no reason to do so. Puritans and Cavaliers . . . it was inconceivable that they could long coexist within the same republic; the tension between the two would result in civil war in England—and eventually in America, as well. Since this antithesis of opinion on the fundamental issues of life would eventually divide the house of America against itself, it might be advisable to trace the origins of the conflict.

God's will or my will—from the time when Adam and Eve made the wrong choice, life on earth has been a matter of such decisions. Whenever people have chosen to obey God and have honestly tried to put

Him first in their lives, He has poured out His enabling grace on them and honored their obedience with blessings. Thousands of years ago, He gave to Moses the Law, to reveal His righteousness and to guide mankind in the right paths. Ultimately, He gave His Son, that whoever by faith chooses to follow Him and to believe in His atoning death and resurrection receives forgiveness of sins and eternal life. And after Christ ascended, the Holy Spirit was given, to inspire and comfort and to empower us to live no longer for ourselves but for God.

It is not natural to go God's way; we naturally prefer our own. Yet even with His infinite grace and mercy available to us, to choose God over self, the selfless way over the selfish way, is an extraordinarily difficult thing to do. Which was why those who choose to go that way usually do so in the company of others so inclined and why God often calls groups of people to go His way together, that they might support one another along the path and show the way to others.

It is in this community of fellow believers in Christ that His followers have daily opportunity to put into practice this new covenant life based on the two great commandments: "Thou shalt love the Lord thy God with all thy heart, soul, mind, and strength, and thou shalt love thy neighbor as thy self" (*see* Matthew 22:37). It was a dual covenant, with a vertical relationship with God and a horizontal relationship with other people.

Whenever anyone sets his will to follow in Christ's footsteps, that person becomes a powerful instrument of the Light—and thus an active threat to the Prince of Darkness. For his example may well lead others into the same commitment. So that person—or group of people or church—comes under the harassment of the evil one, who will do all in his power to thwart and divert, tempt and seduce, discourage and destroy this newfound determination to walk in the Light.

And God allows it: He permits the devil to try the determination of the pilgrim, for without this testing, the Christian's faith cannot be refined and matured. As much as he knows in his head that Jesus is Victor, as much as he reads it in the Bible and hears of it in the testimony of others, until he walks through the fire himself, he will not own it in his heart. As John Bunyan dramatically narrated, there will be wide and joyous places in the path of the pilgrim, to balance the hard and narrow ones, and God's grace will always be commensurate to the task or challenge. But there are no shortcuts to the Celestial City, no painless, easy ways. Those determined to live in the Light must be prepared to walk through valleys of darkness. Indeed, to some extent, the rest of their lives will be a struggle between the Light and the darkness.

In England, by the seventeenth-century, the Protestant Reformation had produced a movement of such men and women who actually tried to live according to the example set forth in the New Testament. The majority were convinced that, by living as Christ had called them to, they could purify the Church of England from within. The trouble was, the established bishops of that church saw nothing that needed purifying and resented these would-be reformers, derisively dubbing them "Puritans." And with the cooperation of the civil authorities, the bishops set about making life exceedingly difficult for them.

A minority of these determined Christians considered that the Church of England was beyond purification and therefore separated themselves from it, setting up churches of their own, as closely as possible following the model laid out in the New Testament. Prayerfully they elected their pastors and elders and then abided by their decisions and direction, thus practicing the first modern example of democracy—government by the consent of the governed. Though small in number, these Separatists nonetheless represented a serious threat to the established church, for they were attracting new converts all the time, and by their very existence indicated that all was indeed not well within the Church of England. As a result, they were persecuted even more heavily than the Puritans. Finally, when it reached the point where Separatist ministers were arrested for preaching treason, they had no choice but to go into exile. Of all the countries of Europe, Holland was the most tolerant, and there they found a haven. Some of the Separatist churches remained there until it was safe to go home again. One congregation, however, in 1620, after having endured eleven years of hardship, felt God calling them to risk all that they had and set sail for the New World. So leaving family and friends behind, they entrusted their lives into the hands of Almighty God, who brought them safely across the ocean and planted them in "a garden in the wilderness," to show others that it was possible to live out New Testament Christianity.

Eight years later, as the persecution of the Puritans in England intensified, they, too, came to the New World. Still determined to purify the Church of England by their example, they now intended to accomplish this at a safe, 3,000-mile remove, where they would have the freedom to obey their call from God: to establish a Bible-based commonwealth. On the voyage, their elected leader, John Winthrop, had time to collect his thoughts and write down their mission, to become "A Modell of Christian Charity" or "a city set on a hill":

> This love among Christians is a real thing, not imaginary . . . We are a company, professing ourselves knit together by this bond of love . . . Thus stands the cause between God and us: we are entered into covenant with Him for this work. We have taken out a Commission; the Lord hath given us leave to draw our own articles. . . . to do justly, to love mercy, to walk humbly with our God; For this end, we must be knit together in this work as one man. . . . We must delight in each other, make one another's condition our own, rejoice together, mourn together, labor and suffer together, always having before our eyes our commission and Community in this work, as members of the same body. So shall we keep the unity of the Spirit in the bond of peace.[9]

As they went about setting up their colony in a place they called Boston, on Massachusetts Bay, the outlook on life of these men and women was almost identical to their Pilgrim cousins at Plymouth, forty miles distant. In fact, so impressed were they with the proven feasibility of these other covenanters' governments, both civil and religious, that they adopted them as their own. The Old Colony and the Bay Colony were good neighbors and eventually incorporated and became one, in 1695. As their numbers grew and multiplied and they went further into the wilderness, each would-be settlement first formed itself into a church and elected a pastor, with the approval of the other pastors of the colony. When they found the site God seemed to have for them, the first building they built was their church.

The Cavaliers, who came to Virginia around the same time, had a different outlook on life. Believing that God's affairs were best left to the bishops duly appointed by the monarch, they arrived at Jamestown in search of gold, not God. They were well aware of the staggering quantities of the yellow metal ripped out of the heart of Central America by the Spanish conquistadors, and rumors abounded that the northern Indians were privy to similar caches. Indeed, one story was repeated on board the first ship bound for Virginia, until it became an article of faith: the Indians they were approaching used chamber pots of solid gold, encrusted with rubies and diamonds![10] In addition, there was the fabled Northwest Passage—the first syndicate to locate it would control a trade route that would take weeks off of the Magellan route around the Cape of Good Hope. No wonder, then, that the first men to make the voyage were adventurers—soldiers of fortune, gentlemen in straitened circumstances, second-born sons of noble families not in line for inheritance, freebooters, and hired servants. And whereas the settlements to the north were for all intents classless, a definite class distinction was brought to Jamestown and encouraged there. The gentlemen on board refused to do manual labor; they would rather die than betray their class by soiling their hands, and indeed some literally starved to death rather than work at planting or hunting, or for wages.[11] The first thing the gentlemen did on shore, while the servants offloaded the ship, was to dig oysters, which they eagerly pried open for pearls. Moreover, while some went exploring for the Northwest Passage, those remaining in camp became convinced by some glittering iron pyrites (that would one day earn the sobriquet "fool's gold") that they had by chance literally landed on a goldfield.[12] Working feverishly, they filled their ship's hull with ore and dispatched it to their waiting adventurer partners in England, where it was assayed as worthless dirt. As for settling? No attempt at farming was made; everyone was too busy digging or exploring. Besides, it was easier to buy corn from the Indians than grow one's own, and when the glass beads and trinkets ran out, it was still easier to simply raid the Indian settlements and take their corn.

There did not appear to be much grace on Jamestown; for years the settlement suffered a horrendous death rate amongst the newcomers, from the nearby fever-infested swamp and later from Indian massacres. While the Indians were friendly enough at first, the white attitude gradually turned them increasingly hostile. Nevertheless, the second and third sons of wealthy English aristocrats, who had an inclination to try their hand at planting in the New World, tended to head for the rich, rolling fields and softer climate of Virginia, rather than the rocky soil and harsh winters of New England.

These adventurers did include a Church of England clergyman with the first boatload, almost as an afterthought. Named Robert Hunt, he was a sincere man who worked hard for the betterment of others and was generally held in high regard. But the message he preached had little impact on the lives of those he served. And in years to come, most of the first churches in Virginia were originally chapels built on large plantations by owners who liked to continue the tradition of going to church on Sunday. The foundations of the planter class and the laborer class were thus established, with no middle class.

In New England, the middle class thrived. Men who could not afford passage to America indentured themselves to do seven years' labor in exchange, and when that time was up, they were as free as the next man, to rise as high as they were able. The majority of settlers, free and indentured, were still Puritans and still primarily motivated by living for God's will. Periodically, they would lose sight of this common goal, and periodically circumstances—a drought, or a plague of grasshoppers, or possibly an Indian uprising—would serve to remind them of their need for and dependence upon God. Later, there would be revivals to remind and return, but in the first generations the tradition of New England town meeting democracy became deeply rooted, for all men were equal at the foot of the Cross. It was a truly classless society, with the lineage of its civil government easily traceable back to the model of the New Testament church. The greater the light and maturity that an individual possessed, the greater the service God expected him to render to his neighbors.

Meanwhile, back in England, the struggle between Puritan and Cavalier had reached the boiling point. Under Elizabeth I, the power of the church had grown to the point where the bishops now ruled the land like an ecclesiastical nobility. There was no tolerance for the Puritan desire to elect their own ministers and hear a living, dynamic Gospel preached. Yet because of their life-giving, life-changing faith, despite increasingly heavy persecution, the Puritans attracted new converts by the thousands. Arrayed against them were the Cavaliers, supporters of the reign of the aristocracy and the principle of the monarch as the head of the church. These men looked upon the growing popularity of the Puritans with alarm, viewing it as the precursor of nothing less than social revolution—as indeed it was. They pressed the king to implement ever harsher restrictions on the dissenters, and when, in 1642, he attempted to force the Scottish Presbyterians to adopt the Anglican *Book of Common Prayer* and then tried to arrest five objecting members of Parliament for treason, civil war broke out. Their glorious revolution was at last underway. It would continue, in one form or another, for ten years, with the Puritans ultimately victorious. The monarchy was abolished and a republican government, with a truly representative Parliament, was erected in its place. Eventually the monarchy would be restored, but thereafter Puritan and Cavalier would live together in peace, their differences resolved and their accord formalized in the Toleration Act of 1689.

In the New World, that tension would not be resolved for another two centuries—indeed, it would not come to a head for a century and a half. But the difference in outlooks and the sectional character they produced was so marked that Jefferson summed them up for his friend the Marquis de Chastellux: northerners were "cool, sober, laborious, persevering, independent, jealous of their liberties and those of others, interested, chicaning, superstitious and hypocritical in their religion." (Jefferson was incensed by evangelical Christianity.) The one trait southerners shared with northerners was their independence. In all other aspects they were in sharp contrast, being "fiery, voluptuary, indolent, unsteady, zealous for their own liberties but trampling on those of others, generous, candid, and without attachment of pretension to any religion but that of the heart."[13]

With the landing of the first slaves in Virginia in 1619, future conflict between the two outlooks became inevitable. Aristocracy bred contempt for the underclasses, and nothing hardened the cement of a class-ordered society faster than slavery, for now a bottom rung appeared on the ladder that everyone, even "poor white trash," could look down on. An even more insidious evil flowered: the effect of slavery on the psyche of the slave owner. But these are subtleties of sufficient intricacy as to require future chapters of their own.

Every delegate to the Constitutional Convention in 1787 acknowledged the evil of slavery. But not all were prepared to agree with those who demanded that it be abolished forthwith. The antislavery voices had a strong case: what could be crueler than to tear men and women from their ancestral homes and families, transport them under hideous, murderous conditions halfway around the world, there to break their wills and force them to do another man's bidding, for no recompense? This, in the world's newest republic, which prided itself on being a model of democratic freedom. How did the Declaration of Independence put it? "We hold these truths to be self-evident, that all men are created equal, that they are endowed by their Creator with certain unalienable rights, that among these are Life, Liberty, and the pursuit of Happiness. . . ." What hypocrisy, for Americans to hold up their system as a light to the rest of the world, when they held thousands of their fellowmen and women in subjection!

Most southern slave owners failed to see this hypocrisy. They regarded their slaves as they did their livestock—as property they had paid good money for and that represented a sizeable investment. When it came to reckoning population to determine how many Congressmen a given state would be sending to Washington, they were perfectly willing to regard their slaves as fellow inhabitants of their fair state. But considering that the black population of more than .5 million was nearly all in the South, and there were only 5 million people, black or white, in America (about a third the population of the British Isles), of which only 1 million adult males were eligible to vote, the vehemence of the North's objection was not surprising.[14] Eventually, they struck a compromise: five black slaves would equal three white men in such a tally. But, insisted the southern delegates, that recognition was not to be misconstrued as an acknowledgment of equal or almost equal status: the moment the census taker departed, the slaves' status would revert to that of two-footed property.

In the height of the debate, Gouverneur Morris leaped to his feet: "The Southern gentlemen will not be satisfied unless they see the way open to their gaining a majority in the public councils!" To which Pierce Butler of South Carolina retorted: "The security the Southern states want is that their negroes may not be taken from them, which some gentlemen, within or without doors, have a very good mind to do!"[15]

Several men stood, shouting, despite the oppressive humidity which had all the delegates soaked and dripping with perspiration. Whereas at the beginning of the session, several men had privately complained that their biggest problem was maintaining an adequate supply of fresh shirts and undergarments (since half an hour after stepping outside they might as well go back in and change clothes), now all present momentarily became impervious to the humidity. The heat they generated, rather than that in which they had recently suffered, held everyone's attention. It was a dark omen for the future that nothing in all the time they had been gathered had so stirred passions as the question of slavery. Commenting on the Northwest Ordinance, which Congress had just passed, and which was based on Jefferson's plan, providing that the law should allow "neither slavery nor involuntary servitude" in the territory bounded by the Mississippi, the Ohio, and the Great Lakes, Gouverneur Morris commented that it had been a mistake from the beginning to ever consider joining eight northern republics to five southern oligarchies.[16] That slur could not go unchallenged, and the proceedings descended to a new level of invective. No one was wrong here, just wrongly accused—and righteously indignant.

At length, Virginia, which had provided such a high caliber of leadership before, during, and after the Revolutionary War, once again endeavored to show the way. It had been Virginia that had seen the need for this convention in the first place and Virginia whose plan for proportional representation had been accepted, including Madison's proposition that the national legislature they were in the process of forming would have the right "to negative [veto] all laws passed by the several States, contravening in the opinion of the National Legislature the articles of Union; and to call forth the force of the Union against any member of the Union failing to fulfill its duty under the articles thereof."[17] (And this from the state that would one day lead the battle for state sovereignty!) Now, on slavery, the Virginians were equally firm and nationally minded.

Years before, Jefferson had condemned the slave trade in his rough draft of the Declaration of Independence: the "King of Great Britain kept open a market where *men* were bought and sold . . . suppressing Virginia's legislative attempts to restrain this execrable commerce."[18] The Continental Congress struck these fiery words from the final version, but Jefferson's antipathy toward slavery remained unabated, and in his will he arranged for the emancipation of his own slaves upon his death. Washington did the same, declaring that he wished "to get quit" of his slaves, and writing in 1786: "I never mean . . . to possess another slave by purchase, it being among my first wishes to see some plan adopted by which slavery in this country may be abolished. . . ."[19] But George Mason's words at this convention would be most often quoted. White haired and, despite his aristocratic bearing, a spirited champion of the common people, Mason owned one of the largest and best-kept plantations in Virginia—5,000 acres with 200 slaves to maintain it. As the debate shifted to restricting the importation of slaves, he rose and declared:

"The present question concerns not the importing States alone, but the whole Union.... Slavery discourages arts and manufactures. The poor despise labor when performed by slaves. . . . [Slaves] produce a pernicious effect on manners: every master is born a petty tyrant. They bring the judgment of heaven on a country." And he held it "essential from every point of view that the general Government shall have the power to prevent the increase of slavery."[20] Then he looked over at the Massachusetts delegation and added: "I lament that some of our Eastern brethren have, from a lust of gain, embarked on this nefarious traffic."[21] The New Englanders winced; it was true that some members of their shipping fraternity were ready to turn a coin on any cargo.

Mason had put the case squarely where it belonged: in the dock of national principle. But for once, not all southerners were willing to follow the Old Dominion's lead. There was visible consternation amongst the three-man delegation from South Carolina: they were disagreeing, but not on their position, merely on who would rise to speak first. That privilege was duly accorded that state's youngest delegate, Charles Pinckney, who recalled, for the benefit of the assembly, the examples of Greece and Rome and the modern nations of England, France, and Holland who still permitted slavery within their colonies. "In all ages," he concluded, "one half of mankind have been slaves. If the Southern States were let alone, they will probably of themselves stop importation."[22] Before any northern delegate could rise to vehemently object, Pinckney's older cousin, the illustrious General Charles Cotesworth Pinckney, pointed out the hard truth: even if he and his colleagues agreed to a new Constitution on those terms, their constituents would never ratify it. "South Carolina and Georgia cannot do without slaves," he stated.

But James Wilson of Pennsylvania could not let the younger Pinckney's allusion go unchallenged: if South Carolina and Georgia were indeed so disposed to voluntarily eschew slave traffic in as short a time as possible, they would never refuse to enter the Union merely because importation might be prohibited.

Butler and the Pinckneys put their heads together and emerged adamant. They *did* want slavery mentioned in the Constitution, all right, but on their terms: they wanted positive confirmation of their rights to their Negro property. And if this were not granted, they would walkout. As for abolishing the slave trade? They did eventually agree to that—on the proviso that it could not happen for another twenty years.

The antislavery delegates were furious, with Elbridge Gerry of Massachusetts predicting "civil war," if he took such a Constitution home for ratification. South Carolina and Georgia were holding a gun to the head of the republic, and they knew it. Some cried, let them go! They would apply for readmission soon enough—perhaps the moment a British squadron loomed over the horizon. But by this time, as the convention dragged into its fourth month and the humidity of the most unbearable summer in memory showed no signs of breaking, the delegates were exhausted, mentally and spiritually, as well as physically. Men who might have stood for their principles two months before had wilted to the point where they were counseling appeasement. Let them have what they wanted. Slavery was gradually dying out, anyway; it was almost gone in Virginia, except in the Tidewater country, and the world trend was decidedly against it. No progressive, civilized, Christian society would condone it much longer. First get the Constitution ratified, with all thirteen states included, and then at some future time let Congress deal with the question of slavery.

So for the sake of harmony, men who might have stood—and should have stood—for their principles, gave in to other men who demanded to have their own way. And thus were the seeds of darkness sown. Young Rufus King of Massachusetts wanted his bitter opposition a matter of record: that the Constitution gave even the shadow of legitimacy to slaveholding was "a most grating circumstance to his mind, and he believed would be so to a great part of the people of America." And Morris joined him, exclaiming that he:

> . . . Never would concur in upholding domestic slavery. It was a nefarious institution. It was the curse of heaven, where it prevailed. Compare the free regions of the Middle States, where a rich and noble cultivation marks the prosperity and happiness of the people, with the misery and poverty which overspread the barren wastes of Virginia and Maryland and other States having slaves. . . . Proceed southwardly, and every step you take through the great region of slaves presents a desert increasing, with the increasing proportion of these wretched beings. . . . The admission of slaves into the Representation, when fairly explained comes to this: that the inhabitant of Georgia and South Carolina who goes to the coast of Africa, and in defiance of the most sacred laws of humanity tears away his fellow creatures

from their dearest connections and damns them to the most cruel bondages, shall have more votes in a Government instituted for protection of the rights of mankind, than the citizen of Pennsylvania or New Jersey who views with laudable horror so nefarious a practice."[23]

2

Heading West

Down in Fairfield, Connecticut, you could hear the rumbling of wheels and the creaking of axles a good two hours before sunup. All day long, the dust seemed to hang like smoke over the road, nor did it settle until long after nightfall. Some of the wagons were shaded by canvas stretched over hoops, while others merely had their loads covered and lashed down, the husband driving with his wife beside him, the children perched on the load in back. Some were horse drawn, others were pulled by yoked oxen, and a number had extra livestock trailing along behind—a cow or two or possibly a saddle horse. But all were covered with dust and so travel-weary that even the children rocked along in silence. From the north they came, and the east, from around Hartford and Norwich, and as far away as Lexington and Concord, from countless four corners that no one had ever heard of and no map listed. They came down the feeder roads, propelled along as if caught in tributaries during a spring flood, west and south down into the main river, which was the Boston Post Road. If you stood there long enough, from before sunup till well after sundown, you might count half a thousand in a single day, heading west.

For this was 1796, and with "Mad Anthony" Wayne's victory two years before over the combined Indian tribes at the Battle of Fallen Timbers, the menace of scalping parties was considerably lessened—at least in the Northwest Territory. And the Ordinance of 1787 had guaranteed that there would be several states between the Ohio and the Mississippi admitted to the Union with full-fledged status, as soon as they reached the requisite 60,000 free population, which meant all comers, as the ordinance had banned slavery in the territory. The way Yankee pioneers were pouring in, statehood would come to Ohio in less than a decade. In New England, the exodus was given added impetus by the fresh arrival of immigrants in Boston. The Appalachian mountain range had previously kept nearly everyone pinned on the seacoast, but at last the psychological barrier of the mountains had been broken, and the three main arteries that funneled streams of pioneers westward were becoming rivers. The Cumberland Gap opened Kentucky to Virginians, and the Great Pittsburgh Road made southern Ohio accessible to New England. The south shore of Lake Erie could be best reached by hiring or building a flatboat to go up the Hudson to Albany, then heading overland to Buffalo and taking a packet from there. That sounded arduous, but it was a popular route: during the previous winter, an observer counted five hundred westbound sleighs passing through Albany on a single day.[1]

In New England, the best farmland had long ago been taken, and the marginal land was now taken as well, with the result that each ensuing wave of newcomers was driving the price of land so high that the best farms were fetching as much as $50 an acre, when they could be had at all. And what was to become of the farmer who had more than one son, and whose farm would be able to support only the eldest, when the time came?

The truth was, it was doubtful that many farms could do even that for much longer. For the rocky soil of New England was well-nigh exhausted. As canny as the Yankee farmers were, no one had taught them yet about contour plowing—to plow their hills horizontally, so that each furrow formed a miniature terrace to catch and hold the downward-flowing rainwater until it soaked into the ground, instead of washing all the topsoil down the hillsides and into the creeks. No one had taught them yet about crop rotation, so that they wouldn't wear out the soil by planting the same crop in the same place year after year, just as their fathers and grandfathers had before them. . . despite the Bible's admonition to give each field a rest every seven years.

So, gradually, imperceptibly, the land simply gave out—until the rocks began to show through like a starving man's bones. Where once four acres could support a cow, now it took eight or ten. Each year, the yield was a little bit less and the taxes a little bit more, and a farmer could work himself old before his time or until his health broke, just trying to stay even. And his son, the one to whom he had intended to leave the farm, would oftentimes be driven to despair. In Granville, Massachusetts, a young lad named Alfred Avery went out with his hoe to do what he could to help his father plant corn. Before long, he was sobbing, and when his father asked him what the matter was, he cried, "I can't get enough dirt to cover the corn!"[2] Not long after that, the

Averys joined the rest of their congregation and pastor and moved en masse to Ohio in the Northwest Territory, where they founded a new town of Granville. In doing so, they were following a time-honored Puritan tradition—of a pioneering people going into the wilderness together as a church. Having formally organized themselves into a congregation of 176 members, they set forth with pastor and deacon, and when they arrived at the chosen site, they turned loose their oxen and listened to a sermon by their pastor: "O Lord, Thou hast delivered us safe through the valleys and shadows. . . ."[3]

Another group who moved west under God's guidance was the Ohio Company, who made plans for settlement by former Revolutionary War soldiers and officers and approached Congress to lobby for effective government in the territory west of the Ohio. Blessedly free from the greed and feverish speculation that would grip later land companies, the Ohio Company, in return for presentation of detailed plans, suggestions, and proposals, was granted by Congress 1.5 million acres of territorial land at eight cents an acre. With typical military precision, two of the company's partners, General Rufus Putnam and Benjamin Tupper, organized the first settling expedition to southeastern Ohio, to a place they called Marietta. They laid out a carefully planned town, reminiscent of the original Plymouth Plantation, with eight acres per farmer outside of town, and the log cabin dwellings inside a strong palisade with blockhouses at the four corners.

From the first day the settlers arrived, the Gospel was preached by the Reverend David Story of Boston, who thanked God for their safe passage and prompt arrival. Most of the settlers were from Massachusetts, and straight away they established a school, which became Muskingum Academy, and eventually Marietta College. It was a community enterprise, as was what became locally renowned as the Coonskin Library—lacking cash, the people of Marietta traded raccoon pelts for books, among them, Locke's essays and Gibbon's *Decline and Fall of the Roman Empire.* In sum, the combination of faith, go-ahead zeal, and fortuitous planning made Marietta an astonishing success—and probably doubled the pace of settlement west of the Ohio.

Another former general, Moses Cleveland, set up two more well-planned and efficiently executed settlements on the south shore of Lake Erie, in Connecticut's Western Reserve, and naturally most of the first settlers came from Connecticut. Ohio land seemed to pay back hard work very quickly, and it wasn't handbills or flyers that brought the next wave of settlers out; it was word of mouth. A sober, straight-laced hardshell Baptist elder from Standish, Maine, named Morris Witham, went out to Ohio in '96, bought a tract of land, and came back the next year to astound his lifelong friends with descriptions of tall chestnut trees from which a fence rail could be split with a single stroke of the ax and potatoes that grew as large as "Caleb Kimball's foot."[4]

But by the end of the eighteenth century, exchanging old Granvilles for new was not the norm. The vast majority of pioneer families went out alone or in response to the encouragement of friends or relatives who had gone before them. The average Yankee farmer back east, though sociable enough, was fiercely independent and self-reliant and not much given to religion or to churchgoing. His wife might get after him for that or might try to hold onto the vestiges of the religious tradition in which they had grown up, by reading the Bible to their children. But for the most part, without the cement of shared Christian worship and fellowship, they were entirely on their own—and preferred it that way. That continued to be so, even when times were at their worst and men were most tempted to give up and the whiskey jug came out of the cupboard more frequently. Most Yankees were instinctively ready to help someone else in need, as best they were able, for that was how they had all survived the desperate hardships in the beginning. The bonds forged by these shared trials were lasting; they could not be forgotten in a few years or even a few generations. Yet their pride was such that they or one of theirs would have to be practically at death's door, before they would ask for help. Besides, most of their neighbors were pretty much in the same condition. We can imagine a Connecticut farmer, let's call him Caleb Hotchkiss, on a cold winter's evening, with the kids bundled off to bed, and the wife knitting by the fireside, sitting and staring into the flames, and thinking the unthinkable—of leaving the land that had been in his family for generations and heading west.

It was a hard thing to contemplate. Caleb knew every tree on the place, every bend in the creek. Some of the trees he had planted with his father, and some of them—the twelve old apples on the leeward side of the barn—his father had planted with his grandfather. And there was the post on the barnyard gate—as a lad he had marveled at how smooth it had been worn, like polished leather. Callused hands had done that, opening and closing the gate day after day, year after year . . . hands that had grown their calluses on the handles of plow, hoe, and spade . . . hands that had wrestled endless rocks and boulders out of fields and placed them in neat border walls. He himself had cleared the pasture bordering Amos Finley's land. It wasn't Amos's any longer, he reminded himself; it belonged to some Dutchman who was trying to raise a dairy herd. Amos had left in the spring of '95. He had offered Caleb the land, but Caleb hadn't had two extra dollars to rub together.

Caleb looked at the gatepost and ran his hand over the satin finish. A lot of the men he had grown up with had already left, and the letters that came back from the frontier were incredible. "The corn out here is fourteen feet high!"[5] "Over in Marietta, they're getting a hundred bushels to the acre!" "The grass is so rich, two acres will support a cow!" But the one that really got to him was: "There are fields out here as flat as a barn floor, with nary a single stone from one end to the other." To be able to farm without having to first spend precious weeks loading and dragging the stone boat. . . . It was surprising what a man would believe, if he wanted to badly enough. Caleb went in to the kitchen, opened a drawer, and took out Amos's well-thumbed letter. He didn't need to read it; he knew every word by heart. But seeing the words written there by his old friend somehow made them more real. Sitting down, he put the letter on the table, smoothing out the creases carefully. It was Amos, all right:

> Well, it's true. Everything we heard and couldn't believe. You know me; I don't garnish. Less than four miles across the Ohio, I could have sworn we were back home. There are shade trees aplenty, and creeks and gentle hills. But this is different: the soil isn't red; it's black as gunpowder, and so deep, you can put a shovel in to the hilt and not come to the end of it. You had best pack up Rachel and your young ones and get out here while there is still plenty of bottom land. Come to East Liverpool, Martha says, who misses you all. I have 120 acres eight miles west of the river, and there's another piece the same size alongside, which I put some money down on, to hold for you. Cost

> you $2 an acre, which is what I paid for mine. It took us about six weeks to get here, but should take you less, if you come in the spring, now that they have extended the turnpike. If you leave in April, you will have time to get some corn in and a cabin up before it turns cold. . . .

Leave in April—the words turned over and over in his mind, as he replaced the letter in the drawer. But how could he leave? His parents were buried over in the churchyard, and their parents, too. . . . In the end, the decision was made for him. They had a long, dry spell in April, and when the first shoots of wheat came up, they were so puny, he could dislodge them with a nudge of his toe. The land was finished—and they were finished with it.

In the morning, he went over to see Piet Vanderpoel, his new neighbor, and found him in the barn, just finishing the milking. The big Dutchman straightened and wiped his hands on his work apron. "*Ja, Herr* Hotchkiss?"

"Came to see if you'd be interested in buying my land," Caleb replied, getting right to the point.

"Be you heading west, then?" Caleb nodded. "Well, we'll be sorry to see you go; you've been good neighbors."

Caleb was surprised at that, since they'd never socialized. The Dutchman was smiling, arms folded on his chest, but the words did not come easily to Caleb. "I've got thirty-six acres," he finally managed. "It's not much for growing wheat anymore, but I expect it would still be good for grazing."

"Thirty-four and a half acres," the Dutchman corrected him.

"Yep," Caleb nodded, "if you don't count the creek bed, and half the track we share."

Both men fell silent again, until Vanderpoel asked, "How much be you wanting for it?"

Caleb had done the figuring many times. "Well, I reckon the land is worth fifteen dollars an acre, plus three hundred dollars for the house and one hundred dollars for the barn, and throw in another fifty dollars for the corncribs, and I'll leave the harrow and the plow, and the other implements."

Vanderpoel rubbed the red stubble on his chin. "Your fields have rocks coming through, like the top of a bald man's head." He chuckled, but Caleb just looked at him. "Well," the Dutchman said, "the barn I can use, but the house. . . ." His voice trailed off as his brows furrowed. At length, he took a deep breath and nodded. "God has been good to us, and having you as neighbors has been part of that. I will give you twelve hundred dollars—hard money."

Caleb's mouth fell open. "My price was fair, but that's more than—"

The big Dutchman's eyes suddenly brimmed. "I will never forget how your Rachel helped us last winter, when Tinike had the pox." He held out his hand. Caleb shook it, then turned away so that Vanderpoel could not see his eyes.

Now that the deal was struck, there was much to do. During the next few days, it was Rachel who had to make the hard decisions, for there was only so much room in the wagon. Tables and chairs and bureaus would have to be left behind—furniture that the men of the Hotchkiss family had fashioned over countless long winters and that had been worn smooth by half a century's elbows and britches. In the end, she elected to leave almost everything behind, but she could not bear to part with their bed. Caleb had agreed that they could take the cherry head and foot boards, with their beautifully turned posts. And now they were making the final adjustments to the load, distributing the weight evenly over both axles, strapping it down securely, and folding the hooked rug Caleb's grandmother had made, to make a nest for the two children to curl up in. Caleb had considered making a frame to stretch the large piece of sailcloth over, but it would be necessary only in the hottest months, and if all went well, they should be there by the middle of June. Besides, this way, they could use the cloth as a tent, if they had to, instead of having to sleep under the wagon or in it.

He took one more inventory of tools—a new ax and two spare handles, the new plow, his long rifle and ammunition and powder horn and wadding and extra powder, the scythe, the crosscut saw, the hammer and small keg of nails, the adze—

"Ready, Pa," his son's words cut across his thoughts. Looking up, he checked his son's work: team harnessed, milk cow and horse tied behind, axles well greased. . . . Caleb nodded and called for the others to get up on the wagon.

"No looking back now," he said gruffly, slapping the reins on the left horse's back. The team leaned into the harness, and the heavy wagon started to roll. In the back, he could hear Rebecca crying and Aaron trying to stifle his own tears. He couldn't be too hard on his son; the lump in his own throat was too large to swallow. He felt tempted to look back himself, for one last glimpse of their home. But there was no need to; he knew the scene by heart—the two-bedroom, white-clapboard house with the dark green shutters, the stone path to the front door, the rose arbor he had made for Rachel just last summer, the wisteria at the side of the barn beginning to bud. . . .

They turned out the gate and away toward Greenfield Hill. "Bye, Mr. Vanderpoel," shouted Aaron from the back, at the Dutchman and his wife, who were standing by their fence, waving. "Take care of Pepper for me. I'll be back to see her in a year or two." Caleb shook his head. There was no way they could have taken the dog; they would have trouble enough just feeding themselves, as it was. And as for coming back, he didn't say so to Aaron, but he doubted very much that any of them would ever see Aspetuck Corners again.

They rode along in silence, and he sighed as he reached Greenfield Hill, for the dogwoods were in full bloom, spreading their delicate white blossoms. Were there any dogwoods where they were going? The team had settled into a slow and steady pace, which nonetheless would see thirty miles pass beneath them before nightfall. At that rate, they might even wind up a little ahead of Amos's estimate, though the New Haven *Gazette* said that Connecticut's roads were the best in America. Anyway, there wasn't much to do but relax and enjoy the trip. They were sad now, but time would fix that; it always did. In a couple of days, they would be thinking forward, instead of back. Come to think of it, none of them had ever been more than a couple of days from home. . . .

The others were lost in their thoughts, and he let his own mind gather wool. There wasn't much to driving the team; after all these years, they almost seemed to know which way he wanted them to go before he did. Well, there would be new fields for them to learn, once they got to East Liverpool. What would he plant? Potatoes right away, and oats for the team, but mostly corn, as Amos had said. It kept well and could be ground into meal, which also kept well. But mainly it could be easily converted into whiskey, which was compact, convenient, and easily shipped. In fact, he'd heard that most of the freight wagons returning east were filled with kegs of whiskey, for that was the frontiersman's main cash crop, and was also his main currency of barter. What was the saying? "A horse can carry four bushels of rye, or the whiskey made from twenty-four bushels."[6] In three or four years, when he'd cleared enough land to make the farm begin to pay, then they could raise wheat and some cattle and do just about anything they had a mind to. But in the beginning, a man made whiskey—that is, if he wanted to survive.

Survival—in the end, it came down to one's health. As long as he was sound of limb and had enough to eat to keep going, they would make it. If something happened to one of the horses, he could still plow with the other one alone. And if it came to that, he could pull the plow himself. But not for very long, he had to admit; he was forty-five now, not twenty-five, and while he still felt as strong as ever, when they had pulled the stump out of the north pasture last summer, his muscles were shaking for a long time afterwards, and he was stiff for several days. No, the one thing they couldn't cope with was if anything happened to him, sickness or an accident. . . . He had taught Aaron a great deal, but the lad was only eleven.

They came to a fork, and before he could twitch the reins, the horses took the road to the right; they seemed to know he wanted to go towards Fairfield. He smiled to himself; as Rachel would say, they were all in God's hands. His mother used to talk that way. She had even gotten him to pray with her, when he was a boy. But she had died in the winter of '63, and he hadn't thought much about God after that. Oh, there was that winter in Valley Forge, when he'd nearly died of whooping cough; he had prayed some then. . . . But now, on a Sunday, he was not about to drop everything and drive six miles to hear some young squirt from Yale expounding vague philosophy. Rachel had wanted to keep going, of course, for the children's sake. But the few times she'd pressed him, he'd gotten short with her. If she wanted to talk to God that badly, she could do it just as easily in the kitchen as in a church pew. Besides, he needed the boy's help with the farm work.

So that had settled it. He would leave the praying to Rachel. For him, God would remain a remote supreme being—Divine Providence, as the General used to refer to Him. And on his part, he would raise his children never to lie or cheat or steal, to work hard and honor their word, just as he had been raised. And he would teach the boy enough so that with his hands he could make or do or fix whatever was needed. He would also teach him to use his head—how to judge an angle or a furrow, how to tell the weather by the look of the sky or the shift of the wind, how to look at a field and reckon the number of days it would take to clear it, plow it, and plant it. He would teach the boy to look at a stand of trees and see the one-room cabin it could produce. He would teach him to figure how long it would take to build that cabin—weeks, not days, because the clearing, plowing and planting had to come first. Meanwhile, they would make a permanent tent out of the sailcloth. . . .

"My, look at the wagons!" Rachel exclaimed, as they came in sight of the post road. "Why, they must stretch all the way back to Bridgeport!"

"New London, more likely," Caleb muttered, waiting for an opening in the line. He eased the team in and noted that the pace was slower now, with interminable stops and starts. It should go faster, though, once they got to the Hudson. Many of these wagons would turn north and head up the river to Albany before going west. Others would cross the river at New York and keeping going west through the Jerseys and the gap cut by the Delaware. But a lot of them would probably go the way they were going, turning south and heading for Philadelphia and then taking the great turnpike west to Pittsburgh. Maybe some, like them, would travel by water from there, where the Allegheny and the Monongahela came together to form the Ohio. He hoped that not too many would be landing at East Liverpool. If the land was as good as Amos said, there was more than enough there for Aaron to have a farm of his own someday. . . .

Such were the thoughts that must have run through the minds of many of the thousands of pioneers who headed west in 1796. Each had his own reasons, but they all shared a common dream—a better standard of living that could be achieved relatively quickly by dint of hard work and resourcefulness. From all over New England they came, selling out for whatever they could get or simply abandoning unsalable homesteads. Indeed, it was not unusual to find the remains of an abandoned farmhouse on a barren hilltop, its roof caved in and only the stone chimney standing above the vines and new growth—mute testimony to the warmth and life that had once been shared there. New England was a harsh, unyielding land, and it produced a breed of men who bore a number of traits similar to another race against whom elements and terrain had seemed in perpetual conspiracy—the Scottish Highlanders. Such was Yankee frugality and shrewdness that it became legendary, especially as they began to travel through more gentle climes on their way west. The "stone soup" gambit was typical, and while it enjoyed infinite variations on the theme, the following may be the first recorded account, from the 1798 journal of the Reverend Benjamin Mortimer, who heard it from an innkeeper in Bedford, on the Great Pittsburgh Road.[7]

It seemed that an emigrant family from Connecticut, having spent nearly all of the meager sum they had with them and still facing at least a fortnight before they reached their destination, was in desperate straits. One of their children had been very sick with a fever and needed some light nourishment, when one morning they passed by a "neat and comfortable-looking dwelling," not far from the inn. Noting the handsome vegetable garden and seeing through the kitchen window a leg of meat on the table, the Yankee husband and wife had a brief consultation, and the father knocked at the door. The lady of the house opened it, and seeing that he was a Yankee, shooed him off before he could say a word, informing him that she was not running an inn and that there had been entirely too many Yankees knocking at her door for a free handout.

The husband withdrew, and he and his wife had another consultation. Now she came to the window and, with "a great deal of that ready tact so peculiar to the New England character," she asked if she might borrow a kettle with which to make her ailing child some stone soup.

"Stone soup! You must be joking. I never heard of such a thing."

The mother replied that it was exceedingly delicious, and just the thing for someone who was getting over the fever. The lady of the house was intrigued; her husband was often sickly, and at such times had a very poor appetite. She invited the mother in, and the latter offered to let her watch her make it, so that she would be able to see how to do it herself. The lady of the house agreed, and the two women began.

The first ingredient was a large, flat, smooth stone from a neighboring brook. The Yankee woman carefully placed it in the bottom of the kettle, which was put over the fire with plenty of water and a little salt. After the water had been brought to a boil, the mother tasted it and allowed as how some turnips, potatoes, leeks, and carrots would certainly improve the taste. These were cheerfully provided, and after more low boiling, the mother again tasted and nodded, "It is becoming very good, but it would be first rate if it had some meat in it."

No sooner said than done: her assistant produced a shinbone of beef, which she added to the pot. After a long while of simmering and various spices added, the mother gave a final taste and pronounced the stone soup ready. Just then, the man of the house arrived, and he and his wife and the family of Yankees sat down to a delicious meal. The man of the house exclaimed that stone soup was the best thing he had ever put in his mouth, and he urged his wife to get the recipe from their guests, which she did:

"Take a large, flat, smooth stone from a spring—put it into a pot with water and vegetables to suit your taste, and a bone of meat. Flavor this to your liking, and boil it for several hours. Note: The same stone will answer a number of times, but it must be kept clean."

It was not just New Englanders who were heading west; the migration seemed to be coming from up and down the eastern seaboard. By 1796, 100,000 Virginians had already moved to Kentucky, Tennessee, and southern Ohio. For in Virginia, the land was tired, too. Even Thomas Jefferson despaired that he could get no more than six or eight bushels of wheat from an acre. And this was a state where Jefferson and the other leaders had made a conscious decision to eschew the coming industrial growth that the North seemed to be embracing. To them, agriculture was the noblest pursuit of a democratic republic, and they saw themselves as akin to English gentlemen farmers.

The trouble was, the noble pursuit of agriculture was not always successful. An Englishman named Robert Sutcliffe, traveling in Virginia and Pennsylvania during this period, observed:

> In Pennsylvania, we meet great numbers of wagons drawn by four or more fine fat horses, the carriages firm and well made, and covered with stout good linen, bleached almost white. . . . Many of these come more than three hundred miles to [the central market in] Philadelphia, and . . . more than a thousand covered carriages frequently come to Philadelphia market. . . . The appearance of things in the slave States is quite the reverse of this. We sometimes meet a ragged black boy or girl, driving a team consisting of a lean cow and a mule. . . ."[8]

There was no question which of the two states was more prosperous. According to nineteenth-century historian Henry Adams, in 1796, even the Old Dominion's most illustrious son, President Washington, "admitted that the land in Virginia was lower in price than land of the same quality in Pennsylvania. [To explain] this inferiority he suggested, among other reasons, that Pennsylvania had made laws for the gradual abolition of slavery, and he declared nothing more certain than that Virginia must adopt similar laws at a period not remote."[9]

But some Virginia gentlemen became adept at avoiding such unpleasant realities, pursuing sensual pleasures or steeping themselves in the classics and ignoring the growing disparities on their foremen's balance sheets. Renowned for their political skills, they were the best orators in America, as well as being charming and genial hosts, whose hospitality became legendary. One visitor from Massachusetts was embarrassed by the preoccupation with prosperity of his friends back home. From Richmond, William Ellery Channing wrote:

> I blush for my own people, when I compare the selfish prudence of a Yankee with the generous confidence of a Virginian. Here I find great vices, but greater virtues than I left behind me. There is one single trait which attaches me to the people I live with more than all the virtues of New England: they *love money less* than we do, they are more disinterested, their patriotism is not tied to their purse-strings. Could I only take from Virginians their sensuality and their slaves, I should think them the greatest people in the world. As it is, with a few great virtues, they have innumerable vices.[10]

The patricians of Virginia often dined on British china and drank from crystal goblets—while broken windows let in drafts behind them. The panes had been missing for years and would remain missing for years more, because there was no money for a glazier.[11] For those who finally faced reality, the heavy, elegant family silver would pay for a wagon, supplies, and provisions, and a quarter-mile square in the Virginia Military Reserve. For others, whose families had never owned such silver or who had already squandered it away at cards and wenching, the West held the only hope for the future. So they left the crumbling and peeling, pillared and porticoed mansions and set their course for the Cumberland Gap.

The Virginian ideal of the gentleman farmer, promulgated by Jefferson and subscribed to by gentlemen (and would-be gentlemen) throughout the South, so caught the imagination that it became the bedrock on which the cherished "southern way of life" would be built.

Even the hardworking dirt farmer looked forward to that time when he could spend much of the day on horseback or hunting, as the plantation owners did, leaving their field hands to toil in the unrelenting sun. The trouble was, the further south one got, the harder it was to find field hands who were willing to toil all day long under the sun, no matter how high the wages. Why work on someone else's land, when for almost nothing one could have his own piece of land a hundred miles or so to the west? To fulfill his dream, then, the dirt farmer had to resort to the one source of labor that couldn't head west. If he could ever get $400 together, he could buy one slave, and that would start him on the road to becoming a gentleman. If he couldn't, he might as well consider heading west himself, to a territory where good land was cheap and he and his family could make a fresh start.

The westward migration was something that nearly all thirteen states shared, but New Yorkers were quite different from New Englanders, being far less concerned with moral rectitude and far more concerned with politics. Pennsylvanians, with all the different religious groups that had settled in their state, were by far the most tolerant and not at all concerned with democracy's possible extremes.

In the North, the driving ambition was not to join the leisure class, but to get ahead in whatever one's calling was. There were so many industrious tradesmen that they sounded like a litany of Anglo-Saxon surnames—wainwrights and wheelers, smiths and taylors, carpenters and coopers, millers and sawyers, weavers and bakers. . . . And as they plumbed the mysteries of mass production, they made everything the South needed, from barrels to shoes, plows to wagons. If there was a guiding term to define the spirit of the North, it would be *industrious optimism.* Up north, America was indeed the land of opportunity: all you needed to prosper was a strong back or nimble fingers, a stout and willing heart, and a reasonably quick mind. You didn't even need to speak the language, at first; you could pick it up along the way. And if it was farming you were interested in (as 95 percent of all Americans, north and south, were), the land in western New York, Ohio, or Pennsylvania seemed to respond as readily to German or Dutch as it did to English. In the cities and towns, if a man were willing to apprentice himself and work hard, he could look forward to owning his own shop one day. And not that far away, either; indeed, the harder he was willing to work, the sooner he would have something to show for it.

In the Northwest Territory, the social life of new towns formed around the local churches. But in the South, the many farm families were isolated from one another and, as Jefferson had indicated, essentially nonreligious. With the exception of enclaves of Moravians, Huguenots, and Scotch-Irish Presbyterians, who came to the New World much as the Pilgrims and Puritans had, largely in response to the call of God, southern farmers could trace their spiritual legacy or lack of same back to Jamestown. In the South, the established church was the American counterpart of the Church of England, the American Episcopal Church: you could worship anywhere or way you liked, or not at all, but you would be taxed to support the Episcopal Church. There was a way to avoid this tax, by making formal application to be recognized as a "dissenter." But the Episcopal Church was the church of the aristocracy, and in a class-conscious society, choosing the status of a dissenter was choosing the status of a social outcast. An anecdote of that era summed it up:

A young lad asked his rector, "Sir, is it possible to become a Christian outside of the Episcopal Church?"

The minister thought for a moment, before replying. "Well, perhaps, but no gentleman would ever consider it."[12]

In 1795, the true temper of spirituality in the Old Dominion was shown in the way Virginians admired the religious freedom of Pennsylvania and how well it worked, and considered their own state to be at least as progressive and high-minded. They were confident that the same freedom would thrive in their state, too, where every plantation was connected to a parish and regular attendance at church services had always been a tradition of the First Families of Virginia. Despite a wave of antidisestablishmentarianism, the legislature voted to disestablish the church, making its financial support no longer mandatory.

They were stunned at what happened: the church collapsed. "The Virginia gentry stood by and watched their churches closed, the roofs rot, the aisles and pews become a refuge for sheep and foxes, the tombstones of their ancestry built into strange walls or turned into flagging to be worn by the feet of slaves. By the year 1800, Episcopal Bishop James Madison found his diocese left so nearly bare of clergy and communicants that after a few feeble efforts to revive interest, he abandoned the struggle. . . ."[13]

Despite the collapse of the Episcopal churches, evangelicals (especially the Methodists and Baptists), still found themselves outside the mainstream of social and political leadership. In contrast, in the North, the prominent denominations had been reform minded from the beginning, and nearly all leadership in society had arisen from their congregations. In the next three decades, of all the differences between North and South, this would prove to be the most crucial. For as God began to pour out His Spirit upon the whole land and the newly revived and converted became filled with holy zeal, those in northern churches had the legacy of the Puritans, who believed that loving one's neighbor as oneself entailed an obligation to continually reform society and help those less well off.

Southern evangelicals, on the other hand, being dissenters, were hardly in a position to provide the social leadership that reform required. If anything, they would be inclined to leave the social responsibility to those who claimed it—and did nothing about it. For the southern aristocracy had no interest in reforming or improving society; on the contrary, their sole commitment was to maintaining things exactly as they were. Hence the weakness of the evangelical antislavery movement in the South: it could never acquire a broad social power base from which to operate.[14]

"America, America, God shed His grace on thee"—and the country desperately needed it at the end of the eighteenth century. There was a tragic irony here: in the beginning, when the Creator had first raised the curtain on this undiscovered continent, it was a land of shadows, where the prince of darkness reigned unchallenged. But gradually the Light advanced—up the rivers, on solitary horseback, in the hearts of missionaries who had first come with the conquistadors and who had stayed to win the hearts of the Indians they met. Generations passed, and the Light advanced further.

Then, during a time of great unsuspected need, there had been a nationwide lightning storm of the Spirit of God. The lightning of awakened faith had fallen first in Northampton, Massachusetts, in 1735, in the parish of America's most prominent theologian, Jonathan Edwards, who in despair at the spiritual complacency of his congregation, began preaching about the dreadful reality of an afterlife for the unregenerate. He made the fires of hell so convincing that his listeners squirmed in their pews—and many began to think seriously for the first time about where they would be spending eternity. Into this plowed field, God poured His Spirit, and revival broke out in the most wondrous fashion, spreading from town to town like wildfire. First New England, then west and south until, in a matter of weeks, the entire Atlantic seaboard was aflame, with preachers like Whitefield and Brainerd and other New Lights carrying the message wherever horse could travel. Where the coals of religion had formerly been so banked that there was no visible glow to them at all, now, under the wind of the Spirit, they gleamed red-hot. The revival came to be known as the Great Awakening, and it brought the thirteen colonies together, as nothing else could have; salvation was for everyone who yearned for it, and all were equal at the foot of the Cross.

The timing was God's, for Americans had grown somnolent, and the Awakening arrived just in time to raise up a generation of devout believers who would have the commitment and spiritual backbone to stand up to the onslaught of the British. But now, in 1800, with America at peace and all external threat for the moment removed, man forgot that the main source of darkness lay not without, but within. Without a common foe and a common objective, the national mood relapsed into selfishness. Where once the Light of Christ had traveled inland with men, now lust for land became their focus, and their only concern was which route over the mountains was the quickest. The spiritual state of the nation might be described as the "Great Asleepening."

Many families now crossed the mountains with no thought of God or Christian fellowship; where a church was once the first building to go up in a settlement, now it was often erected almost as an afterthought, if at all. With a few exceptions it was essentially a godless migration. As Henry Adams put it:

> The Pilgrims of Plymouth, the Puritans of Boston, the Quakers of Pennsylvania, all avowed a moral purpose, and began by making institutions that consciously reflected a moral idea. No such character belonged to the colonization of 1800. From Lake Erie to Florida, in a long, unbroken line, pioneers were at work, cutting into the forests with the energy of so many beavers, and

> with no more express moral purpose than the beavers they drove away.[15]

In 1798, the General Assembly of the Presbyterian Church was so alarmed at the backslidden state of religion in America that it expressed its concern in the form of a pastoral letter, which was to be read from every Presbyterian pulpit in the country:

> Formidable innovations and convulsions in Europe threaten destruction to morals and religion; scenes of devastation and bloodshed, unparalleled in the history of modern nations, have convulsed the world, and our country is threatened with similar calamities. . . .
>
> We perceive, with pain and fearful apprehension, a general dereliction of religious principle and practice among our fellow-citizens, a visible and prevailing impiety and contempt for the laws and institutions of religion, and an abounding infidelity which in many instances tends to Atheism itself. . . .
>
> The profligacy and corruption of the public morals have advanced with a progress proportionate to our declension in religion. Profaneness, pride, luxury, injustice, intemperance, lewdness, and every species of debauchery and loose indulgence greatly abound. . . .[16]
>
> The eternal God has a controversy with this nation.[17]

The young republic slept on. But God did not intend for her sleep to remain long undisturbed; He had other plans for America, plans that would begin with a second lightning storm even greater than the first.

3

Like a Mighty River

A thin column of blue-white smoke rose straight up in the crisp, perfectly still, morning air. It was coming from the stone chimney of a two-room log cabin in a densely wooded valley in western Kentucky. A fresh covering of snow lay on the ground, and the nearby creek was silenced in the icy grip of winter. Around the cabin the woods were as still as the air, as if holding tight to the last vestiges of sleep, before the eastern sky began to turn pink. But nothing could hold back the dawn. The sky reddened, silhouettes took on colors, squirrels and ground animals awakened, stretched, and began to take stock of the new day. In the shed adjacent to the cabin, a horse began to stamp its feet, and from the chimney a puff of smoke signaled that the hearth fire had been freshly fueled. In a few minutes, a man bundled in a heavy wool jacket emerged from the cabin and headed out back, while from the cabin now emerged the aroma of frying bacon and brewing coffee. . . .

Life on the frontier—how romanticized it has been in best-selling fiction and film! Swiss Family Robinson in the American wilderness; the return to lost innocence, to ultimate and lasting values, to family solidarity; the incomparable challenge of confronting nature and taming it; the chance for a man to be a man, to be the absolute captain of one's ship and master of one's fate, and *never be told what to do by anyone. . . .* Practically everyone who has written popular fiction about life on the frontier has slipped into the same pitfall that once claimed Jean-Jacques Rousseau and the vicomte de Chateaubriand and their ilk who extolled the noble savage—without ever having actually met one. Just as distinguished historians have presented a far richer and more positive portrait of the Puritans than the popular stereotype, so they show us that what life was really like in that two-room log cabin was far from the romantic image that most of us carry.

To be sure, the beauty of the rolling hills was breathtakingly, and for years Kentucky would be known as "the Garden of the West."[1] An Ohio boatman who knew both sides of the river intimately was quoted by Charles Fenno Hoffman: "No, stranger, there's no place on the universal earth like old Kaintuck. She whips all 'out-west' in prettiness, and you might boil down Creation and not get such another State out of it."[2] Kentucky was commonly equated with Paradise and a new Eden, and some likened it to the perfect setting of the anticipated creation of the Kingdom of God on earth. In a meetinghouse near Paint Lick, a Baptist preacher, trying to give his listeners an idea of what heaven was like, exclaimed, "O my dear honeys, heaven is a Kentucky of a place."[3]

But—the aroma of frying bacon was in the air *every* morning—and noon and evening, for salt pork was the staple of frontier life in Kentucky. An Englishman named Ashe unquestionably exaggerated when he wrote in 1806:

> The Kentuckians eat nothing but bacon, which indeed is the favorite diet of all the inhabitants of that State. . . . No people on earth live with less regard to regimen. They eat salt meat three times a day, seldom or never have any vegetables, and drink ardent spirits from morning till night. They not only have an aversion to fresh meat, but a vulgar predjudice that it is unwholesome. The truth is, their stomachs are depraved by burning liquors, and they have no appetite for anything but what is highly flavored and strongly impregnated by salt.[4]

But despite its disdainful condescension, his observation is in the main confirmed by none other than James Fenimore Cooper, who related the opinion of a Kentucky mother in 1784:

> As for bread, I count that for nothing. We always have bread and potatoes enough; but I hold a family to be in a desperate way, when the mother can see the bottom of the pork barrel. Give me the children that's raised on good sound pork before all the game in the country. Game's good as a relish, and so's bread, but pork is the staff of life. . . . My children I calculate to bring up on pork.[5]

As for burning liquors, the Kentuckians probably consumed more whiskey per capita than any people on earth. On the Kentucky frontier, whiskey was as much a way of life as pork, and since it was also the principal means of barter, it was in constant supply. Other than common sense (which was not always in constant supply), the one check on excessive consumption would have been the moral conscience which springs from a dynamic, shared faith. But unlike the northern frontier, that was a pretty rare commodity in Kentucky. Most of the population had come from Virginia, where disestablishment had painfully revealed the long-term spiritual bankruptcy of the Church there. As Francis Asbury recorded in Kentucky in 1797: "When I reflect that not one in a hundred came here to get religion, but rather to get plenty of good land, I think it will be well if some or many do not eventually lose their souls."[6]

Without God to turn to in moments of crisis or despair, the jug came out frequently; indeed, it was practically the only form of diversion to alleviate the crushing monotony of the same tasks day in and day out and especially the winters, when it was too cold to do anything outside. Then there was the loneliness. In settlements north of the Ohio, the neighborhood church provided social as well as spiritual focus to the lives of the farmers. But down in the Kentucky hills, their much prized independence came at a price, and that price was seldom seeing any but one's own kin, often for several weeks at a time. A man's own family had to meet all his social needs, and he theirs, and as nerves began to fray, a pull on the jug was often needed to set oneself up for the day, and a dram in the morning was a sign of a young lad's passage into manhood.

In his book, *Westward Ho!,* James Kirke Paulding summed up the effect of the frontier on Kentuckians:

> The result of their peculiar situation, habits, and modes of thinking has been a race of men uniting in a fearlessness of danger, a hardy spirit of enterprise, a power of supporting fatigues and privations, and an independence of thought which perhaps were never associated with the pursuits and acquirements of civilized life in any other country than the United States.[7]

These "peculiarly American tendencies" were, in the opinion of Frederick Jackson Turner, "much intensified by the Kentuckians by isolation." But perhaps the best summary of the Kentucky mind-set is provided by Arthur Moore:

> Reckless, exuberant, lawless, violent, brave, the frontiersman of Kentucky acted the part of the utterly free agent and by word or gesture expressed a lively contempt for artificial ethical prescriptions. Admittedly, the cords which bind the individual to a given cultural frame may be snapped by prolonged danger and isolation, but such a consequence is by no means inevitable, at least not to an extreme degree, as witness the Puritan experience in New England. . . . Most of those who trudged over the Wilderness Road, while not officially rebellious against society, probably intended to achieve in the Garden of Kentucky a way of life conspicuously free of the impediments familiar to the East. Such an expectation of unalloyed freedom, intensified by and involved in myth, inevitably precipitated irresponsible acts ranging from gross to foolish and eventuated in an unusual state of mind—the frontier mind.[8]

Man's sense of society—of belonging to a community of other men—at the deepest level comes from the wellspring of shared religion—which the Puritan pioneers had and the Kentuckians initially lacked. Modern sociologists point to the importance of permanent neighborhoods and ethnic compatibility, of families putting down roots in one place. Yet how often have families lived in neighborhoods or apartment buildings for years, without ever developing mutual, caring relationships with their neighbors? As historian Page Smith has noted, there are two sides to the American psyche, perpetually in conflict: at war with man's instinctive desire to dwell in community is his desire for competitive individualism. Today, that individualism has largely won out in America. Many of us live in metropolises of millions—and can count our meaningful nonfamily relationships on the fingers of one hand. We pay enormous fees to psychiatrists, just to have someone who appears to care listen to us attentively for an hour or two a week. In our buildings, we don't know anyone on the floor above or below us—and don't want to. It was not always thus; there was a time early in this century, when apartment dwellings were vertical neighborhoods, and everyone knew everyone else. But many modern Americans have made an idol out of privacy, and once we can afford the isolation we desire—once we have truly become islands unto ourselves—we expect to find at least a measure of the happiness that has thus far eluded us. But it is not there, and then our children choose to leave our islands, and our lives are even emptier than before.

What begins to fill the emptiness—what draws people together with others—is a common enthusiasm, a favorite club or a team. But of all possible shared enthusiasms, the one which most causes men to want to worship together, live together, and become involved in one anothers' lives is the love of Jesus Christ. This shared love continually renews our closest relationships, daily making our lives together fresh and challenging. You can have it in a prayer group or a church, on a college campus or in a factory, on board a ship or in a residential Christian community.

Yet even an active Christian faith is no guarantee against isolation. How many of our fellow church members do we Christians truly care about? How many people do we ask how they are—and are inwardly relieved when they don't tell us? It comforts us to think of ourselves as caring, but how often are we compassionate when it is inconvenient? How many of us prefer to concentrate on the first great commandment and let the second take care of itself?

Of all the untamed territory in America, settlers in Kentucky were the most isolated. Most of the pioneers who headed there were convinced they needed *no one.* For them, Kentucky meant a life of complete freedom. Partly as a result of living that way, they became in many cases a little crazy and more than a little lawless, but they also became extraordinarily proficient at coping with the extremities of their situation. Their prowess with the long rifle was legendary, and their skill with an ax, while less well-known, was every bit its equal. The Kentucky ax was light, sharp, and durable, and the precision with which men wielded it was testified to by the tightness of the log cabins they built. Each log was notched at the end, to receive the notch of the log that would go crossways, and the better the fit, the less mud packing would be necessary to fill the gaps. The Kentucky cabins were remarkably mud free.[9] These axmen were also fast; many of them could split 200 rails a day.

The struggle to carve out a living was a dawn-to-dusk affair. Nor was there any time to waste on such frills as floorboards or glazed windows or a vegetable patch. Any variation from pork three times a day would have to come from the frontiersman's game bag. Fortunately, game was prevalent in Kentucky; in the beginning, there were even herds of buffalo and elk, but these were soon driven west. Happily, the wild turkeys remained behind—because, said some, they were too fat to fly very far—and the forest teemed with rabbits and squirrels. Turkey, however, was everyone's favorite, and they were so plump that sometimes they broke off the limbs on which they landed, and some even split open, when they hit the ground. (Kentuckians were sometimes known to embellish their tales a bit, even Kentucky's most famous son, Colonel D. Boone, who passed that gem along).[10]

In any event, the knowledge that his wife and children would go to sleep hungry that night, if he did not return with something in his rucksack, was a potent incentive for the Kentucky backwoodsman to perfect his marksmanship until he could hit the eye of a squirrel at sixty yards (although he preferred to aim just above the squirrel's head, so that it would be knocked senseless by flying bark). In that way, none of the eating meat was messed up with bone or bullet fragments. For the same reason, in shooting turkeys, the object was to sever the neck, which could be done at a hundred yards. Moreover, there are documented accounts of Kentucky riflemen felling birds on the wing, and even two birds with one shot.[11]

As hunters and woodsmen, these buckskin-clad Kentuckians soon became a match for the Indians, who were bent on getting rid of them. In the first years of the frontier, to live on the farm was to live in a combat zone. Before opening your front door in the morning, you climbed a ladder to look out a peephole, to see if any Indians were in sight. But you did not stop there; you craned your neck to look directly below at the front door itself. For Indian war parties had been known to have one of their number sleep leaning against the door all night long, so that when it was incautiously opened, he would be awakened and gain access to the house, whereupon the rest of his party would burst from concealment and follow him in. Daniel Boone recalls a similar ruse in his memoir. The Indians would have one among them who could speak English, and in the evening he would approach the door and say, "Who keeps house?" which was the standard greeting of a frontier stranger. Too often, loneliness and hospitality would get the better of caution, and the door would be opened wide—to a guest with a paint-streaked face and a raised tomahawk.[12]

If your house did come under attack and no chance to escape presented itself, you had better go down fighting than be taken alive. The savagery of the Indians to their captives was so horrible that if many diaries and published narratives of those who did manage to escape did not document it, in this modern age none would believe the truth. For the Indians were accomplished masters at inflicting physical and psychological pain up to the threshold of consciousness, then backing off just enough to keep the victim from merciful unconsciousness or insanity. Periodically, they would let him rest, for they felt cheated if their victims died too soon. Skilled torturers could skin their victims alive and then carefully filet them, with captured friends or relatives forced to watch, as they prolonged life for hour after hour of sobbing, shrieking agony. That the Indians derived such pleasure from the pain they thus inflicted was nothing short of satanic. Indeed, some of the accounts are so gruesome they make modern methods of torture seem almost humane.

One of the milder ones is the account of Thomas Baldwin, who lived in west Kentucky, in the spring of 1791:

> They now appeared almost daily in still greater numbers, in view of our little settlement, and the more to provoke us there amused themselves by brandishing their scalping knives and imitating the dying groans of such of our unfortunate friends as had fallen into their hands, and on whom, in all probability they had, in their last moments, inflicted the most savage cruelty.[13]

Baldwin and his family were subsequently attacked in their home by a band of Indians, who set their roof afire and then slaughtered his wife and son and daughter, as they fled the flames. He himself, another son, and a daughter were taken prisoner. He and his daughter were forced to watch his son be burned alive at the stake, and twice when he passed out they threw water in his face so he would not miss the "enjoyment" of his son's agony. After his son finally died, the Indians got drunk, and Baldwin was able to escape, but he could not rescue his daughter. He came back for her with a posse, but was unable to find her and learned later that she had died in captivity.

Nor was river travel any safer. Along the banks of the Ohio, Indians formed ambushes, firing upon the hapless settlers as they drifted by on their flatboats. Frequently they sent out false signals to lure the boats ashore, capturing or murdering everyone on board and plundering the contents of the boat. Occasionally, they would dress in their victims' clothes and man the boat themselves, heading downriver among the other vessels like wolves attacking a herd of sheep.[14] For the early settlers embarking on a river voyage down the Ohio, getting there was definitely not half the fun. In the seven years after 1783, no less than 1,500 men, women, and children were slaughtered in Kentucky alone. When a treaty was attempted with the Indians at the Miami River in western Ohio, the Indians' request for thirty days to think it over was granted. They made good use of the time; they killed or captured another 120 people, slowly roasting several alive. When two more federal representatives were sent to talk with them, the Indians pretended to negotiate with them, and when the agents relaxed, they murdered them.

Finally, by 1794, Congress had had enough. They sent the commander-in-chief of the United States Army, Anthony Wayne, together with 2,000 regulars (practically the entire army) to pacify the Indians. A former Congressman from Georgia, Wayne had proven himself to be among the best field generals in the Revolutionary War, especially when it came to fighting Indians. He tracked a large body of warriors of approximately equal size and finally caught up with them near what is today the city of Toledo. The Indians were waiting for him, well concealed behind trees felled by a tornado. They opened fire, and the United States Infantry charged. In the fierce hand-to-hand fighting that ensued, the Indians were soundly defeated, and the British fort which had supplied them with weapons and incited the uprising was neutralized.[15] After the Battle of Fallen Timbers, definitive treaties were concluded, and for all intents and purposes, 1794 brought an end to Indian aggression.

Ironically, while Kentuckian families breathed a sigh of relief and were grateful to be able to focus their full attention on farming, a good many men in this crazy-quilt collection of individualists were almost sorry for the sudden removal of imminent peril that followed the burying of the hatchet. They had been forced to become as adept in the woods as the Indians who stalked them, and many were even more so—powerful, lethal killing machines, living with the expectation that death could be lurking behind the next tree. As such, they depended on honed, lightning-quick reflexes to buy them the split-second edge that would save their lives. Few warriors in history were their equal, and for such men the transition to hoeing corn and planting wheat was difficult at best. Still, they knew that was what they were there for (their wives reminded them), though they looked forward to the fortnightly trips to town for supplies. There they invariably found a saloon where whiskey was as plentiful, and almost as cheap, as water.

Backwoodsmen did not have much restraint to begin with, and liquor tended to remove what little there was. They spoke whatever they thought, and as facing down fear had become so much a part of their lives, it was inevitable that their words would take on bravado. Their idea of a good time was a roaring drunk, and roar they did, bellowing at a potential adversary like a bull discovering another bull in the same field. One foreign traveler on the Mississippi wrote down the following exchange, which took place between two drunken Kentuckians on a nearby flatboat, their voices escalating at each outrage.

"I am a man; I am a horse; I am a team!" cried one, "I can whip any man in Kentucky, by God!"

"I am an alligator," cried the other, "half man, half horse; can whip any man on the Mississippi, by God!"

"I am a man," shouted the first, "have the best horse, best dog, best gun, and handsomest wife in all Kentucky, by God!"

"I am a Mississippi snapping-turtle, have bear's claws, alligator's teeth, and the devil's tail, can whip any man, by God!"[16]

A listener might smile, but it would be a grave and possibly fatal mistake to discount such roaring as empty epithets. Such men had few personal possessions—really not much more than their pride—but to them that was a priceless commodity, to be defended at all costs, including life itself. Therefore, the slightest slur, real or imagined, could not go unanswered. Such roarings, then, were not substitutes for combat; they were preambles, like football linemen psyching themselves up for a sustained test of their courage. And when the fighting began, these adversaries had never heard of the marquis of Queensberry, much less his rules for civilized hand-to-hand warfare. They had learned to survive against scalping knife and tomahawk by neutralizing their savage attackers as quickly and decisively as possible. And so, they were like gamecocks: once pitted against one another, there was no quitting until one or the other was immobilized. A broken arm or jaw was not enough to end one of these rip-roarers, especially with a heavy load of alcohol anesthetizing the pain. It usually took something more drastic, and you could tell a Kentucky brawler by the absence of an ear or a nose—or an eye, for anyone who drank in a saloon had better know how to gouge an eye out of its socket in a hurry.

This practice was as shocking to civilized observers of that era as it is today, yet it was intrinsic to survival. The Reverend James B. Finley, one of the most respected frontier preachers and himself a great hunter, told of a settler who, while cutting wood, chanced upon a bear. The bears, being far less savory than the buffalo that once populated Kentucky, and having no natural predators, were the last large animals to leave. They were extraordinarily dangerous and canny, and they particularly resented the two-footed adversaries who were crowding into their territory. The woodsman had only his ax with which to defend himself, and this the bear knocked away with a swipe of his paw that severely lacerated the settler's arm. It was fight or flee, and the settler, furious at the inflicted wound, chose to fight. He leaped on the bear, caught its nose in his teeth, and jammed his thumbs into the bear's eyes. When asked about bears some years later, he responded: "They can't stand Kentucky play. Biting and gouging are too hard for them."[17]

According to the New York *Courier,* not even a Florida alligator was an equal match for such a man.

> A Kentuckian, belonging to a survey party under an officer of U.S. Engineers swimming in St. John's River, was seized by a large alligator and taken under the water. In a short time, the Kentuckian and the alligator rose to the surface, the latter having the right leg of the former in his mouth, and the former having his thumbs in the eyes of his antagonist. The officer immediately gave orders to his party, who were in a boat a few yards from the combatants, to go to the relief of their comrade, but the Kentuckian peremptorily forbade any interference, saying, "Give the fellow fair play." It is needless to add that the gouger obtained a complete victory. Having taken out one of the eyes of his adversary, the latter, in order to save his other eye, relinquished his hold upon the Kentuckian's leg, who returned to shore in triumph.[18]

One of the roughest counties in all Kentucky was Logan County, out in the southwest corner. Technically, it was under United States law, even before Kentucky was admitted to the Union in 1796. The trouble was, no one on the frontier was designated to enforce the law, with the result that, as Congress would state, "the immunity which offenders experience attracts as to an asylum, the most vile and abandoned criminals, and at the same time deters useful and virtuous persons from making settlements in such society."[19] Logan County attracted so many murderers, horse thieves, highway robbers, and counterfeiters (one-quarter of the money then in circulation in America was counterfeit) that it was nicknamed "Rogues' Harbor" by the outlaws who fled there to escape justice back east. Some virtuous folks lived there; they had even built a few tiny churches. And they themselves tried to do something about the lawlessness that swirled about them. As Peter Cartwright, who grew up there, recalled: "Those who favored a better state of morals were called 'Regulators.' But they encountered fierce opposition from the 'Rogues,' and a battle was fought with guns, pistols, dirks, knives and clubs, in which the Regulators were defeated."[20]

Into Rogues' Harbor in 1798, rode the Reverend James McGready, a Scotch-Irish Presbyterian who wore buckskin breeches like any other frontiersman, and who preached in a vivid, plain-spoken style. He modified old-style Calvinism somewhat by stressing the necessity for experiencing the "new birth," and he described heaven in such detail that his listeners could "almost see its glories and longed to be there." Conversely, borrowing a page from Jonathan Edwards's book, he would also "so array hell and its horrors before the wicked, that they would tremble and quake, imagining a lake of fire and brimstone yawning to overwhelm them, and the wrath of God thrusting them down the horrible abyss."[21] While his powerful delivery had once engendered increasing opposition in South Carolina, here in Logan County it was much appreciated; even the rogues, when they weren't drunk, seemed to regard him as one of their own.

In 1797, the Lord raised up three small congregations for McGready, located on three of the rivers in Logan county, the Muddy, the Red, and the Gasper. Aside from his impassioned preaching and diligent pastoral efforts, McGready had a secret weapon, a covenant, part of which read as follows:

> When we consider the Word and promises of a compassionate God, to the poor lost family of Adam, we find the strongest encouragement for Christians to pray in faith—to ask in the name

> of Jesus for the conversion of their fellow men. . . . With these promises before us, we feel encouraged to unite our supplications to a prayer-hearing God, for the out-pouring of His Spirit, that His people may be quickened and comforted, and that our children, and sinners generally, may be converted.[22]

All those who were willing to sign the covenant agreed to pray every Saturday evening and Sunday morning and to devote the third Saturday of each month to prayer and fasting. The focus of this concerted prayer campaign was for the Lord to cause a religious awakening in the county,[23] and month after month they importuned the gates of heaven. It may have seemed to them that it was in vain, for if anything, matters appeared to be getting worse. But McGready urged them to keep praying, reminding them that God did hear the prayers of the righteous. So they prayed and asked God to search their own hearts and show them where they needed to repent, that they might truly be righteous in His eyes.

Within a year, revival began to break out. The first instance was in the Red River congregation during the quarterly communion service of July, 1799, where "some of the boldest, most daring sinners in the county covered their faces and wept bitterly."[24] The following month, McGready similarly celebrated the Lord's Supper at the Gasper River church, with similar results. But according to him, these were but "a few scattering drops before a mighty rain—the overflowing floods of salvation" that would commence the following summer.[25] The frontier folk of Kentucky had no training in theology, no patience for rational deduction, no tradition of decorum that had been passed down for generations. They were a people of strong emotions running close to the surface, and they respected physical power, in whatever form it took. God was about to give them what they needed.

In June of 1800, it was once again time for the quarterly communion services at the Red River church. News of what had taken place the year before had traveled far and wide, and to McGready's astonishment, more than five hundred people showed up, a number traveling from as far as a hundred miles away. Some came spiritually hungry, others were merely curious, but none went away disappointed. The meetings were scheduled to run from Friday to Monday, with the Lord's Supper being celebrated on Sunday. During the first two meeting days, the congregation was reduced to tears several times, but not until the last service on the final day had concluded did God pour out

His Spirit on all flesh. Several ministers had joined McGready, and three of these had already left the church when the Spirit fell on the assembly. As they sat in reflection, a "solemn weeping fell over the house," and one Methodist minister, John McGee, from the Cumberland Valley in Tennessee, managed to compose himself for one final appeal.

> I exhorted them to let the Lord Omnipotent reign in their hearts and submit to Him, and their souls should live. Many broke silence. The woman in the east end of the house shouted tremendously. I left the pulpit to go to her. . . . Several spoke to me: "You know these people. Presbyterians are much for order, they will not bear this confusion, go back and be quiet." I turned to go back—and was near falling, the power of God was strong upon me. I turned again and losing sight of fear of man, I went through the house exhorting with all possible ecstasy and energy.[26]

With that, the dam broke, and the floods of salvation swept through the assembly. In a moment, the floor was "covered with the slain; their screams for mercy pierced the heavens," and according to McGready, one could see "profane swearers and Sabbath-breakers pricked to the heart and crying out 'What shall we do to be saved?' "[27]

From there, McGready went on to Muddy River and held meetings with similar results. Word of mouth spread through the land like wildfire: things were happening at McGready's meetings that had not happened since the Book of Acts! And for frontier families who had spent long, lonely winters in cabin isolation, followed by springs of grinding labor, getting the season's crops planted, the news was like a magnet drawing them. They headed for Gasper River where in July there was to be a four-day sacramental meeting. Realizing that many people might come, McGready sent out word for people to bring wagons and supplies and prepare to camp, for his little congregation would never be able to house all the visitors. Similarly, woodsmen cut a great clearing in the forest, built a preaching stand eight feet in the air, and split logs for rough-hewn benches. Yet even McGready was dumbfounded when *ten thousand* people showed up! For Logan County was so far back in the woods that the nearest major town, Lexington, the biggest in the whole state, was more than a hundred miles away to the northeast. And even Lexington, if you counted every woman, child, and slave, numbered only eighteen hundred inhabitants. People had obviously traveled for days to be there.

McGready had invited several backwoods ministers to join him, for frontier preachers were such a rarity that they all knew one another. The McGee brothers came, and the Reverend Barton W. Stone, who himself had been converted under McGready's preaching in North Carolina a dozen years before. Stone had two congregations of his own halfway back across the state, in Bourbon County, but after hearing what had happened at Red River and Muddy River, a week-long journey through the backwoods did not seem too far to travel, to see for oneself. Reverend Stone was soon exceedingly glad that he had made the trek:

> There, on the edge of a prairie in Logan County, Kentucky, the multitudes came together and continued a number of days and nights encamped on the ground, during which time the worship was carried on in some part of the encampment. The scene was new to me and passing strange. It baffled description. Many, very many, fell down as men slain in battle, and continued for hours together in an apparently breathless and motionless state, sometimes for a few minutes reviving and exhibiting symptoms of life by a deep groan or a piercing shriek, or by a prayer for mercy fervently uttered. After lying there for hours, they obtained deliverance. The gloomy cloud that had covered their faces seemed gradually and visibly to disappear, and hope in smiles brightened into joy. They would rise, shouting deliverance, and then would address the surrounding multitude in language truly eloquent and impressive. With astonishment did I hear men, women, and children declaring the wonderful works of God, and the glorious mysteries of the Gospel.[28]

With crowds so large, several ministers could preach at once without interfering with one another, and they did—Baptists and Methodists, as well as Presbyterians, in what might be called the first massive ecumenical Christian rally in history. McGready was overjoyed: "No one seemed to want to go home—hunger and sleep seemed to affect nobody—eternal things were the vast concern. Here awakening and converting work was to be found in every part of the multitude!" Indeed, when the meeting finally broke up and the worshipers dispersed, most of the ministers went away buoyed up in their faith and zeal, as they had never been before. In each of their home congregations, they immediately organized camp meetings that met with similar success. Word of mouth of what was happening seemed to be carried by the wind of the Spirit. It spread throughout Kentucky, south into Tennes-

Revival - Kentucky - 1800

see and beyond into North Carolina, it jumped the Ohio and went north, and it went back east through the Cumberland Gap—the Great Revival of 1800 was underway!

Looking back, McGready would declare:

> The present summer has been the most glorious time that our guilty eyes have ever beheld. All the blessed displays of Almighty power and grace, all the sweet gales of the divine Spirit and soul-reviving showers of the blessings of heaven which we enjoyed before, and which we considered wonderful beyond conception, were but like a few scattering drops before the mighty rain which Jehovah has poured out like a mighty river upon this, our guilty, unworthy country. The Lord has indeed showed Himself a prayer-hearing God; He has given His people a praying spirit and a lively faith, and then He has answered their prayers far beyond their highest expectations. This wilderness and solitary place has been made glad, this dreary desert now rejoices and blossoms like the rose; yea, it blossoms abundantly, and rejoices even with joy and singing.[29]

Like the rest, Barton Stone returned home to Bourbon County and astounded his congregations with his account of what had transpired. And with his Cane Ridge congregation, he began to lay plans for a camp meeting the following summer, the likes of which the world had never seen.

For days before the meeting at Cane Ridge was scheduled to begin, family wagons had begun arriving. Indeed, they choked all the approach roads, and the dust they raised coated everything. The first men to arrive were set to clearing and then enlarging a vast open space in the woods. In the manner of the first camp meetings, men fashioned rough benches from felled logs that they then flattened on top by adze and ax. Speaking platforms were also erected around the perimeter of the clearing—for this one, no less than seven—so that voices could carry over the assembly and preachers could be easily seen. Stone had invited other preachers to help—Presbyterians, Baptists, Methodists; denominational background did not seem to matter much in the trenches, and these frontier preachers were seasoned veterans. "They were of one mind and soul," wrote Stone, "the salvation of sinners was the one object. We all engaged in singing the same songs, all united in prayer, all preached the same things."[30] They were of one mind and one accord—as is always the case when true revival breaks out.

The clearing at Cane Ridge was enormous, for it would have to hold literally thousands, but no one foresaw that there would be some twenty-five thousand in all[31]—more than an eighth of the state's entire free population. Everyone came prepared to camp out, either in their wagons or under them, and hundreds of wagons were circled around the outer perimeter of the clearing. As for food, most brought an ample supply for several days, and makeshift tent shops set up behind the wagons could answer many needs. There were also merchants who would sell whiskey by the cupful from barrels hidden in the bushes, to those with a thirst that could not be assuaged by water. The meeting was open to all, and that included the dregs of Kentucky society, who were just as curious as the sober. There was, therefore, some drunkenness in evidence, but these unfortunates became regarded as prime objects for special prayer and soon learned to keep their peace or be converted, as many were. The ministers and those who had already been converted at camp meetings the previous summer proved sufficient to keep the rowdy element under control. Basically, one could describe this as a gathering of the curious—who had heard and wondered and come to see for themselves. It was also a unique opportunity to socialize for many folk who had seen no more than half a dozen people outside their immediate families. For them, Cane Ridge would be the social high point of the year. And also present would be some scoffers and brawlers and hard cases, but they would make up a decided minority of the gathering.

When at last it was time for the meeting to begin, the clearing was filled to overflowing. The pews had long since been taken, but it didn't matter, for everyone felt too excited to sit down anyway, and those with places on the benches used them to stand on. One by one, the preachers either mounted the platforms or stood on stumps, and often several preached at once, spaced far enough from one another so that their voices did not conflict. Each had a crowd gathered in front, some numbering more than a thousand, and a great many people drifted from group to group, as if sampling a divine smorgasbord.

It was not long before the Spirit fell. People began to come under the conviction of the Holy Spirit and began to call out, "What must I do to be saved?" Others fell to the ground, "slain in the Spirit," and still others exhibited all manner of bizarre behavior. For as powerful as the outpouring of the Holy Spirit was, the unholy spirit was present also. Indeed, Satan prowled around the perimeter of the clearing like a mighty lion, seeking whom he might devour. Powerful emotions had been unleashed, and as has been noted, these were uncomplicated people whose feelings sometimes got the better of them. Invariably some got carried away, and there were reports of lascivious behavior in the underbrush out beyond the wagons. The preachers in charge assigned elders to patrol there, but they were wise enough not to be stampeded into drastic action against all spontaneous outbursts, as some of the Presbyterians present were calling for. Better to let the wheat and the tares grow together for a season than to risk quenching the Holy Spirit, let alone grieving Him into departing. What was genuine and what was sham or self-generated exhilaration would be apparent soon enough.

Among the preachers present were Methodist John McGee and his Presbyterian brother William. The latter "would sometimes exhort after the sermons, standing on the floor, or sitting, or lying in the dust, his eyes streaming, and his heart so full that he could only cry out 'Jesus, Jesus.' "[32] His brother John, who had been so used by God at McGready's meeting at Red River the summer before, described the awesome scene at night: "The camp ground was well illuminated; the people were differently exercised all over the ground, some exhorting, some shouting, some praying, and some crying for mercy, while others lay as dead men on the ground."[33]

There were many instances of hard cases and scoffers falling at the continual services "as suddenly as if struck by lightning," sometimes at the very moment they were cursing the proceedings. One tried to prove that the fallen were faking their experience and began prodding them with a nail on a stick, but to no avail. Frustrated, he went and purchased several cupfuls of whiskey, then returned and shouted that he, at least, would not fall. The words were scarcely out of his mouth before he found himself flat on his back. When he regained his speech, the first words out of his mouth "acknowledged himself a great sinner, and hoped for pardon through Christ."[34]

The meeting continued all night long and into the next day and the next night. As people were converted they would spell the preachers, giving their own testimonies in the most vibrant terms. More fell, and all manner of manifestations were given vent, but the most unaccountable—and moving—to chief preacher Barton Stone was the "singing exercise." With a sublime countenance, the individual "would sing most melodiously, not from the mouth or nose, but entirely in the breast, the sounds issuing thence. . . . It was most heavenly. None could ever be tired of hearing it."[35]

Now small groups were forming and singing Watts's and Hart's hymns, until the next preacher arose. William Burke described one instance of his own preaching, as he got up on a log bench and

> . . . commenced reading a hymn with an audible voice, and by the time we concluded singing and praying, we had around us, standing on their feet, by fair calculation ten thousand people. I gave out my text in the following words: "For we must all stand before the judgment seat of Christ," and before I concluded, my voice was not to be heard for the groans of the distressed and the shouts of triumph. . . . Here I remained Sunday night, and Monday and Monday night, and during that time there was not a single moment's cessation, but the work went on.[36]

At times, when more than a thousand were shouting at once, the sound could be heard for miles. The overwhelming impact of this deafening uproar was described by James B. Finley, who had come as a skeptic:

> The noise was like the roar of Niagara. The vast sea of human beings seemed to be agitated as if by a storm. I counted seven ministers, all preaching at one time, some on stumps, others in wagons. . . . Some of the people were singing, others praying, some crying for mercy in the most piteous accents, while others were shouting most vociferously. While witnessing these scenes, a peculiarly-strange sensation, such as I had never felt before, came over me. My heart beat tumultuously, my knees trembled, my lip quivered, and I felt as though I must fall to the ground. A strange supernatural power seemed to pervade the entire mass of mind there collected. . . . Soon after, I left and went into the woods, and there I strove to rally and man up my courage.

After some time, I returned to the scene of the excitement, the waves of which, if possible, had risen still higher. The same awfulness of feeling came over me. . . I saw at least five hundred swept down in a moment, as if a battery of a thousand guns had been opened upon them, and then immediately followed shrieks and shouts that rent the very heavens. My hair rose up on my head. . . .I fled into the woods a second time, and wished I had stayed at home."[37] [Finley survived, to become one of the strongest preachers on the frontier.]

If the Cane Ridge meeting had an apex, it was when the Lord's Supper was served on Sunday morning to approximately a thousand Presbyterians and an indeterminate number of Methodists and Baptists. Once again, the wind of the Spirit swept through the assembly like a mighty, unseen scythe, and this time no less than three thousand, by conservative estimate, were mown down. Showers of blessings continued to rain down upon them all, until the food ran out, the meeting wound down, and the wagons began to leave. Finally, they were all gone; the empty, sun-dappled clearing heard only the song of birds and the rustle of small animals who wondered perhaps at the incredible thing that had happened here.

And what of the aftermath? Did the Great Revival in the West have a permanent effect on Kentucky? If one were to judge by the exploding church membership rolls, it did. In three years, Baptist congregations in Kentucky gained more than ten thousand members, the Methodists gained approximately the same, and the Presbyterians also gained vast numbers. More significantly, foreign travelers who had been to Kentucky before could hardly believe that they were in the same state. Whereas before, isolation and drunken brawling had been among the most memorable aspects of the people who lived there, now there were churches and churchgoers who behaved like good Christians elsewhere on the frontier. Now there were fellowship and neighbors caring for one another, raising barns and clearing fields together. In the wake of God's lightning storm, many Kentuckians (though by no means all) now behaved remarkably like the early Puritan pioneers.

The final assessment belongs with perhaps the most skeptical observer of all: Dr. George Baxter, of Washington Academy in Virginia. Hearing the amazing stories and disapproving of the reported excesses, this Presbyterian minister was of a mind to discredit the revival at its source, and in the name of religion he journeyed to Kentucky in November, 1801, for this express purpose. The report he sent the prominent Presbyterian leader, the Reverend Archibald Alexander, in Princeton, was not at all what the latter expected—or the sender, for that matter. The report was subsequently published and widely circulated in the *Connecticut Evangelical Magazine,* and thus served to further spread the good news. Wrote Baxter:

> The power with which this revival has spread, and its influence in moralizing the people, are difficult for you to conceive, and more so for me to describe. . . . I found Kentucky, to appearance, the most moral place I had ever seen. A profane expression was hardly ever heard. A religious awe seemed to pervade the country. . . . Never in my life have I seen more genuine marks of that humility which . . . looks to the Lord Jesus Christ as the only way of acceptance with God. I was indeed highly pleased to find that Christ was all and in all in their religion. . . . and it was truly affecting to hear with what agonizing anxiety awakened sinners inquired for Christ, as the only physician who could give them any help.
>
> Those who call these things "enthusiasm," ought to tell us what they understand by the Spirit of Christianity. . . . Upon the whole, sir, I think the revival in Kentucky among the most extraordinary that have ever visited the Church of Christ, and all things considered, peculiarly adapted to the circumstances of that country. . . . Something of an extraordinary nature seemed necessary to arrest the attention of a giddy people, who were ready to conclude that Christianity was a fable, and futurity a dream. This revival has done it; it has confounded infidelity, awed vice to silence, and brought numbers beyond calculation under serious impressions."[38]

The Second Great Awakening was underway. It would spread through the gaps and over the turnpikes and down the rivers—wherever men traveled, whose lives had been profoundly altered by what happened in Kentucky. It would take different forms and different substances, according to local circumstances, and while nowhere would the results be quite as spectacular as they had been at the early camp meetings, they would go deeper and last longer.

The sleeping adolescent giant who had been rudely and wondrously awakened now had a choice, another option, instead of just living for self. Awesomely powerful when his attention was focused, yet alarmingly impetuous in the grip of his emotions, he was now aware of the One who gave purpose and direction to all life. Now, in his life there was the possibility of wholeness, balance, and maturity. The choice would still be his, but now he had a choice.

Once more, God had intervened in order that the covenant the Pilgrams and Puritans had made with Him could still be kept—if the republic chose to do so. The temptations would still be there—all the myriad opportunities to forsake our inheritance for a mess of pottage. From now on, there would be a counterforce of Light to offset the darkness that had seemed to have gained the upper hand. The choice was up to the people as to which way they would go.

In the meantime, it was the turn of a small band of selfless men of faith who would give their lives to carrying the revival to the homes of those who had not been able to get to the camp meetings, and to solidly grounding the faith of those who had. They were a new generation of men passionately devoted to God and delighting in His service.

4

"On the Stretch for God"

The young rider drew his black cloak tighter about him as he leaned into the November sleet. Feeling his horse shiver beneath him, he patted her neck and promised her a barn and all the oats she could eat, before darkness closed in on them. And then he looked up at the gray sky and beseeched his heavenly Father, whose business he was about, to provide for the mare that night. Tilting his head so that the brim of his black hat would keep the rain from his eyes, he added a postscript for himself, affirming that God's grace was sufficient and worth riding to the ends of the earth for.

They came to a stream, swollen from the downpour. Gingerly the mare started across, feeling for sure footing in the dark, swirling waters. Deeper they went, and faster rushed the water around them. It was over the rider's feet now, filling his boots and soaking his last pair of dry socks. The mare stumbled, and for an instant it looked as if they would both be swimming for their lives. Anger and self-pity gnawed at the edges of the rider's heart—then he laughed out loud and praised God. He shouted encouragement to the mare over the noise of the wind and rain, and she regained her footing and clambered up the bank. Only four more miles to go, he assured her, to the cabin of a family he had brought to salvation the previous summer, and he broke into a hymn. . . .

A new breed of lightning rods emerged from that Great Revival in the West, men who would spend much of their lives "on the stretch for God," as George Whitefield, the original circuit rider, had put it. The lightning had fallen suddenly and astoundingly on camp meetings throughout the frontier, and now these saddlebag evangelists had committed their lives to carrying the light of Christ to all who had been unable to attend the meetings. They would ride deep into uncharted territory, and later, on repeating circuits, they would water the wilderness seeds that they had planted. These were the black-cloaked Methodist missionaries, assigned to a circuit of frontier settlements that would usually take them six to eight weeks to complete. They practically lived in the saddle, taking lodging wherever a family invited them into house or barn, and taking every possible opportunity to pray with them and cheerfully share the good news that Jesus Christ came for all sinners, even one's host.

As a result, much of the frontier was converted to Methodism, for even if these young preachers were not oratorically gifted, they more than made up in enthusiasm what they might have lacked in pulpit polish. What won their converts to Christ was not so much what they said as how they lived their faith. For the circuit riders were the only men on earth who drove themselves as hard or even harder than the American pioneers. And if there was one thing the frontiersman respected, it was hard work. Consequently, if he were inside on a day so foul that not even a dog would venture out and chanced to look out the window and see a Methodist circuit rider passing, he would have to wonder at the commitment that impelled the preacher onward. Later, over a hot meal, to hear that preacher make light of the vicissitudes of his journey . . . well, it was enough to give a strong man cause to think. They would joke among themselves about the circuit riders, saying of a bitterly cold January day, "There's nothing out today but crows and Methodist preachers."[1] They would chuckle, but they would also ponder, and when the preacher was in their own cabin and asking them if they wanted to accept Christ into their hearts, as often as not, they would agree.

So bit by bit at the beginning of the nineteenth century, a new Light counterbalanced the new darkness, and men whose main recreation had been drinking and brawling now mended their ways. They might not go so far as to join the church choir, but they would begin to read aloud from the Good Book to their families, and open their doors to itinerant preachers of any persuasion. Not many other books made their way across the mountains, but among those that did and that found a place in the new convert's home were *Pilgrim's Progress, The Westminster Confession,* and Knox's *History of the Church of Scotland,* along with some bound sermons and journals of godly men.[2] School was usually opened with singing and Scripture reading, and prayer was not uncommon.

Sooner or later in the course of making their appointed rounds, the circuit riders had to surmount practically every conceivable obstacle—even bears. One chanced upon a bear beset by dogs and felt compelled to put a stop to it. Remembering "how we used to kill salmon with a club by hitting them on the nose just below the eyes," he waded into the thick of it and "hit the bear on the nose just below the eyes, and he died instantly."[3] More often, they chose the nonviolent approach, as in the case of another itinerant preacher, who, coming across a bear that "must have been as large as a good-sized yearling steer," sitting in the middle of the wooded path, addressed the creature: "Mr. Bruin, I do not wish to trespass upon your rights, but really I want to go just where you are now sitting. If you can make it quite convenient to get out of my way, I shall be much obliged to you; but if you cannot, or will not, why then I must give you the path, and get out of the way myself."

The bear ruminated on this discourse for a while, then got up and ambled off into the woods.[4]

Not all the obstacles were ursine, however; often the worst were upright, on two legs. The New England backwoods was different from the Kentucky frontier, in that here a nimble wit was often as necessary as physical courage and endurance. One day, Methodist circuit rider Jesse Lee found himself accosted by two lawyers:

"You are a preacher, sir?"

"Yes, I generally pass for one," replied Lee.

"You preach very often, I suppose?"

"Generally every day; frequently twice a day, or more."

"How do you find time to study, when you preach so often?"

"I study when riding," said Lee. "And read when resting," he added, maintaining a smile, though he could see now where they were heading.

The first lawyer feigned incredulity. "But do you not write your sermons?"

"No, not very often, at least."

"Do you not often make mistakes, preaching extemporaneously?" the second lawyer queried.

Lee nodded. "I do, sometimes."

"Well, do you correct them?"

"That depends on the character of the mistake. I was preaching the other day, and I went to quote the text, 'All liars shall have their part in the lake that burneth with fire and brimstone,' and by mistake I said, 'All lawyers shall have their part—' "

The first lawyer interrupted him. "What did you do with that? Did you correct it?"

"Oh, no, it was so nearly true I didn't bother."

"Humph!" said one of the lawyers looking at the other, "I don't know whether you are more a knave than a fool!"

"Neither," replied Lee smiling, and looking at the one on his right and then the one on his left, "I'd say I was just between the two."[5]

If a circuit rider were accustomed to spending long hours in the saddle, sometimes from dawn till dusk, regardless of the weather, and had been doing it for years, the only thing that kept him going was the grace of God—and a cheerful spirit. The latter could turn just about any situation into one that was at least tolerable. And sometimes it was a blessing to both him and the recipient. One minister, applying for lodging at a tavern, was addressed by the landlord: "Stranger, I perceive that you are a clergyman. Please let me know whether you are a Presbyterian or a Methodist."

"Why do you ask?" responded the preacher.

"Because I wish to please my guests, and I have observed that a Presbyterian minister is very particular about his food and his bed and a Methodist about the care and feeding of his horse."

"Very well," replied the minister, "I am a Presbyterian, but my horse is a Methodist."[6]

The saddlebag preachers took William Penn's caution literally: "No Cross, no crown."[7] Perhaps the best-known of them all, Peter Cartwright, looking back years later, recalled:

> A Methodist preacher in those days, when he felt that God had called him to preach, instead of hunting up a college or Biblical institute, hunted up a hardy pony of a horse, and some traveling apparatus, and with his library always at hand, namely Bible, Hymn Book, and [Methodist] Discipline, he started, and with a text that never wore out or grew stale, he cried: "Behold the Lamb of God, that taketh away the sin of the world." In this way, he went through storms of wind, hail, snow, and rain; climbed hills and mountains, traversed valleys, plunged through swamps, swam swollen streams, lay out all night, wet, weary, and hungry. . . . This was old-fashioned Methodist preacher fare and fortune. Under such circumstances, who among us would now say, "Here I am, Lord, send me?"[8]

So they rode, moving like needles across the fabric of America, quilting regions together with the common thread of a shared faith. This sewing was needed not only to prepare the nation for the heart-rending Civil War that would come in two generations; it was needed right now. For without the spiritual needlework of the evangelical ministers of all major denominations, the fabric of the young republic would not have survived ten years, let alone sixty.

Most of Christ's cavalrymen were Methodists, but there would have been precious few of them, were it not for the lifelong example and steadfast determination of Francis Asbury. At five foot nine (which in those days was tall), Asbury was rail thin, with a rugged, intelligent countenance and penetrating blue eyes. When, in 1771, John Wesley, the renowned leader of the Methodists, called for volunteers to go to America, this young itinerant preacher was the first to respond. Well-organized and possessed of deep reserves of zeal for Christ and a passion for travel, Asbury preached wherever he found people who would listen—in inns, jails, or by the wayside. Such were his drive and his success that before long Wesley made him his general assistant in the colonies. But when the American Revolution broke out, and all Methodist ministers were recalled to England, after much prayer, Asbury elected to remain. He felt called to America, whatever her fate.

Asbury seemed to thrive on adversity—especially in terms of impossible distances to travel and impassable road conditions or foul weather to be overcome en route. At a time when a wilderness trail was little more than an indication of direction through the bush, he drove himself unmercifully, even after his health started to break down. "I seldom mount my horse for a ride of less distance than twenty miles on ordinary occasions, and frequently have forty or fifty, in moving from one circuit to another," he once confided in his journal, adding, "In traveling thus, I suffer much from hunger and cold."[9] Moreover, this increased, rather than eased, as the years passed, for as the frontier grew ever larger, so did Asbury's "parish." In the end, it was about the size of western Europe, and when he took the time to add up his horseback mileage, it generally worked out to four to six thousand miles a year.

Asbury was a gifted field general—expertly marshaling his forces and leading his officers, the Methodist circuit riders, mainly by his personal example. His preaching was inspired and often touched his listeners deeply, but it was as bishop and ultimately as general superintendent of the American Methodist Episcopal Church that his gifts truly shone. No young circuit rider, on fire for the Lord, could fail to be powerfully moved by Asbury, who thought nothing of riding 200 miles in a week; preaching every other day, usually for at least an hour; getting up at four in the morning, in order to have two uninterrupted hours of prayer and meditation with the Lord, before the day began. In addition, whenever he was riding, he was reading—he would read the Bible through in about four months and knew the New Testament by heart, but he would also peruse history, biography, and mounds of devotional material.

One thing Asbury could not do on horseback was write letters, but somehow he found time to faithfully and thoughtfully answer every one of the letters he received each week (years later he figured that he received around a thousand a year). This was the mark of Asbury: He *cared.* He loved to "deal closely" with people, as he put it, and would gladly spend extravagantly of the time in his busy schedule for the sake of helping one individual in his Christian walk. Any family with whom Asbury spent the night could expect to be led in prayers, to be exhorted in Christian living, and to be examined, one by one, in their progress toward sanctification. Indeed, as his biographer, L. C. Rudolph, points out, "He preached wherever his horse stopped! If he did not give all men the Gospel, their blood might be on his hands. Extraordinary times demanded extraordinary means."[10]

Asbury's boundless love of the Lord was contagious; he inspired those who were close to him, and his selfless actions spoke even more dramatically than his words.

As Bishop Asbury gradually became a legend, people all up and down America, from back east right out to the western edge of the frontier, came to know by sight the erect, commanding figure who came riding on horseback. The blue eyes, the long white hair, the strong chin and nose and mouth all combined to create a compelling impression. As one of his contemporaries described him: "There was as much native dignity about him, as any man I ever knew. He seemed born to sway others . . . . His countenance had a cast of severity, but this was probably owing to his habitual gravity and seriousness; his look was remarkably penetrating. In a word, I cannot recollect ever seeing a man of more grave, venerable, and dignified appearance."[11]

Indeed, such was the impression that he made, and the ground that he covered, that it was generally reckoned he was instantly recognizable to more people than any man in the country, including President Madison. (Indeed, a friend once sent him a letter addressed: "The Reverend Bishop Asbury, North America," and it was promptly delivered.)

Following his itinerary for a typical year (1791-92), it was not hard to see why. Leaving New York in the early part of September, he proceeded to Philadelphia, Wilmington, and Baltimore; from there to Alexandria, Petersburg, and Norfolk, Virginia; then down to Raleigh and further south to Charleston, and over to Washington, Georgia; back up through the Carolinas again, and on into the west he went, crossing the mountains (which he called "the Alps") to the Holston River in Tennessee; further west he rode, into the Kentucky wilderness as far as Lexington (Indians were a very real danger at that time); then back through Tennessee and over the mountains again, going up the west side of the Alleghenies this time, through the whole breadth of Virginia, into Uniontown, Pennsylvania; now across the Alleghenies by Laurel Hill and Cumberland to Baltimore, and then on to New York; continuing east through Connecticut to Lynn, Massachusetts, then back through the valley of the Connecticut, stopping at Northampton; now over the Berkshires by Pittsfield to Albany; and finally down the Hudson to New York City.[12] The trip took a full year (and one feels vaguely saddlesore, just thinking about it).

Organized in all things, Asbury meticulously kept a detailed journal, most of which was given to comments on that day's travels.

> I was unwell: the clouds were lowering. We had ridden but a mile when the rain began. . . . Hard necessity made us move forward. The western branch of the Toe River, that comes down from the Yellow Mountain, was rapidly filling, and was rocky, rolling and roaring like the sea, and we were compelled to cross it several times. Then when we came to ascend the mountain, we had a skirmish of rain, thunder and lightning. . . ."[13]

Or "We have had rain for eighteen days successively, and I have ridden about two hundred miles in eight or nine days—a most trying time indeed."[14] Or "At night we were poorly provided against the weather; the house was unfinished; and to make matters worse, a horse kicked the door open, and I had a cold and a bad tooth ache, with a high fever."[15]

If the mountains were the bane of the West, undrained land was the bane of the South. Instead of "crossing the Alps," he was "crossing the swamps," and this journal entry from Virginia, in 1787, was typical: "Brother Poythress frightened me with the idea of the Great Swamp, as the east end of the Dismal, but I could not consent to ride sixty miles around, so we ventured through. Neither we, nor our horses, received any injury, praise the Lord!" Then, in North Carolina, he was traveling "three miles on the water, and three more on roads under the water."[16]

Asbury wore out three horses, Jane, Fox, and Spark, underneath him, and finally took to riding light but strong carts, often over roads that were little more that a swath cut by lopping off saplings at a foot and a half—just short enough to let a wagon pass over them. He was proud of his skill as a bush driver, as this journal entry suggests:

> We set out for Crump's, over rocks, hills, creeks, and pathless woods and low land. . . The young man with me had lost heart before we had traveled a mile, but when he saw how I could bush it and sometimes force my way through a thicket, and make young saplings bend before me, and turn out of the way when there was no proper road, he took courage. With great difficulty, we came in at two o'clock after traveling eight or nine hours. The people looked almost as wild as the deer in the woods; I preached on Titus 2:10-12."[17]

The bishop paid little heed to his physical well-being and suffered cruelly from all manner of ailments, including inflammatory rheumatism, fever, boils, bronchitis, asthma, neuralgia, and finally galloping consumption. Yet as he said, he "gladly bore all these things for the sake of the elect" and the ministers for whom he was responsible, exclaiming "I am willing to travel and preach as long as I live, and I hope that I shall not live long after I am unable to travel."[18]

Asbury loved to preach. To him, a perfect Sunday was one that afforded an unexpected third opportunity, in the evening, after a potluck supper. While he came to urge circuit riders to give their all on Sundays and then take Monday off for a rest, Asbury seldom did so himself. He was well aware that his talents as a preacher were no more than "respectable" or "able and systematic," and he prayed, "Lord, keep me from all superfluity of dress, and from preaching empty stuff to please the ear, instead of changing the heart!"[19]

What was the circuit rider's theology? Bishops Coke and Asbury summed it up succinctly in their 1798 edition of the Methodist *Discipline,* when they charged him to: "Convince the sinner of his dangerous condition. . . . He must set forth the depth of original sin, and show the sinner how far he is gone from original righteousness; he must describe the vices of the world in their just and most striking colors, and enter into all the sinner's pleas and excuses for sin, and drive him from all his subterfuges and strongholds." Then, the preacher should go on to "bring the mourner to a *present* Saviour: he must show the willingness of Christ *this moment* to bless him, and bring a present salvation *home* to his soul."[20]

What was the worst thing that could happen to a circuit rider? According to Bishop Asbury, it was falling in love. Until that happened, his men fought on as true soldiers for Christ—going sixteen, eighteen hours a day, year in and year out, and glad to do so for a ridiculous salary that only barely covered their most urgent expenses, like horseshoes. They married their work—until one of those willowy, unmarried Kentucky belles started to flutter her eyelids at the guest preacher, and. . . . Asbury himself never wed, and like the Apostle Paul, he would not require his riders to forego settling down ("locating," he called it), although he confided to his journal, "Marriage is honorable in all—but to me it is a ceremony awful as death. Well it may be so, when I calculate we have lost the traveling labors of about two hundred of the best men in America, or the world, by marriage and consequent location."[21] On another occasion, caught by surprise at the news that one of his favorites in the "thundering legion" was betrothed, he exclaimed: "I believe the devil and the women will get all my preachers!"[22]

Self-denial was something that Asbury was thoroughly familiar with and wished that his young charges were more familiar with. As he expressed it in the General Conference of 1812:

> The important duty of fasting has become almost obsolete. This we are afraid will be productive of melancholy effects. We yet have abundant cause for deep humiliation before God and one another. Our country is threatened, calamities stare us in the face, iniquity abounds, and the love of many waxes cold. O let us again resort to fasting and humiliation.[23]

Nor was Asbury averse to any method, short of direct coercion, to correct his ministers' spiritual perspective. Listening to some preachers complain about their poor support and hard work, he called them to prayer:

> Lord, we are in Thy hands and in Thy work. Thou knowest what is best for us and for thy work, whether poverty or plenty. The hearts of all men are in thy hands. If it is best for us, and for thy Church that we should be cramped and straitened, let the people's hearts and hands be closed. If it is better for us—for the Church—and more to Thy glory that we should abound in the comforts of life, do thou dispose the hearts of those we serve to give accordingly; and may we learn to be content, whether we abound, or suffer need.[24]

But always, he was hardest by far on himself. "O Lord, help me to watch and pray! I am afraid of losing the sweetness that I feel: for months I have felt as if in the possession of perfect love; not a moment's desire of anything but God." Or, "My body is weak, but this does not concern me like the want of more grace. My heart is too cool towards God; I want to feel it like a holy flame." Or when some friends made the mistake of commending him: "Satan, ready for every advantage, seized the opportunity and assaulted me with self-pleasing, self-exalting ideas. But the Lord enabled me to discover the danger, and the snare was broken. May He ever keep me humble, and little, and mean, in my own eyes!"[25]

In his later years, he became increasingly concerned with the need for sanctification, and preached on it in practically every sermon, and he always readily saw himself as the one most in need of perfecting. Indeed, he had a tendency to slip into despair, not only where he was concerned, but for the well-being of Methodism in America. His antidote, hard work, never failed to rouse him. "It is by this that Satan tries to come in: it is my constitutional weakness to be gloomy and dejected. The work of God puts life into me—and why despond? The land is before us, and nothing can hurt us but divisions among ourselves."[26]

Inevitably, there were those who were jealous of the effectiveness of his ministry and the tremendous affection shown him by Methodists everywhere, and these tried to claim he was power hungry. Normally, he simply ignored cutting comments and innuendos, but when one Christian brother compared him to the pope, he felt compelled to respond:

> For myself, I pity those who cannot distinguish between a Pope of Rome, and an old, worn man of about sixty years, who has the power given him of riding five thousand miles a year, at a salary of eighty dollars, through summer's heat and winter's cold, traveling in all weather, preaching in all places, his best covering from rain often but a blanket; the surest sharpener of his wit, hunger, from fasts voluntary and involuntary; his best fare for six months out of twelve, coarse kindness; and his reward—suspicion, envy, and murmurings all the year around.[27]

Bishop Asbury continued, unperturbed, to be faithful to his call, and God honored his obedience: Methodism took flame. The frontier camp meetings, with their inevitable excesses and the spiritual counterfeiting of the enemy, proved too hot for most of the Presbyterians to handle. But the Methodists thrived on the heat. They seemed to be able to channel and direct a camp meeting's energy without quenching the Spirit. Now, when a young man burned to live totally for God, forsaking all the things of the world and all carnal enticements, instead of becoming a Jesuit missionary, as his European counterparts had two centuries before, he could become a Methodist circuit rider. The existence would be every bit as demanding, and he would be challenged to the limit of his endurance and beyond. But the call was also incredibly fulfilling for those who were willing to pay the price.

So these knights of the second lightning donned the whole armor of God and rode forth on their appointed circuits. They were not all cast in the image of Francis Asbury, though they sought to emulate his sacrifice and obedience. They were very much their own men, and while they submitted willingly to their superintendent's authority, how they conducted their ministry remained pretty much their own business. It became Asbury's business when they strayed out of line in their private lives or departed from sound doctrine, but they exhibited very few instances of this—the call was so demanding and the corresponding commitment so great, that the temptations that harass the divided heart obtained little access to them.

Thirteen years after he first packed his Bible into his saddlebag and rode off into the wilderness, Francis Asbury was consecrated bishop at the Methodists' annual convention in 1784. Immediately he had to deal with the greatest crisis he would face: the debate over the Methodist position on slavery. The dispute was exacerbated by the fact that located ministers, who had themselves taken slaves or married wives with slaves, were resisting emancipating them. Asbury himself hated slavery and felt that its continued maintenance, when a man had a chance to stop it, was utterly repugnant in God's eyes. But even by 1784 it had become such a part of the fabric of American life in the South that he was fighting an uphill battle. Nevertheless, he had never shied away from a fight, and he waded into this one, jaw set.

The key man here was actually Bishop Thomas Coke, whom Wesley had assigned with Asbury as "joint superintendent," and Coke was also unequivocally antislavery. Together the two of them, joined by the vast majority of American Methodist ministers, laid down a cornerstone policy for the newly formed Methodist Episcopal Church. They declared slavery "contrary to the golden law of God . . . and the inalienable Rights of Mankind, as well as every Principle of the Revolution" which America had so recently won. Slaveholding Methodist laymen who refused "to extirpate this Abomination from among us" were given twelve months to free their slaves or withdraw from the Methodist societies, or they would be put out. Grudging exception was made for layman and ministers in Georgia and the Carolinas, where it was illegal to free slaves. And ministers from Virginia, where slavery had gotten its start and was a deeply ingrained tradition, had another year to free their charges. Ah, but woe unto the slaveholding preachers of Pennsylvania, New Jersey, Delaware, and Maryland! For they would be suspended, if they did not release their slaves at once. An impressive proclamation—were it not for the fact that there were almost no preachers in that category in those states.[28]

It *was* a powerful edict—and it elicited a powerful backlash. Asbury and Coke did their best. They circulated petitions to the Virginia State Assembly and the Legislature of North Carolina, calling for emancipation, either immediate or gradual. Asbury called on the Governor of North Carolina and appeared to have won him over (though no legislation was subsequently forthcoming). Asbury and Coke together called on George Washington, who deplored slavery—but would not lend the weight of his name to their petition. Coke preached so strongly against slavery in Virginia pulpits that he was threatened with mob violence. And everywhere, for the sake of harmony, more and more middle-of-the-roaders in the Methodist Church decided not to back their leadership on this issue.

Coke began to bend before the pressure, moderating his stand until by the conference of 1785, on the eve of his departure home to England, he stated that he should not have used the pulpit to attack slavery. Coke recorded the fate of their antislavery declaration, which was not even a year old: "We thought it prudent to suspend the minute concerning slavery, on account of the great opposition that had been given it, our work being in too infantile a state to push things to extremity."[29]

Was the newborn Methodist Church in America in too infantile a state to push the antislavery cause to its conclusion? Only God knows for certain. One wonders what might have happened, had Coke, like Asbury, adopted America for his native land or if Asbury alone had persevered. He wanted to. He was at that point strongly tempted to concentrate on working against the "peculiar institution," for as he observed in his frequent crossing into South Carolina in 1801: "I cannot record great things upon religion in this quarter, *but cotton sells high*. I fear there is more gold than grace—more of silver than of 'that wisdom that cometh from above.' "[30] And two years earlier he had written of the Old Dominion: "I am brought to conclude that slavery will exist in Virginia perhaps for ages; there is not a sufficient sense of religion nor of liberty to destroy it."[31] And two years before that he had privately noted in Georgia: "I saw how [a] flood had ploughed up the streets of Augusta; I walked over the ruins for nearly two miles, viewing the deep gulfs in the main street. I suppose they would crucify me, if I were to tell them that it is the African flood, but if they could hear me think, they would discover this to be my sentiment."[32]

So then, where did the general superintendent stand, and what would be his lead?

> Polygamy, slavery, and such like were never commanded under this dispensation, but only tolerated, and accompanied by strict injunctions to prevent men from running to greater lengths

> in these practices. . . . Moses, as a man, suffered this, a less evil, to prevent a greater. But it was not so from the beginning; it is the fall which hath done this, not a holy God. It is man's work, of two evils to choose the least. But God is not tempted of us to evil, neither tempteth He any man. Christians, of two evils should not choose or use either, if they would be like God.[33]

Alas, not enough Methodists were willing to join him in total abstinence, and Asbury now had to decide: would the Methodist clergy expend their energies working against slavery or in evangelizing the South? In all probability, they themselves could not eradicate slavery. But they could bring thousands of slaves to Christ, making their circumstances slightly less intolerable, and could at the same time change the hearts of many slaveholders, which should result in a marked improvement in the living conditions of their slaves. Evangelization had to come first. They would go South.

Having overlooked his health for an entire lifetime, it came as no surprise to Asbury, when, in his seventy-second year, his body finally gave out. Even then he continued to travel everywhere, although now he had to be carried in, wherever he went, always to tears and tumultuous applause. The end came on March 31, 1816, and such was the grief of the Methodists that funeral services were conducted in many cities, chief among them being Baltimore, which saw some twenty thousand mourners escort his remains to their resting place. That previous October he had written: "My eyes fail. I will resign the stations to Bishop McKendree [his successor]—I will take away my feet. It is my fifty-fifth year of ministry, and forty-fifth year of labor in America. My mind enjoys great peace and divine consolation."[34]

How does one evaluate a life like Asbury's? Not easily—although the hard evidence is there: when he arrived in Philadelphia in 1771, there were but 300 communicant Methodists in America. He personally ordained more than 4,000 preachers, traveled more than a quarter of a million miles mostly on horseback, and preached more than 16,500 sermons. At the time of his death, the recorded membership of the Methodist Episcopal Church in America was 214,235.[35] Still, it is difficult to assess its full impact, because it coincided with the Great Revival in the West, and how much one influenced the other, only God knows.

One historian has nevertheless gone on record that Asbury was as much a Founding Father of America as the then president, James

Madison, was. And we can look at his obedience and givenness with awe and realize that he taught two generations of circuit riders and pulpit ministers what it meant to give one's utmost. The cardinal rule of leadership is: never ask those under you to do what you yourself are not prepared to do. Not only was Asbury prepared, he *did* what hardly anyone else of his own volition would have called upon himself to do. In this, he and his circuit riders taught a whole nation what it truly meant to be on the stretch for God. Finally, looking at Asbury from the perspective of God's plan for America, one is grateful that every so often the right man *does* arrive in the right place at the right time. We had seen it before, in the cases of Governor Bradford of Plymouth, Governor Winthrop of Massachusetts, Governor Hooker of Connecticut, and George Whitefield of America, and of course, above all, George Washington, who truly deserves to be called the father of our country. Seen against the tapestry of the end of the eighteenth century and the beginning of the nineteenth, Asbury merits inclusion in that elect company.

A number of Methodist circuit riders under Asbury's generalship earned reputations well beyond their circuits. One of them, Peter Cartwright, became something of a legend. A solid 200 pounds on a medium frame, he possessed considerable physical strength, as well as unruly hair, a resolute jaw, and piercing black eyes that could look right through a man. In all, he presented "a very bold and formidable look."[36] Born in Virginia in 1785, at the age of nine he accompanied his family to Kentucky, where his father settled in Logan County, not realizing why it was nicknamed "Rogues' Harbor."

Here Cartwright was raised, and he well remembered the showdown between Rogues and Regulators. Unfortunately, history did not follow the subsequent Hollywood scenarios; the "bad guys" soundly thrashed the "good guys," which meant that any Logan County lad had to learn to use his fists if he was going to survive. Young Cartwright learned. By the time he was fifteen, he was, in his own words, "a wild, wicked boy, and delighted in horse-racing, card-playing, and dancing. My father restrained me but little, though my mother often talked to me, wept over me, and prayed for me."[37] Young Cartwright had a fast mount and liked nothing better than a challenge on the open road. But his favorite pastime of all was a party—until one evening in his sixteenth year, when he and his father and brother had come home from attending a wedding celebration, at which there had been drinking and dancing, as was the custom.

> I began to reflect on the manner in which I had spent the day and the evening. I felt guilty and condemned. I rose and walked the floor. My mother was in bed. It seemed to me, all of a sudden my blood rushed to my head, my heart palpitated, in a few minutes I turned blind. An awful impression rested on my mind that death had come, and I was unprepared to die. I fell on my knees and began to ask God to have mercy on me. My mother sprang from her bed, and was soon on her knees by my side, praying for me and exhorting me to look to Christ for mercy. Then and there, I promised the Lord that if He would spare me, I would seek and serve Him.[38]

The seeking continued for several days, with Cartwright undissuaded of his desperate, fallen condition. And then one afternoon, he described himself as "walking and wringing my hands in great anguish, trying to pray, on the borders of utter despair. It appeared to me that I heard a voice from heaven, saying, *Peter, look at me.* A feeling of relief passed over me, quick as an electric shock. It gave me hopeful feelings and some encouragement to seek mercy, but still my load of guilt remained." The search went on. It ended three months later, at a camp meeting three miles away, presided over by the Presbyterian minister James McGready, who had invited several Methodist preachers to attend with him, among them John Page. Ten times the number of people that McGready's church could hold arrived for the meeting, some traveling by wagon for several days to get there. Cartwright responded to the first altar call.

> I went with weeping multitudes and bowed before the stand, and earnestly prayed for mercy. In the midst of a solemn struggle of soul, an impression was made upon my mind, as though a voice said to me: "Thy sins are all forgiven thee." Divine light

> flashed all around me, unspeakable joy sprang up in my soul. I rose to my feet, opened my eyes, and it really seemed as if I was in heaven—the trees, the leaves of them, and everything seemed to be, and I really thought they were, praising God. My mother raised the shout, and my Christian friends crowded round me and joined me in praising God.[39]

Young Cartwright joined John Page's Methodist church and soon became a preacher himself, specializing in the camp meetings he loved. Of them, he wrote: "Some sinners mocked, some of the dry old professors [believers] opposed, some of the old starched Presbyterians preached against these exercises, but still the work went on and spread in almost every direction, gathering additional force, until our country seemed all coming home to God."[40]

Perhaps because of his bare-knuckled upbringing in Rogues' Harbor, Cartwright was almost universally accepted, by brawlers and hard cases, as well as by regular churchgoing folks and pillars of the community. Contemporaries recorded that he had a booming voice that made women weep and strong men tremble.[41] And if any strong drunks and reprobates ever got obstreperous in his meetings and prayer and admonishment did not quiet them, as a last resort he did not hesitate to chastise them by hand. Legends began to grow up around this two-fisted preacher, even to the point of claiming that he had once bested the notorious frontier brawler Mike Fink in hand-to-hand combat, though Cartwright denied this. Nevertheless, where there was smoke, there was some fire; he did admit to sometimes using a club, if it was absolutely necessary to restore order, but only to get the miscreant's attention.

Ross Phares reports one incident, however (not in a Cartwright congregation), which occurred before any club could have been produced. Fittingly, it was on Temperance Sunday, and after inveighing in traditional terms against demon whiskey, the minister decided to offer shocking visual evidence. From his pulpit he produced a glass of water, a glass of whiskey, and a worm. He dropped the worm in the glass of water, where it wriggled around in apparent delight. The he fished it out and dropped it in the glass of whiskey. It died instantly. "Now what does this prove?" beamed the minister.

A red-eyed brother in the back staggered to his feet: "If you drink plenty of whiskey," he mumbled, "you'll never have worms!"[42]

In his concern for maintaining order, Cartwright's reprimands were not limited to the stronger sex, for he brooked disturbances from *no one.* Sometimes the interruption was unintended or the sort of benign nuisance that occasionally plagues every congregation. One such cross he had to bear was an old lady, as outspoken as she was pious, who often disturbed his meetings by "going off on a high key." In a class meeting one day, when her soul was filled with joy to overflowing, she rapturously cried out, "If I had one more feather in my wing of faith, I would fly away and be with my Saviour!"

"Stick in the other feather, Lord," exclaimed Cartwright, "and let her go!"[43]

He was bold—far bolder than most preachers today, and it was a holy boldness. There was, for instance, the time he was returning from a session of the General Conference and found himself overtaken by nightfall, in the Cumberland Mountains. Arriving at an inn, he was informed that they were going to have a dance there that evening. He considered leaving, but on receiving their assurance of civil treatment, he decided to remain, after all. That evening, as the dance went on, he noted the condition of the revelers and felt a powerful desire to preach to them rising deep within him. Just then, a striking mountain beauty came up to him and asked him to dance. To the astonishment and delight of the company, Cartwright stood, bowed to her, and taking her proffered hand, led her to the center of the floor. The fiddler tuned a string and raised his bow—but Cartwright held up his other hand. For years, he told them, he had never taken an important step without first asking the Lord's blessing on it. Now, he desired to ask God's blessing on the beautiful young woman and on all the rest, for the kindness that they had shown a stranger. And holding fast to the woman's hand, he dropped to his knees and began praying vehemently for the conversion of the entire company.

Stunned silence followed, then pandemonium—some fled, others wept, and still others fell to their knees. The young woman tried to pull away, but Cartwright's grip on her hand was too strong to break, and she wound up joining him on her knees. Having finished his prayer, he arose and commenced exhorting them to turn from their wicked ways and give their lives to the Lord, and when he finished, he burst into a hymn. The young woman, now prostrate on the floor, began crying out to God for mercy, and this so encouraged Cartwright that he redoubled his efforts and prayed and exhorted and sang all night long. Of those who stayed, many were converted, and thus further encouraged, the hard-knuckled preacher tarried two more days. Revival broke out. By the time he was finally ready to leave, Cartwright had organized a society, received thirty-two into membership, and appointed the inn-keeper class leader! The revival was now spreading out into the whole region, and Cartwright promised to send them a preacher. Musing later on the events of that extraordinary evening, he commented, "Several of the young men converted at this Methodist preacher dance became useful ministers of Jesus Christ."[44]

At the age of twenty-seven, much against his will, Cartwright was elevated to presiding elder of the Green River District, and he labored long and fruitfully in the Lord's vineyard. At the end of his life, it was reckoned that 10,000 souls came to the Lord under his ministry, and more than 20,000 were received into the church.[45]

One key footnote to Cartwright's illustrious career concerns his stand on the ominous dark cloud of slavery. No bigger than a man's hand at the birth of the republic, slavery now blanketed the South and was rapidly spreading west, to the despair of Christians of all backgrounds. Unlike his superiors who had reached an accommodation with powerful Methodist slave owners, Cartwright could not bring himself to compromise, and also unlike them he was free to resettle, to avoid the institution. In 1824 he moved his family to Illinois, "to get clear of the evil of slavery" and to ensure that his children would not marry into slaveholding families. Yet, despite this deep-seated loathing, Cartwright had no stomach for the wild extremism of the Abolitionists, who were now making themselves known:

> I have never seen a rabid abolition or free-soil society that I could join, because they resort to unjustifiable agitation, and the means they employ are generally unchristian. They condemn and confound the innocent with the guilty, and the means they employ are not truthful at all times. And if force [which they are calling for] is resorted to, this glorious Union will be dissolved, a civil war will follow, death and carnage will ensue, and the only free nation on the earth will be destroyed.[46]

Therefore, despite his initial disagreement with his denomination's policy of not excommunicating slaveholders but attempting to reach them through what had been termed "moral suasion," he set his will to be obedient. But he remained as outspoken as ever, when it came to some of his fellow preachers who had themselves taken slaves: "It is clear to my mind that if Methodist preachers had kept clear of slavery themselves, and had gone on bearing honest testimony against it, thousands upon thousands more souls would have been emancipated who are now groaning under an oppression almost too intolerable to be borne." Nonetheless, before long, God began to honor his obedience with fruit, and it seemed clear to him that once again their general superintendent had heard God correctly. Cartwright began to have considerable success, reaching blacks and whites on the same plantations, and eventually he was of the opinion:

> I believe that the most successful way to ameliorate the condition of the slaves, and Christianize them, and finally secure their freedom, is to treat their owners kindly, and not to meddle politically with slavery. Let their owners see and know that your whole mission is the salvation of the slaves, as well as their owners. . . . In this way, more is to be done for the final extirpation of American slavery than all others put together, for these ultraists [Abolitionists] breathe nothing but death and slaughter.[47]

Therefore:

> Let moral suasion be used to the last degree for the sake of the salvation of the slaveholder, and the salvation of the slaves. Let us not take a course that will cut off the Gospel from them, and deliver them over to the uncovenanted mercies of God, or the anathemas of the devil. I have had glorious revivals of religion among the slaves, and have seen thousands of them soundly converted to God."[48]

For, as he would often later say, "If the religion of Jesus Christ will not finally bring about emancipation of the slaves, nothing else will. . . . and unless freedom for the slaves is accomplished, under the redeeming influence of religion, this happy Union will be split from center to circumference, and then there will be an end to our happy and glorious republic. And if we do not carry the Gospel to these slaves and their masters, who will? Surely not the ministers who justify slavery by perverting the Word of God, and still more surely not by abolition preachers, who by political action have cut themselves off from any access to slaveholders or slaves."[49]

Before he left Kentucky, he presided over a Breckenridge Circuit camp meeting, at which the following incident took place:

> There were a Brother S. and family, who were the owners of a good many slaves. It was a fine family, and Sister S. was a very intelligent lady and an exemplary Christian. She had long sought the blessing of perfect love, but she said the idea of holding her fellow beings in bondage stood out in her way. Many at this meeting sought and obtained the blessing of sanctification. Sister S. said her whole soul was in agony for that blessing, and it seemed to her at times that she could almost lay hold and claim the promise, but she said her slaves would seem to step right in between her and her Saviour, and prevent its reception. But while on her knees and struggling as in an agony for a clean heart, she then and there covenanted with the Lord, that if He would give her the blessing, she would give up her slaves and set them free. She said that this covenant had hardly been made one moment, when God filled her soul with such an overwhelming sense of divine love that she did not really know whether she was in or out of the body. She rose from her knees and proclaimed to listening hundreds that she had obtained the blessing, and also the terms on which she had obtained it. She went through the vast crowd with holy shouts of joy, exhorting all to taste and see that the Lord was gracious, and such a power attended her words that hundreds fell to the ground, and scores of souls were happily born into the Kingdom of God that afternoon and during the night. Shortly after this, they set their slaves free, and the end of that family was peace.[50]

Efforts to legalize slavery in Illinois compelled Cartwright to enter politics, and in 1828 and 1832, he was elected to the lower house of the Illinois General Assembly. His opponent in the latter election was another former Kentuckian, a young rail splitter and lawyer, recently returned from the Black Hawk War, who would later write: "It was the only time that I have ever been beaten by the people," and sign himself, A. Lincoln.

As the sun rose on the nineteenth century, the revival continued to spread—and in the West it became a conflagration that changed the land. There were excesses and irregularities, and once again the timid of spirit would seek to get rid of the smoke by smothering the flame, as they had before, in the days of Whitefield and Wesley. The elders of the Presbyterian Church spoke solemn warnings about the new emotionalism, but Cumberland Presbyterians, who had had such success with camp meetings, were loathe to give them up when ordered to do so and split away to form their own denomination. Similarly, the overly enthusiastic of other denominations would leave the mainstream to form new churches. But despite all the defects and all the opposition, the purifying flame burned on, and the movement was ultimately vindicated by the peaceable fruits of righteousness that it yielded.

Back east, on the other side of the mountains, the sun had also risen. . . .

5

Needles of Light

In the last decade of the eighteenth century, east of the Hudson River darkness prevailed. Here and there, in isolated communities that still had old-fashioned, persevering preachers, lights flickered on—lone candles in the enveloping gloom. But for the most part, New England, once the fountainhead of the spiritual Light that had burst forth upon this continent, slumbered on as if caught in a spell from which she could not arouse herself. Gone was the Puritan sense of the need for personal and corporate repentance. Gone was the enthusiasm for all things Christian, which had swept the colonies three generations earlier at the time of the Great Awakening.

In its place was a deadness that pervaded practically every church in the East. People came and listened to dry, theological expositions of salvation and went away unenlightened, unmoved, and unimpressed. The following Sunday, fewer bothered to come back. A Methodist preacher named Francis Aspinwell, making a northern pilgrimage to the land of the Puritans, wrote these words as he passed through Connecticut: "I do feel as if there had been a religion in this country once, and I apprehend there a little form and theory left. There may have been a praying ministry and people there, but I fear they are now dead."[1]

What had so radically altered the prevailing mood and sentiment of New England? For one thing, the military crisis was over. After seven long years of perilous fighting, often against overwhelming, hopeless odds and with far more losses than victories, nevertheless the Americans had finally, miraculously, prevailed. By force of arms they had won their independence. The newborn country went mad with joy. For the first time in more than a century and a half, they were free—truly free! They would have their own government, decide their own destiny. The time of peril was over. Now minutemen could put up their rifles on pegs over mantel or door and know that they would not be taking them down again, unless to go deer hunting, and mothers and wives need fret no longer for the safety of sons and husbands. Many could look ahead to a time of unbroken prosperity and growth. For those with bottom land, now was the time to clear and plant new acreage, to buy new land, a new team, a new harrow.

Now, more than ever, was the time to give profound thanks to God for His miraculous deliverance, but where once they had been committed to living for Christ, instead of self, and later were committed to defending the land God had given to them, now they wholly committed themselves to accumulating—for themselves and their offspring. If they thought of God at all anymore, it was little more than a quick prayer to ask His blessing on their next purchase or on the neighboring farm that they just acquired. To those still concerned about such things, it seemed that spiritual life in New England was at a desperately low ebb. The Reverend Nathan Perkins despaired: "Piety seemed to be flying away from our land. . . . Religion declined . . . morality languished . . . vice grew bold . . . profaneness, reveling, dishonesty, and sinful amusements increased."[2] James Morris of Litchfield, Connecticut, observed in his *Memoirs:* "The Church . . . was made up of numbers of ignorant, unprincipled, and unexemplary men. . . . Profane swearing and open Sabbath-breaking and drunkenness were not uncommon among professors of religion. The young people were clownish, ignorant, and uncivil in their amusements."

Nor did the clergy call them sternly to task and rebuke them for their unchristian ways, for the pastors had lost the ability to lead their flocks. The openhearted evangelical zeal of the Great Awakening had gradually given way to a dour and dismal orthodox school of thought which held that an unsaved man could do absolutely nothing to put himself "in the way of salvation." These so-called "consistent Calvinists" believed that the human efforts of their parishioners to obtain God's grace were for naught. All these unfortunates could do was to hope that God had chosen them for salvation and not damnation and await divine lightning bolts of inspiration that would change their hearts toward faith in Christ.

There was even a school of hyper-Calvinists who held that the true test of an individual's love of God was his willingness to suffer eternal damnation, should that happen to be God's will for him. These severe doctrines, known collectively as the New Divinity, gained increasing favor among many of the clergy of the day, with Samuel Hopkins and

Nathanael Emmons as its leading spokesmen. A young lady named Harriet Beecher Stowe, whose father, Lyman Beecher, would shortly preach a powerful antidote to this insidious poison, summed up Mr. Emmons's theology succinctly: "a skillful engine of torture calculated to produce all the mental anguish of the most perfect sense of helplessness, with the most torturing sense of responsibility."[3]

She did not exaggerate. Told that those serious about obtaining salvation must pray much, read their Bibles, and regularly attend public worship, yet simultaneously told that strict attendance to these duties would in no way ensure their eventual salvation, it is no wonder that even the most ardent seekers after God grew discouraged and apathetic. What was worse, this indifference began to harden into a negative and even hostile attitude toward the clergy, the church, and all things Christian. Hearing the talk of their elders, the young people of the time began passing this derisive bit of doggerel to one another, about attending church:

> You can and you can't,
> You will and you won't,
> You're damned if you do,
> And damned if you don't.[4]

With a strange perversity, the New Divinity adherents seemed bent on harkening back to a Calvinism more rigorous than the most demanding Puritanical system—at a time when the spirit of the age was going in exactly the opposite direction. After all, this was the new nation that had fought Britain to a standstill, the land of virtually limitless opportunity! This was a free and independent republic, where free men could decide their own destiny. No man would be king, and no man need submit to having anyone else tell him what to do—not even a preacher! (Not even God.) They endured their pastors' haranguing for a season, because their wives and mothers insisted on keeping the tradition of churchgoing, but eventually they took to ignoring or actually dismissing preachers who were too dreary and sometimes even took to physically lowering their lofty pulpits.[5] As historian Stephen Berk pointed out, the concept of God's absolute sovereignty seemed somehow despotic; a predestined elect smacked of aristocracy; and a theology that disparaged human effort sounded as if it were against entrepreneurial democracy.

But there was (and is) no such thing as a spiritual vacuum, and with conventional Christianity seeming ever more remote at the end of the eighteenth century, the enemy had a shiny new substitute all dressed up and waiting in the wings. Actually, the belief system known as Deism first made its appearance in America in the middle of the century. Expounded in England by the third earl of Shaftesbury and others, it left God in the role of creator of the universe, but it denied that He took a personal interest in the souls of men, let alone intervened in their affairs—or heeded their prayers. Deism emphatically rejected the Triune God of Holy Scripture. It renounced the divinity of Jesus Christ, His sacrifice on the Cross to atone for the sins of men, and His resurrection. Indeed, according to the Deists, there was nothing to atone for: to them, the concept of man's nature as sinful and fallen was repugnant and absurd. They exalted reason and intellect, and anything that was not logical or rational they summarily rejected—including all the supernatural elements of the Christian faith. In sum, Deism offered a more appealing deity—a comforting abstract, the Prime Cause to which all effects could be traced, an ever gentle, loving and kind Supreme Being—quite different from the righteous authoritarian of the extreme Calvinists.[6]

How could such a weed have taken root at the very heart of what was once a Bible commonwealth? We have already seen two parts of the answer: with independence won and prosperity the common goal, men's hearts were turned toward self, instead of Christ, at the same time that their spiritual shepherds were putting God farther and farther out of reach with their extremist dogma. The third part had to do with a young nation's eagerness to prove itself worthy of inclusion in the sophisticated councils of Europe. America was wide open to foreign ideas, and French Rationalists and Deists were quick to seize the opportunity. When their soldiers had come over to help fight the British, they were contemptuous of Christianity—an attitude young American soldiers had never encountered before. More urbane than the British, these French Deists were well versed in squelching contrary opinion with a knowing or condescending look. After all, hadn't they been our allies in our life-or-death struggle for independence? "They perfectly knew," observed Timothy Dwight, president of Yale, "how to insinuate the grossest sentiments in a delicate and inoffensive manner, to put arguments to flight with a sneer, to stifle conscience with a smile, and to overbear investigation by confronting it with the voice and authority of the great world."[7]

General sympathy for the French had continued in most quarters after the war and was enhanced in 1789, when they launched their own revolution to overthrow the monarchy and aristocracy and become a democratic republic like their former ally, the United States. Many Americans simply assumed that the two causes were identical and questioned no further. But in New England, increasing numbers of academic clergy were expressing grave alarm at the growing influence of the French philosophy—the New Age of Rationalism, as it called itself, or the French Infidelity, as Timothy Dwight dubbed it. He considered it one of the deadliest evils the world had faced since the betrayal of Christ, because it was so seductive. For what Voltaire and Rousseau were claiming—what, indeed, they had built *their* revolution on, as opposed to America's—was that, because of the potential power of man's mind and virtue of his heart, it *was* possible to have the Brotherhood of Man, without first having the Fatherhood of God. In other words, if one concentrated on the second great commandment, one could safely ignore the first—man's "innate goodness" would carry the day.

Many respected American thinkers and statesmen agreed with them, and ironically those most susceptible to this "Enlightenment" were the young men at colleges originally founded to provide future American ministers an education at home, so that they would not have to sail to England, to attend Oxford or Cambridge. Here, the new Rationalism spawned like bacteria in warm milk, for it seduced the intellect through flattery, and the intellects of these teenage students did not have the benefit of the balance and discernment that comes with a lifetime of seasoned faith. As Dwight observed:

> Youths particularly, who had been liberally educated, and who, with strong passions and feeble principles were votaries of sensuality and ambition, delighted with the prospect of unrestrained gratification and panting to be enrolled with men of fashion and splendor, became enamored of these new doctrines. . . . Striplings, scarcely fledged, suddenly found that the world had been involved in a general darkness through the long succession of preceding ages and that the light of wisdom had but just begun to dawn upon the human race. . . . Men reluctantly conscious of their own inferiority of understanding, rejoiced to see themselves without an effort to become in a moment wiser than those who had spent life in laborious investigation.[8]

Why were Dwight and the others coming on like voices crying in the wilderness? Because they had actually *read* the things that these French prophets of Enlightenment were promulgating. Wrote Voltaire of Jesus: "Among the Jews, there have always been men from the rabble who played at being prophets in order to distinguish themselves from the mob: here, then, is the one who made the most noise, and who was turned into a god."[9] It was when this scurrilousness began to infect American writers that the New England clergy reacted so vehemently. In 1784, Ethan Allen, hero of Fort Ticonderoga, published his book, *Reason the Only Oracle of Man,* in which he asserted: "The doctrine of the Trinity is destitute of foundation, and tends manifestly to superstition and idolatry." He dismissed the atonement: "There could be no justice or goodness in one being's suffering for another, nor is it at all compatible with reason to suppose that God was the contriver of such a propitiation." Antichristian authors were rapidly gaining a certain fashion in literary circles, and their ranks were soon joined by Elihu Palmer, a Baptist clergyman who had been defrocked and driven from his pulpit for preaching against the deity of Christ. In his *Principles of Nature,* Palmer maintained: "The simple truth is, their pretended Saviour is nothing more than an illegitimate Jew, and their hopes of salvation through him rest on no better foundation than that of fornication or adultery," and he referred to the Bible as "a book whose indecency and immorality shock all common sense and common honesty."

But the crown prince of American Deists was Tom Paine, the famous pamphleteer who had been a hero of the revolution. When General Washington became America's first President, Paine had privately gone to him and asked him for the job of postmaster general, as payment for services rendered to the revolution. Washington, after carefully reviewing the writer's qualifications, had regretfully turned him down, whereupon Paine launched a vicious personal attack against the President.[10] To Paine's surprise, his slander backfired, and with a growing number of Americans souring on him, he found it a convenient time to go to Europe, to raise capital for the construction of a pierless iron bridge that he had invented. While there, he became infatuated with the new Rationalism and saw it as the perfect means to extract a measure of revenge against the American establishment. For what gave civil authority its power in a democratic society? The moral influence of that society's religion—in America's case, Christianity. Presenting the tenets of Deism in his own words, Paine set about the systematic destruction of Christianity.

The result was *The Age of Reason,* an enormous edition of which, in 1794, was printed in English in France and then shipped to America and dumped on the market for a few cents a copy. Like the other Deist works, it was widely read and contained such profundities as: "The Christian mythologists, calling themselves the Christian Church, have erected their fable which, for absurdity and extravagance, is not exceeded by anything that is to be found in the mythology of the ancients."[11] And "Take away from Genesis the belief that Moses was the author, on which only the strange belief that it is the word of God has stood, and there remains nothing of Genesis but an anonymous book of stories, fables, and traditional or invented absurdities, or of downright lies. The story of Eve and the serpent, and of Noah and his ark, drop to a level with the Arabian Nights, without the merit of being entertaining."[12] Nor was he any less vitriolic about the New Testament, referring to the Gospel as "the fable of Jesus Christ" and calling the Virgin Birth "blasphemously obscene."

When such a well-known American aligned himself with the devil, it was a grave matter indeed, and clergy everywhere denounced his latest work, pointing out that it had been written in France, where Paine himself was serving as an elected member of the revolutionary French Convention. Their condemnation only seemed to pique curiosity, and not surprisingly Paine's ideas found some of their strongest supporters on college campuses, where Jacobin clubs formed, modeled after the radical deistic societies in France, which had fueled the revolution and sustained the Reign of Terror. Within weeks after the arrival of *The Age of Reason,* there were not one, but *two* Tom Paine societies at Yale.

In one sense, what was happening on that New Haven campus in the last decade of the eighteenth century was typical of the few colleges in America; but in another, it was pivotal, for with Harvard (and indeed, all of Boston) lost to Unitarianism (Deism's whitewashed, intellectual cousin), Yale was the last bastion of Puritan orthodoxy, the source of the few remaining new ministers who could be counted on to preach the Gospel as it used to be preached. But Yale was now turning out more lawyers than ministers; only five members of the class of 1799 were willing to profess that Jesus Christ was their Lord and Saviour. A year later, that figure had dropped to one.

One wonders what the founders would have thought had they lived to see their institution at its nadir. It was God's mercy that Abraham Pierson, Yale's first rector, and Elihu Yale, its chief benefactor, and the other Connecticut leaders who used to gather in Saybrook for those early commencements were long dead. For the college that had once produced earnest young ministers, eager to serve the Lord wherever He called them, was now producing young wastrels dedicated to the pursuit of pleasure and selfishness. Well before the sun went down, the elm-shaded campus rang with boisterous carousing, and young men in the red knitted caps of the French Jacobins lolled on the old post-and-hole fence that surrounded the common and referred to one another as *Voltaire* or *Rousseau* or *D'Alembert,* or names of other heros of the French Revolution. Undergraduates kept well-stocked liquor supplies in their rooms and entertained at all hours, in general disporting themselves as much like Parisian *bon vivants* as possible. They aped everything French, bent on outdoing one another in outrageous conduct.[13]

What was happening at Yale was happening everywhere. Dr. Ashbel Green, president of Princeton, had experienced the same situation when he was an undergraduate there: "While I was a member of the college, there were but two professors of religion among the students, and not more than five or six who scrupled the use of profane language in common conversation, and sometimes it was of a very shocking kind. To the influence of the American war, succeeded that of the French Revolution, still more pernicious, and I think more general."[14] One Yale undergraduate summed it all up in a brief entry in his diary for May 3, 1797: "The world is coming either to Christianity or infidelity."[15]

From all available evidence, it seemed that darkness had clearly gained the upper hand and would soon vanquish the Light entirely. And then, once again, God intervened. This time the lightning fell sporadically at first, but everywhere it hit, small revival fires broke out—East Haddam and Lyme in 1792, Farmington and New Hartford in 1795, Milford in 1796. And the fascinating thing was: it happened in churches where the same minister had preached in the same die-hard evangelical fashion for years. One Sunday morning, heads would be nodding and yawns stifled and children squirming, and the next Sunday, the congregation was suddenly attentive, aware of the presence of God and coming under conviction. At such times, no one would be more surprised than the minister himself!

A thrill of excitement ran through the towns as local revivals began to break out and then spread and join others all over Connecticut. Ironically, it was Litchfield County, the very seat of the "New Divinity," which had so restricted access to salvation, that now experienced the greatest revival. Said the Reverend E. D. Griffin: "I saw a continued succession of heavenly sprinklings . . . until, in 1799, I could stand at my door in New Hartford, Litchfield County, and number fifty or sixty contiguous congregations laid down in one field of divine wonders, and as many more in different parts of New England."[16] Just one year after the Presbyterian General Assembly had deplored "God's controversy with the nation" in its annual pastoral letter, now they would exclaim: "We have heard from different parts, the glad tidings of the outpourings of the Spirit, and of times of refreshing from the presence of the Lord. . . . From the east, from the west, and from the south have these joyful tidings reached our ears."[17] The Holy Spirit was on the move, just as He had been, three generations before!

Soon the lightning spread out across Connecticut, Massachusetts, and Rhode Island, and up into Maine, New Hampshire, and Vermont. In Shaftsbury, Vermont, the local minister wrote this account of what happened in his congregation in 1797:

> In the month of April last, there appeared nothing among this people but the most rapid increase of every species of vice and immorality, and even professors had grown cold as to religious exercises. Then, towards the end of that month, it pleased God to visit my poor soul with some sense of my own vileness and shortcomings, and how little I had done for God and the good of souls. At this time I think I had a glimpse of the infinite character of Jehovah, which made me shrink into nothing in my own esteem. Then, to my astonishment, my soul was strangely drawn forth at particular times, in secret prayer for the salvation of sinners. Repeated exercises of this kind gave me a strong confidence, that the Lord would soon work salvation in this place.
>
> There were, however, no favorable symptoms among the people until the month of July, when a young woman who had been converted some years before was stirred up and came forward in baptism. Her conversion was made the means of the awaken-

> ing of a number of young people, and thus the work began. In August four more persons were baptized. In September, I baptized seventeen. . . The whole number added to this church since last May is 175.[18]

Three aspects of this account, so typical of narratives recorded in New England at that time, are significant: first, earnest prayer for revival preceded the move of the Holy Spirit. Second, God did not require a "superstar" evangelist to come in from the outside, to act as the lightning rod. He used the same shepherd whom He had planted there. Third, the wind of the Holy Spirit did not come in as a tornado, as it was doing at the same time out in Kentucky; it came in almost as a gentle breeze—uniquely suited to the temperament of the Congregational churchgoers, who would have been frightened and put off by the power unleashed at the huge camp meetings of Cane Ridge and elsewhere. What happened in Connecticut was just right for that state, which, after all, was known as the "Land of Steady Habits." The point was, lightning *was* falling, churches were coming alive, and the Second Great Awakening was underway in the East.

The focus and leadership of the Awakening was, of all places, that scene of modest colonial brick buildings and elm-shaded fences, the Yale campus, which was undergoing an extraordinary mental and spiritual transformation. For into that cauldron of infidelity and rebellion, God introduced His man of the hour—Timothy Dwight. A graduate of the class of 1769 and grandson of Jonathan Edwards, the leading theologian of the first Great Awakening, Dwight came from solid Puritan preaching stock. From the moment in 1795 that he set foot in New Haven as Yale's new president, he confronted infidelity straight on.

Undergraduate Lyman Beecher (who would become one of the nineteenth century's outstanding men of God), describes what pre-Dwight Yale was like: "Before he came, college was in a most ungodly state. The college church was almost extinct. Most of the students were skeptical, and rowdies were plenty. . . ."[19] The first thing President Dwight did was fire all faculty members espousing the French Rationalist point of view. Then, with the windows of Connecticut Hall thrown open and the sounds of spring mixing with the streams of sunlight coming through them, he started holding frank and open-ended discussions with the undergraduates. He encouraged the young men in his charge to speak their minds, and by his willingness to listen carefully to their side, with no recriminations for anything they would say, he elicited rare candor from them. But then, they were obligated to pay him the same courtesy, and he presented cogent, well-reasoned rebuttals of all the Rationalist arguments, following with strong appeals for life-changing Christianity, which, as president and an ordained minister, it was his place to give. On Sunday, his sermons followed similar lines, and his voice carried out the open windows of the student-filled Brick Church:

> Contempt is the spirit and ridicule the weapon, with which Christianity has long been principally opposed. . . . The cause which needs these weapons cannot be just; the doctrine which cannot be supported without them must be false. . . . You will dread to become the objects of scorn, and to be wounded by the shafts of derision. You will be afraid to declare yourselves friends to a cause which has been the standing jest of so many men of wit, and which has been so often and so publically held up to systematized contempt, to which insult is merit, and mockery a fashion."[20]

He was right, of course, and the students sensed it. Yet while increasing numbers began to apply what he was saying to their own lives, few in those first years were willing to admit it to their peers. Nevertheless, with resolute patience, Dwight persevered. Speaking of the French Infidelity and the subsequent Reign of Terror, to which the French Revolution had degenerated, he said:

> The spirit of infidelity has the heart of a wolf, the fangs of a tiger, and the talons of a vulture. Blood is its proper nourishment, and it scents its prey with the nerves of a hound, and cowers over the field of death on the sooty pinions of a fiend. Unlike all other animals of prey, it feeds upon its own kind; when glutted with the blood of others, it turns back on those who have been its coadjutors. . . Between ninety and a hundred of those who were leaders in this mighty work of destruction fell by the hand of violence. Enemies to all men, they were, of course, enemies to each other. Butchers of the human race, they soon whetted the knife for each other's throat.[21]

Dwight never let up on infidelity: she was the foe, and once he had identified her, he was relentless: "Infidelity was the genuine source, the Vesuvius, from whose mouth issued rivers of destruction, which deluged and ruined all things in their way . . . Christians saw their God denied, their Saviour blasphemed, and war formally declared against Heaven."[22] Nor would he allow his students to equivocate. They had to choose that day which master they would serve:

> There can be here no halting between two opinions. . . You must meet face to face the bands of disorder, of falsehood, and of sin. Between them and you there is, there can be, no natural, real, or lasting harmony. What communion hath light with darkness? What concord hath Christ with Belial? Or what part hath he that believeth, with an Infidel? From a connection with them, what can you gain? What will you not lose? Their neighborhood is contagious; their friendship is a blast; their communion is death. Will you imbibe their principles? Will you copy their practices? Will you teach your children that death is an eternal sleep? That the end sanctifies the means? That moral obligation is a dream? Religion a farce? . . . Will you become the rulers of Sodom, and the people of Gomorrah? . . . Will you enthrone a Goddess of Reason before the tale of Christ? Will you burn your Bibles? Will you crucify anew your Redeemer? Will you deny your god?

It seems likely that after such a confrontation many red caps were left in closets or discreetly disposed of. Dwight's sermons were not all hammer and anvil, for in closing he offered his listeners a potent alternative to infidelity. He reminded them of the enduring joy of sweet Christianity, of God's enabling grace, and of prayers heard and answered. He reminded them that the time of harvest was nearly past for them, that every year they held back from God, their hearts would be that much harder and more difficult to yield. He described the peace of a cleansed spirit, the joy of fulfillment that came with laboring for Christ, the strength to choose the right that came with a pure heart:

> With these blessings in view, you will, I trust without a sigh, leave to the Infidel his peculiar gratifications. In every innocent enjoyment, you can partake at least as largely as he. You will not, therefore, repine that you cannot shine at a horse race, bet at a cockpit, win at a gaming table, riot at the board of intemperance, drink deep at the midnight debauch, steal to infamous enjoyments at the brothel. But the most important consideration is yet to be suggested, a consideration infinitely awful and glorious: *There may be an Hereafter*. . . . The course of sin, begun here,

> may continue forever. The seed of virtue, sown in the present world and raised to a young and feeble item, may be destined to growth immortal.[23]

In advocating that a sinner take advantage of "the means of grace" and pray earnestly for God to save him, Dwight was moving radically away from the consistent Calvinist position which had so frozen the membership of the elect. He observed: "Perhaps no one who has persisted in his efforts to gain eternal life was ever finally deserted by the Spirit of grace." Convicted sinners, feeling their "danger of ruin," proceed to inquire "what they shall do to be saved."[24]

"Heresy!" cried the Hopkinsians, whose own position, taken to its ultimate extreme, held that salvation was so far from a sinner's reach that he should accept eternal damnation with gratitude, should that turn out to be God's will for him. But fewer and fewer people were paying any attention to them. What Dwight had to say rang true: "Willingness to suffer perdition is no part of Christian resignation." The "controlling anguish of a sinner's heart" decides whether or not he "shall be directed to pray" for grace. If sinners cannot be directed to pray for a new heart, who can? Saints have no need of one.

If the hearts of his young listeners responded to this message, few made open professions of faith in these first years. Nevertheless, as his illustrious grandfather had before him, Dwight toiled on in the vineyard, never compromising, never flagging. And finally, in 1802, his efforts were rewarded. Like a thunderclap, revival fell upon Yale. In March the first new student confessed his faith in Christ as his Saviour, and in April there was the second. By the end of that summer there were no less than fifty! And by the time the senior class was ready for graduation half of them had committed their lives to Christ, and a third went on to careers in the ministry. Indeed, Dwight personally witnessed the formal conversion of half the student body. Dr. Heman Humphrey, later to become president of Amherst College, was a student at Yale, when the storm broke.

> It came with such power as had never been witnessed within those walls before. It was in the Freshman year of my own class. It was like a mighty rushing wind. The whole college was shaken. It seemed for a time as if the whole mass of the students would press into the kingdom. . . . It put a new face on the college. It sent a thrill of joy and thanksgiving far and wide into the

> hearts of its friends who had been praying that the waters of salvation might be poured into the fountain from which so many streams were annually sent out. . . . In the four preceding classes, only thirteen names of ministers stand, against sixty-nine in the next four years—nearly, if not quite all, of them brought in by the Great Revival.[25]

Undergraduates pressed forward to profess Christ and redirect their lives to the ministry. Instead of dying away, the revival seemed to renew itself in waves, continuing long after Dwight's death in 1817 and sending many hundreds of dedicated young ministers into churches and to the mission field. Humphrey was not the only one to report Yale's transformation. As Benjamin Silliman, then a tutor, wrote to his mother: "Yale College is a little temple; prayer and praise seem to be the delight of the greater part of the students, while those who are still unfeeling are awed with respectful silence."[26]

If at first the Yale students were slow to heed their president, the rest of New England was not. In those days, significant sermons were picked up by the newspapers, and most of Dwight's were considered significant by the editors of his time. And as the editors of all the major papers in America exchanged subscriptions with one another and often reprinted the best from each paper, what Dwight had to say on infidelity was soon published by practically every paper in the country. Hundreds of thousands who had read Paine's words now had to weigh them against Dwight's. Indeed, such was his influence that Thomas Jefferson, back in America and the leader of the Democratic Republicans, to whom the Deists and Rationalists naturally flocked, was soon referring to Dwight as "the pope in New Haven." Bishop Hurst delightedly exclaimed: "From the day that the young president faced his students in the chapel of Yale College, infidelity has been a vanishing force in the history of the American people."[27]

Why were so many students attracted to the Democratic Republican banner? Young people, then as now, find much that is appealing in the combination of idealism and rebellion, and no one personified that combination better than Jefferson. There seemed to be a subtle streak of rebellion in the man who penned the Declaration of Independence. Upon his return home, he became a champion of the states relinquishing as few rights as possible in order to establish a federal government.

In the presidential election of 1800, the independence of this refined and erudite Virginia gentleman farmer appealed not only to the youth, but to all the most recent arrivals in America, who had none of the traditions or sense of divine call upon their lives that the First Comers had. Indeed, many of these newcomers had left England precisely to get out from under the rigid class system that they saw the French Republicans overthrowing. They identified totally with the French Republican cause and thus identified with Thomas Jefferson, whose blanket espousal of that cause was enough to make them forget his own patrician ways and background. On his part, Jefferson was pleased to think of himself as spokesman for the common man. The people were mad for democracy, and the Federalists were voted out, but when the electoral college votes were counted, Jefferson had managed no more than a tie with Aaron Burr. Who would be president would have to be decided by the House of Representatives, and Alexander Hamilton reluctantly threw his considerable Federalist influence behind the lesser of two evils. Jefferson was elected president—just before public awareness of the realities of the French Revolution finally broke.

For years, Dwight had been patiently, painstakingly exposing Deism for what it was, and now, concurrent with the outbreak of revival in the East in 1802, horrendous details of the French Reign of Terror were at last surfacing and finding their way to these shores. In France, Americans learned, all law and order had broken down and no property was safe any longer, no matter to whom it belonged; mobs went in anywhere they pleased, to search or rob. The Catholic Church was massively assaulted, its buildings sacked and razed and hundreds of priests and nuns murdered. And then the king and all his family were guillotined, and after them, wave upon wave of innocent people whose only crime might have been falling afoul one of those who were for the moment in power. As for those, jealousy and hatred reigned supreme at the top of the pyramid, for hundreds of others were lusting for their places and were prepared to do anything to get them. The tumbrils—those two-wheeled farm carts used to transport the condemned to their places of execution—were heard clattering over the cobblestones of Paris at all hours of the day and night, for the thirsty guillotines never rested.

Shocked Americans heard one verified account after another of depravity that knew no bounds. And the great cry throughout the brutal events was "Reason"—which put man's mind in the position of ultimate authority. "God" was a figment of man's imagination, and religion a system of superstitions that had kept man in bondage for centuries. And so they made a mockery of the sacraments of the Church, actually dressing up a whore and worshiping her, taking sacramental vessels from churches and parading them through the streets on the back of an ass, in mockery of Christ's entry into Jerusalem. To observe the Sabbath became an act of treason against the people's government, and clergy were reduced to having to beg for food.[28]

The American artist John Trumbull, son of the Connecticut governor, was there at that time, serving as secretary to Ambassador John Jay. He was stunned by what he saw: "When the National Assembly of France, the elected rulers of a great nation, formed a procession to [the cathedral of] Notre Dame . . . and there in mock solemnity bowed their knees before a common courtesan, basely worshipping her as the Goddess of Reason, still there were those, and not a few in America who threw up their caps and cried, 'Glorious, glorious sister republic!' "[29]

But if the French Revolution had been unmasked in America and blatant Deism put to rout, the antichristian attitude that had given it a warm reception remained prevalent, despite the beginnings of a Second Great Awakening. Jefferson, after all, was in the White House, and one of his first acts in office was to announce that he would no longer proclaim national days of fasting, humiliation, and prayer, "as my predecessors did."[30] In this he was referring specifically to the fast day John Adams had declared in 1799. Jefferson's supporters at that time had labeled the national fast day as a calculated Federalist ploy to ensnare Democratic Republicans into praying for President Adams. Now their leader justified his act by interpreting the Constitution as prohibiting the federal government from intermeddling with religious institutions. Openly declaring the doctrines of church fathers Athanasius and Calvin to be the "deliria of crazed imaginations,"[31] Jefferson called for the unequivocal separation of church and state. Yet as the two were already separate, what he was really calling for was a drastic de-emphasis of church's traditional influence upon state.

The braying of Deism may have been silenced, but the subtler, more seductive melodies of Unitarianism daily soothed greater numbers of itching ears. Unitarianism was a close neighbor of Deism, for if there was one abstract God, then why not one benevolent, universal Intelligence, embodying love? Why this compulsion for discouraging man with the heavy concept of original sin and man's fallen nature? Why the need for a radical allegiance to a Saviour? If God made man, then a bit of His Spirit must dwell in every man, which meant that man was inherently good and therefore perfectable, if only given the right environment, encouragement, and inspiration—"God as universal spirit, indwelling in man, the essential worth and dignity of the individual."[32] Having denied the concept of original sin, Unitarians saw no need for Christ to have died for our sins. There existed no great holy mystery concerning His shed blood expiating sin; indeed, sacrificing Himself on the Cross became simply not the sort of thing a supreme being, a supremely rational being, would do. No, Jesus was just a man, after all—the greatest who ever lived, perhaps, and eminently worthy of emulation—but still just a man.

Unitarianism, having consolidated its beachhead in Massachusetts, expanded westward in soft, undulating waves of its own. In Virginia, men like Jefferson, indifferent to the collapse of their disestablished churches, welcomed its approach. "That doctrine has not yet been preached here to us," wrote the Sage of Monticello from Charlottesville, "but the breeze begins to be felt which precedes the storm, and fanaticism [that is, Christianity] is all in a bustle, shutting its doors to keep it out."[33]

Jefferson and Dwight personified the contest between Unitarianism and Christianity. A decade before Dwight went to Yale, Jefferson, as a brilliant undergraduate at William and Mary College, was being steeped in the new French Rationalism and developing deep doubts about Christianity. During his years in France with the Deist *philosophes* (1783-1789), these hardened into loathing. Back in America, he went to great pains to keep his feelings about Christianity from the voting public, yet they were clearly discerned by Dwight and the evangelical clergy, nearly all of whom denounced Jefferson as an infidel and made the direst predictions of what would happen to America, if "that man" should ever get into the White House. They depicted him as harboring a hidden agenda of introducing to America the same godless anarchy that was rampant in France. Were the Democratic Republicans to win the election, everything that so many had struggled and prayed, fought and died for, would be lost.

But God's ways are often hidden from men—even from those who claim to know Him best. For the times were changing. As noble and selfless as they were, the Federalist leaders, who had been present at the creation of the republic, and who, through the Constitution, had ensured its continuation, were passing from the stage. Those that were left fought a rearguard action, despairing that the new order did not seem to catch the same vision or be motivated by the same ideals of country and service. The sad truth was that the time of the Federalists had passed, and the time of unrestricted democracy, no longer influenced by custom, tradition or religion, was at hand. Unlimited power to the people was a potent brew—France was still recovering from a ten-year bender—and every newly arrived settler wanted his share.

A century and a half before, the two strongest Puritan leaders, John Winthrop and Thomas Hooker, had argued the merits of unlimited democracy in a society called into being by God. Anxious to persuade Hooker to stay, Winthrop had argued in favor of restricting democracy, that the leadership of the Massachusetts Bay Colony might be passed on to those with maturity who understood and accepted the selfless obligations of what it meant to be a servant-leader, after the example of Christ. Hooker replied that, as long as the leaders understood that, there would be no problem, but that there was no guarantee that they *would* always appreciate that—and no way to get rid of them, if they didn't. He said that, like it or not, they would have to trust the operation of the Holy Spirit through the expressed will of the people. While unrestricted democracy might be responsible for some gross excesses and the occasional tyranny of the majority, it was the only system that ensured that in the long run God would have His way. So Hooker left the Bay Colony and founded Connecticut, incorporating his democratic principles into that colony's constitution, which became the model for the Bay Colony's revised constitution and ultimately for the Constitution of the United States.

Once again, in 1800, it was time to trust the operation of the Holy Spirit through unrestricted democracy, even though its champion was Thomas Jefferson. Ironically, Jefferson himself echoed part of this truth when he wrote in Paris, casually dismissing the horrors of the revolution as passing aberrations: "The mass possesses such a degree of good sense as to enable them to decide well."[34] The truth was, they didn't, but a mass with enough Christians at its center would. As it turned out, President Jefferson, through a unilateral embargo imposed against trading with all warring European countries—a measure that practically ruined the economy of the embryonic republic and that no Federalist administration would ever have enacted—probably kept the United States out of a war that it could not have then survived. It was also Jefferson who had the vision and courage to accept the Louisiana Purchase, which effectively doubled the size of the United States—at a time when the Federalists were clamoring for America to reduce, not expand, her territorial responsibilities. Jefferson, as President, may not have had a close relationship with God, but there was no question that God used him anyway—as He often does those leaders who have no personal knowledge of Him.

Yet even Jefferson, securely ensconced in the White House, could go too far. When he offered Tom Paine free passage home on a United States ship, as if he were some sort of national hero, the response from moderates of all political stripes was so furious that he was forced to backpedal and distance himself from the offer. His own opinion remained unchanged, however, and while dwelling in the White House, he compiled the "Jefferson Bible" for his children: a narrative of the life of Christ, from which he had removed every vestige of the supernatural—the Virgin Birth, the Resurrection, the raising of Lazarus, and all other miracles.[35] In the closing years of his life, he considered himself a Unitarian, a belief system which, he was confident, was about to eclipse Christianity. He confided to his friend Benjamin Waterhouse: "I trust that there is not a young man now living in the United States, who will not die a Unitarian."[36] And to John Adams he wrote: "The day will come when the mystical generation of Jesus, by the supreme being as his father in the womb of a virgin, will be classed with the fable of the generation of Minerva in the brain of Jupiter."[37]

Unitarianism and Christianity were bound to clash head on, and one man whom God raised up to be His standard bearer on that battlefield was a prototypical Yankee preacher, Dwight's favorite student, Lyman Beecher. Angular, sinewy and ungraceful, Beecher possessed an infectious enthusiasm and a wry sense of humor that took delight in poking fun at himself, for he was a humble man at heart, acutely aware of the many places where he fell short of the Lord's example. Because he knew himself, he had a canny awareness of what motivated others, and a shrewd and nimble intellect when it came to debate—which it frequently did, because Beecher had a passionate temperament, especially concerning the things of God.[38]

He had been a student at Yale when Dwight became that institution's president, and he gravitated to Dwight as the best living model of what a preacher should be. Recalling Dwight in his memoirs, Beecher wrote: "There was a pith and power of doctrine there that has not been since surpassed, if equalled. I took notes of all his discourses, condensing and forming skeletons. He was of noble form, with a noble head and body, and he had one of the sweetest smiles that ever you saw. He always met me with a smile. Oh, how I loved him! I loved him as my own soul, and he loved me as a son."[39]

Dwight was instrumental in Beecher's coming to the Lord, during his junior year. "I rose to pray and had not spoken five words before I was under as deep a conviction as ever I was in my life. The sinking of the shaft was instantaneous, I understood the law and my heart as well as I do now, or shall in the Day of Judgment, I believe. The commandment came, sin revived, and I died, quick as a flash of lightning."[40] At just this point, a sermon by Dwight on the theme "The harvest is past, the summer is ended, and we are not saved," plunged young Beecher into despair. But Dwight, a veteran of harvesting souls as well as harrowing them, soon rescued the young man and sent him on his way to conversion.

Beecher became Dwight's protégé, and although he rose to equal if not greater heights as a leader of the Awakening and patriarch of one of the most influential families in nineteenth century America, his loyalty to his mentor and his love for him never faltered. His son Charles described how he took the news of Dwight's death, when it was brought to him in the pulpit: "A man came in suddenly and went up into the pulpit and whispered to him. Father turned from the messenger to the congregation and said, 'Dr. Dwight is gone!' Then, raising his hands, with a burst of tears, as if he beheld the translation, he said, 'My father, my father! The chariots of Israel and the horsemen thereof!' The congregation, with an electric impulse, rose to their feet, and many eyes were bathed in tears. It was one of the most impressive scenes I ever witnessed."[41]

Looking back on his own life, Beecher summed up his credo:

> I was made for action. The Lord drove me, but I was ready. I have always been going at full speed . . . From the beginning my

> mind has taken in the Church of God, my country, and the world, as given to Christ. It is this that has widened the scope of my activities beyond the common sphere of pastoral labor. For I soon found myself harnessed to the Chariot of Christ, whose wheels of fire have rolled onward, high and dreadful to His foes and glorious to His friends. I could not stop. . . .[42]

The chariot of Christ rolled resolutely forward in his first church, in East Hampton, Long Island, where Beecher declared: "I always preached right to the conscience. Every sermon with my eye on the gun to hit somebody. Went through the doctrines, showed what they didn't mean, what they did, then the argument, knocked away the objections, and drove home on the conscience."[43]

The first instance of his ministry widening beyond his pastoral labors in East Hampton occurred soon enough, in 1806, at the age of thirty. Stunned by the loss of one of the brightest Federalist leaders, Alexander Hamilton, his grief turned to outrage when he learned that the man who had killed him, Aaron Burr, had faithfully practiced pistol marksmanship for *three months* before goading Hamilton into a duel. "When I read about it in the paper," wrote Beecher in his journal, "a feeling of indignation was aroused in me. I kept thinking and thinking, and my indignation did not go to sleep. It kept working and working, and finally I began to write."[44] After several months of meditation and research on the "honorable" *code duello,* Beecher found it and the code of chivalry that produced it to be a perversion of the code of honorable Christian living. He delivered his "Sermon on Dueling" to his congregation and then repeated it for a presbytery of ministers and laymen, astonishing that august body with his departure from theological themes. "Dueling is a great national sin," he announced.

> The whole land is defiled with blood . . . This work of desolation is performed by men in office, by appointed guardians of life and liberty. On the floor of Congress challenges have been threatened, if not given, and thus powder and ball have been introduced as the auxiliaries of deliberation and argument . . . a duelist may be a gambler, a prodigal or fornicator, an adulterer, a drunkard and a murderer, and not violate the laws of honor. . . . We are a nation of murderers, while we tolerate and reward the perpetrators of the crime.[45]

The sermon was published, and more than forty thousand copies were distributed. Lyman Beecher's national reputation was established. He would remain at East Hampton for seventeen more years, and when he finally left, his farewell sermon was mainly directed at those few holdouts who had not come forward and given their lives to Christ:

> And what shall I say to you, my dear hearers, of decent lives and impenitent hearts, to whom, through the whole period of my ministry, God by me has called in vain? God is my witness that I have greatly desired and earnestly sought the salvation of your souls, and I had hoped before the close of my ministry to be able to present you as dear children to God. But I shall not. My ministry is ended, and you are not saved. . . . Once more I call upon you to repent and spread before you the unsearchable riches of Christ, testifying to all of you that there is no other name under heaven whereby we must be saved, and that he that believeth shall be saved. And now I have finished the work which God has given me to do. I am no longer your pastor, nor you the people of my care. To the God who committed your souls to my care, I give you up. And with a love which will not cease to glow till the lamp of life expires, I bid you all farewell.[46]

A footnote to that moving adieu: thirty-six years later, one of Beecher's sons called upon a widow who had been in the congregation that morning. He asked her if she had been a member of his father's church. "Oh, no," she answered, tears coming to her eyes, "it was his leaving that was the cause of my conversion. I thought when he went that the harvest was past, the summer ended, and my soul not saved."

Beecher's next pulpit was in Litchfield, Connecticut, and here he came into even greater national prominence, founding temperance societies to deal with what was then (and is today) one of the biggest social problems of the age—alcohol. It is hard to imagine how widespread and ruinous alcoholic consumption was a century and a half ago. We have seen how frontiersmen started their days with drams of whiskey and introduced their sons to the habit, when they were big enough to do a man's work. But steady drinking was hardly restricted to the rough-and-tumble life of the frontier. Back East, in all walks of life, the habit was similarly ingrained. Beecher deplored the pernicious usage which "breaks down the moral government of God over men. . .

emancipates them from the restraint of the divine sanctions, and lets them loose upon society to obey, as they may be tempted, the impulse of passion and a depraved inclination."[47] Once he began his campaign, thousands of New Englanders "took the pledge," vowing to abstain for life from alcoholic beverages. Temperance societies sprang up everywhere, and "the experience of one year had furnished lucid evidence that nothing was impossible to faith."[48]

Thus did Lyman Beecher, along with evangelical pastors Nathaniel Taylor and Asahel Nettleton, inherit from Timothy Dwight the leadership of the Second Great Awakening in New England. At the height of his career, we have this endearing portrait by the best-known of his offspring, daughter Harriet, of a typical Sunday morning, getting Father to the church on time:

> The bells would begin to ring, and still he would write [his sermon notes]. They would toll loud and long, and his wife would say, "He will certainly be late," and then would be the running up and down stairs of messengers to see that he was finished, till, just as the last stroke of the bell was dying away, he would emerge from the study with his coat very much awry, come down the stairs like a hurricane, stand impatiently protesting while female hands that ever lay in wait, adjusted his cravat and settled his coat collar, calling loudly the while for a pin to fasten together the stubbed bits of paper [his notes], which being duly dropped into the crown of his hat, and hooking wife or daughter like a satchel on his arm, away he would start on such a race through the streets as left neither brain nor breath till the church was gained."[49]

In 1826, Beecher was offered—and accepted—his greatest challenge: the pulpit of the Congregational church on Hanover Street in old Boston. As Harriet recorded, when her father "came to Boston, Calvinism, or orthodoxy [Christianity], was the despised and persecuted form of faith. It was the dethroned royal family, wandering like a permitted mendicant in the city where it had once held court, and Unitarianism reigned in its stead. All the literary men of Massachusetts were Unitarian. All the trustees and professors of Harvard College were Unitarians. All the elite of wealth and fashion crowded Unitarian churches. The judges on the bench were Unitarian, giving decisions by which the peculiar features of church organization, so carefully ordained by the Pilgrim fathers, had been nullified."[50] In short, the reception Dr.

Beecher received in the heart of the Unitarian stronghold could scarcely have been colder.

At first, they chose to simply ignore him. No matter; when he had preached revival in Connecticut, the Lord had graced his efforts, and revival had come in the wake of his preaching. He would preach revival here. Upon his arrival, there were thirty-seven professing members of the church. "I began with prudence, because a minister, however well-known at home, and however wise and successful he *has* been, has to make himself a character anew, and find out what material is around him."[51]

Beecher began by a careful propounding of basic doctrine, in order that there could be no mistaking the foundations of his faith. But his own enthusiasm for the new life awaiting those who came to Christ was contagious, as was the gravity of the alternative. He was getting through.

> From the beginning, my preaching was attended with interest . . . There was very earnest hearing in the congregation. I saw it was taking hold—deep solemnity, not mere novelty. I felt in my own soul that the word went forth with power. It was a happy season, hopeful and auspicious.

New faces began to appear in the congregation, and soon whole families.

> I kept watch from the first among my hearers. They told me of a young lady who had been awakened. I found her out, conversed with her, and she was converted. . . . I tell you this, that you may know how to *begin* a revival. I always took it by word of mouth first, talking with single cases and praying with them. Went on so till I found twelve, by watching and picking them out. I visited them and explained what an inquiry meeting was and engaged them . . . to agree to come. I never would risk a blank attempt."[52]

Before long, the church on Sundays was packed out. Beecher was well familiar with the course of revival; he had experienced it often enough before and knew what was coming next. "I began to say to the church: 'I think there is a work begun. Fire in the leaves—not only among us, but in the community.' I made no attack on Unitarians. I carried the state of warm revival feeling I had had in Litchfield for years. . . . They came to hear, and came again, till they were snared and taken. Many that came to scoff remained to pray."

Finally, he invited the whole congregation to an inquiry meeting, where people could explore the meaning of the Christian faith. Fifteen came the first week, twenty the second, thirty-five the third, and three hundred the fourth. And God moved mightily among them. Now the Baptists began to come, and the revival spread to their churches. But not the Unitarians. When Beecher set up evening meetings, because the church could not hold all those who wished to come on Sundays, his church's bell was the only one that was ringing. But when the Unitarian ministers discovered that some of their people were beginning to attend, they started calling their own evening meetings at the same time, until the peel of Beecher's bell seemed to set off a veritable tintinnabulation of Unitarian church bells.

"I used to laugh to hear the bells going all around," wrote Beecher. "In this thing of revivals, you would find all these things came by showers. Each shower would increase, increase, increase; and when I saw it was about used up by conversion, I would preach so as to make a new attack on mind and conscience, varying with circumstances, and calculated to strike home with reference to other classes, and bring in a new shower. The work never stopped for five years."

Ultimately, the revival reached the point that seventy converts at a time were being admitted to communion, and in desperation the Unitarians changed their tactics. Up to that point they had relied on their chief weapon, ridicule, but now they sent spies, and things began to get ugly. This, too, Beecher had foreseen.

> As the work deepened, I told my church one of two things would come: either revival would burst out through all these churches, or else there would be an outbreak of assault upon us such as could not be conceived. It was the latter. In one day after the seventy joined, the press belched and bellowed, and all of the mud in the streets was flying at us. . . . There was an intense, malignant enragement for a time. Showers of lies were rained about us every day. The Unitarians, with all their principles of toleration, were as persecuting a power, while they had the ascendancy, as ever existed. Wives and daughters were forbidden to attend our meetings; and the whole weight of political, literary, and social influence was turned against us, and the lash of ridicule laid on without stint. "Well," I said to the church, "I

have only one thing to say; don't let your fears be excited about *me.* God helping, I shall take care of myself. But watch your own hearts and pray" . . . and they did. As for me, I cared for it all no more than for the wind. I knew where I was, and what I was doing, and knew that I was right."[53]

For two solid years the Unitarians pressed their attack, and when they finally saw that it was to no avail, they began to treat Beecher and his Christians with civility. In the meantime, the good doctor had done some preaching on temperance, and the tract society had purchased the copyright to his sermons, and soon he had all the notoriety, pro and con, that a preacher could ever use.

Beecher never entirely defeated Unitarianism, as Dwight had Infidelity, for just as he was pressing home the advantage in the enemy's heartland, so to speak, the Body of Christ once again became divided as a fresh round of doctrinal squabbles broke out. Much of Beecher's concentration was diverted to expounding enlivened Calvinism as he understood and practiced it. As Beecher himself put it in one of the many letters he would write to satisfy this or that self-appointed judge:

> The enemy employs influential friends of Christ to wound one another, and to propagate distrust, and alienation, and acrimony, almost as injurious to the cause of Christ as heresy itself. The strength of the Church depends upon our concentrated action, and this, like credit in the mercantile world, depends on confidence; whatever, therefore, propagates suspicion and distrust among brethren who have long acted together paralyzes their power as the failure of great capitalists undermines public confidence and propagates alarm in cities. Of this, the great enemy of the Church is perfectly aware, and has never failed, when the concentration of forces against him had become too formidable for direct resistance, to ease himself of his adversaries by dividing them."[54]

Nevertheless, much of the remainder of his career was spent in sound and sober disquisition on the basic tenets of Christianity, trying all the while to keep the door open to salvation, when others determined to shut it. While he did not defeat Unitarianism, it can honestly be said that he so blunted its effectiveness that from that time forth, while it did lead to the Transcendental School of New England intellectuals like Thoreau and Emerson, it ceased to be a serious threat or viable alternative to Christianity.

The final chapter in Beecher's illustrious ministry saw a radical departure. Lyman Beecher was offered the presidency of Lane Seminary in Cincinnati, and anticipating the great westward migration of tens of thousands of Americans, he accepted the position and the pastorate of the Second Presbyterian Church there. His reason: "The moral destiny of our nation, and all our institutions and hopes, and the world's hopes, turns on the character of the West, and the competition now is for that preoccupancy in the education of the rising generation. . . . If we gain the West, all is safe; if we lose it, all is lost."[55]

Perhaps the most significant fruit of the Second Great Awakening in New England was the strengthening of the loving one's neighbor aspect of American Christianity. We have already seen the powerful reestablishment of the loving God aspect, through the lightning storm on the frontier and the waves of the Spirit back East. Yet nowhere did awakened Christianity manifest itself so dramatically in the love of one's neighbor as it did in New England, where caring for the needs of others had once been regarded not merely as a spiritual obligation but as a physical necessity for survival. Where the Puritans and Pilgrims had looked after the poor and the widows and orphans in their midst, as a matter of course, now reawakened Christians of all denominations established orphanages and old people's homes, sanitariums and hospitals, and all manner of benevolent societies—for everything from improving morals and combating alcoholism, to distributing tracts and Bibles, starting Sunday schools, and supporting missionaries.

In Connecticut, for instance, it was law that every child coming of age be given a Bible, and early in 1811, Beecher wrote to his friend Asahel Hooker: "We are succeeding remarkably in . . . getting subscribers to the Connecticut Bible Society, especially in this town. . . . Churchmen and Democrats, Christians and men of the world, all fall into the ranks on this occasion. The thing is the most popular of any public charity ever attempted in Connecticut."[56] Where once it had been feared that the disestablishment of the church would pauper the charitable impulse, the opposite was now proving to be the case: in the wake of the revival, any good cause received support—not only financially but with committed lives. Denominational barriers seemed to melt away, and excitement mounted as Christians began to believe that society actually could be changed by the power of Christ. "A Christianized America"—maybe it was not just a naive dream, after all!

In New Haven, in 1815, Thomas Gallaudet, fresh out of Yale College and Andover Seminary, met with some strong Connecticut ministers to pray together and lay plans for founding the Connecticut Asylum for the Deaf and Dumb. Such was the response (including a $5,000 grant from the state legislature) that in less than two years construction was completed, and it was ready to receive patients. During the same period, the American Asylum for treating the mentally ill opened in Hartford, and prison reform began at Newgate Prison in East Granby. Christians were also discovering that the printing press was the ideal means to reach both the lone pioneer and the newly arrived immigrant with the good news of Jesus Christ. The American Tract Society was formed, and during its first twenty-five years it published 48 million tracts. These, plus their devotionals and periodicals for young and old alike, were carried and passed out both at home and abroad—"from the shores of the Baltic to the Cape of Good Hope, through the whole of Europe and India, and were pressing upon the inhabitants of China."[57]

Much of the credit for such grass-roots enthusiasm must be given to young Samuel Mills, who, in 1806, entered Williams College on fire for the Lord, and whose coals were not banked with the passage of time. One day that summer, he and four of his friends were walking through the countryside when a sudden thunderstorm drove them to seek shelter in a large haystack. Held captive by the rain, they fell to talking about the "moral darkness of Asia," when one of them suggested that they pray for that continent. One prayer led to another, and the more they prayed and talked, the more they became seized with the desire to go to Asia as missionaries. Thus was born this nation's foreign missionary movement. Two years later, Mills and his friends formed a private society, called the Brethren, the members of which pledged their lives to missionary service.

The problem was, the Brethren had no funds to support a missionary outreach to Asia, so Mills, aged twenty-seven and a graduate student at Yale now, and three of his young colleagues made an appeal to the General Association of Massachusetts, a newly formed body of evangelically minded Congregational ministers, asking for their "advice, direction, and prayers."[58] The result was the formation in 1810 of the American Board of Commissioners for Foreign Missions. Within two years the first five foreign missionaries set sail from these shores, determined to bear the light of Christ westward to India—a little over three centuries after Christopher Columbus had set sail from Spain with the identical intent. The Light that America had so abundantly received she had now herself begun to give.

To his acute disappointment, Mills did not accompany them. The same mission board that he had been primarily responsible for creating now ruled that his unique abilities would be far better spent at home, recruiting other on-fire young ministers for the mission field. With every reason to be resentful and embittered, Mills instead chose to accept their decision and cheerfully threw himself into his assignment—with remarkable results. A steady stream of missionaries went forth, to Africa, India, China, Japan, and the islands of the Pacific. One of these islands, in the Sandwich group, which later became known as Hawaii, was the birthplace of a native lad named Henry Obookiah. His family had been killed in a tribal war, and a sea captain had rescued him and brought him to New Haven. Here Mills encountered him and undertook the task of converting him and educating him—in other words, doing the work of a missionary, right in his own backyard. His hope was that Obookiah would one day return to his homeland as a Christian missionary himself, and toward that end Mills established a Foreign Mission School, under the auspices of the Board of Missions. But as it turned out, Obookiah himself became an effective recruiter, as he was now able to tell earnest young New England Christians how badly the Gospel was needed on the other side of the world, and his own sincere faith spoke for itself.

Mills never completely gave up his desire to go on the mission field himself, and finally he got his chance, though once again, it was not exactly what he had originally envisioned. By now, the East was well familiar with the miracles of revival that were taking place beyond the mountains, but the more they heard, the more New England leaders realized how little was really known about the status of the frontier. So Samuel Mills and John Schermerhorn were dispatched together by the Missionary Societies of Massachusetts and Connecticut on a two-year fact-finding tour, which took them from Ohio to Kentucky, and then through Indiana, Illinois, and Tennessee. Traveling down the Mississippi with General Andrew Jackson and his troops, they finally reached New Orleans in May, 1813.[59] With methodical, dispassionate care, they counted inhabitants, preachers, and Bibles, set up Bible societies for the future propagation of the Word, and upon their return they published their findings.

At first, their report reads like a dry assemblage of data and statistics, but as one begins to read between the lines, it comes vividly to life.

> In the ten counties which this district [western Pennsylvania] comprises, is a population of only 21,255 souls, which must necessarily be very scattered. There are only three ministers, six churches supplied with preaching part of the time, and three vacant societies of the Presbyterian order. . . . Eight of these counties, it will be perceived, are entirely destitute of preachers, unless they are occasionally visited by an itinerant Methodist. . . . This part of the country is a proper field for missionary labor."[60]

Of the Mississippi, they wrote: "The state of society in this Mississippi Territory is truly deplorable. Most of the emigrants to this country came here for the purpose of amassing wealth, and that object seems to have absorbed their souls."[61] Everywhere they went they inquired as to the availability of Bibles, and upon their return Mills estimated that some 76,000 Bibles were needed immediately, with as many more to follow as possible. Said Mills, the lack of Bibles (which were not inexpensive in those days) among the destitute in America was "a foul blot on our national character. Christian America must arise and wipe it away."[62]

Christian America did arise: the American Bible Society was immediately founded in New York in 1816, and soon 750 Bible societies sprang up, most of them affiliated with the parent society in New York, hard at work distributing the Scriptures all over the country. The work of Mills and Schermerhorn also served to galvanize the zeal of the hundreds of newly enlisted Christian soldiers, inspiring them to go out into the home mission field, as well as to foreign lands.

Once again, in the wake of the Second Great Awakening, as in the wake of the first, with renewed urgency the Light spread inland from the Atlantic, wherever men were carving out homesteads in the wilderness or trades in the towns and cities. As before, the timing was vital: in the middle of the last century the colonies had to be stitched together so tightly that their fabric could withstand the tension that would come with pulling away from Great Britain. Only the needles of Light—stitching the thread of a shared, vital, common faith could do that, and in the nick of time, by a tremendous outpouring of the Holy Spirit, it was accomplished. Despite the fact that fully a third of all Americans were in some degree sympathetic to the Crown, the fabric held.

Now the young republic was about to face a similar wrenching as an unconvinced Britannia sought to regain her property in the New World. Only this time the United States were far less united in spirit than the colonies had been; in fact, most of the spiritual leaders in America were so anti-French that it left them pro-British and therefore vehemently opposed to "Mr. Madison's war." But once again the needles of light were darting and stitching, sewing the patchwork quilt together with the luminescent thread of a faith that transcended region and denomination.

6

"Don't Give Up the Ship!"

The blue ensign with the white stars on it seemed iridescent in the first rays of the morning sun. An offshore wind straightened the ensign out from the mizzenmast as the *USS Chesapeake* crowded on sail and set course for the Mediterranean, where she was due to relieve the *USS Constitution* on patrol duty. The ship had a fresh-scrubbed look as mates hollered orders and barefoot tars scrambled up her rigging and out on her arms to unfurl her mainsails. The heavy canvas billowed out, and the ship's three masts began to thrum with tension as she gathered speed. Her bow rose and fell in the rhythm of the sea, her lines humming as she ran before the wind. One of the mates started a chanty that gave expression to what they were feeling in their hearts.

Commanding her from the quarterdeck was Commodore James Barron, who now passed the order to clear the decks as quickly as possible. This was a shakedown cruise for both ship and crew—and piles of equipment and provisions, the remains of her fitting out in Norfolk, still littered her decks. The commodore passed another order to his first lieutenant, who shouted it to the boatswain's mate; he would not rest easy until all the loose gear was below and the decks were squared away. He had no real reason to feel uneasy. The date above their departure time in the ship's log was June 22, 1807; with the exception of subduing the Barbary Coast pirates, America had not fired a shot in anger in more than twenty years. Still, the *Chesapeake* was a ship of war, and as such, she should be ready for action at a moment's notice.

"Sail ho!" came the cry from the mainmast lookout.

"Where away?" called the first lieutenant.

"Two points off the larboard bow—and closing." The commodore nodded to his first lieutenant, who climbed partway up the rigging and extended his spyglass. In a few moments he called down: "A frigate, sir, about forty-four guns. Appears to be British."

The commodore thanked the lieutenant without further comment. Technically, there was no cause for alarm, and yet. . . . Other than stopping merchant ships suspected of harboring deserters or carrying contraband cargo to the French, the British left the Americans pretty much alone. At least they had, until the war with Napoleon had become a struggle to the death. Now the stoppings of American merchantmen had become much more frequent, and the British were using the pretext of getting back deserting sailors to take seamen by force, to serve in the Royal Navy. Britannia did indeed rule the waves, but it meant maintaining 644 warships on active duty, with another 936 in reserve.[1] To man such an armada, she could hardly count on volunteers, for conditions in the British fleet were appalling—the pay was negligible, the food was barely edible and infested with weevils and maggots, and the lash was used so liberally that discipline was enforced by fear. As a result, 80 percent of a ship's company had to be rounded up by press gangs, roaming the docks and taverns with an eye out for drunken sailors—or any able-bodied men, for that matter. It was not wise to be out after dark in any port where a British warship lay at anchor.

Nor did it matter if it was an American port and a man confronted by a press gang could prove that he was American born. For Britain was desperate. Napoleon had conquered all Europe and was planning to invade England; the only way he could be countered was by blockading the entire continent of Europe. Every ship in the Royal Navy was drastically undermanned, and it reached the point where they were stopping American ships on the high seas, mustering their crews, and taking away any sailors who spoke with English accents, instead of the Yankee twang. If the "English" sailor had papers on him, proving him to be a naturalized American citizen, more often than not, the British officer in charge would tear them up before his eyes and cast them to the wind.

The American government repeatedly expressed its outrage, but the onetime colony had no navy to speak of, and the British government had little but contempt for the upstart, ragtag nation that had slipped out from under its dominion. In the British view, their failure to squash the American Rebellion was just bad luck and wretched timing. Burgoyne and Cornwallis had gotten themselves into such messes through their poor generalship. Even the gifted General Washington could not have prevailed for long against the full weight of the British

Army. Let the Yankee Doodles make all they wanted to about God being on their side; that was one place where the British would have to agree with Voltaire. God was on the side of the army with the biggest battalions.

So Britain ignored American protests and kept right on impressing American seamen when and wherever they felt like it. And American citizens demanded that a navy be built. So it was—amounting in 1807 to all of ten ships on active duty. Up to this point, no American warship had ever been stopped and searched, yet as the British frigate bore down on him, there was cause for Commodore Barron to be concerned. Three months earlier, two groups of British seamen had stolen longboats and deserted their frigate in Norfolk harbor. Several of these sailors immediately sought asylum on American soil and volunteered for service aboard the warship that was then being fitted out. The Americans paid much better, their new ships were all manned by volunteers, so that one's messmates were not the wharf rats and convicts one served with under the Union Jack, and the officers and mates treated you like human beings. Given the opportunity, who wouldn't jump ship?

Three of the men who left the British frigate claimed to be American citizens who had been impressed by the British, and these three were allowed to join the roster of the *Chesapeake*. The British captain, when he learned, was furious and lodged a formal protest through the British consul at Norfolk, who forwarded it to the United States Secretary of the Navy, who made inquiry of Commodore Barron, who confirmed that two of the three men were freed slaves, one from Virginia, the other from Maryland, and the third had been born on the eastern shore of Maryland. The British demanded that the three be returned at once. Their demand was denied.[2]

Normally, it would take five years of living in America before an immigrant would be eligible for the status of naturalized citizen, but America had always made a special exception of granting immediate political asylum. It was this special status that a fourth man from the British ship now claimed—one Jenkin Ratford, who had been a tailor in London when he had been impressed. He, too, signed aboard the *Chesapeake* and so jubilant was he at his newly acquired immunity that he mocked and derided British officers in the streets and on the quays of Norfolk.[3] The more indignant they became, the more he insulted them, until a formal demand was also issued for his return, in addition to the others. Again, the request was refused, and the British captain now referred the case to his supreme commander on the North American station, Vice Admiral Sir George Berkeley, based in Halifax, Nova Scotia. Berkeley shared his officers' indignation and sent his own flagship, *HMS Leopard,* to Norfolk with orders to search the *Chesapeake* for the deserters.

It was the *Leopard* that the *Chesapeake*'s lookout had sighted and that was now dispatching a longboat with a lieutenant on board to the *Chesapeake,* to present the British demands to Commodore Barron. Barron refused, and as soon as the British lieutenant was off the deck, he called for all hands to try to get the ship ready for action. It was a hopeless task; the gun crews had never practiced and had not even gotten their guns unlimbered. The captain of the *Leopard* now brought his ship alongside and spoke directly to Barron through a loud-hailer, informing him that he himself would come aboard and muster the Americans on the foredeck and take the deserters. Barron replied that no one but the captain or the first lieutenant mustered an American crew aboard an American warship, and he was not about to do so. His men knew that he was playing for time, and they worked even faster to clear the *Chesapeake*'s decks, but the British captain must have sensed it, too, for he shouted "Fire!" A deafening roar, a billow of white smoke, and the *Chesapeake* was staggered by a full broadside at point-blank range. The *Leopard* fired a second unanswered broadside, and then a third. The *Chesapeake* was being destroyed. With three men dead and eighteen wounded, still she had not been able to fire a round. Barron had no choice but to strike his colors. The British sent over a boarding party, took the men, including Ratford, whom they had to drag out of hiding, and departed, sailing back to Nova Scotia, where Ratford was hanged.

Outrage swept the eastern seaboard. Americans were quickly informed by the astonishing network of daily newspapers, as editors exchanged papers with their colleagues by fast riders and reprinted one another's major articles and editorials the next day—as well as pertinent pieces from the London papers. The average American was well and quickly informed—and vitally interested in the *Chesapeake* affair. So important was that story that Thomas Ritchie, the editor of the Richmond *Enquirer,* cut short his wedding trip in order to get back to his office to write scathing editorials.[4]

British ships in Norfolk harbor immediately canceled all shore leave and got their crews back on board on the double, as the Americans cut off all supplies to the Royal Navy. In New York, a mob savaged a docked British warship, and the British consul's house had to be put under police protection. Even in Federalist Boston, where British sympathy was running strong, due to long-established mercantile ties, thousands of people gathered to clamor for war. Across the ocean in London, the *Times* responded by calling for a naval bombardment of America's seacoast towns, to bring them to their senses.

In Washington, the pressure mounted on President Jefferson to declare war, and had Congress not been on summer recess, it might have been almost impossible to avoid. It was an ironic situation for Jefferson, who had made no secret of his preference for the French over the British in their seemingly endless controversy. Now he had to stand against his own bellicose Democratic Republicans, who were demanding that America go to war as a matter of national honor. Jefferson, who had opposed the creation of a navy and the maintenance of even a token standing army, now had to admit that America was in no condition to go to war with anyone, least of all Great Britain. So he put off the decision, and by September, when Congress reconvened, the ardor for war had died down—somewhat. Nevertheless, from the moment of the firing on the *Chesapeake,* the balance had tilted toward war with England, and many were saying that it was only a question of time.

Impressment was not the only grievance Americans felt was serious enough to go to war over, although it may have been the only one that affected all regions of the fledgling nation equally. The North was incensed at the increasing restrictions that Britain, in its attempts to blockade France, was imposing on American trade. At first, the only goods restricted were those that could aid the French militarily, but then they tightened the screws, issuing Orders in Council, which stated that only ships that stopped in English ports and had their cargoes scrutinized and approved would be allowed to proceed. In November of 1807, these orders were tightened still further: *all* shipments bound for France were curtailed, and any ship even suspected of heading in that direction would be confiscated. In effect, Britain was declaring that henceforth she would control American trade. In the South, where sympathy for the French was the strongest, people had apparently forgotten the horrors of the French Revolution. To them, France symbolized the new age, the age of democracy, with no more aristocracy, no more elitism, no more class consciousness—no more of all the things Great Britain seemed to stand for.

In the West, on the frontier, the problem was still Indians, although now it centered further to the west, in the territory known as Indiana. To the continuing shame of America, one sequence kept repeating itself: the Indians and the territorial government of the United States would make a treaty whereby the Indians would cede over millions of acres of hunting land. For a year or so, the treaty would stand. But then the temptation of all that "free land" would become too much to resist, and pioneers and land developers would start to encroach on the Indians' territory. Thicker and thicker their numbers would become, driving away the wild game the Indians depended upon, until the Indians would make formal complaint. At that point, American agents would find one pretext or another to nullify the existing treaty and either impose a new one or threaten force. So the Indians would make another treaty, ceding away still more millions of acres. In the end, they became desperate, and a Shawnee chief named Tecumseh started rallying them, pointing out that only by uniting as one did they ever stand a chance of driving the white man back. He saw a vision of a separate Indian nation, for which he was prepared to go to Washington, to meet with President Madison.

For their part the British anxiously desired to see Tecumseh's plan succeed. The Hudson's Bay Company had a number of trading posts, backed by forts, in the Northwest Territory, from Illinois clear out to the Pacific. Over the years, they had built up a lucrative fur trade with the Indians and were not inclined to stop the sale of firearms to those Indians, even when it appeared that the latter were getting ready to go on the warpath. For the Indians represented the one tangible obstruction to the onslaught of white Americans. British support had already been implicated in the Battle of Fallen Timbers, and hard evidence—in the form of documents offering bounties for American scalps—convinced farmers on the western frontier that the British were inciting the Indians to an uprising.

Everyone in America, it seemed, wanted war, except the pious Federalists, mostly in New England, who despite the continuing effrontery of British arrogance, nonetheless considered it unthinkable that they would ever align themselves with the infidel French against the only other English-speaking, God-fearing, mission-supporting nation on earth. As Timothy Dwight put it: "To ally America to France is to chain living health and beauty to a corpse dissolving with the plague. . . . The touch of France is pollution. Her embrace is death. . . . Those who unite with the enemies of God in their hostilities against Him, His church, and their fellow-men will perish with those enemies."[5] Moreover, many of the New England clergy were now openly preaching that Napoleon was the antichrist.

Now approaching the end of his second term as President, Jefferson was heartily sick of the whole affair and growing increasingly grieved by the incredible factionalism in America. Never in its brief history had the "United" States been so split, and now, in that winter of 1807–1808, it seemed that *secession* was on the lips of Americans at all points of the compass. In New England, such talk had begun when Napoleon had retaliated against the new British Orders in Council by issuing his own decree, which stated that any American ship examined by the British would be considered an enemy vessel and would be confiscated by the French. Suddenly, Jefferson faced the suicidal prospect of having to declare war on Britain *and* France simultaneously. He did the next best thing: he declared an embargo against United States shipping to *any* foreign port. Now the merchants really had something to holler about. It was bad enough having to elude both British and French warships, but to be denied even the remote chance of getting a cargo through—and by one's own President—that was too much!

Jefferson, who had repeatedly declared that the government that governed best was the one which governed least, was behaving as much like a dictator as George III or Napoleon ever had! Most of the shipping merchants affected were located in New England and they openly wondered if Jefferson would have been so zealous in the imposition of federal will had the affected region been his beloved Virginia. Moreover, Jefferson, who had been against building any naval vessels for national defense, now spent vast sums of federal funds to build up a fleet of little gunboats, not to defend our shores, but to make sure that Yankee shippers did not disobey his embargo. Indeed, to them it felt as if he had already declared war—on New England. Eventually, they would go so far as to call and convene a convention in Hartford for the purpose of considering New England's seceding from the Union, although there were still too many Patriots with long memories in New England for anything to actually come of it.

They were not the only ones contemplating secession. To the westerners, it seemed as if the Jefferson administration had turned a deaf ear to their repeated expressions of concern over Indian unrest. And now the one marketing avenue left open to them—the shipping of their produce down the Ohio and the Mississippi for sale to brokers in New Orleans—had been effectively closed by the embargo. For with no ships going to Europe and precious few being allowed up the coast, for fear that they might veer off eastward, the brokers had no one to sell to. America's population had increased 50 percent in the first decade of the nineteenth century, but the war in Europe and the embargo had combined to reduce the flood tide of immigration to a mere trickle. The year before, so many newcomers had arrived on the frontier that there would have been a large enough market for farm produce right there and fresh cash to pay for it, too. Now the loss of the Mississippi as a trade route was a crippling blow. Western farmers felt desperate—desperate enough to murmur that they would be better off on their own, but not quite desperate enough to take matters into their own hands.

In the South, while the question of slavery no longer had a place in the front-page news, it had hardly died away. Southerners needed only to look to the Northwest and Indian Territories, where most of the immigrants were settling, see the sort of states that would be formed from them—most of them admitted with constitutions banning slavery. How long would it be before they were overwhelmed, in Senate and House? Right now, one of their own, indeed their champion, was imposing his will on the North—how long before the shoe was on the other foot? Jefferson's embargo was hurting them, too; countless bales of cotton remained piled on the docks and levees, with no place to send them. Something had to be done. . . .

By the grace of God, literally, the republic stayed together. The nation stumbled on, with Jefferson's protégé, James Madison, now at the helm. But the situation was not improving. On the Continent, Napoleon appeared to be invincible. The Austrians fell to him, and the Spaniards, and the Italians, and now he was turning towards Russia; it appeared he was about to add the Bear to his list of conquests. The greater his success, the greater the threat he posed to the island race to his west. And the greater measures Britain took to protect herself. Now *any* American ship found on the high seas was likely to be taken and her crew impressed. As A. L. Burt put it:

The independence of the United States was being frittered away. The country was losing its self-respect, the most precious possession a nation can have, as it failed to command the respect of the belligerents. More and more the feebleness of the American government's policy had been teaching these embattled giants of the Old World that they could trample with impugnity upon American rights, American interests, and American feelings."[6]

Finally, by the summer of 1812, there had been too many ignominies, too many outrages; it was reported that more than 6,000 American citizens had been kidnapped and forced to serve in the Royal Navy, which had to replace some 2,500 deserters a year and simply refused to curtail impressment. If America was to retain any semblance of honor, she had no further alternative but to fight. Crying, "Free Trade and Sailors Rights," the War Hawks in Congress won the vote for war seventy-nine to forty-nine, and on June 18, President Madison proclaimed that a state of war existed between Great Britain and the United States. The American cause was summed up by the commander of Western Tennessee Militia:

> We are going to fight for the re-establishment of our national character, misunderstood and villified at home and abroad; for the protection of our maritime citizens, impressed on board British ships of war and compelled to fight the battles of our enemies against ourselves; to vindicate our right to a free trade, and open the market for the productions of our soil, now perishing on our hands because the "mistress of the ocean" forbids us to carry them to any foreign nation.[7]
>
> ANDREW JACKSON

On land, from the very beginning, nothing seemed to go right. Once again, as in the Revolutionary War, America made a land grab at Canada—this time, at least, with the excuse of avenging the incessant inciting of the Indians and striking a blow at the only enemy possession within reach. But as the anti-war Christians pointed out, it was still aggression of the sort that Scripture condemned.

To those who believed that God took a hand in the affairs of nations, it seemed abundantly clear that God did not intend America to annex Canada. He had His own plan for Canada, and the moment American soldiers began to interfere with it, His grace, which had in the previous conflict so favored the American cause, suddenly was lifted.

In the summer of 1812, the commander of the 2,000-man force approaching the British fort at Detroit, was perhaps the least gifted American general. William Hull, governor of the Michigan Territory, remained preoccupied not with the smaller British force approaching under General Isaac Brock, but with the Sioux and Ottawa Indians that intelligence reports convinced him were encircling them in great numbers. When informed that Tecumseh was at the outskirts of Detroit, he gasped, "My God! What of the women and children?" And with that, he surrendered, learning afterwards that all but thirty of the Indians had previously departed, to spend the winter at home.[8]

Still America did not learn. A month later, a second thrust was authorized, this time under the command of General Stephen Van Rensselaer of the New York militia with fully seven thousand men at his command. His plan: to attack across the Niagara River at the tiny Canadian settlement of Queenston, initially defended by a garrison of perhaps 300 troops. For some inexplicable reason, General Van Rensselaer chose to attack with only 600 of his men and thirteen of the eighty boats available to him.[9] The battle began, and after several hours, Van Rensselaer spotted some British reinforcements coming and belatedly decided that it was time to commit his main force. But they, too, could see the advancing British soldiers and abruptly decided that their short-term enlistment did not cover invading a foreign country. Refusing to cross, they all stood on the shore and watched while the newly reinforced defenders cut down their comrades in arms. Finally, with more than a third of the invading force either killed or wounded, the stranded remainder surrendered, and the darkest day in American military history ended.

Van Rensselaer resigned his commission, and command of the army devolved to one General Alexander Smyth. With a great deal of bombast about the changes that would occur now that a *real* general was in charge, he assumed command. A month later, the army discovered what would occur. Smyth's target was the British post at Fort Erie, on the Canadian side of the Niagara. He spent all morning putting his men into small boats to cross the river, and when they were all embarked, he demanded the surrender of the British fort. To his dumbfoundment, the British refused. Smyth ordered his men back to shore and back to camp. The men rioted. "A scene of confusion ensued which is difficult to describe," recalled one officer, "about four thousand men discharging their muskets in every direction."[10] Most of them shot in the direction of the general's tent! Hastily informing his second in command of his desire to visit his family, Smyth disappeared—from the Niagara, and from the United States Army.

Naturally, Britain took great comfort in the tidings from Canada; their deepest convictions about the lack of backbone and leadership of the American military were confirmed. Obviously previous British defeats at Trenton, Saratoga, and Yorktown were unlucky flukes, aberations from the true strain, and the upstarts would now gladly sue for peace. Most Federalists regarded the debacles on the Canadian border as further proof of the wrongness of Mr. Madison's war. But the rest of the country, though humiliated, remained unconvinced. Now Henry Clay, the young Senator from Kentucky who was a leader of the War Hawks, set about recruiting a new army, this one made up primarily of Kentucky riflemen, whom he claimed were the best fighting men in the world. At their head he installed a general who had already proven himself in combat under the most difficult of circumstances—William Henry Harrison, the hero of Tippicanoe. In that battle, a night attack by a superior force of Indians under Tecumseh's brother, the old brigadier had kept his wits about him and, with masterful courage and tenacity, had beaten off repeated attacks of the enemy. But he would need all these traits and more in a war that was getting progressively more vicious.

In January, 1813, an advance detachment of Harrison's force under General James Winchester, a hundred miles ahead of Harrison, was taken by surprise at the village of Frenchtown on the River Raisin. The Americans were routed, and Winchester himself was captured, and as a prisoner, surrendered the rest of his force. Many, however, barricaded themselves in the town, preferring to hold out until Harrison could relieve them. But before the remaining troops would surrender, they demanded the guarantee of the British commander, General George Proctor, that they and their wounded would be protected from the Indians, who had gained a reputation for slaughtering and scalping prisoners of war. Proctor gave the guarantee and the defenders obeyed their commanding officer and surrendered. The American wounded were left behind in the town without a guard, and after the British left, the Indians, wild drunk, fell upon them, killing and scalping them. Then they set fire to the village and beat the survivors back into the flames as they tried to get out of doors. When the Indians rejoined the British, fresh with their bloody scalps, General Proctor congratulated them on their bravery.[11] Several American prisoners of war overheard him, and they vowed never to forget. It was going to be a grim campaign.

Meanwhile, on Lake Erie, the situation was, as they say, developing. Britannia might rule the oceans, but the "inland sea" of Lake Erie, separating the United States and Canada, was another matter. Until now, the American reconnaissance schooner *Scorpion* had to turn tail and run for it every time she sighted the British brigs of war *Queen Charlotte* or the *Lady Prevost*. But now Lieutenant Oliver Hazard Perry, the ranking United States naval officer on Lake Erie, was constructing a squadron at Erie—specifically two large brigs of 480 tons each, the *Lawrence* and the *Niagara,* and two support ships. Work proceeded at a frantic pace, for with these vessels afloat the American navy's vessels would be roughly equal in tonnage to the British, who had ruled Lake Erie unopposed.

But Perry needed men to man the new ships, and the twenty-seven-year-old lieutenant went in person to Brigadier General Harrison, to plead for riflemen to train as seamen and marines. Control of the lake meant everything: without it, the British would not move their troops along the shore. Moreover, their ships protected the two British-held forts at either end of the lake, and these forts at Detroit and Niagara controlled two of the three invasion routes south. If the British lost control of the lake, these forts would become untenable, and they would then have only one other invasion route: down Lake Champlain to the Hudson and down it to the city of New York. If the Americans could somehow check them on Champlain, as by the grace of God they had in the previous war, to further prosecute this contest, the British would have to resort to direct amphibious assault, which if met with force, would prove disastrous.

The other reason Perry went to personally plead his case was the requirement of speed: the situation on the Continent was shifting so rapidly that it was about to radically alter the balance of power in North America. Ever since Napoleon's retreat from Moscow the past winter, things had been going from bad to worse for "the little corporal." His so-called allies, seeing which way the wind blew, were turning against him one by one, so that Britain, far from going it alone, had now gained so much support that a significant portion of Wellington's seasoned regulars would shortly be available for North American service. At the moment, the British military presence in Canada was still a token one, augmented mainly by Canadian volunteers and the tribes who had united under Tecumseh. It was a force to be reckoned with, for Tecumseh was a master tactician as well as a wise and courageous leader of considerable charisma. But the Americans, under a combat-proven general for the first time since the Revolutionary War, enjoyed the advantage, however slight.

All that, of course, would tilt irrevocably with the arrival of 15,000 to 20,000 thousand of Wellington's best troops, possibly with Wellington himself in command. Wellington had once said of Napoleon that his presence on a battlefield was worth 40,000 troops. The same could be said of the Iron Duke. In less than a month, the British would take everything west of the Ohio River, and even if the Americans could hold them there and sue for peace, the western border of the United States would be forever delineated by the Ohio and the Mississippi. In sum, an incalculable amount depended upon four small ships, five "cockleshells," and some four hundred men—*if* Perry was able to persuade Harrison to give him that many.

Fortunately Harrison could appreciate the delicate, shifting balance and the need for immediate action every bit as well as the fiesty young lieutenant who faced him. Without hesitation, the grizzled old brigadier drafted dozens of able-bodied potential seamen from his ranks, and as substitutes for marines he gave Perry 100 of his finest Kentucky marksmen from the famed McArthur Brigade.[12] Jubilantly Perry returned to Erie and urged the shipwrights to increase their efforts. They did so, working by torchlight far into the night, and by the beginning of August, they had the new brigs finished and off the stays, ready to be fitted out. Gunnery practice now became the first order of the day, every day, as Perry drilled his new crews until he knew he could count on them for rapid, effective fire, especially at close range. At first, the buckskin "marines" had difficulty adapting to the rigors of seagoing discipline, but Perry himself patiently explained to them that in combat at sea every man had a series of precise and demanding responsibilities that required instant, unquestioning obedience. At length, he was able to get these extremely independent Indian fighters to see it his way.

By mid-August, the lieutenant judged his ships and crews seaworthy and moved the squadron to an advance base at the harbor of Put-in-Bay on South Bass Island, about fifteen miles northwest of Sandusky, directly in the sea-lane of any traffic heading into or coming out of the Detroit River. The British occupied forts on both sides of the narrow river, and well aware of the buildup in American naval strength, the British positioned their fleet in the middle. It was highly unlikely that the Americans would risk sailing into the river, where the longer range of the British guns and the lack of maneuvering space would put them at a serious disadvantage.

The situation was a standoff, which was exactly what the British commander, Captain Robert Heriot Barclay, wanted. The river and the rim of the lake would freeze over in early December, immobilizing both fleets until the spring thaw, by which time Wellington's troops should be on hand. And as Barclay, too, had been building and was himself severely shorthanded, nothing suited him better than to play the waiting game, until the first thin film of ice began to form on the Detroit River. . . .

Unfortunately for Barclay, his commanding officer, General Proctor, was of the honor-above-all school. He ordered Barclay to put the American upstarts in their place and strongly implied that Barclay's personal courage would be held in question, if he failed to do so. Ironically, this was the reverse of the situation with the Americans. Perry, one of the Navy's new breed of "fighting lieutenants," was spoiling for a fight, confident that all the training and gunnery practice and their seamanship would stand them in good stead. His superior, Commodore Chauncey, in charge of all the Great Lakes, repeatedly warned Perry not to put his ships in harm's way and to fight only with the greatest caution, for the loss of a single vessel would upset the balance of power.

Several times in late August, Perry took his fleet to the mouth of the Detroit River, hoping to entice the British out to fight, and finally he determined that if they would not come out, he would go in after them. He summoned his ship captains to a council of war in his cabin and there assigned each American captain a specific ship in the British squadron to fight. Regardless of their line of battle or the longer range of some of their guns, each captain was to seek out his opposite number, lay alongside, and destroy her. He himself, aboard the *Lawrence,* would fight the new British flagship, the *Detroit*. Captain Elliott of the *Niagara* boasted that he would reduce the *Queen Charlotte* to floating wreckage in ten minutes. As they concluded, Perry reminded them of the words of Britain's greatest naval commander, Lord Nelson: "If you lay your enemy close alongside, you cannot be out of position."[13]

The morning of September 10 dawned bright and clear, and as they tacked out of Put-in-Bay, they were greeted with the sight of six British ships on the horizon, in line of battle. The Americans had three more ships than the British, but they were lightweight schooners. More significantly, the British had sixty-three guns to the Americans' fifty-four, and concentration of firepower was more important than a few extra schooners, with one or two guns on each. Perry glanced up at the pennants on the masts: the wind was from the southwest, which meant that they would have to engage from leeward. This gave the British a decided advantage, as they would come down on the Americans and dictate which way the battle would be fought. As Perry's sailing master mentioned this to him, he just smiled and said, "To windward or leeward, they shall fight today."

"Clear for action!" came the command from the first lieutenant, and all gear not essential to fighting was stowed below. The decks were then heavily sanded—fresh blood was slippery, and there would be a lot of it, for the science of ballistics and gunnery had outstripped the capacity of wooden bulkheads to afford adequate protection. Hammocks were slung inside the bulkheads to attempt to cut down some of the large flying splinters, which were as deadly as grapeshot or the cannisters of iron scrap and nails. When they had completed all the preparations, about three hours remained before the wind finally brought the two fleets together.

They must have been hard hours for the buckskin marines. On land, if the artillery got too bad, a man could always back off a bit to get some breathing space, or at least dig into the ground. On land, if it looked like you were hopelessly outnumbered or about to be surrounded, a wise officer would withdraw his men, to keep his fighting force intact. On land, there were a dozen honorable alternatives to standing toe to toe with a superior foe who was certain to annihilate you. Surely, skill was a key factor at sea, as the contest began at long range. Ship handling and accurate gunnery could sometimes decide the outcome before the combatants ever closed to within rifle range.

But—if you had two determined captains, inevitably the range would close. Then full broadsides would begin to take devastating effect. Hulls would be torn open, masts would come thundering down, heavy guns would be tossed about like woodchips, grapeshot would literally sweep the decks, and all the while, up above in the rigging, sharpshooters would pour down a withering fire on anyone still standing. No protection existed, no trees or earthworks to hide behind, no place to run to; indeed, there was no running at all. The decision was not even the individual's; the captain or senior surviving officer decided whether or not to strike colors and surrender or send a boarding party over the side. Either way, there was no breaking off; once the battle was joined, it was to the death.[14]

A ragged cry arose from the deck as the sailors pointed aloft. The pennants had shifted; they would be fighting from windward! Morale picked up markedly after that. At 10:30, a little more than an hour before the battle was likely to begin, Perry had a meal served to the men at their battle stations. Just as they finished, they could hear a bugle aboard the *Detroit,* and her ship's band, joined by bands on all the British ships, struck up "Rule, Britannia." With Union Jacks flying and their hulls freshly painted bright red, they made an imposing sight. But the psychological moment for intimidation had already passed. As soon as they finished playing, Perry had a surprise of his own—a personal battle flag with the dying words of Captain Lawrence of the ill-fated *Chesapeake* emblazoned on them: DON'T GIVE UP THE SHIP. It was a large flag, easily visible from the decks of the rest of the squadron, and a mighty cheer greeted its hoisting.

At 11:50, the long guns of the *Detroit* opened fire. They hit the *Lawrence* and shivered her timbers, and from the quarterdeck, Perry steadied his crew, reminding them that they would get their chance, soon enough. But the way the battle lines came together, the *Lawrence* was leading the American line and thus forced to sail down the entire British line, before she finally came abreast of the *Detroit*. Every British ship fired into the *Lawrence* now, and their strategy became apparent: concentrate on the American flagship, until she was subdued, then shift fire to the *Niagara,* reduce it, and then mop up the rest of their fleet, lingering behind.

But the *Lawrence* inflicted heavy damage of her own. Perry had released the gun captains to choose targets of opportunity, and the gunners chose well. One by one, they would aim, put torch to touchhole, clap hands over ears, and stand clear as the gun trundled backwards with the recoil. Then they would reload, run the gun out, check the elevation, and wait until an opposing gun or mast or rudder came into the line of sight.

Time seemed to slow almost to a standstill as the entire British fleet poured their fire into the *Lawrence.* The main deck was chaotic: men were screaming, shrapnel flying, canvas and rigging coming down, another gun was knocked off its carriage—twelve of their eighteen were already out of commission. And still the bombardment continued. As more and more men were hit, Perry kept passing the word for them to be taken below, where the surgeon would do what he could for them, but the decks ran red with blood.

"Mr. Yarnell," Perry cried, momentarily losing his control. "Where is the *Niagara*?"

"To leeward, sir. She seems to be holding out of range."

"Well, signal her up here, mister!" The executive officer called for the bugler to do so, but he received no apparent response from the *Niagara.* Furious, Perry concentrated on directing the fire of the last three guns still operable. The endless hours of gun-laying practice now paid off: as they slowly drifted astern, the incoming rounds from the *Detroit* and the *Queen Charlotte* diminished notably; the *Lawrence* had taken quite a toll of its own.

With the American flagship rudderless and nearly silenced and her sister ship apparently avoiding combat, surely, thought Barclay, the American commander would strike his colors. And everyone in both fleets expected at any moment to see the blue ensign with the white stars lowered. But though four out of every five of his men had been killed or wounded, Perry still had one small gun they could remount and fire. With the help of two unwounded men, he himself got it upright, loaded it, aimed it at the enemy flagship's quarterdeck, where his counterpart was no doubt observing him through his glass, and fired. The shot hit its target, and Barclay died.

Incredibly, in a contest that should have been decided in minutes, well over an hour had passed. The American schooners had inflicted significant damage on their British opposites, but there was no question that victory would shortly go to the British. Still the *Niagara* hung back, maneuvering now to put the *Lawrence* between herself and the British broadsides. Staring at her, Perry, in cold rage, informed the handful of men still standing that he would go over there and take command of the *Niagara,* and would sail her into battle himself. Instructing his thrice-wounded executive officer, Mr. Yarnell, not to strike the *Lawrence*'s colors until he was well clear of her, Perry hauled down his battle ensign, DON'T GIVE UP THE SHIP, clamped it under his arm, and ordered the longboat lowered away.

The four seamen started rowing furiously, as soon as the longboat settled into the water. Once the British caught sight of them, the *Detroit* fired a broadside at the longboat and called up repeated volleys from their marines, but while shot and musket balls rained down about them, miraculously not one hit their vessel or its occupants. When they reached the *Niagara* and climbed aboard, the first thing Perry did was have his battle ensign raised. "I've been sacrificed!" he shouted at Elliott, who stared at him as if he were looking at a ghost. Elliott then offered to take the boat and go fetch the two schooners that had lagged behind, and while this was a task any junior officer could have done, Perry was glad to let him go. He assumed command of the *Niagara* immediately and crowded on sail. The ship leapt forward.

Virtually unscathed, with her men cheering as the range closed, the *Niagara* entered the fray. Perry executed a classic maneuver, cutting the enemy's battle line and pouring larboard and starboard broadsides into British bow and stern simultaneously. "Double load—stand by all guns—fire as your guns bear!" came the stream of commands from the quarterdeck, and a great rippling roar belched forth from both sides of the *Niagara.*

In eight minutes, the *Detroit,* the *Queen Charlotte,* and the *Lady Prevost* lay dead in the water. With a hand that was still shaking, Perry wrote out a brief dispatch for Brigadier General Harrison.

> We have met the enemy, and they are ours:
> two ships, two brigs, one schooner, and one sloop.
>
> Yours, with greatest respect and esteem,
>
> O. H. PERRY.

Calming somewhat, he sent a second dispatch to the Secretary of the Navy: "It has pleased the Almighty to give the arms of the United States a signal victory over their enemies on this lake. The British squadron, consisting of two ships, two brigs, one schooner, and one sloop have this moment surrendered to the force of my command after a sharp conflict."[15]

Then and only then, as he looked astern at the floating hulk of the *Lawrence,* did it apparently dawn on him that he had come through the inferno unscathed. Those standing near him saw him bow his head and heard him say, "The prayers of my wife are answered."

All America celebrated Perry's victory, the more astonishing—and uplifting—since eyewitness reports of the action were unanimous in the estimation of his certain defeat. There had been celebrations of naval victories before, the previous summer, when the *Constitution,* now known affectionately as Old Ironsides, through superior gunnery, handling and ship design, had not just defeated but completely destroyed the *Guerrière* in single combat, and later his majesty's ships *Java, Macedonian,* and *Peacock* had similarly fallen. These, of course, had been little more than fleabites to the Royal Navy, whose fighting ships outnumbered America's by more than a hundred to one.

Nonetheless, they had taken a toll psychologically, for after Lord Nelson's victory at Trafalgar, the British had thought themselves invincible at sea. Wrote the London *Times*: "It has cast a gloom over the city which is painful to see . . . ," and an article in the British journal the *Pilot,* stated:

> Any man who had foretold such disasters this day last year would have been treated as a madman or a traitor. He would have been told that ere seven months had gone by, the American flag would have been swept from the ocean, the American navy destroyed, and the maritime arsenals reduced to ashes. Yet not one of the American frigates has struck her colors . . . Nothing chases them, nothing intercepts them, nothing engages them, except to yield. . ."[16]

Perry's incredible victory had surpassed these, and now, even in staid New England, there were fireworks and banquets. It seemed almost like a second Fourth of July—and in a sense it was, for the heroism of a handful of American sailors, led by an intrepid young officer who did not know the meaning of surrender, had altered the balance of power in the West. For with the American lake flotilla effectively doubled and the enemy's annihilated, regardless of what else transpired, the western invasion routes were now permanently sealed.

It remained only to secure the land, and there, too, the outlook was drastically altered. The British defeat had a profoundly demoralizing influence on their Indian allies, who began to slip away in ever increasing numbers. Not even Tecumseh could hold them, though he tried. Indeed, this noble warrior now emerged as the last major threat Harrison faced. For Proctor, who had inherited the overall British command when General Brock was killed, had lost all taste for combat, and was now fearful that the rapidly advancing Americans had but one purpose in mind: avenging the River Raisin Massacre and his treachery there. In fact, Proctor made ready to abandon his troops. Tecumseh, whose men had heard the great naval guns and had noted that the British fleet had failed to return, confronted him.

"Our ships have gone one way," he said, looking the British general in the eye, "and we are very much astonished to see you tying up everything and preparing to run the other way. . . . You always told us you would never draw your foot off British ground. . . . We must compare your conduct to a fat dog that carries its tail upon its back, but when affrightened, drops it between its legs and runs off."[17]

Tecumseh's words stiffened Proctor's backbone to the point where the British withdrawal was orderly, rather than a rout. But both the British regulars and their Indian allies knew that Proctor only felt concern for his personal safety, and Tecumseh had to watch him constantly, to make sure he did not run away. Each day, more Indians left and went home. Finally, the retreating British were backed up against the Thames River and forced to make a stand. The night before the battle, Tecumseh was deeply pessimistic. Staring into the flickering campfire, he confided to his remaining chiefs, "When General Brock was in command, he used to say, 'Tecumseh, come and fight the Americans,' but General Proctor always says, 'Tecumseh, go and fight the Americans'. . . . Brothers, we are about to enter an engagement from which I shall never return. My body will remain on the field of battle."[18]

Early the following morning, Harrison sent his mounted Kentuckians into the woods against Proctor. Shouting, "Remember the River Raisin!" they charged the British lines, which caved in and broke—and as Proctor abandoned his men and fled for his life, some of them escaped, but the vast majority surrendered. It was a different story for the Indians under Tecumseh; as the Kentuckians came yelling toward them, they themselves gave the war cry and charged. The two forces came together with a violent shock, and it was tomahawk versus hunting knife. Wounded and bleeding profusely, the leader of the Kentuckians, Colonel Richard Johnson, was rushed by an Indian with raised tomahawk. Just before he passed out, he fired his pistol and put a ball through the brave's head. Though Tecumseh's body was never found, witnesses later claimed that Tecumseh was the attacker whom Johnson killed.

The land war in the west was concluded; all the territory south of the Great Lakes now lay in American hands. Once again, America celebrated. Yet in the orgy of self-congratulation, there was almost no public call to pause for a moment, to give thanks to the Almighty Deliverer. In a single generation, the republic seemed to have forgotten that spiritual lesson it had vowed never to forget.

7

The Dawn's Early Light

The first sunlight bathed Baltimore harbor in a soft golden haze, just reaching the peaks of the pitched roofs of the clapboard houses nestled around the bay. The houses still had their eyes closed against the sun, but in the harbor, half a dozen low, sleek gunships made preparations to weigh anchor with the tide. Their decks piled with fresh provisions, one by one they ghosted through the morning mist that was rising off the water and passed close by the massive earthwork ramparts of the fort that guarded the harbor entrance. A lone sentinel waved to them, but the sailors were too busy to wave back. Refitted and supplied, they were bound for the Irish Sea, riches and glory—or death by hanging. For these were privateers—the fastest, deadliest ships in the world, and the scourge of the English sea-lanes.

In the winter of 1813–14, Napoleon's fortunes steadily worsened. Unable to defend France's borders, he found himself toppled from his throne and exiled to Elba. For the first time, the British could devote their full attention to the situation in America. They tried to persuade Wellington to assume command of the war effort there, but he would have none of it, stating unequivocally that the Americans could not be beaten on their homeland. Nevertheless, a major portion of the British fleet was now free to concentrate on America and its accursed privateers. Until now, the British had not been overly concerned by the war in America. They had undertaken it to punish the rebel colonists and teach them the lesson they should have been taught in the previous war. The blockade formed their principal instrument of punishment, and it had indeed crippled the maritime industry of New England. Since the British found that relatively easy to maintain and in harmony with the main priority of waging war against Napoleon, they saw no reason to curtail hostilities. It would cost them precious little to let the war go on indefinitely.

Except for one thing: the Americans had an instrument of punishment of their own—the privateer. Some called privateering legalized piracy; others saw it as the only recourse of a fledgling nation with a navy of ten capital ships against a force of more than nine hundred. A privateer carried enough guns to fight or subdue, but her primary tactic was to evade. She carried a letter of marque from the government she represented and was allowed to keep and sell any ships of the declared enemy nation that she captured. Thus privateering greatly appealed to the intrepid Yankee sailor who from birth had an appreciation of the dollar. It also attracted solid businessmen with a little money to invest, for the rewards could be extraordinary: a swift, well-captained privateer could capture two or three prizes a week, and when these were sold and the shares divided, it resulted in a handsome return for those who had put up the money to put her to sea.

There were privateers everywhere. They hunted solo or in wolf packs, taking British ships wherever they could find them, even plucking them out of the English Channel. They forced the British to concentrate their merchant ships into convoys; then they would trail the convoy, hovering about the fringes and picking off the stragglers. And there were enough of them so that the English merchants cried out in rage at the Admiralty for being unable to protect their nation's trade. Baltimore had emerged as the principal port of the privateers; from that place alone ships had accounted for the staggering loss of 556 vessels![1] Lloyd's of London, the great maritime insurance company, was driven to despair by the amount of claims it had to meet. Finally it flatly refused to insure any vessel sailing from England to Ireland—a sign of how unsafe Britannia's home waters had become. In 1814, the *Perry* captured twenty-two British ships in a two-month cruise, while the *Governor Tompkin* seized and burned fourteen ships in a single sweep through the English Channel. Thomas Boyle, captain of the *Chasseur,* dispatched a handbill to Lloyd's that declared his own personal retaliatory blockade of "all ports, harbors, bays, creeks, rivers, inlets, outlets, islands and sea-coast of the United Kingdom."[2] The London *Times* summed up the nation's frustration and her fury: "May no false liberality, no mistaken lenity, no weak or cowardly policy interpose to save them from the blow. . . . Strike! Chastise the savages!"[3]

With their singular ability to affront and offend without any awareness of doing so, simply by the very nature of their appalling haughtiness, the British still could not understand why the Americans had declared war in the first place. Was Napoleon not the antichrist, a monster bent on world domination? They perceived their war with him as a battle to the death between light and darkness, with themselves the last hope of free Europe. Therefore, they regarded America's declaration of war, just as Russia was falling under Napoleon's heel, as an act of extreme perfidy—nothing less than attempted national matricide at a time when England stood in the greatest danger she had faced since the Spanish Armada. For her offspring to have chosen that moment to plunge in the knife. . . . All these sentiments were now recalled, as the knife finally began to cut deep.

But with Napoleon now gone, the opportunity to start paying back loomed before them. Squadrons received their specific assignment of punishment—razing and pillaging undefended coastal ports and towns. One leader of such raids was Rear Admiral Sir George Cockburn, who had a personal score to settle with the Yankees. He had been senior naval officer in Canada when an American raiding party landed at York (now Toronto), the undefended capital of Upper Canada. After beating off the local militia—though in the process they lost perhaps the finest field grade officer in the United States Army, General Zebulon Pike—the Americans systematically savaged the civilian population, looting and putting the torch to everything in their path, government buildings as well as private dwellings, including the Parliament Building. For this act of barbarity and cowardice Cockburn swore revenge—in kind. He vowed that one day he would lead just such a raiding party against the American capital at Washington and that when the time came he would show no more mercy or compassion than had been shown the women and children and homes of the Canadian capital.

The time came far sooner than he or anyone else imagined. One year and four months later as English raiding parties under Cockburn and others ravaged the coast of Maryland (that state specifically, for it was home base for the majority of privateers) there was a curious contrast between the outlook of the citizens of Baltimore and those of Washington, thirty-seven miles away. For the citizens of Baltimore, the privateering capital, the handwriting was on the wall. But the citizens of Washington retained a peculiar penchant for unreality. Directly in the path of the marauding squadrons, hardly anyone there seemed to take the danger seriously, except perhaps, the President himself. Madison made preparations to remove and preserve the papers of state and did his utmost to build a fire under General William Winder, the commander of the local militia. But the predominant mind-set for the rest of the dwellers in the nation's capital was that it couldn't happen there.

It did happen there, on August 24, 1814. The British invasion force, under the leadership of one of their ablest commanders, Major General Robert Ross, accompanied by Cockburn, advanced on Washington from the head of the Patuxent River. Taken by surprise, Winder frantically tried to organize the hastily assembled militia, belatedly deciding to make a stand at Bladensburg, Maryland, in the path of the oncoming British regulars. Winder then refused the advice to set up defensive positions in the town's buildings and behind cover, and determined to face them in the open, European style. The British could not have been happier. Scouting forward, Ross ascertained that the defenders had distinct superiority in numbers (approximately 6,000 to 2,600), as well as artillery, cavalry, and position—but they were, after all, militia, unseasoned in actual combat. For them, the British had a secret weapon—the Congreve rocket. In actuality, it was largely ineffectual, being little more than a pipe stuffed with gunpowder, capped with a warhead, and launched out of another pipe; but it made a wildly whooshing and flaming projectile that badly unnerved any soldiers who had never seen it before.

Long before Ross's light infantry came in range, the American gunners opened fire, their shots plowing up the dirt road well in front of the vanguard. Closer and closer came the Redcoats, the sun glinting on their fixed bayonets. Now the cannon began to take a real toll, but the British kept closing ranks and kept coming. Suddenly, the Congreve rockets roared and whistled overhead, and the British front line charged. The militia began to flee. In their excitement, a gun crew rammed in wadding before the powder, and to get it out depressed the muzzle of the cannon so far that it toppled into a ditch. By then, the British were almost on top of them, and the crew ran after the others who had already left.[4] Winder panicked and ordered the second line to withdraw without firing a shot. Then he sent troops forward and changed his mind and recalled them, in a blizzard of contradictory commands. Back and forth the troops marched, becoming increasingly demoralized, as it became patently obvious that their commander did not have any idea what he was doing.

One force of men requited themselves with unalloyed gallantry—Commodore Joshua Barney's 600 flotillamen. Having been ordered to burn their gunboats to keep them from falling into British hands, these hardened veterans of naval combat fought on land as they did at sea. They ignored Winder's order for a full-scale retreat and trotted forward with five naval guns. Setting them up, Barney's troops promptly cleared the road of Britishers with an eighteen pounder; then charging a superior British force behind a fence row, they jumped over the fence, crying, "Board 'em!" They alone checked the British advance, and held them for half an hour, until Barney was hit and their guns overrun.

Regardless of the grit of the flotillamen and those militiamen with competent unit commanders, appalling generalship and galloping panic combined to throw the American forces into a rout that British reports later dubbed "the Bladensburg Races." At dusk, General Ross and Admiral Cockburn led the first troops into the American capital. A few short hours before, these streets had been teeming with fleeing families, screaming women, and wagons rushing every which way. One who had kept her head was Dolley Madison, who had had the presence of mind to remove Gilbert Stuart's portrait of Washington, though she had to leave most of the White House valuables behind. But now silence reigned in the hot, sultry evening, until the boots of the British grenadiers echoed in the empty streets.

Slowly approaching the Capitol, Ross commanded the drummer to beat a roll to indicate that they wanted a parley, but no one came forth. They had just paused beside Robert Sewall's house, when suddenly a flurry of shots rang out. A soldier toppled forward, and Ross's horse went down, the second he had lost that day. By the time the British broke in, the house was deserted. Nevertheless, the soldiers retaliated swiftly and brutally: thenceforth, anyone caught with a weapon, there or anywhere else, would be summarily executed, and his house burnt to the ground, as Sewall's was immediately. No further incidents occurred as Cockburn kept his vow to avenge the razing of York. The British torched the incomplete Capitol building and systematically looted and vandalized the White House and surrounding dwellings despite the pleading of those women and children still on the premises. As the night sky turned an angry red-orange with the leaping flames, Ross kept the grim score: buildings "totally consumed" included the Capitol, the House of Representatives, the arsenal, dockyards, shipping, and numerous other public and private establishments. Estimated value: £4 million sterling (1814). Suffice it to say that the burning of Washington was such a shock that it even stunned the customarily hostile British press.

From the vantage point of nearly two centuries, one wonders if divine retribution was not at work here. For when Providence finally *did* intervene, it called an abrupt halt to the razing with a violent thunderstorm. The next day, when the British attempted to resume their depradations, a tornado struck the city with such force that in many places the soldiers were unable to remain on their feet, and a collapsing building buried a squad of men. General Ross ordered his men back to the Patuxent without delay.[5] It would seem that, if God had allowed the retribution for the equally ruthless razing of Upper Canada's capital, He had also prescribed its limits.

In any event, Baltimore came next. Just prior to this second action, a minor incident occurred in Chesapeake Bay. A Methodist missionary named Joshua Thomas was stationed on Tangier Island in the bay, about a hundred miles south of Baltimore, where the British had quartered their 12,000 troops. On the Sunday before embarking for the assault on Baltimore, they had ordered Thomas to hold a public meeting to exhort the troops. Thomas considered refusing, but when he prayed about it, "It came to me that I must stand up for Jesus, as a good soldier in the fight of faith, and as some of these men might be killed in battle and never have another opportunity of worship, it was my duty and privilege to obey their order."

His exhortation was hardly what the British officers had in mind. When the 12,000 were assembled, Thomas told them that sin caused war and fighting among nations, but that "this is a faithful saying and worthy of all acceptation, that Jesus Christ came into the world to save sinners. . . ." (1 Timothy 1:15). He went on to tell them "what kind of a sinner I was, and how He saved me from sin," and that He was "able to save to the uttermost, all them that come unto God, by Him." But then he felt compelled to go on. "I told them that it was given to me by the Almighty that they could not take Baltimore, and would not succeed in their expedition," and he said that he feared that many had that morning received their last call to salvation and were about to perish by the sword. When the meeting ended, many came up to him and "thanked him for his faithful warnings and hoped that it would not go as hard for them, as he had foretold." But the parson was unable to offer them any more encouragement privately than he had in his sermon.[6]

At dawn on the day of the attack, Admiral Cockburn and General

Ross accompanied their advance units forward, commandeering a farmhouse along the way and stopping for a leisurely breakfast, while they waited for the main body of their troops to catch up with them. When asked if they would also be requiring dinner that evening, Ross replied with a smile: "I'll eat in Baltimore tonight—or in hell."[7]

In Baltimore, the response to the approach of this uninvited dinner guest was somewhat different from what had it been in Washington. Once again, the bulk of the defenders were unseasoned militia, yet they had an excellent commander in one Sam Smith, who had served as a young combat officer during the Revolutionary War. There was also a fort named McHenry commanding the entrance to Baltimore's harbor: vast earthworks in the shape of a star, reinforced by logs—the most difficult of all structures to reduce by naval bombardment. In addition, Smith had taken an ingenious step to keep the deep draft British vessels at a distance: he had sunk many old ships, nose to stern, creating a picket fence of masts across the mouth of the harbor.

In Ross and Cockburn's path, General John Stricker had lined three regiments of militia, and as the first British troops came into sight, the Americans opened fire. When the British returned fire, the Americans melted back into the woods. A lull in the firing followed, and Ross announced that he himself would go back to hurry along the light infantry, coming up the road behind them. The general wheeled and spurred his horse, when abruptly his dinner plans were changed. An American sharpshooter sent a rifle bullet after him, which pierced his arm and buried itself in his chest. Ross reeled in the saddle and fell from his horse, lying in the dust until an aide rushed up to him. "Send immediately for Colonel Brooke," he gasped and died within an hour.

Arthur Brooke, commander of the Forty-fourth Foot and the second-ranking officer in the expeditionary force, may have lacked the panache and ability of his predecessor, yet as he came against Stricker's forces he had more than 4,000 combat-seasoned veterans, against 1,700 untested militia. On came the massed Redcoats, in places forty deep, their fixed bayonets pointed forward as they emerged from the dirty yellow powder smoke. Fear shuddered through the ranks of the waiting Marylanders, and their officers, sensing it, called out to them over the bombardment: "Hold your fire, boys! Let 'em get closer! Remember, aim just below that buckle on their chests, and shoot the officers first . . . hold steady . . . now, *fire!*" A volley roared out. The red line stopped—not to retreat, but to return a volley of their own. As their first rank reloaded, the second stepped past them, paused, and fired a second volley, and the defenders responded in kind. British soldiers fell, but they kept on coming, scarlet ghosts advancing through the smoke. They were almost upon them now; there was time for only one more volley, before they had to give way. But this time there would be no Bladensburg Races; the British won the field, but at a casualty rate more than twice as high as the Americans'.[8] In the face of this unexpectedly stiff resistance, Brooke decided not to advance further without naval support.

What stood in the way of that support was Fort McHenry, guarding the entrance to Baltimore's harbor and flying the largest American flag ever seen. In Baltimore, there dwelled a widow named Mary Pickersgill, whose specialty was making flags and who had done many for the city's privateers. Recently she had been asked by the fort's young commander, Major George Armistead, to make a battle flag that measured twenty-nine feet by thirty-six feet (or thirty-one feet by forty feet, or thirty feet by forty-two feet, depending on which historian one consults)—in any event, it was one that any British invaders could see for miles, for Armistead was confident that the fort could not be taken.

On the other hand, the British were about to concentrate more firepower than had ever been leveled at the United States in one place. The flagship of Vice Admiral Sir Alexander Cochrane, overall commander of the expedition, was HMS *Tonnant,* which mounted an incredible ninety guns (America's largest ship, the *Constitution,* carried forty-four). In all, there were thirty-five British men-of-war, and five of the Royal Navy's eight new bomb vessels, the most infernal weapon system yet devised. For they lofted aerial bombs—ballistic missiles of high trajectory that would burst directly over the heads of the defenders, instantly filling the air with flying shrapnel and death.

As the first light of dawn on Tuesday, September 13, 1814, started to burn away the morning mist, the peace of Baltimore harbor was shattered by the earth-shaking reports of the *Tonnant*'s heavy guns. Standing just out of range of the fort's twenty-four pounders, the other British men-of-war joined in, raining down hell on the fort for hour after hour. Finally, Cochrane, convinced that the fort's batteries had been put out of action, sent the bomb ships in closer, to finish the job. But as these vessels lobbed their aerial bombs and huge, deadly mortars into the air, suddenly the sea around them erupted with spouting white plumes. One bomb ship was hit and then another as the American gunners found their range. Stunned at the realization that hardly any of the American guns had been silenced, Cochrane signaled the bomb ships to withdraw immediately, for he dared not risk two-thirds of the Royal Navy's supply of such vessels.

No matter how horrendous an experience may be, if it continues long enough, man's nerve ends numb out, and thus anesthetized, he endures. The worst part about an impending bombardment was the waiting. Did one of the shells on one of those ships out there at the mouth of the harbor have your name on it? Would you be blown to smithereens? Would you lose control and start bawling or running? Would you have an arm torn off—or a leg? To look over the parapet and see the masts of forty ships, whose sole intent was to destroy you. . . . Unquestionably, the worst part was the waiting.

The first shells to fall struck terror into the hearts of all save those few who had been cannonaded before. The whistle of incoming shells, the deafening, breathtaking, earth-shaking concussion of the exploding round, and the fiery fragments flying everywhere—these would cause any man to hug the earth, his senses reeling, his body shaking and out of control. Before you could catch your breath and collect yourself, in would come another shell and another, with the ground jumping and fire spewing and men screaming. There you were, trapped in this hell pit, fingers clawing the dirt, and wondering if these were the last sights and sounds you would see on earth. But gradually you realized that the madman shrieking in your ear was you, and that while the shelling had not stopped, neither had your breathing. You were still alive, still sane, still whole. If you kept your head, you might just go on that way.

So you and your mates endured. Gradually, you got so you didn't flinch at each impact and forgot about the ringing in your ears or your eyes watering from the smoke. You also got so that you could gauge the proximity of an incoming round by its whistle, many of which did not merit diving for deeper cover. Every three or four minutes one of the mortars would arrive—a giant, 200-pound sphere that instead of exploding on impact plunged into the rain-softened mud, where it sat, either entirely out of sight or half buried, an evil wisp of smoke curling up from its fuse hole. Sometimes it would just sputter out, but still you got as far away from it as you could, because of the deadly splinters in the shower of mud that would erupt with it.[9]

If you were a praying man, you thanked God for the rain that had turned the ground inside the fort into a quagmire that simply absorbed so many of the shells and rendered the earthworks outside like a sponge, which did the same. You also thanked Him for the banty rooster that came out of nowhere, mounted a parapet, and hurled defiance at the British, to the cheers of the exhausted defenders.[10] But most of all, you thanked Him for such obvious interventions as the mortar that landed directly on top of the powder magazine and dented in its roof—but did not explode. And you thanked Him that, after a whole day in this living inferno, you and most of your comrades were still alive.

In the meantime, on land, the advance of the three regiments of British regulars—the same who had successfully stormed the bastions of Tarragona, Badajoz, and Bayonne—had for the moment bogged down. The Americans had gradually reoccupied the earthworks that had been carefully prepared, and as always, when they had their confidence back, their superb marksmanship took a fearful toll. The British could not expose themselves, let alone advance. But under the cover of darkness, Colonel Brooke devised a bold plan: a coordinated night attack that would void the advantage of the American gunnery, both rifles and artillery. All it required was for the fleet to neutralize the strong battery in the earthworks that anchored the American right flank.

Cochrane, however, was not about to risk sending any of his ships close enough to accomplish this, until the covering guns of McHenry were silenced. Instead, the admiral offered a diversion: an amphibious assault on the bastion in question, which would enhance the prospects of Brooke's night attack. Brooke agreed, and the plan was put into effect. But once again, "luck" turned against the British: it began to rain heavily. The most immediate effect this had was to so obscure the vision of the landing force that part of it took a wrong turn and got lost. The other effect the rain had was to soak the firelocks of Brooke's infantry, and to make matters worse, the main landing force was spotted long before it could reach the shore. The fort's batteries opened fire, and from midnight until two o'clock the unequal contest continued, until finally the landing party, what was left of it, turned and rowed back to the fleet. Half the ships sent out never returned, and with the sight of the last boats receding in the distance, Brooke's resolve failed him. Despite the fact that his main assault would probably have succeeded, he ordered a withdrawal, and the threat to Baltimore was over.

But not the bombardment of Fort McHenry. Now, more than ever, Admiral Cochrane felt determined to subdue this earthwork affliction. All through the night, rocket ships arced their missiles into the fort, aerial bombs burst, mortars thudded in. In the small hours of early morning, another fierce storm came up, further obscuring the vision of two Americans who were on board a British ship under flag of truce, to negotiate the exchange of prisoners. One of these was Francis Scott Key. He did not write the words that would become etched in every American's heart the following morning, as has popularly been supposed. He wrote them in the middle of the night, when the outcome was still very much in doubt. The giant flag that had been flying over the fort at "twilight's last gleaming" was still occasionally visible by "the rockets' red glare" and the "bombs bursting in air." Through the night, these gave proof "that our flag was still there." But the rain occluded their vision, and then the bombardment seemed to stop. Had the fort fallen? Francis Scott Key paced the deck and wrote down the lines that had been coming to him. Would that "star-spangled banner" still be there when morning came? Would "dawn's early light" reveal victory or defeat for the attacking British? As light came, Mary Pickersgill's flag remained, its inspiration having lasted through the "perilous night" to be enshrined in what would someday become the nation's national anthem. The battle had ended and the defeated British fleet slunk away, carrying on board General Ross's body, preserved in a barrel of rum.

When the British invasion army returned to Tangier Island, Parson Thomas inquired of the first officers ashore if they had taken Baltimore. "They looked at me and said, 'No, but hundreds of our brave men have been slain, and our best general is killed. It turned out just as you told us, the Sunday before we left: we have had a bloody battle, and all the time we were fighting, we thought of you, and what you told us. You seemed to be standing right before us, warning us against our attempt to take Baltimore.' " One soldier told of a friend whose last words were "God bless Parson Thomas. He showed me the way to Christ, and now, though I die, I hope for mercy and salvation through the name of Jesus, and expect to meet that good man in heaven." Another wounded grenadier told Thomas, "I never felt my sinfulness before God, until that Sunday you preached to us; and while the bullets were flying, and my comrades were falling on every hand . . . I cast myself on the merits of the Lamb of God, and now feel at peace."[11]

On the other side of the Atlantic Ocean, in neutral Belgium, five Americans had precious little to give thanks for. Henry Clay, Jonathan Russell, Albert Gallatin, James Bayard, and John Quincy Adams had been sent to the city of Ghent to negotiate the best possible terms for a peace treaty with Britain. So far, the gentlemen on the other side of the table had dictated the terms. Indeed, they had, in effect, presented the Americans with a five-part ultimatum:

1. Abandonment of America's claim to immunity from impressment.
2. On the Great Lakes, the complete disarmament, naval and military, of all forts and ships and recognition of Great Britain's exclusive right to arm and garrison the frontier.
3. The turning over to Britain of the northern half of Maine, the south bank of the Saint Lawrence, the region around Fort Niagara, and the island bastion of Michilimackinack.
4. Acceptance of the Mississippi as an Anglo-American river and the surrender of the territory between that river and the Canadian border to Lake Superior.
5. The ceding of the state of Ohio and the Indian Territory (the present states of Indiana, Michigan, Illinois, Wisconsin, and part of Minnesota), which would become an independent Indian state, as a buffer between the United States and the possessions of Great Britain.

The American commissioners' reply to George III's ministers was brief: such terms would never be considered "till the people of the United States were ready to give up their liberty and their independence."[12] The British reply was even briefer and came in the form of a *Times* editorial: "Our demands may be couched in a single word—submission!"

So the war dragged on—just as the British intended. Well aware that there was not the remotest possibility of the Americans accepting their terms, they played for much higher stakes: conquest was the name of the game now, and they intended to keep every bit of land that they could conquer. For the first time in modern memory, all Europe was at peace. That meant that Wellington's Invincibles, *all* of them, were now at Britain's disposal. In secret council, the crown's military advisors proposed a new three-pronged thrust, with the first objective already achieved: as of August 24, a British army held the capital of the United States. On the northern frontier, a second expeditionary force was poised ready to take Burgoyne's old invasion route down Lake Champlain and the Hudson River. This would split off the dissident New England states from the rest of the Union, and a separate peace could then be made with them. (The British Foreign Office suffered from the same myopia that has traditionally afflicted those responsible for assessing prevailing moods in other countries: they believed what they wanted to believe, reading only the Federalist papers, which were very vocal about their disaffection with the war.)

The third expeditionary force was already at sea and bound for New Orleans, where it would take the port and drive a wedge up the Mississippi and the Ohio, before heading east over the turnpike. There, the army from the north would meet it, and another army would drive up from the south, thus effectively quartering what remained of the United States. Maintaining three major forces in the field simultaneously was an enormously expensive undertaking, especially in the wake of the protracted land campaign against Napoleon, but the potential for victory seemed well worth the risk.

While the American commissioners did not know the details of the strategy, the general intent was not hard to surmise. Clearly they were now in the end game, and they gathered in increasing gloom, to attempt to discern what, if any, moves were left open to them. Surprised at first that the British did not break off negotiations upon the rejection of the ultimatum, the Americans came to realize that their adversaries wanted them there when the news of fresh British victories from across the sea would give them the maximum psychological advantage. With the news of the debacle at Bladensburg and the burning of Washington, it appeared that that moment might be at hand.

But unbeknownst to them, Fort McHenry had withstood the greatest bombardment in naval history, and two days before that, an even greater miracle had taken place on Lake Champlain. Outside Plattsburg, the garrison town for the lake, the British prepared to attack with 18,000 men—cavalry, heavy artillery, grenadiers, hussars, the cream of the Iron Duke's Invincibles, who had beaten the finest troops in Europe. Neither Wolfe nor Burgoyne, Amherst nor Cornwallis had ever commanded such a force. Nor did the British have any shortage of experienced field commanders, for there were two lieutenant generals and five major generals, all under the overall command of the Governor General of Canada, Sir George Prevost. Against this formidable engine of war was arrayed a rag-tag collection of 3,300 Americans, of which there was only one professional battalion amongst them—four companies of the Sixth Infantry. Certain disaster was only hours away.

One small matter needed to be taken care of first—the American flotilla of four brigs and eight gunboats, which had taken refuge in Plattsburg Bay, to avoid the British flotilla of equal size but considerably longer gun range. Meeting the British in open water would have proved suicidal; the British would have picked them to pieces at long range before they could ever get close enough to use their own cannon. They were no threat to the British ships and precious little threat to the land forces, who could easily have outgunned them. Yet Prevost intended to leave nothing to chance and would not move until he had secured his sea flank. He ordered his naval commander, Captain Downie, into the bay to dispatch the Americans. When Downie pointed out that this would put them in the only circumstances that might give the Americans an even chance, Prevost, almost exactly as Proctor had to Barclay at Detroit, impugned Downie's personal courage and the honor of the British navy. Hardly lacking in the right stuff, Downie was nonetheless young and so stung by Prevost's slurs that he ignored the warnings of his senior officers and led his flotilla full tilt into the bay.

As had happened so many times in the past, when British and American forces came together, a fluke in the weather proved the deciding factor. The moment Downie entered the bay, the wind dropped away, leaving him and the ships behind him to glide the full length of the American battle line, receiving one well-aimed broadside after another at close range. He gave as good as he got. His first broadside put one fifth of the *Saratoga*'s crew out of action. But American gunnery, under the command of another of the fighting lieutenants, John MacDonough, once again proved superior. In fifteen minutes, Downie was dead, and two of the British craft were disabled. Though the battle lasted two full hours, the outcome was decided at the outset when the wind died, for the Americans had put out anchors, which enabled them to turn and fire fresh broadsides, without the aid of the wind. Prevost, watching the entire action, became so disheartened that he withdrew his army back toward the frontier, without firing a shot. His men were so furious and disgusted that 800 deserted to the American side, and Prevost himself was subsequently recalled for incompetence.[13] On his part, MacDonough sent a report to President Madison that indicated that the fighting lieutenants were also praying lieutenants: "The Almighty has been pleased to grant us a signal victory."

America had just sealed the last invasion route from the north, and the arrival of this sensational news, coupled with that of Fort McHenry, abruptly reversed the mood at Ghent. The five commissioners enjoyed their own Fourth of July celebration, while in London, gloom settled in. A fresh appeal was made to Wellington to assume chief command in America as soon as possible, but the Duke again refused: "That which appears to me to be wanting in America is not a general, or general officers and troops, but a naval superiority on the lakes; without it, I could do little more than sign a peace which might as well be signed now."[14] The vast majority of Englishmen agreed with him, having lost all stomach for prolonging the war. Now at Ghent, the tables were turned, and the British became anxious for peace. They allowed the Americans to remove every term they objected to. The British agreed to abandon impressment and to respect America as a proper nation.

They signed the treaty on Christmas Eve, and a sloop of war was dispatched to New York with the news. But before it could get there, other sails approached the Mississippi delta and the prize of New Orleans. Seven thousand picked troops under Sir Edward Pakenham, Wellington's brother-in-law, went ashore just two hours' march from the city that controlled half the commerce that flowed out of the New World. His superiors exerted a great deal of pressure on Pakenham not only to take the city, but all of Louisiana and the Mississippi Valley as well. Unquestionably, enthusiasm for further prosecution of the war was on the wane, yet the government saw one remaining opportunity to salvage a ruinously expensive campaign from being a total loss. So far, they had absolutely nothing to show for having committed all those men and ships at a time when the protracted struggle with Napoleon had bled the country white. Yet to take the Mississippi would be worth far more, in the long run, than all the immense treasure they had already squandered. So Pakenham sailed with a commission installing him as Governor of Louisiana—and secret orders to carry out his mission, regardless of any rumor he might hear of a peace treaty between Britain and the United States. For even if the rumor proved true, by the time any such treaty could be formally ratified by both sides, Great Britain would be in firm possession of the heart of central North America.[15]

One man stood in his path—perhaps the most effective American military leader since Washington. Old Hickory his devoted soldiers called him. And though he was only forty-seven, the name seemed to fit this lean, hard Tennessean with the shock of gray hair and deep blue eyes, who carried two bullets in his body from old dueling wounds and who suffered from dysentery that wracked his innards. Of all the generals then available in America, Andrew Jackson had the most abiding, deep-rooted hatred of the British. In the spring of 1781, as the Revolutionary War entered its sixth year, the Redcoats had shifted their focus to South Carolina, and raiding parties swarmed over the countryside. One of them captured Jackson and his brother, and a dragoon officer commanded the fourteen-year-old to clean his boots. Jackson refused. When the cavalryman drew his saber and repeated the order. Again Jackson refused, and the officer slashed him viciously across the face. He then made the same demand of Jackson's brother, who likewise refused and received a similar gash.

The raiders took the boys with them and held them prisoner in Camden. The boys' wounds became infected, and both contracted the smallpox that was spreading through the prison stockade. Their mother was able to get them released, but Andrew's brother died, and he himself nearly did. That summer, his mother went to Charleston, to nurse American soldiers held on British prison ships in the harbor. Her parting words to her son were: "Make friends by being honest and keep them by being steadfast. . . . Andy, never tell a lie, nor take what is not your own, nor sue for slander. . . . settle them cases yourself."[16] He never saw her again, for she succumbed to "ship fever" and was buried in an unmarked grave, leaving her son an orphan, and one moved by deep passion.

Jackson studied law in Salisbury, North Carolina, reading hard—and playing hard. He established a reputation as a leading figure at wild drinking parties and high-stakes gambling. The proper citizens of Salisbury were scandalized by this tall, good-looking rowdy, yet there was something compelling about him at the same time—"a presence," as one young lady described it, and most of the young ladies he met were taken with him.[17] To the surprise of everyone except his senior law partner, Jackson became an able lawyer and an extremely forceful speaker who impressed those who heard him as "a young man of promise, bold and candid, with a notable sense of justice and the self-assured air of one born to leadership."[18]

With age, Jackson mellowed some—but only some. He owned a very finely honed sense of chivalry and honor at a time when affairs of honor were so common that a strong movement had grown up to banish dueling—too many of the country's promising young men were being wasted. On more than one occasion, Jackson came perilously close to being wasted himself. Indeed, whether on the field of honor or the field of battle, many said that he led a charmed life, surviving clashes with Indians that saw every man around him killed—almost as if he were being saved for some later assignment. Politics was his natural arena, for while he had amassed sizable land holdings and become something of a frontier aristocrat, with courtly manners and a racing stable, he remained immensely popular with his fellow Tennesseans. As soon as Tennessee achieved statehood in 1796, they sent him to Congress as their first representative. He resigned after a brief period, to tend to the neglected affairs of his estate, but was later returned as one of their Senators. In the Senate, he gained much respect for his blunt, straightforward speaking, but public life in far-off Washington held no appeal for him, and he resigned after a year.

He accepted the post of judge on the superior court in Tennessee, yet there was a sense of biding time, of still not having found his calling. Then came the War of 1812, and suddenly he knew exactly what he wanted to do, what he was born to do. With no trouble, he raised a large regiment of militia and offered his services to the federal government. But Jackson had made jealous enemies in Washington, as everywhere else, for he made no attempt to modulate his opinion of how the Madison administration was running the country. As a result, the government ignored his offer when it devised its grand plan for the conquest of Canada. And when they finally gave him an opportunity to fight, it was not against the British, but the Creek Indians in Alabama, who had been incited to war by Tecumseh. These he defeated so thoroughly that they ceased to be a force in the Indian wars. Then, acting under orders for the United States government and ostensibly to recover the cost of the Indian campaign, Jackson concluded a peace treaty with them that confiscated one-half of the ancestral Creek lands—23 million acres in all, comprising approximately a fifth of Georgia and three-fifths of Alabama. Jackson's biographer Burke Davis would call it "the most rapacious treaty in the history of Indian-white relations."[19]

But there was no arguing with Jackson's military ability, and in 1814 the administration was forced to acknowledge it, commissioning him a major general in the United States Army. His next assignment would take him south. The British were rumored to be mounting a major assault at either Mobile or New Orleans, and there was no one else to send but Jackson. The rumors proved true. Admiral Cochrane, with an invasion fleet now twice as large as that with which he had sailed up the Chesapeake and with a landing force in excess of ten thousand men under General Pakenham, now approached New Orleans, which reportedly had $15 million worth of cotton, tobacco, and whiskey in her warehouses.

Jackson arrived barely in time to organize the city's defenses. In fact, on December 23 he learned that some 1,700 British had already landed and were making camp by the Mississippi, eight miles from New Orleans. Indeed, a deserter informed him that Pakenham had boasted that he would eat his Christmas dinner in New Orleans. "If so," retorted Old Hickory, "he'll find me at the head of the table."[20]

Immediately, Jackson decided on a surprise night attack and, as if made to order, a low-lying fog rolled in, covering their advance. The British were at supper, completely relaxed, for this was a war in which the Americans never attacked. With idle curiosity, they watched as a small, two-masted schooner emerged from the fog and slowly swung broadside to their encampment on the bank of the river. Suddenly an awful noise shattered the peaceful stillness of the evening, as a seven-gun broadside belched fire and filled the air with a hurricane of iron—pieces of horseshoes, nails, scraps of every description. Stacks of weapons, tents, cooking fires—and men—were blown apart. Chaos reigned as the night sky filled with screams of the wounded. Another broadside erupted and another and then Jackson moved forward with his men, firing into the confusion. Soon the fighting became hand to hand, rifle butt and bayonet. The British fell back, but they did not break and run, for these were Wellington's regulars; they rallied and began to organize volleys.

At midnight the action died away inconclusively. One would think that after achieving perfect surprise and successfully withstanding the British counterattack, the buckskinned Americans might have earned a measure of respect from their adversaries. Not so. So strong was the assumption of natural superiority among the senior British officers that they were notoriously slow in accurately esteeming their adversaries. They continued to hold the American "dirty shirts" in the utmost contempt and over the next few days prepared to fight them as if they were waging a land campaign in Europe. They would have to advance on New Orleans along the comparatively narrow high ground that formed the east bank of the Mississippi, and Jackson chose to place his main line of defense across that ground, just beyond the Rodriguez Canal.

All day long his men dug trenches and solidified earthworks, and as the British had learned, if there was one thing the Americans did exceptionally well, it was digging. Their earthwork forts and redoubts had proven nearly impregnable, and Jackson determined that this line should not fail, as well. But he was also a realist: just in case, he prepared two additional fall-back lines, between the canal and the city.

As it turned out, the city fathers also took a realistic look at things; in a secret session of the assembly they decided that in the event Jackson's first line was broken they would turn New Orleans over to the British without further resistance. When he heard this, Jackson flew into a rage and sent word to the Governor that if there were any more such treasonous activity, he would blow up the assembly. Meanwhile, his men kept digging.

On the first day of 1815, Pakenham decided to test Jackson's defenses. Previous infantry sallies had only resulted in unwarranted casualties, and he now decided to solve this with an attack of heavy artillery. With enormous effort, and under the cover of darkness and a dense fog, he had thirty heavy guns brought from the ships, and these he managed to set up European style, in front of his infantry, a mere 700 yards from the American line. With his artillery now outweighing the Americans' by more than two to one, he planned to put the most exposed American batteries out of action, whereupon the British light infantry would pour through the breaches, and the contest would be quickly decided.

When the fog lifted, the artillery duel began. In about twenty minutes, it became apparent that the Americans—specifically the "Baratarians," a motley assortment of pirates and freebooters of all nationalities, serving under Jean Lafitte—were infinitely better gunners. Five of the British guns had been dismounted, and sixteen others had suffered so much damage that they could not be aimed. With only nine guns left in action, Pakenham ordered a withdrawal. He spent the next few days resting his men and building up their numbers for the main assault. But there was to be no rest for the weary. Every night Tennessee volunteers, natural experts at guerrilla warfare, went on sorties that wrought havoc in the British camp. Every couple of hours, they would put up enough hollering and firing to convince the edgy British that they were under another nighttime attack and they would sound general quarters. Pakenham's officers felt outrage at such barbaric tactics. One lieutenant said, "Thus the entire night was spent without obtaining any sound or refreshing sleep . . . we never closed our eyes in peace, for we were sure to be awakened before many minutes by the splash of a round shot or shell in the mud beside us. . . . From the first moment of our landing, not a man had undressed, excepting to bathe, and many had worn the same shirt for weeks."[21]

In the meantime, the American force was growing. More Tennessee volunteers arrived all the time, having traveled night and day so as not to miss out on what promised to be the final and best battle of the war. And on January 3, 2,400 Kentuckians arrived, under General John Adair. These last were most welcome, for 600 had brought their own rifles, and these were now added to Colonel Carroll's 1,400 on the weaker left flank, where Jackson anticipated the heaviest attack. All told, they now had some 4,000 men on the east bank, with another 1,000 guarding their guns across the river. Facing them, the British had some 8,000 troops, 1,400 of which were to be dispatched across the river to take the guns there and turn them on the American positions.

Pakenham held a council of war with his top generals, and they decided that on January 8, they would make their main attack. The key to their plan was to make the canal more fordable by laying down bundles of green sugarcane and then to put up the ten-foot scaling ladders they would need to take the ramparts. The generals congratulated themselves on their operation plan—and were a little put out with Lieutenant Colonel Thomas Mullens, whose Forty-fourth Regiment was assigned to carry the cane bundles and the scaling ladders. He was heard to murmur, "My regiment has been ordered to execution. Their dead bodies are to be used as a bridge for the rest of the army to march over."[22]

Any totally mobilized, massive military attack, involving thousands of men, be it an amphibious assault, like D-Day, or a frontal action like Pakenham's, is like a huge juggernaut that, once set in motion, is impossible to recall. Late-arriving intelligence might warn of far stronger defensive positions than had previously been supposed, indeed, of almost certain disaster; yet once the final signal is given and the assault has begun, it has a momentum of its own. Everything then depends on the care of the planning, the wisdom and courage of the Commander in Chief, the resourcefulness of the unit commanders—and Divine Providence.

From the moment the British assault got underway at midnight, things started going wrong. The flanking detachment had enough flatboats to cross the Mississippi, but no access to the river. A canal had been dug in the riverbank to float the boats to the river itself, but earlier in the night a dam had broken, and the water level in the canal subsequently dropped so low that most of the boats ended hopelessly mired in the mud. Less than a quarter of the 1,400 could now cross, yet they pressed on, as quietly as possible, hoping to cross unnoticed. At 1:00 A.M., Jackson was aroused with the report that men in boats had been sighted starting across the river. His response was brief and typical: "Gentlemen, we have slept enough," and with that, he took his senior officers with him to inspect the lines.

By 3:30, the Forty-fourth Regiment was in motion, advancing through the darkness. Colonel Mullens led his troops to the forward British battery, where the scaling ladders and cane bundles were supposed to have been stored. When he did not find them there, he realized his mistake: his orders had been to pick them up at the forward *redoubt,* now some 400 yards behind them. He sent 300 men back on the double to fetch them, although they would not now get back before daybreak. But they still could break off the attack, and now Pakenham's aide, Captain Harry Smith, urged the British commander to do so, for Pakenham himself had just acknowledged that the abortive flanking thrust across the river would now be of no use to them. But

Pakenham shook his head. "I have twice deferred the attack. Order the rocket to be fired."[23] So, as the first streaks of pink and gray spread across the horizon behind him, a signal flare arched into the heavens, and the awesome machine of war was set in motion.

Behind the American breastworks, everything was calm as word was passed along the line to shoot the officers first. In the dim half light, three columns of British regulars could be seen steadily advancing. They were 500 yards distant, when the American Long Tom twelve pounders opened fire. Their shots punched holes in the first rows, but the British stepped over the fallen, closed ranks, and continued forward. Now the enemy batteries opened up, firing at the flashes of the American cannon, barely visible in the swirling morning mist. When the British columns approached 300 yards, Jackson turned to Adair and General Coffee and had them hold the American artillery fire; the smoke would prevent the waiting riflemen from finding their marks. In the eerie silence that followed, he said, "Gentlemen, they're near enough now. Fire when ready."[24]

Adair turned to a Kentucky sharpshooter named Morgan Ballard. "Morg, see that officer on a gray horse?"

The rifleman nodded.

"Snuff his candle."

Ballard bent to his sight, allowed for windage, elevation, the direction and speed of the horse, and squeezed off a round. The bullet, barely a third the diameter of the standard issue, bone-crushing British musket ball, struck the officer just above the ear. Major John Anthony Whitaker of the Twenty-first Foot was dead before he hit the ground.

The British were appalled. The shot had come from more than three hundred yards away! A stunned British observer reported what happened next: "Instantly the whole American line, from the swamp to a point past its center, was ablaze," he wrote. (These were mainly the Kentucky riflemen, standing in four rows of 150 each, aiming, firing, and moving to the rear to reload, while the next rank stepped up and took its turn.) "In less time than one can write it, the Forty-fourth Foot was literally swept from the face of the earth. The regiment seemed to vanish from sight, except the half of it that lay stricken on the ground. Every mounted officer was down at the first fire. No such execution by small arms has ever been seen or heard of."[25]

Now the entire American line fired in the Kentuckians' manner, in relays of four. The Forty-fourth scattered, their scaling ladders and bundles forgotten, and all along the British ranks, men went down as wheat before a scythe. Yet these were the Invincibles, and they kept on coming, now only 200 yards away. The Americans marveled, for the British did not fire a shot, just kept marching with their bayonets grimly fixed. Less than half the center column was left, and every mounted officer had disappeared. Lieutenant Leavock of the Twenty-first Foot actually reached the canal in front of the American ramparts with a band of his men, only to look about in dismay for any logs or boards on which to cross the canal. Several of his men jumped into water and started wading across, only to be shot down from above. But somehow Leavock managed to reach the other side. Scrambling to the top of the breastwork, he found himself face-to-face with two American officers and commanded them to surrender their swords to him. They just cocked their heads and smiled, and Leavock, looking around, discovered there was no one else behind him—and turned over his own sword.

Other men were reaching the canal now and wading toward the ramparts. Foes they never saw killed them, for now the defenders were holding their rifles above their heads, pointing them over the breastwork, and shooting down into the canal without ever exposing themselves. Colonel Rennie, leading the left column, managed to make it to the earthworks; he climbed to the top, only to receive a bullet in the face. At the center, General Keene fell, and with that, the British assault, now virtually leaderless, hesitated and began to fall back.

From his vantage point, Pakenham sent an order for the Forty-fourth to get their scaling ladders to the ramparts, and when their commander, Lieutenant Colonel Mullens, could not be found, he determined to lead them himself. The delay was causing the entire assault to falter—and with it, Britain's grand design for the conquest of the Mississippi Valley. All, including his reputation, stood in jeopardy, slipping away before his eyes. In desperation, Wellington's brother-in-law spurred his horse forward to rally his men himself. A cannonball struck his horse, killing it and wounding him in the knee. He went down, but struggled to his feet and looked about for a riderless horse. Finding one, he somehow got up on it and resumed his charge. He had reached the rear ranks now and stood in his stirrups, shouting encouragement to them and waving them forward with his hat. He was a gallant figure—as several Kentuckians undoubtedly noted as they lined up the sights of their hunting rifles on him and began the deadly squeeze. Two bullets hit Pakenham simultaneously. With his last words, he called up the reserves, and in a few seconds his life had seeped away into the sand.

Command now devolved to General Gibbs, the only remaining field-grade officer left alive. In a rage, he spurred his horse toward the American line, charging alone across a battlefield thick with the bodies of men and horses. Shaking their heads, the riflemen went back to their grim work. Four bullets brought Gibbs down, and he was carried to the rear, cursing violently before he died. With no leaders left, the British assault was finished. Those troops, who had proven their courage in battle countless times, saw no further reason to be added to the welter of human debris piling up around them. They turned and began putting as much distance as possible between themselves and the unerring marksmen.

The Americans ignored Jackson's order that none should expose himself unnecessarily and clambered up on top of the breastworks to get better aim. As the British began to run they started to cheer, and some even jumped down to pursue them, before Jackson sternly ordered the rest back. He needed to hold his force intact, for there was no telling what the British might do next. But the enemy had lost his heart for the fight. A two-hour truce was declared, and the Americans helped the British remove their fallen from the field. All told, they had suffered 1,971 casualties, while American losses numbered 7 killed and 6 wounded. The British quartermaster noted that nearly all their dead had been killed by rifles, not cannon, and an "appalling proportion were shot through the head," something never seen before on European fields of battle.

The last battle of the War of 1812 had been fought, and the victory was the greatest triumph of arms since the defeat of Cornwallis at Yorktown. American honor was avenged, word of peace arrived, and the nation went wild with joy. Newspaper headlines trumpeted the news, and Jackson became a national hero. Everyone was jubilant that now, at last, they were Americans first, and then southerners or New Englanders or westerners. One of the signers of the Treaty of Ghent, James Bayard, wrote to his son, right after signing: "The war has raised our reputation in Europe, and it excites astonishment that we should have been able for one campaign to have fought the British single-handed. I think it will be a long time before we are disturbed again by any of the powers of Europe."[26] And from Washington, the French foreign minister, Louis Seurier, summarized for Tallyrand: "Finally, the war has given the Americans what they so essentially lacked, a national character founded on a glory common to all."[27] And Augustus Foster would eventually write: "In the opinion of the Speaker, Mr. Clay, and his friends, the war was as necessary to America, as a duel is to a young naval officer, to prevent his being bullied and elbowed in society. Baleful as the war has been, I must confess that I think in this respect something has been gained by it."[28] Something had indeed—for the British had a new respect for their American cousins, and from that time forth to the present day, their interests would be closely linked. As historian Page Smith noted, the war "ratified" the Revolution.

The banquets and bonfires, ceremonies and fireworks, speeches and proclamations went on for days. But save for a few dour preachers, there was no general call to give thanks to God for deliverance, as there had been after the previous conflict. Jackson himself was practically the only public figure to emphasize the role of the Almighty in what he came to regard as a miraculous deliverance. He spoke to Major Davezac of a premonition the Lord had given him, that the canal would be held. "I was sure of success, for I knew that God would not give me previsions of disaster, but signs of victory. He said this ditch can never be passed. It cannot be done." To Robert Hays he wrote: "It appears that the unerring hand of Providence shielded my men from the shower of balls, bombs, and rockets, when every ball and bomb from our guns carried with them a mission of death." And finally to Secretary of War James Monroe, he reported: "Heaven, to be sure, has interposed most wonderfully in our behalf, and I am filled with gratitude, when I look back to what we have escaped."[29]

Regardless of most Americans' ingratitude toward the Father who had seen fit to preserve the possibility of His plan for them, the young republic had come through the gravest external crisis that she would face in two centuries. The real threat, however, was not external but internal. For while the surge of victorious patriotism had for the moment covered the regional differences, the root causes of division still existed and someday would have to be dealt with. The nation was not yet strong enough to survive that dealing; the wheat and the tares needed to grow together a while longer. In the meantime, to hold her together would take the quiet courage, leadership, and tenacity of a few key men totally given to the vision of what America was meant to become. First, that meant seeing her through that deceptive period euphemistically known as "the Era of Good Feelings."

8

The Last Puritan

The onlookers had to shade their eyes with their hands, to shield them from the sun on that first Tuesday in March, 1817. From the rise on which they stood, they could see the row of rude wooden dwellings stretching away into the grassy marshland and the silvery Potomac, shimmering beyond. In the distance, they could just make out the White House, whose elegant, columned facade accentuated the contrast between the lowly structures before them and the magnificent Capitol behind them. Indeed, were it not for these two edifices, the nation's capital would indeed be a seedy place to live. Dolley Madison used to look out her window at the White House and shake her head at the cows grazing on the "Mall," and with scathing wit Gouverneur Morris, Senator from Pennsylvania, summed up what serving in Washington was like: "We only need here houses, cellars, kitchens, scholarly men, amiable women, and a few other such trifles to possess a perfect city."[1]

Everyone longed for the amenities of Philadelphia, which used to be the capital—the paved streets, the sophisticated salons, the elegant dinner parties and generally cosmopolitan atmosphere. Here, during a heavy rain, the chuckholes in the unpaved roads filled with water up to the hubs of the carriage wheels and were almost as full of dust when it was dry. One diplomat on his way to an appointment with the president, in a downpour, had to abandon his carriage in sticky clay within four blocks of the White House. Secretary of State John Quincy Adams was returning from a formal occasion in his carriage one evening when it hit a hole and tipped over. But perhaps the most arresting observation was made by Harrison Gray Otis in a letter to his wife, after fording the nearby Bladensburg Run in a stagecoach. "As we passed through, the driver pointed out to us the spot, right under our wheels, where all the stage horses last year were drowned, but then he consoled us by showing the tree on which all passengers but one were saved."[2]

But on this particular day, the sun was warm and the smiles warmer, for the dignified assembly had gathered to witness the inauguration of the fifth President of the United States. Among the senators and congressmen, the cabinet members and their wives, the senior military men and invited guests (and uninvited passersby) were foreign ambassadors and dignitaries, resplendent in full-dress uniforms and formal attire. As they gazed impassively at the diminutive, elderly president-elect in waistcoat and breeches long out of fashion, a hint of amusement might have flickered across their faces, for their own capitals were already old when wild savages roamed this place.

Yet as the man in the outmoded breeches raised his right hand and solemnly received the oath, the unseasonable warmth of that day in 1817 conspired with the golden haze of the sun to soften the details of the framed lodging houses and make them almost appealing. A gentle breeze carried birdsong to the hill, and it was possible to believe its promise of an early spring. Listening to the buoyant words of James Monroe, one could even believe that the political and economic climates were experiencing early spring as well.

> We find cause to felicitate ourselves in the excellence of our institutions . . . our citizens have been individually happy and the nation prosperous . . . one great family with a common interest. . . . Never did a government commence under auspices so favorable, nor ever was success so complete. If we look to the history of other nations, ancient or modern, we find no example of a growth so rapid, so gigantic of a people so prosperous and happy. In contemplating what we still have to perform, the heart of every citizen must expand with joy, when he reflects on how near our Government has approached to perfection. . . . If we persevere in the career which we have advanced so far, in the path already traced, we cannot fail, under the favor of a gracious Providence, to attain the high destiny which seems to await us.[3]

Even the visiting ambassadors had to nod assent to that. Compared to the rest of the world, it did seem that a gracious Providence had favored America. Even Britain now regarded her opponent with something approaching respect. America was now shipping her goods all over the world, and at home her Constitution worked so well that other emerging democracies used it as their model.

Only in one corner of America did the sun not shine. Down in Georgia, near the Florida border, farms and plantations were being terrorized by marauding bands of Seminoles and Creeks, who would sneak up from Spanish Florida, steal produce and cattle, and then hightail it back across the border to the sanctuary of territorial immunity. If a Georgia farmer and his sons tried to protect their property, they would be shot with weapons sold to the Indians by British agents and then promptly scalped. United States citizens in Georgia were enraged and repeatedly called upon the federal government to have Spain put a stop to it.

But Spain had grown weak and corrupt. Her South American colonies were in revolt and what remaining force she could still project would be expended there, not on the worthless province of Florida. She maintained no more than token garrisons at the forts of San Marcos in East Florida and San Michel in West Florida, and when the Americans complained of the raiding parties, the Spaniards merely shrugged and said they were powerless to prevent them. Yet at the suggestion that they allow the Americans to pursue the thieves and murderers across the border, the Spanish became indignant: foreign troops invading Spanish soil? Never! The Americans did not press the point, for delicate negotiations were underway for the formal ceding of Florida to the United States. At times, however, the Spanish seemed content to sit at the negotiating table forever, if that alone kept the Americans from crossing over the border. Meanwhile, more families were slaughtered and their livestock stolen, more plantations were burned and their crops destroyed. . . .

Not everyone in America felt content to leave matters as they lay. Andrew Jackson had cleaned the British out of Florida once, en route to New Orleans, and he was more than willing to go back to do whatever was necessary to ensure the safety of American citizens. He had told the new President so, when Monroe was still Secretary of State. Twice, the two of them had talked long into the night by a crackling fire. They looked like an incongruous pair—Jackson, lean and hatchet-faced; Monroe, the opposite, called by his detractors "a dull, sleepy, insignificant-looking man, who hasn't got brains enough to hold his hat on."[4] But Jackson found nothing sleepy or dull about Monroe's patriotism or the vision for America that they both shared. That vision included Florida becoming American land; indeed, the way things were now, as Jackson put it, any foreign power holding Florida held a gun at the heart of the South. The negotiations that Jefferson had begun and Madison had carried on were going nowhere. The matter could be decided quickly by a single preemptive strike, and Monroe evidently agreed, for Jackson returned home expecting to be recalled to active duty momentarily.

But the weeks turned to months, and Jackson wearied of listening for the approaching hoofbeats of an express rider from Washington. When the papers announced that Monroe had won the Democratic nomination, a delighted Jackson wrote him about one of the greatest dangers he saw threatening the young republic that they both loved: "Now is the time to exterminate the monster called party spirit. By selecting characters most conspicuous for their probity, virtue, capacity and firmness, without any regard to party, you will go far to . . . eradicate those feelings which, on former occasions, threw so many obstacles in the way of government; and perhaps have the pleasure of uniting a people heretofore divided."[5]

Monroe responded with equal candor, stating that he firmly believed that "the Chief Magistrate of the country ought not to be the head of a party [as in British Parliament], but the head of a nation."[6] He soon proved it by taking Jackson's advice and filling his cabinet with the ablest men he could find, starting with John Quincy Adams for Secretary of State. When it came to the post of Secretary of War, Jackson's own name was at the top of the list, but the latter begged off, pleading that he was a field general and lacked the patience to endure the hours of desk work and debate.

So it happened that on the day that the new President stood on the hill before the Capitol building and took the oath of office, Andrew Jackson sat at his writing desk on the front porch of the large log cabin he called the Hermitage and wrote his friend another letter of congratulation. From where he sat, he could look up and see his adopted son Andrew playing in the field with his friend Lincoyer, a Creek Indian orphan whom Jackson had rescued. He looked up often, because the letter was becoming longer than he had expected. In it, he tried not to let his impatience show, but it was almost impossible; it had now been two years since he had stood on the rampart of Rodriguez Canal, gauging the advance of the British Grenadiers—two years of total inactivity. The army of the Southern District had been instructed to stand down, and his Tennessee Volunteers had gone back to their homes, as he himself had. But he knew his men and knew that a thousand would rise and join him in an instant. All he had to do was ask. He intimated as much in the letter and felt compelled to mention something that had rankled him for some time, but that the new President could take care of quickly enough. During the previous administration, the acting Secretary of War had recalled one of his army engineers to Washington without consulting him. Undoubtedly it was an oversight, but he believed that, as commander of the Southern District, he was due that courtesy.

Giving Mr. Monroe a chance to settle in, Jackson expected to hear from him in about a month. But the fifth week went by with no approaching hoofbeats—and the sixth. The papers were full of Monroe's tour of coastal fortifications and frontier outposts, which had rapidly turned into a "presidential jubilee," with crowds turning out in ever greater numbers to cheer him. By the time he reached Boston, that citadel of Federalism which had once been so furious with Secretary of State Monroe for his part in getting the country into the war with Britain had climbed totally on the bandwagon. The same *Colombian Sentinel* that had berated him and openly called for New England to secede from the Union now hailed his visit with the headline:

ERA OF GOOD FEELINGS

That phrase summed up a lot of people's feelings, and it caught on around the country. But down in Tennessee, Jackson's feelings were badly hurt. Seven weeks had now passed since he had written the President, and not so much as a note had he received in reply. This, from the man with whom he had thought he had a special understanding! Well, he was still commander of the Southern District, and he issued an order: henceforth, no subordinate of his was to obey any order received directly from the War Department, unless it bore his personal endorsement.

When the press learned of Jackson's order, they had a field day, one paper even reporting that General Winfield Scott considered Jackson's act nothing short of mutiny. That was a grave accusation for one professional soldier to level at another, particularly someone with a code of honor as finely honed as Jackson's. Jackson wrote a restrained note to Scott, assuring him that he put no stock in the irresponsible newspaper report, but asking him for clarification, nonetheless. Scott replied that he *did* consider Jackson's order mutinous, and what was more, "a reprimand to the President."

Jackson could hardly believe his eyes. Immediately, despite his wife Rachel's pleading, he got out his writing desk and dashed off a reply. Calling Scott, who outranked him, a "hectoring bully" and one of the "intermeddling pimps and spies of the War Department,"[7] he added that the aforementioned insults were intended and deserved, and if Scott felt that they required satisfaction, Jackson awaited his pleasure.

Scott responded that he could not match Jackson's vulgar language and declined the challenge on the grounds that it was against his Christian principles, adding that he preferred to risk his life on the field of battle. Jackson did not reply, since his temper had had a chance to cool somewhat, but to Monroe he had already declared that he would resign his commission before he rescinded his order. The President, in turn on the advice of his new Secretary of War, John C. Calhoun, had decided to take a mollifying approach. He had written to Jackson, declining to grant him absolute control over the Southern District, since the issue involved "the naked principle of the power of the Executive over the officers of the army."[8] He urged him instead to remain in the service, particularly in view of the Florida crisis, which threatened war with Spain. And Tennessee Congressman John Rhea, an old friend of Jackson's, assured Jackson that the administration was unanimous in its support of him. For the truth was, something did have to be done about the Seminoles—in fact, about the whole Florida question—and no one could do it better than Jackson.

His honor satisfied, Jackson felt immensely relieved that he was not forced to give up his commission for he liked nothing on earth so much as being at the head of a column of men on the march or going into battle. But the rest of the year dragged by with no further call to action. Unchecked, the Indian raids grew worse than ever, until finally the War Department authorized General Gaines, the on-site commander, to follow the Indians into Florida in hot pursuit, regardless of Spain's objection. Yet still there was no general mobilization. At last, Jackson could stand it no longer: he sent a note to the President and suggested that not only could he put down the Indian incursions once and for all, but he could seize the whole of East Florida . . . without implicating the government. "Let it be signified through a channel [he suggested

Congressman Rhea] that the possession of the Floridas would be desirable . . . and in sixty days it will be accomplished."[9]

The effect of this note on Monroe must have been electrifying. How tempting to cut through the Gordian knot of the Florida situation, which had frustrated presidents for years, with one decisive stroke! But could a President authorize a military incursion against the province of a nation with which America was at peace? Of course not . . . at least, not in so many words. It might, however, be intimated . . . and even before the Commander in Chief received Jackson's confidential communication, he had sent one of his own, intimating that Florida was to be taken now or never, and that no risk was too great for the prize. "The movement . . . against the Seminoles . . . will bring you on a theatre where you may possibly have other services to perform. . . . This is not a time for repose . . . until our cause is carried triumphantly through."[10]

Our cause—there was no mistaking the inference there. Action at last! Feeling years younger, Jackson summoned his senior officers to the Hermitage, told them the good news, and sent them off to raise the army. He himself swore in 200 troops, and advanced $4,000 of his own funds to pay the expenses of the march, so that they would not have to wait for a paymaster from the War Department. It was considerably later, while marching through Georgia, that further confirming orders arrived from Secretary of War Calhoun, instructing him in rather broad language to: "adopt the necessary measures to terminate the conflict."[11] In the same pouch, Jackson later insisted, arrived the signal he had requested, in the form of a letter from Congressman Rhea assuring him of the President's support.

On March 10, 1818, Jackson crossed the border into Florida, at the head of a fast-moving column of 1,100 men. Hacking their way through underbrush "as virgin forest as in the days of De Soto," they nevertheless made good time—too good, as far as their commissariat was concerned. Their supply boat was unable to keep up with them, and they had to forage for "pork on the hoof"—wild pigs. One incident goaded them to great speed. After inconclusive skirmishes with the Indians, they had come upon an Indian village with the still-dripping scalps of forty white men and women on display. After that, they forgot about their hunger.

Learning that the Seminoles were now fleeing to the west to seek the protection of the Spanish governor at Pensacola, Jackson called on his half-starved men for another forced march. On they pressed through the subtropical wilderness until they came in sight of Pensacola where Jackson received a communique from Governor Masot demanding that he retire, or "I shall repel force with force."[12] Never one to turn from a challenge, Jackson stormed Fort San Michel on May 24 and pursued the fleeing Spanish governor to Fort Barrancas on the Gulf Coast. There, Masot, with nowhere else to go, prepared to defend himself to the death. Jackson obliged the latter's honor by firing a single cannon volley at the fort, after which Masot was able to raise the white flag with dignity. Leaving one of his senior officers in command of Pensacola, Jackson now returned to the States, recrossing the border on May 30. The expedition had taken eighty days—twenty more than his original estimate.

When the news of what he had done reached Washington, the capital was in a furor. America now faced the real possibility that Spain, out of pride, would declare war on the United States, and that Britain, out of outrage at the trial and execution of two of her agents whom Jackson had caught warning and supplying the Seminoles, would join her. The press was in an uproar. In Congress, Henry Clay rallied opposition and everyone in the administration who had been involved, started backpeddling furiously. The President swore that he had never given Jackson any order to take Florida or any such signal through Rhea, who also denied sending any letter, though he would later equivocate on that point. Jackson insisted that he *had* received such a letter from Rhea and that in any event his actions were in conformity with the orders he had received from the President and the Secretary of War. Privately, Monroe asked Jackson to change his story or at least to allow them to alter the wording of the dispatches he had sent them during the Florida campaign.

But Jackson refused. He was not a liar, and personal honor had always been of the highest consequence to him; he was not about to compromise it now. Nor would he be made a scapegoat. He came to Washington himself to answer the charges flying around the capital. Foremost among his accusers was the War Hawk of Kentucky, Speaker of the House Henry Clay. Until the Battle of New Orleans, Clay had been the sole hero and champion of the West. But Old Hickory had eclipsed him, and now Clay saw an opportunity to deal a mortal blow to the man he viewed as his chief rival to become Monroe's successor in 1824. Speaking of Monroe, Clay was still furious at him for not having made him Secretary of State, the traditional stepping-stone to the presidency, and he had already set himself to oppose every policy of Monroe's administration. Here he overstepped himself, for as he started lamenting the plight of the Indians at the hands of Jackson, he lost most of his credibility with his western constituency. Anyone who had pioneered in the wilderness, or whose parents had, could remember the horror stories of what renegade Indians had done. The gambit backfired on Clay, and in the process earned him the lifelong enmity of a man who was fiercely loyal to his friends but could be an implacable foe when crossed.

On July 15, the President summoned the cabinet to the White House, to an extraordinary session which would last five hours. The subject: what exactly was to be done about Jackson? There was no question but that the Spanish forts should be returned immediately, but should Jackson be punished, as Don Luis de Onís, the Spanish minister, demanded? Should he be stripped of his rank and drummed out of the army in disgrace, as it were? Short of that, should he receive a formal censure, or merely a reprimand? According to the meticulous diary of the Secretary of State, everyone in that long session had an ax to grind against Jackson. Secretary of War Calhoun took Jackson's refusal to come under the authority of the War Department as a personal affront. William Crawford, Secretary of the Treasury, had his own designs upon the presidency in 1824 and demanded the repudiation of Jackson and all his works. Attorney General William Wirt concurred. Even the President, who had implicitly encouraged the general, was now inclined to go with the consensus. . . . It seemed expedient that one man should be sacrificed for the good of the state. . . .

But that opinion was not unanimous. Jackson had a champion in that sweltering council chamber into which servants brought relays of cool drinks on silver trays. Moreover, his defender was the least likely of them all, the man who stood to gain the most by Jackson's destruction, who, as Secretary of State, was in the best position to succeed Monroe. That in itself was ironic, for John Quincy Adams was the only one who had never actively sought public office and had no designs on the presidency. JQA, as we will call him, recorded in his diary: "The President and all the members of the Cabinet except myself are of the opinion that Jackson acted not only without, but against, his instructions, that he has committed war upon Spain, which cannot be justified. . . ."[13]

That was how matters stood, and were it not for the adamant refusal of the Secretary of State to go along, no doubt the administration, scrambling to save itself, would have thrown Jackson to the wolves. But the diarist *was* there, and never in his life had he let popularity or peer pressure sway him from his principles. In fact, his whole life was a monument to that credo; for that reason he, a former Federalist, had been appointed Secretary of State over such staunch Republicans as Clay and Calhoun.

The life of John Quincy Adams began in a home steeped in patriotism: his earliest memories of his father were of him in the company of other Massachusetts men, dreaming of a day when the colonies might be free. When he was seven, he and his mother had watched the smoke rising from the Battle of Bunker Hill; a week shy of John Quincy Adam's ninth birthday, his father signed the Declaration of Independence. He idolized his father, who took him along with him to Europe, where he learned French. Upon returning home, JQA entered Harvard, and after graduating, was admitted to the Massachusetts bar and began practicing law.

Here JQA first demonstrated that he had a mind and will of his own, writing a series of widely reprinted articles rebutting Thomas Paine's *Rights of Man,* then at the height of its popularity. He wrote another series defending President Washington's policy of neutrality in the war that broke out between France and England, and these caught the eye of the President, who asked him to go back to Holland as America's minister to that country. Young Adams performed brilliantly at that post and several other European assignments, returning home soon after Jefferson swept into power on the cresting tide of Republicanism. JQA was elected to the Massachusetts state senate in 1801, and two years later was elected by that body to be one of the United States senators from Massachusetts. His constituency assumed that he would vote the Federalist Party line, but people soon learned of the danger in assuming anything about this Adams, particularly if it involved not thinking for himself. For when Jefferson invoked his embargo against both France and Britain in 1807, JQA supported the act, exclaiming: "The President has recommended the measure on his high responsibility. I would not consider, I would not deliberate; I would act!" It was not the first time and would certainly not be the last that JQA put the national interest ahead of party politics, but in so doing he was voting against the shipping and ship-building interests of his constituency. It cost him his seat in the Senate and his Federalist affiliation. The latter he considered no great loss, for he had long been chafing at the narrow factionalism of his father's party. Young Adams became an independent, perhaps the first of that unique breed in America, and he spent his enforced absence from public service as a professor of rhetoric and oratory at Harvard.

In 1809, President Madison, who needed someone qualified to be America's minister to Russia, recalled him to active duty. Adams was still at Saint Petersburg when the War of 1812 broke out. He was dispatched forthwith to Belgium, to work out a peace treaty with the British, where Albert Gallatin, Henry Clay, James Bayard, and Jonathan Russell joined him. At forty-five, although not the most senior commissioner in terms of age, he was in terms of experience and, as he would soon demonstrate, in terms of negotiating skill as well. The negotiations in Ghent tested JQA to the limit of his ability, and here, too, his true character began to emerge.

As we have seen, the circumstances could hardly have appeared less favorable for the American commissioners. There seemed to be no stopping the British or any doubt about the eventual outcome. But surrender, diplomatic or military, was something quite foreign to the nature of John Quincy Adams; even in the face of overwhelming odds, he displayed an extraordinary, unshakable fortitude. When it boiled down to a test of will (as diplomacy does far more often than most people realize) and the pressure became unbearable, he would dig in and refuse to yield another inch. As one Englishman put it, after an encounter with JQA, when he was the United States minister to Russia, "With a vinegar aspect, cotton in his leathern ears, and hatred to England in his heart. . . . he sat in the frivolous assemblies of Petersburg like a bulldog among spaniels. . . ."[14]

Those who knew him only fleetingly might have been tempted to write him off as an irascible, antisocial Yankee, but the truth about John Quincy Adams ran much deeper: he was one of the most moral statesmen America has ever produced. Historians hesitate to apply the word *Puritan* to him, as the Puritans had long since passed from the New England scene. Yet in a profound sense, Adams properly deserves to be called the last Puritan.

One of his Calvinist characteristics was to rise early, to spend predawn hours reading the Bible. In Berlin, he read Luther's version in the original German; in Paris, he read the French translation. His diary not only accurately chronicled the day's events; there, too, in Puritan tradition, he honestly recorded his sins and shortcomings. His diary reveals his remarkable relationship with a righteous and loving God—the source of his inner strength. On the last day of 1812, shortly before departing for Belgium, he wrote:

> I offer to a merciful God at the close of this year my humble tribute of gratitude for the blessings with which He has, in the course of it, favored me and those dear to me. . . . My endeavors to quell the rebellion of the heart have been sincere, and have been assisted with the blessing from above. As I advance in life, its evils multiply, and the instances of mortality become more frequent and approach nearer to myself. The greater is the need for fortitude to encounter the woes that flesh is heir to, and of religion to support pains for which there is no other remedy.[15]

In the privacy of his diary, he was often hard on his colleagues but every bit as hard on himself: "I am a man of reserved, cold, austere, and forbidding manners; my political adversaries say, a gloomy misanthropist, and my personal enemies, an unsocial savage."[16]

Adams's Puritan heritage was further revealed in his attitude toward public service. Like Bradford and Winthrop and Hooker, he regarded it as a sacred trust, a call of God to serve his fellowman. Hardly any of his peers saw it that way anymore; indeed, most lusted after political position and prominence in a far different manner. But he would not compromise, for in one other area JQA resembled his forebears of an earlier century: he shared their vision for America and felt strongly that God did have a plan for her and that they had a part to play in that plan.

So when the British commissioner Goulburn, negotiating from apparent strength, insisted that one clause in any treaty must be that American expansion would be curtailed by a north-south boundary that ran through the Illinois Territory, beyond which a buffer state of Indians would exist, JQA answered him with quiet force. According to the census of 1810, the population of the United States had passed 7 million and was probably past 8 million by now. If the British commissioner thought for one moment that any demarcation line would put a stop to the westward surge of that burgeoning population, it would be "tantamount to trying to stop a torrent with a feather." Any war concluded by such a treaty "would immediately be followed by another, and Great Britain would ultimately find that she must substitute the project of exterminating the whole American people, for that of opposing against them her barrier of savages."

"What!" exclaimed Goulburn, "Is it, then, the inevitable nature of things that the United States must conquer Canada?"

"No."

"But what security, then, can Great Britain have for her possession of it?"

"If Great Britain does not think a liberal and amicable course of policy towards America would be the best security, as it certainly would, she must rely on her general strength . . . ,"[17] which she was already doing with inconclusive effect.

Not all of JQA's exchanges with the British commissioners were white-knuckle affairs; two weeks earlier, at a dinner which the Americans hosted (and from which that Goulburn was absent due to illness), Lord Gambier mentioned that he had visited Boston in 1770 with his father, who was naval commander there. At that time, and later when he had commanded a frigate that was stationed in New York harbor "during our contest," Gambier commented that he had known JQA's father. He also mentioned that he was vice-president of the English Bible Society and recalled a correspondence with the Bible Society of Boston, of which JQA was a member. It seemed that an American privateer had captured a British ship bound for Halifax, which was carrying, among other things, a shipment of Bibles. The moment the Bible Society of Boston heard this, they had taken up a subscription and sent it to their English counterpart, to cover the loss of the Bibles, a course of action that pleased both men very much.[18]

But social occasions, for the most part, were not JQA's forte. Conversant in many languages, he had never mastered the art of polite social conversation and was generally regarded to be as cold as a Massachusetts codfish. Over the years, a few men who worked closely with him and gained his confidence saw glimpses of the passion that surged in his diary. But for the most part, he appeared aloof and formal, a smile never becoming a comfortable expression for him. On the other hand, when it came to work, few could match his pace or output, and none could match his skill in negotiating. In short, to reverse the old adage, he was respected but not loved.

In Ghent, his fellow commissioners were friendly enough; they had to be, since they and their assistants were practically the only company they had for almost three years. But their life-styles could hardly have been more different. Henry Clay was a Kentuckian—a tall, graceful gentleman with a great deal of charm and a natural eloquence, who made friends easily and whose favorite way to end an evening was with a bottle of brandy, a deck of cards, and some boon companions. JQA played whist, too, and took an occasional glass of wine, but he did so mainly for conformity's sake at state receptions, and his whist was usually with some elder statesman's wife, while others danced or chatted gaily. When the American contingent retired to their rooms, Clay would invite JQA to join them for a nightcap, but if he accepted, he would soon thereafter take his leave. For he was an early riser; indeed, his arising sometimes coincided with (or was occasioned by) his colleagues finally calling it a night. This, too, he duly noted in his diary, and while he refrained from making any judgmental comment on their deportment, he could not resist adding the hour of his entry: "*September 8, 3:45*: Just before rising, I heard Mr. Clay's company returning from his chamber. I had left him with Mr. Russell, Mr. Bentzon, and Mr. Todd at cards. They parted as I was about to rise. I was up nearly half an hour, before I had daylight to read or write. . . ."[19] Or, "*September 21, 4:30*: . . . another card party in Mr. Clay's chamber last night, and I heard Mr. Bentzon retiring from it, after I had arisen this morning."[20]

Years later, Henry Clay would remark: "A man must be a born fool who voluntarily engages in a controversy with Mr. Adams on a question of fact. I doubt whether he was ever mistaken in his life. And then, if he happens to be in doubt about anything, he has his inevitable diary, in which he has recorded everything that has occurred since the adoption of the Federal Constitution."[21]

For all their differing personalities, they got along remarkably well, each representing a different sector of the country and being especially on guard for that sector's interests. Clay adamantly refused to grant navigation rights to the Mississippi, while Adams and Gallatin were equally determined not to yield fishing rights off American shores. With the resounding news of the victories on Lake Champlain and Fort McHenry, on top of the relentless depredations of the Yankee privateers, they found themselves dealing from strength, instead of weakness. On Christmas Eve, 1814, the commissioners on both sides gathered for the last time and signed the Treaty of Ghent.

Instead of coming directly home, JQA was posted to London, to the Court of Saint James, to negotiate a commerce treaty. Soon after his arrival, he learned of the abortive Hartford Convention, which Federalist extremists had called to consider New England's seceding from the Union. If anything, JQA was even more stricken than his father, to whom he wrote:

> As to our beloved New England. . . her shame is still the disgrace of the nation—faction for patriotism, a whining hypocrisy for political morals, dismemberment for union, and prostitution to the enemy for state sovereignty. You tell me that they are ashamed of it themselves. I rejoice to hear it. As a true New England man and an American, I feel the infection of their shame.[22]

But on one subject John Adams and John Quincy Adams were not in one accord, and JQA hesitated not an instant in pointing out to his parents where he felt they were wrong, even if it meant losing the approval that he cherished above anyone's. We have seen how the incipient spread of Unitarianism gradually, imperceptibly engulfed the upper, more enlightened strata of Boston society. While few would go so far as to espouse the nihilistic extremes of the French Deism, nonetheless it had become unfashionable to adhere to the simple Trinitarian doctrine on which the Bay Colony had been founded. Unitarianism presented God as an abstract, cosmic oneness, flattering the mind with the nobility of man and eschewing any necessity for the sacrifice of Christ to redeem sinful man. To do this, a considerable amount of skewing and distorting of Scripture was necessary, and Dr. Joseph Priestley, the leading Unitarian minister in Boston, handled it deftly. His gentle, bemused condescension toward the miracles attendant to the Gospel was adopted by his followers. Nor could one describe these followers as gullible sheep; they counted among their numbers most of the best educated and leading intellectual lights of Boston and Cambridge, among them, John and Abigail Adams.

The first inkling their son had of what had happened came when he received a letter from his father, mildly remonstrating with him for beginning to gain an unfortunate reputation for being a champion of orthodoxy. That his father could say such a thing, as if it were something undesirable, shocked JQA. Going back through his parents' letters and making inquiries of other Americans who had recently arrived from Boston, he was even more shocked to discover just how far Unitarianism had enveloped the minds of the Puritans' descendants, like some translucent cocoon. He began to read Dr. Priestley's writings, to familiarize himself, and a transatlantic debate now ensued, made no less intense by the month's delay between riposte and reception. As in postal chess, the interim, if anything, sharpened the response. To his father, a Harvard-trained, widely traveled attorney like himself, he bluntly declared:

> I perceive that the Trinitarians and the Unitarians in Boston are sparring together. . . . Most of the Boston Unitarians are my particular friends, but I never thought much of the eloquence or the theology of Priestley. His *Socrates and Jesus Compared* is a wretched performance. Socrates and Jesus! A farthing candle and the sun! I pray you to read Massilon's sermon on the divinity of Christ, and then the whole New Testament, after which be a Socinian if you can.[23]

With his mother, he was more patient, and one can imagine him sitting down at his writing desk and looking out the leaded windows of his apartment through the raindrops at the glistening slate rooftops of nineteenth-century London. His mother had always impressed him as one of the most intelligent, thinking women he had ever known, in an age when most women were not expected to think. . . . At length, he reached inside the desk and extracted a fresh sheet of the writing paper he had just purchased—good, rag-content stuff, made with relatively little acid, so that it would not rapidly yellow or disintegrate. It was an extravagance, but worth it, for the Adamses saved their letters. Feeling the paper, he admired its soft luster and its "tooth"; it would take the ink well. He shook his head; the English still made the best paper in the world. From his vest pocket, he extracted a small penknife and tested its edge on the piece of scratch paper alongside the clean sheet. Satisfied, he took the business end of the goose quill pen and honed it, scraping away the dried ink. Raising the silver top of the cut-crystal inkwell, he dipped the point, primed it by scratching a few lines on the scrap paper, and commenced to write.

> My Dear Mother. . . I find in the New Testament, Jesus Christ accosted in His own presence by one of His disciples as God, without disclaiming the appellation. I see Him explicitly declared by at least two other of the Apostles to be God, expressly and repeatedly announced, not only as having existed before the worlds, but as the Creator of the worlds without beginning

of days or end of years. I see Him named in the great prophecy of Isaiah concerning him to be the mighty God! . . . The texts are too numerous, they are from parts of the Scriptures too diversified, they are sometimes connected by too strong a chain of argument, and the inferences from them are, to my mind, too direct and irresistible, to admit of the explanations which the Unitarians sometimes attempt to give them, or the evasions by which, at others, they endeavor to escape from them.[24]

But John Adams the elder had never been one to enter into any area of thought without careful study, least of all something as important as religious doctrine, and now he challenged his son on academic grounds. He had discussed the matter in recent correspondence with Thomas Jefferson, among others; he had read books and listened to sermons on the subject and was now convinced that Unitarianism was the correct, the only sensible course that a man with an inquiring mind could take. He was surprised that his son should dispute this and wondered how carefully JQA had thought out his own position. His son was quick to respond:

> You ask me *what* Bible I take as the standard of my faith—the Hebrew, the Samaritan, the old English translation, or what? I answer, the Bible containing the Sermon on the Mount—any Bible that I can . . . understand. The New Testament I have repeatedly read in the original Greek, in the Latin, in the Geneva Protestant, in Sacy's Catholic French translations, in Luther's German translation, in the common English Protestant, and in the Douay Catholic translations. I take any one of them for my standard of faith. . . . But the Sermon on the Mount commands me to lay up for myself treasures, not upon earth, but in Heaven. My hopes of a future life are all founded upon the Gospel of Christ. . . . You think it blasphemous that the omnipotent Creator could be crucified. God is a spirit. The spirit was not crucified. The body of Jesus of Nazareth was crucified. The Spirit, whether external or created, was beyond the reach of the cross. You see, my orthodoxy grows on me, and I still unite with you in the doctrine of toleration and benevolence.[25]

In 1817, John Quincy Adams was recalled to assume the responsibilities of Secretary of State. He had not sought the office, but now that it was thrust upon him, he determined to serve his country, as always, to the utmost of his ability. If that meant disagreeing with the President, concerning General Jackson, and with every other cabinet member, if necessary (which in the summer of 1818, it seemed to be), then so be it. JQA refused to go along with the movement to dump Jackson, not even after five hours of deliberation. Previously he had taken the Spanish minister to task, to the effect "that we could not suffer our women and children on the frontiers to be butchered by savages, out of complaisance to the jurisdiction which the King of Spain's officers avowed themselves unable to maintain against those same savages."[26] He now informed the President and cabinet: "My opinion is that there was no real, though an apparent, violation of [Jackson's] instructions; that his proceedings were justified by the necessity of the case, and by the misconduct of the Spanish commanding officers in Florida. . . . My principle is that everything he did was defensive, that, as such, it was neither war against Spain, nor violation of the Constitution."[27] That left the matter deadlocked, for none of them could afford politically to have it known that, of them all, JQA alone supported Jackson. Whatever decision they reached, it had to be unanimous, so they came back the next day . . . and the next . . . and the next. . . .

In the meantime, several realities were beginning to filter through. For one thing, Britain was still too preoccupied with affairs in Europe to go to war over two freebooters in Florida, who were quite obviously up to no good. The spirit for war was there, to be sure; it was said that when Parliament first heard the news, the Prime Minister had but to raise a finger, and war would have been declared. But the finger was not raised; in just three short years of peace, Britain had discovered in America a valuable trading partner. As for Spain, once she had swallowed her pride, she faced the reality of how much more important it was to her to try to hold on to her Latin American colonies. If she declared war on America over the worthless province of Florida, the Americans would undoubtedly help the revolutionary forces to the south and would probably take the Texas territory as well, which she would be powerless to prevent. Into the cabinet's council chamber seeped the great reality of the magnitude of Jackson's popularity. Never mind what the Washington newspaper had said, the rest of America seemed to regard his swift and bold adventure as an even greater achievement than his victory at New Orleans. Whether they liked it or not, Jackson was now by far the most popular man in America. Anyone moving against him would commit political suicide.

So in the end, they unanimously decided that Adams was right, and in response to Spain's demand that Jackson be punished, JQA instructed the American minister in Spain to inform that nation:

> The President will neither inflict punishment, nor pass censure upon General Jackson for that conduct, the motives of which were founded in the purest patriotism . . . the vindication of which is written in every page of the law of nations, as well as the first law of nature—self defense. . . . Spain must immediately make an election, whether to place a force in Florida adequate at once to the protection of her territory, and to the fulfillment of her engagements, or to cede to the United States a province of which she retains nothing but the nominal possession, but which is, in fact, a derelict, open to the occupancy of every enemy, civilized or savage, of the United States, and serving no other earthly purpose than as a post of annoyance to them.[28]

Spain returned to the bargaining table, this time in earnest. Even so, negotiations were to drag on for another year, due mainly to JQA's refusal to yield even the most minor concessions. Finally, in February 1819, he got what America wanted: for $5 million in compensatory damages and the yielding of any United States claims to the Texas territory, Spain ceded Florida to the United States. But there was more: Spain had exploration claims to the west coast of North America, clear up to and including the vast Columbia River basin and had already settled much of the California coastlands. Yet in a cabinet meeting, JQA had shared his vision for an America that stretched from sea to sea, declaring that "the world must be familiarized with the idea of considering our proper dominion to be the continent of North America," which he claimed was "as inevitable as that the Mississippi should flow to the sea."[29] He was specifically seeking a clearly defined southern border, to match the forty-ninth-parallel agreement which he had won from the British, establishing the border between Canada and the United States. In return for the Texas territory and American guarantees of Spain's sovereignty in California, he wanted Spain to relinquish all claims north of the forty-second parallel (which marks the southern border of Oregon and Idaho today). In the end, the Spaniards agreed, and the two nations signed the Transcontinental Treaty, which extended America's southern boundary from the Sabine River to the Pacific Ocean. In 1819, for the first time, the United States had a clearly defined border all the way across the continent.

The Transcontinental Treaty was the greatest single-handed diplomatic achievement in American history, and America duly celebrated it as such. John Quincy Adams became the toast of the nation, and he himself always considered it the most important achievement of his life. But there would be one more diplomatic master stroke during his term as Secretary of State, which would eclipse even that, though it would bear another's name. In 1822, President Monroe and JQA decided that the time had come to recognize the independence of the South American republics who had thrown off the yoke of Spain and won their right to be free. But now Spain threatened to return in force, supported by the Holy Alliance of Russia, Prussia, and Austria, with France joining in belatedly but already planning to establish Bourbon monarchies in the South American republics.

Great Britain, naturally, greatly desired that this not happen, and through her minister in Washington, Stratford Canning, she suggested a joint Anglo-American guarantee of the sovereignty of the newly emergent nations. Any ships sailing the Atlantic for the purpose of subjugating existing governments would be interdicted by the British fleet—and of course, the United States Navy (such as it was), as well. Once again, President Monroe's cabinet was strongly in favor of accepting this proposal, and once more the sole holdout was the Secretary of State. "It would be more candid, as well as more dignified, to avow our principles explicitly to Russia and France, than to come in as a cock-boat in the wake of the British man-of-war,"[30] said JQA, and he proceeded to outline his proposed doctrine of American nonintervention and guarantees of western hemisphere autonomy.

The United States should adopt a policy, he proposed, that no European power would form any new colonies on the western hemisphere; neither would America intervene in any of the wars of the European powers. But nonintervention was also to apply to those powers, vis-à-vis their thrusts into North and South America. From now on, any move on the part of any government to oppress or control the destiny of the independent states of the New World would be regarded as "unfriendly" by the United States. In addition to what the European powers had been planning for Latin America, the Russian tsar was now extending Russian hegemony south of Alaska, claiming significant portions of the Oregon Territory, north of the forty-ninth parallel. This was the only sector of America's borders still in dispute, for Britain also claimed much of the territory; in fact, Stratford Canning had recently had a heated exchange with Adams over who had prior rights to the Columbia River basin. Did Adams (who recorded the incident in his diary) not know that Great Britain claimed the Columbia River? Canning expostulated.

"I do not know," replied JQA, "what you claim nor what you do not claim. You claim India, you claim Africa, you claim—"

"Perhaps a piece of the moon?"

"No, I have not heard that you claim exclusively any part of the moon, but there is no spot on *this* habitable globe that I could affirm you do not claim."[31]

Both men lost their temper at this point, but JQA knew exactly what he was doing, while Stratford Canning, accustomed to being the one who intimidated, was nonplussed. In this, JQA was backed to the hilt by the President, and gradually the Monroe Doctrine, as it came to be called, became a cornerstone of American foreign policy—a declaration of global independence, as it were, completing the vision which John Quincy Adams had labored so long to fulfill.

And what of Andrew Jackson? The debate over his Florida campaign was carried on sporadically for almost two years, being revived by Henry Clay whenever it appeared to be dying out. But national approval had firmed up behind Jackson, and Congress was savvy enough politically to know which way the wind was blowing. As Representative Smyth said to Clay: "Surely there must be an overruling Providence, who directs the destinies of men and nations . . . the English sailed to New Orleans and there they met the dire avenger, the man appointed by Heaven to tread the wine press of Almighty wrath. . . . Let me assure you that the American people will not be pleased to see their great defender, their great avenger, sacrificed."[32]

Was the Florida campaign part of God's overruling providence? God uses military and political leaders, whether or not they are in close personal communion with Him, and it does seem possible that it was part of the unfolding plan for America to have Andrew Jackson take the Floridas when he did. Undeniably the campaign brought to a head the cession issue that seemed destined to drag on unresolved for years; moreover, it was essential to the protection of American life and property and was accomplished with a minimum of bloodshed.

This much we do know: two men of indomitable will, sharing the same vision of one nation under God, free from foreign intervention and intrigue, were raised up and mightily used in charting the young republic's external destiny. But two other men of equally indomitable will remained locked in a contest to see who would chart America's internal destiny.

9

Chief Justice

Two men—both Virginians, distant cousins who were natural leaders (as were so many highborn sons of the Old Dominion)—would play crucial roles in the development of the United States during the early years of the nineteenth century. But the similarities ended with those few facts, for in everything else they were opposed. One saw America as a loose confederacy of sovereign states, any of which would have the right to veto federal legislation that it did not consider constitutional, and if push came to shove, to secede from the Union. The other's vision of America saw a republic under law, created by the whole people and answerable only to them.

The man who would give supreme power to the states was Thomas Jefferson, narrowly elected President on the rising tide of Democratic Republicanism that was eclipsing the classic Federalist cause. During the critical period when America's leaders hammered out and ratified the Constitution, Jefferson—the one man who might have effectively blocked its adoption—was far away in Paris, acting as the United States minister to France. In his absence, Washington, Adams, Hamilton, and other Federalists who felt convinced that America's survival depended on a central government with the states subordinate to it had their way.

When Jefferson came home and carefully studied the documents that would shape the future of America, he realized the magnitude of what had transpired. He envisioned America as a bucolic society, represented by well-educated, thoughtful farmers—rather like himself. Such a society would be so noble of mien and intent that there would be little need for a federal government. To be sure, the Articles of Confederation had needed strengthening, Jefferson conceded, and the machinery of government needed to be made more efficient, if only to raise taxes and defend borders and operate the postal service.

Instead, in his absence these men created a full-blown government structure, complete with executive, legislative, and judicial branches and defined by a Constitution that everyone seemed to regard almost reverently as the highest law in the land—in short, a government so instantly permanent that it had the appearance of being cast in bronze. But the total lack of guarantees of personal rights or protection against the intrusions or incursions of national government upon the lives and property of individuals disturbed Jefferson. He was hardly alone in his concern; it had become obvious to all thinking Americans, including the framers of the Constitution, that they needed a Bill of Rights, and Madison drafted one that eventually became the ten amendments that the states ratified in 1790.

After that, Jefferson felt content enough with the Constitution itself—provided that the federal government assumed no more powers than those explicitly granted it. The trouble was, some chose to interpret the Constitution as granting the federal government *implied* powers, among them the right to pass legislation that superseded the laws of a given state, which meant, in effect, that the federal government could impose its will on the sovereignty of a given state. The Constitution could be amended, of course, but the process was intentionally ponderous: each state had to hold a referendum, and two-thirds of the states had to be in favor of the proposed amendment. (In the two centuries since the Bill of Rights was passed, only sixteen amendments have been added.)

Jefferson refused to accept that the whole people had created and ratified the Constitution. He chose to view it as a compact between the states—a creation of the states, to serve the states.[1] Moreover, Congress itself was "merely the creature of the compact, as subject as to its assumptions of power to the final judgment of those by whom, and for whose use, itself and its powers were created and modified."[2] In other words, the states had sovereignty over Congress, and what the states gave, the states could also take away. If the federal government turned against any of the states that had created it and passed some unreasonable and unacceptable legislation that was not explicitly granted in the Constitution, then one or several states had every right to declare that legislation null and void within their borders. If the federal government objected to the nullification of their laws, then Virginia and any others could simply vote with their feet.

While Madison drafted resolutions for Virginia to that effect, Jefferson initiated them and provided the impetus, predicting that, if the tendency of the federal government to encroach on the rights of the states were not promptly checked, it would "necessarily drive these States into revolution and blood." When the Virginia legislature balked at the implied threat of secession and watered the resolutions down before passing them, Jefferson, furious, drafted even stronger resolutions for the Kentucky legislature, which passed them verbatim. From their inception, the Virginia and Kentucky Resolutions seemed to wield an almost mystical power over the imagination of states' rights extremists, one day becoming the cornerstone on which the architects of secession would lay the foundation of their confederacy. Jefferson's chilling prophecy gradually became self-fulfilling; the man who felt that in statecraft a whiff of rebellion was a healthy thing had sown a wind that would eventually reap a whirlwind.

Two years later, Jefferson was sworn in as the third President of the United States and immediately began dismantling Federalist policies and institutions, starting with the United States Mint and proceeding to the disbanding of the army and the scuttling of plans for a navy. In just four months in the White House, he had achieved so much that New England Federalist George Cabot commented: "We are doomed to suffer all the evils of excessive democracy through the United States. . . . There will be neither justice nor stability in any system, if some parts of it are not independent of popular control."[3]

Only one part remained seemingly beyond the President's reach: the Supreme Court, whose leader, Chief Justice John Marshall, seemed equally determined that Jefferson and his Democratic Republicans would not have their way. Marshall appraised the situation incisively and dispassionately, privately observing: "The Democrats are divided into speculative theorists and absolute terrorists. With the latter I am disposed to class Mr. Jefferson."[4]

For his part, Jefferson, too, remained circumspect about what he said publicly about his cousin. Marshall had many friends in high places, and in low ones as well, for he was universally well thought of. But to his intimates, the third President made no secret of his detestation for the fourth Chief Justice, who seemed intent upon usurping powers never granted by the Constitution and with them laying a foundation, precedent by precedent, for a federal republic ruled by law. Marshall had to be destroyed, or all the Democratic Republican victories and all Jefferson's plans for America would come to naught.

Who was this tall, courtly judge with the twinkle in his eye, causing such consternation? Born in 1755, John Marshall was the son of Thomas Marshall, a gentleman farmer with extensive properties in the Blue Ridge mountain country, who had once gone surveying with Washington and was a member of the House of Burgesses. In 1776, John Marshall's father was given a colonelcy and command of one of the Virginia regiments, and John himself became a lieutenant. He fought with valor at Iron Hill and Brandywine Creek and was with the army in the winter of Valley Forge. Demonstrating a rare ability to analyze legal cases, young Marshall was appointed as Deputy Judge Advocate and promoted to the rank of captain. But his greatest gift was his unflagging sense of gentle humor—a priceless commodity in that dread winter, when nearly half the army was too sick to function, and nearly a quarter more were ill-clothed; men had cut up tents to serve as coats, and blankets to take the place of boots. Indeed, so many men had marched into Valley Forge barefoot that someone observed you could have tracked the army by the bloody footprints in the snow.

Captain Marshall gave his men all the clothes he owned, save for what he was wearing, and each day he would make the rounds of the entire regiment, bringing a joke, a smile, or an amusing story to each campfire. Of him, one of his messmates, Lieutenant Philip Slaughter, wrote: "He was an excellent companion, idolized by the soldiers and his brother officers, whose gloomy hours were enlivened by his inexhaustible fund of anecdotes. . . . John Marshall was the best-tempered man I ever knew."[5]

But when he was alone, and no one needed cheering, he thought about the wagons that never reached camp—the ones carrying supplies that had already been paid for, but which were being diverted to the British over in Philadelphia, who paid in gold. He thought of the Continental Congress, sixty miles away in the town of York, which was making no effort to alleviate the army's appalling conditions, but on the contrary, was berating the army for not driving the British out of Philadelphia, so that the representatives could return to their more comfortable winter quarters. This at a time when rations were almost gone, the cemetery was growing rapidly, and only 5,000 out of 17,000 were well enough or sufficiently clothed to answer roll call.[6]

Continental Congress—what a far cry they were from the men who had signed the Declaration of Independence, just a year and a half before. Where were those signatories? A number of them were here in

Valley Forge with the army, and some, like Franklin, had gone abroad on vital missions. Few had remained in Congress. What of cousin Thomas, who had penned the Declaration? He had resigned from Congress, pleading that "the situation of my domestic affairs renders it indispensably necessary that I should solicit the substitution of some other person" to take his place.[7] Once he had returned home, his domestic crisis seemed to have quickly resolved itself, allowing him to spend the rest of the war doing his favorite thing: drafting legislation in the House of Delegates.

Thinking on such things and contrasting them with the incredible spirit of the men who were sticking it out at Valley Forge, when other armies would simply have disappeared, John Marshall reached the same conclusions that his Commander in Chief had: if America was ever going to be able to protect herself, she could no longer depend on the sovereign states to do so. She needed a strong, central, representational government, with the power to tax, to make national laws, and raise and supply an army. The General, and all his men gathered in this freezing, gnawing misery were not here because they had been promised paltry sums of worthless Continental scrip. They were not here to defend Pennsylvania or to attempt to keep the British out of New Jersey. They were here because they believed in a country called the United States of America, where a man was free to live and work and worship as he chose. Later, Marshall would recall his feelings at that time, "a time when the love of the Union, and the resistance to the claims of Great Britain, were the inseparable inmates of the same bosom; when patriotism and a strong fellow-feeling with our suffering fellow-citizens of Boston were identical; when the maxim 'United we stand, divided we fall' was the maxim of every orthodox American."[8]

When America's independence was won, the General, who had grown fond of this alternately cheerful and pensive deputy advocate, urged him to go into politics, which he did, serving two terms in the House of Delegates. When the states had ratified the Constitution, and Washington was elected America's first President, he offered to make Marshall the United States attorney for Virginia, but the latter declined; he greatly enjoyed practicing law before the brilliant Virginia bar. He was also developing an extraordinary talent, winning nearly all his cases, despite his youth. He did run again for the House of Delegates in 1789, winning handily, despite the fact that he was a Federalist in an increasingly predominant Democratic Republican state; indeed, Marshall was gaining a reputation as their most articulate spokesman outside of New England. In debate, he proved a formidable opponent. One political adversary admitted that he "made it a rule in argument, never to admit any proposition asserted by Marshall, however plain and unquestionable it might seem to be, for if the premises were once admitted, the conclusion, however apparently remote, flowed on with an irresistible certainty."[9]

In 1795, as Washington approached the end of his second term, he was anxious to see Marshall in public service on the national level, and offered to make him Attorney General for the United States. Again Marshall declined, but in 1799, at Washington's urging, he did run for Congress. Such was his popularity with his Richmond constituency that he won easily, despite his Federalist affiliation. A year later, President John Adams, the last Federalist to serve in that office, offered him the post of Secretary of War, which he declined, and not long after, the post of Secretary of State. Marshall would have declined that, too, but a strong appeal from the President caused him to reluctantly change his mind.

With the Democratic Republican spirit growing ever stronger, the man in the President's mansion was increasingly blamed for everything that went wrong. The election of 1800 voted Adams out, and while the Democratic Republicans rejoiced, the Federalists and many committed Christians viewed Jefferson's imminent administration like the coming of Napoleon. But the country might yet be preserved, and before Adams left office, he had one last request of his Secretary of State: accept appointment to the bench of the Supreme Court, as its Chief Justice. John Marshall accepted and began to bring to fruition the vision for America that had come to him that winter in Valley Forge, twenty-three years before.

In those days, the Supreme Court met in a cramped basement room of the Capitol building, which appeared to be an afterthought—and was. So little did the people think of the Supreme Court that no plans had been made for it to meet anywhere. An idle passerby might wander in and find two or three onlookers and a court clerk and several men who had given up trying to find work and felt grateful for a warm place to sit on a cold day. Except for the facts that there were no jury stalls and seven men sat on the bench instead of one and that the top attorneys in the country might be on hand to argue cases, one could not tell he had entered the highest courtroom in the land. No matter; the decisions emanating from this room would soon shake the Capitol at its core.

The man leading the court possessed a dispassionate clarity of vision and logic so persuasive that President Jefferson would groan that it did no good to pack the court with staunch Democratic Republicans: Marshall would soon have them all converted to Federalism. Given "the cunning and sophistry within which he is able to enshroud himself," Jefferson said, "it will be difficult to find a character of firmness enough to preserve his independence on the same bench with Marshall."[10]

Surprisingly, Marshall was not at first perceived to be such a threat, but it only took one crucial case to draw the battle lines: *Marbury* v. *Madison.* During his last days in office, John Adams appointed a number of justices of the peace for the District of Columbia. Some of these commissions still had not been delivered by the time Jefferson took office, and he ordered them stopped. One intended recipient, William Marbury, sued Jefferson's Secretary of State, James Madison, to receive the commission that he felt was rightfully his, and the case went before the Supreme Court.

The case raised several momentous questions: was any man, including the President of the United States, above the law? If the Constitution was the touchstone against which all legislation was to be tried, was the Supreme Court the final arbiter of the constitutionality of that legislation? Did it have the authority to repeal a law passed by Congress if it found it unconstitutional? In sum, would the United States of America become a democracy, subject to the current whim of the majority, or a republic under law? It seems incredible today—and a measure of Marshall's daring—that the judicial order established by that decision, which we today take so much for granted, was so much in question then.

Jefferson and the other Democratic Republican leaders did not take it for granted: for them, the voice of the people as the highest authority in the land, and the people made their will known through elections. They gave men they elected the responsibility of carrying out their wishes, which meant that the new President had the right, indeed a mandate, to stop the wholesale distribution of Federalist appointments. The way Jefferson saw it, the three branches of the federal government were equally balanced, in order to check one another. Marshall, by attempting to elevate the Supreme Court to the role of sole final arbiter of a law's constitutionality, was usurping authority not explicitly granted him. Jefferson felt that both the executive and legislative branches should have a say in the question of constitutionality—indeed, any state's legislature should have the right of final approval—otherwise one only hypocritically called America a democracy.

Marshall, on the other hand, was a Federalist who believed not only in strong central government, but on a deeper level, in the fallen nature of mankind. Man was born sinful, and for his own protection he needed to be under law and not subject to popular opinion that could shift as quickly and unpredictably as the wind.

In the meantime, as no higher court existed to which to appeal the Supreme Court's forthcoming decision, the Democratic Republicans' strategy became, of necessity, guerrilla warfare. There were other ways. . . . and using their substantial majority in Congress, the Democratic Republicans did away with the June and December sessions of the Supreme Court, effectively closing it down—and postponing the *Marbury* v. *Madison* decision—for more than a year. Then, following the lead of Jefferson, who observed, "The Federalists have retired into the judiciary as a stronghold . . . and from that battery, all the works of Republicanism are to be beaten down and erased,"[11] they also managed to repeal the Judiciary Act of 1801. In one stroke, they voided many of the district court and United States marshal appointments that Adams had made shortly before leaving office. In doing so they fired the first salvo of a barrage intended to ultimately reduce the Constitution to a meaningless document.

During the ensuing debate in Congress, threats and counterthreats flew. "There are many now willing to spill their blood to defend the Constitution," exclaimed James Bayard. "Are gentlemen disposed to risk the consequences?" Destroy the independence of the national judiciary, and "the moment is not far when this country is to be desolated by civil war."[12] John Randolph of Roanoke replied that the proper restraint of Congress lay not with the Supreme Court, but with the people themselves, who at the ballot box "could apply the Constitutional corrective. That is the one, true check; every other is at variance with the principle that a free people are capable of self-government."[13] It appeared that the Democratic Republican majority would have its way, nevertheless Roger Griswold of Connecticut warned them: "There are States in this Union who will never consent, and are not doomed to become the humble provinces of Virginia."[14] It was not an empty threat; a few New England Federalist leaders actually approached the British minister to sound him out about the possibility of British aid, if they were to secede.[15]

With the battle joined, neither side would yield, until the issue was decided. When the Supreme Court reconvened in 1803, the House of Representatives had already begun the process of impeaching John Pickering, judge of the United States District Court of New Hampshire, for "high crimes and misdemeanors." Democratic Republicans, tasting blood, vowed that Supreme Court Justice Samuel Chase, who had conducted his circuit court in a partisan, pro-Federalist fashion, would be next. If they successfully removed Chase, everyone knew who the next target would be: none other than the Chief Justice himself. And the moment Marshall was out, the President would replace him with Spencer Roane, who had been Jefferson's candidate all along.

A lesser man than Marshall, aware of the slenderness of the thread that suspended him above the abyss, might have unconsciously modified his pronouncements. But not the veteran of Valley Forge—in the *Marbury* v. *Madison* decision he made it emphatically clear that the Supreme Court could annul an act of Congress. No middle ground existed; the Constitution was either "a superior paramount law," which could not be tampered with by legislation, or "it is on a level with ordinary legislative acts" and can be altered at the will of Congress. If the Constitution is not the highest law of the land, then "written constitutions are absurd attempts on the part of the people to limit a power that is illimitable."[16] He further declared that "the particular phraseology of the Constitution of the United States confirms and strengthens the principle . . . that a law repugnant to the Constitution is void."[17] Had this epochal decision not been made when it was, Congress would not have had its power challenged until the Dred Scott case of 1857. With seventy years of momentum, one doubts that it ever could have been checked.

By fortunate coincidence, precisely at the time the court rendered that decision, the attention of the country and all the newspapers focused on Jefferson's surprise purchase of the Louisiana Territory;

indeed, not even in Congress could anyone think or debate about something else. But eventually, the Democratic Republicans did return their attention to the proposed impeachment of Samuel Chase, who had given them cause by an ill-advised tirade to a grand jury in Baltimore against Maryland's new state constitution. Prodding them to the attack, Jefferson asked, "Ought this seditious and official attack on the principles of our Constitution and on the proceedings of the State. . . . go unpunished?"[18]

The gloves came off, and William Giles of Virginia indicated how raw the contest would be when he told the newly elected Senator from Massachusetts, John Quincy Adams: "We want your [Federalist] offices for the purpose of giving them to men who will fill them better." That night, JQA noted in his diary that the charges "contained in themselves a virtual impeachment of, not only Mr. Chase, but of all the judges of the Supreme Court."[19] The move afoot was nothing less than a naked power play: the Democratic Republicans felt determined to impose their will on the Supreme Court. On the floor of the Senate, Giles rejected the concept of "an independent judiciary," adding, "if the judges of the Supreme Court should dare, as they had done, to declare the acts of Congress unconstitutional . . . it was the undoubted right of the House to impeach them, and of the Senate to remove them for giving such opinions."[20]

The impeachment debate and proceedings dragged on for months, finally coming to a vote in the Senate chamber, on March 1, 1805, before a packed crowd of journalists and observers. One by one, the eight articles of impeachment were read off, and one by one the Senators registered their verdict. "How say you?" asked the Senate secretary, "Is Samuel Chase, the respondent, guilty of high crimes and misdemeanors, as charged in the article just read?" The secretary turned to the Senator from Massachusetts, whose named topped the roll. "John Quincy Adams."

JQA responded with a resounding "Not guilty!" Enough others followed his lead, so that when the vote was completed after the last article had been read, the secretary announced: "It becomes my duty to declare that Samuel Chase, Esq., stands acquitted of all the articles exhibited by the House of Representatives against him."[21] That vote assured the independence of the Supreme Court.

Through it all, Marshall had stood beside Chase, supporting him and being a true friend as well as his leader. He would have done no less for any of his Associate Justices, and the degree to which his loyalty was reciprocated was evident years later in the description of him by one who had served with him the longest, Joseph Story, who attempted to give some explanation of why so many of their decisions were unanimous:

> In strength and depth and comprehensiveness of mind, it would be difficult to name his superior. He sought for truths far beyond the boundaries to which inquisitive and even ambitious minds are accustomed to push their inquiries. He traced them out from their first dim lights and pale glimmers, until they stood embodied before him with a clear and steady brightness. His sagacity was as untiring as it was acute, and he saw the conclusion of his premises at such vast distances, and through such vast reaches of intermediate results, that it burst upon other minds as a sort of instant and miraculous induction. . . . His powers of analysis were indeed marvelous. . . . But what seemed peculiarly his own was the power with which he seized on a principle or argument, apparently presented in the most elementary form, and showed it to be a mere corollary of some more general truth which lay immeasurable distances beyond it. If his mind had been less practical, he would have been the most consummate of metaphysicians, the most skillful of sophists. But his love of dialectics was constantly controlled by his superior love of truth.[22]

Thus did one in close contact with this extraordinary mind describe Marshall, and now others wanted to know more about this tall, stately Virginian in whose eye the resident twinkle could narrow to a discerning gleam. In his native Richmond, a city confident that socially it had no peer, the most envied invitation was to one of his formal dinner parties. At his table, the Chief Justice presided with gracious wit and disarming informality. A first-time guest, perhaps a bit self-conscious, would be quickly put at ease and made to feel at home by his smiling host. Looking about him, he would note the cherrywood sideboard polished to a dark luster and gleaming in the soft glow cast by the silver candelabra and wall sconces. He would admire the delicate carving in the Hepplewhite chairs, the sparkling, cut-crystal wine glasses—and be the more astonished when his host amused the table with a simple country tale that invariably made fun of his own shortcomings. For an instant, the guest would be nonplussed—was the man, after all, a bumpkin? A rude strutfurrow, dressed up in a fancy shirt and brocaded waistcoat that didn't quite fit him? Indeed, with his lanky frame, and arms and legs that seemed rather haphazardly attached to it, he did look rather more like a scarecrow than a gentleman. But then, how did one explain the reaction of the other guests, among them some of the most eminent men in the Old Dominion? For they openly adored Judge Marshall, hanging on his every word.

At length, the newcomer relaxed, and he, too, fell under the spell. For the story his host was relating, though simple, was being exquisitely told—the timing, the inflection, the pauses for effect, the hilarious lines casually thrown away—had there ever been such a raconteur? When it came to an end, the guest would laugh so hard that tears would come to his eyes, and he would join the others in begging their host for another.

The quickness of his wit was renowned. A club in Philadelphia had a rule that all present had to make a rhyme on whatever word was suddenly called out. As Marshall entered the club to attend a meeting, he had noted several Kentucky colonels drinking at the bar. When he entered the meeting room, he was asked to provide a rhyme for the word *paradox*. Glancing across the hall, he immediately replied:

> In the bluegrass region, a paradox is born:
> the corn was full of kernels, and the colonels, full of corn."[23]

Marshall himself was a total paradox. In court, lawyers considered the opportunity to argue before him the high point of their careers and would spend weeks in preparation, yet outside the courtroom he was so homespun and so at ease with common folk that they almost never recognized him. He enjoyed this natural anonymity, as he loved just being with people and felt dismayed if they discovered who he was and started paying deference to him. He liked nothing better than to stop at some log tavern along the road, sup with the family and other guests, and sit by the fireside afterward, just enjoying the conversation. On one occasion, the Chief Justice had gone to town on market day and was passing the time with some friends, when a newcomer to Richmond offered the tall fellow a coin if he would carry home for him a heavy turkey he had just purchased. Marshall nodded in agreement and, with the turkey tucked under one arm, trudged along after his erstwhile employer, while his companions clapped their hands over their mouths to keep from giving him away.[24]

As ready as his sense of fun was, it was gentle, for John Marshall owned a tender side. His wife was afflicted with a disease of the nervous system, which increasingly incapacitated her with the passing years. Marshall's devotion to his "dearest Polly" was legendary, and stories of his care would circulate long after his death.

Summing him up, Justice Story would one day write: "He was a man of the most unaffected modesty. . . . he was far more anxious to know others, than be known by them."[25]

It would seem, if only from how well the system has worked, that God intended America to become a nation under law. In this instance, His instrument was the Supreme Court and specifically its leader, who seemed to have a personal relationship with the Lord, even though he never publicly spoke of Him. One story did appear in the Winchester *Republican,* however, that described an incident in McGuire's Hotel in that city, when Marshall arrived in that hotel's tavern, having suffered a mishap on the road.

> The shafts of his ancient gig were broken and "held together by withes formed from the bark of a hickory sapling." He was negligently dressed, his knee buckles loosened. In the tavern, a discussion arose among some young men, concerning the merits of the Christian religion. . . . No one knew Marshall, who sat quietly listening. Finally, one of the youthful combatants turned to him and said, "Well, my old gentleman, what think you of these things?"
>
> Marshall responded with a "most eloquent and unanswerable appeal." He talked for an hour, answering "every argument urged against" the teachings of Jesus. "In the whole lecture, there was so much simplicity and energy, pathos and sublimity, that not another word was uttered." The listeners wondered who the old man could be. Some thought him a preacher, and great was their surprise when they learned afterwards that he was the Chief Justice of the United States.[26]

"It was the best of times, it was the worst of times"—with those words Dickens began his tale of London and Paris, set during the

French Revolution. They aptly summed up the 1819 American paradox known as the Era of Good Feelings. For while President Monroe had presided over three uneventful years of peace and expansion and the front pages of the newspapers extolled the triumph of his Secretary of State's Transcontinental Treaty, the back pages of the same paper were filled with quiet horror, stories of collapsed banks, unbelievable economic depression, and local currencies run wild. Three years before, in Philadelphia, some thirty businesses there employed 9,672 persons. By 1819, three-fourths of the workers had been let go and more than half the eighty-nine stores on Market Street stood empty. That was just one city; in New England, the heartland of America's fledgling industrial base, the situation seemed even worse. In fact, America was in the throes of the worst depression she would ever suffer, unimaginably worse than the one that would come a century later. The entire middle class was being wiped out by suddenly worthless currency, and wage earners desperately sought to feed their families. Facing the certainty of prison for insurmountable debts, thousands of families headed for the frontier as the only alternative.[27]

What had happened? In the beginning, the bankrupt Continental Congress resorted to printing money with no gold or silver backing, with the result that their dollars became, in the popular phrase, "not worth a Continental"—as many embittered Revolutionary soldiers discovered. In the vacuum, various state banks started printing their own currency, though a Massachusetts dollar might be worth more than a Maryland dollar, depending on the relative soundness of the banks issuing them. After the ratification of the Constitution and a federal election, Congress chartered a federal Bank of the United States under Secretary of the Treasury Alexander Hamilton. In a bold and courageous move, Hamilton redeemed every Continental dollar at full face value with new federal dollars, back by hard currency. This new money soon earned the approbation, "sound as a dollar" and made good, in effect, on the promissory notes of the pre-Constitution government. Thus did American currency finally stabilize under federal banking policies so conservative that foreign nations and private investors had the confidence to do business with the new republic for the first time.

But the Americans of the early nineteenth century did not appreciate the need for fiscal stability. The war was over, the West was beckoning, and the time was now. People needed money to buy tools and new land out West. They needed to take advantage of once-in-a-lifetime opportunities, to do a million and one things *now,* instead of having to establish a credit record or waiting half a lifetime to slowly accumulate the necessary capital, as their parents and grandparents had. The pressure on the Bank of the United States to expand the money supply and loosen its credit policies became intense. When the bank refused to yield, people began to hate it.

Nineteen years before, when the Democratic Republicans swept into power, they determined to get rid of every Federalist in office and every federal institution. After their assault on the national judiciary, they turned their batteries on the United States Bank, founded by that arch Federalist Hamilton and run by Federalist directors. It had to go. In 1811, the bank's charter expired, and a Democratic-Republican-dominated Congress refused to renew it. The bank was dead.

For a while, things continued pretty much as normal. To be sure, the state banks flourished and charters for new ones seemed to be granted to all comers, but they all continued to adhere to the conservative policies established by the Bank of the United States—at first. As the pressure for money continued to build, however, the temptation to loosen credit and to print more notes than one had hard currency or United States dollars on hand to support soon proved overwhelming. The further away from Federalist New England (where banking in America had begun) a state was, the more "democratic" its lending policies were likely to be—and the more its notes would inevitably be discounted. If the banks of the Middle Atlantic States were less sound than those of New England, those in the South were positively shaky, and those in the West and Southwest, where land speculation was most rife, seemed "weird to the point of madness."[28]

Finally, Congress grudgingly admitted that there had to be a national bank, if the country were to survive, and in 1816, they chartered the Second Bank of the United States. But this time, it would be run by Democratic Republicans. In New England, the bank's methods remained conservative—forced to, by the financiers who did business there. But in the South and West, it was a different story. There, the Bank behaved much as did the state banks around it—making speculative loans and extending unrestricted credit. Meanwhile, every private bank that had a charter considered it a license to print money—literally. Many new banks didn't even bother to get a charter. As Hezekiah Niles, publisher of the widely read and respected national newsmagazine *Niles' Weekly,* said, all you need to start a bank was plates, presses, paper, and a suitable site—"a church, a tavern, a blacksmith's shop" would do.[29] The notes that were turned out had a dollar value printed on them, but it was rare that the bank held even 10 percent of that amount in redeemable United States currency or coin. One western bank did possess $27,000 in gold and silver—and issued bank notes against it, amounting to $395,000.[30]

The madness spread like wildfire. In 1818, tiny Zanesville, Ohio, located on one of the main routes west, had 176 banks! Americans believed easy access to capital was the very essence of common-man democracy. As John Quincy Adams had written to Rush a few years before: "The banking infatuation pervades all America. Our whole system of banks is a violation of every honest principle of banks . . . a bank that issues paper at interest, is a pick-pocket or a robber. But the delusion will have its course. You may as well reason with a hurricane."[31]

Now, with all semblance of restraint laid aside, greed consumed both lenders and borrowers, and capitalism turned ugly. For the lenders were now printing money with abandon and sending agents into the street to lend huge sums at marginal interest. You say you have no collateral? Nonsense, my boy, look at those shoulders! They're all the collateral you'll need. You're young and strong, and you want to buy a piece of land and build a farm on it, right? Well, that farm's going to be worth something then someday, isn't it? Sure it is—we'll just call that future collateral. Now you sign right here, and we've got 10,000 brand-new, Sixth Bank of Zanesville dollars for you! What do you think of that? Won't the missus be pleased? You bet she will! Is she going to be proud of you!

So you sign and take the crisp new bills and buy the land and the equipment and start to work. You work hard, you pour a lot of sweat into the ground, and your shoulders are aching, but by the end of the year, you've managed to clear half a dozen acres and planted corn and some wheat; you've put up a two-room cabin and a shed for your horse and pigs. . . . But when you go to town to buy supplies, suddenly the man in the feed and grain store won't give you but fifty cents on the dollar for your Sixth Bank of Zanesville money. So you've got to pay twice as much for supplies, and the interest on your loan has also doubled because the local bank bought your mortgage, and they couldn't care less that Zanesville money isn't what it used to be. So the next year you work even harder, and meanwhile the money you borrowed has dwindled in value to twenty cents on the dollar, which means your interest is now five times as high. You can't pay it, and the local bank, assuring you how sorry they are, gives you two weeks to get off their property. You don't wait that long; you and your family slip out of town that same night, one step ahead of the sheriff. You don't stop till you get across the Mississippi, and there, out in the Missouri Territory, you borrow some more easy money to start again—what else can you do?

All over America, unscrupulous banks accumulated vast quantities of farms and mills, factories and general stores. If anyone refused to accept their currency, the bank would have its other customers boycott him, which would make it impossible for him to do business. Then, to forestall anyone attempting to redeem their bogus money, the banks colluded and organized chains. . . . You want to redeem your Sixth Zanesville notes? Very well, sir, we'll be happy to give you the same amount in Chillicothe dollars. You want silver? Sorry, but our bullion is back in Cincinnati—not safe to keep it out here, you know. I'm afraid it's Chillicothe dollars, or nothing. . . . If you go to them, the Chillicothe bank offers you Canton dollars, and so on, until you give up.

At the same time, counterfeiters had a field day. Why bother even putting up a storefront bank when you could print money on a fictitious bank in another state and no one would be the wiser? Wasn't that basically what the wildcat bankers did anyway? In any event, it was estimated that 40 percent of all the money in circulation in 1819 was counterfeit, with the result that eventually no one trusted money printed anywhere outside of town. They didn't care very much for the local product, either, but at least they could see where it came from. Holders of Ohio bank notes found them discounted anywhere from 10 percent to 50 percent, and Indiana, Illinois, and Missouri bank notes were discounted even more.[32] Poor Hezekiah Niles complained in his weekly that two-thirds of the bank notes sent in to pay for subscriptions could not be passed at all.

While all this went on, two sections of the nation would have been plunged into economic depression, even had the currency been sound. During the War of 1812, British manufactured goods were obviously unavailable, and new American industries sprang up to fill the country's needs for shoes, cloth, tools, and the like. But as soon as the war ended, British products which had piled up for three years with no place to go were now dumped on the American market at distressed prices. Oftentimes the workmanship was shoddy beyond belief, but when they cost a third the price of the homemade equivalent, most people chose them. Moreover, English exporters of farm produce could afford to drastically undercut their American competitors, because their ships picked up more profitable American cargoes for the West Indies, selling them there, and reloading for home.

The second factor was the cotton boom. After the war, English mills were so ravenous for American cotton, that the price soared to an undreamed of thirty-two cents a pound. At that rate, cotton became the most profitable cash crop by far, and any land that looked like it might support cotton went for a premium price, sometimes as much as $100 an acre—in early nineteenth-century United States dollars. But now the price of cotton rose more than the re-export market could absorb, and the English mills turned to India, whose cotton lacked the quality of America's, but cost a lot less. When this news reached New Orleans, the price of cotton began to fall and continued on down to fourteen cents a pound, which threw the Deep South into a severe depression.[33]

The balloon went up in February of 1819, when the head office of the Second Bank of the United States, embarrassed by the wild speculations of its southern and western branches, started calling its loans. This forced many of the state banks to call their own loans, and the string of dominoes started to fall. When it was over, the list of bankrupt businesses covered the entire back page of *Niles' Weekly,* six columns across in fine print.[34] Hundreds of thousands of men were out of work and dependent upon charity. By March, New York City fed 6,640 people daily in soup kitchens.[35] Needless to say, all the blame for the economic collapse was laid at the door of the United States Bank. As before, the Democratic Republican majority went for the quick and easy solution: emergency legislation that would force the banks to accept all paper money at its face value, regardless of the solvency of the bank (or counterfeiter) that printed it. Blocked in this approach, they now called upon the state legislatures to pass laws absolving debtors from further obligation. They were joined in this cry by unscrupulous "professional bankrupts," who would shield their assets, declare bankruptcy, and be back in business in a matter of weeks, leaving their frustrated creditors gnashing their teeth.

In the center of the financial chaos that engulfed America stood a calm, rock-steady institution. At its helm, Chief Justice Marshall could do little to abate the dashing waves, but he could do something to ensure that they would never reach this height again. He and his associates could establish some foundational principles for American business. In February of 1819, the Supreme Court read a unanimous decision that declared unconstitutional any state legislation that impaired the mutual obligations of a contract, including in this case the obligations of a debtor. They further confirmed the sanctity of contracts by the landmark decision in the case of Dartmouth College. Dartmouth had been founded as a private charitable organization, under a grant awarded it by the state of New Hampshire. That state now desired to run the college and had set up a new corporation to do so. But if Dartmouth's charter could be so callously and wantonly revoked or amended, then no private institution would remain immune from national or local takeover—nor, by logical extension, would any private corporation be safe. All such institutions would become subject to the "rise and fall of popular parties . . . and the contention of politics," as the brilliant and articulate young attorney for the college put it. This was Daniel Webster, an alumnus himself and a backwoods lawyer, out to make a name for himself.

Prior to arguing a case before the Supreme Court, lawyers would spend weeks preparing their briefs and tracking down every loose end of their case. Yet preparation alone did not spell success; presence and delivery counted far more than they do today. In fact, before the age of television and microphone amplification, oratory was a highly respected gift, and in the early nineteenth century, a handful of Americans could have held their own with the greatest orators of Parliament, or the Senate of Rome, for that matter. But you had to prepare; if you had done your homework, then your presentation could take on the air of an elegant castle under construction—each turret strategically placed in balance with the whole, each tower topped with a pennant, and the keep saved for last. Daniel Webster, perhaps the finest orator of his era, had done his homework, for this, his first major court appearance.

The cold penetrated the basement of the north wing of the Capitol that day, despite the fire the court clerk kept stoked and fueled in the Franklin stove in the corner. For, according to the "barometer" developed by the French fellow Pascal, the air pressure was unusually high and seemed to be pressing the cold into one's bones. Up on the bench, the seven justices sat in their thick black robes (and one suspected, had their feet tucked in hidden pillows or foot warmers). But the rest of those in the courtroom kept on their cloaks and outer coats, with the first ones in getting the seats closest to the stove. You could almost see the breath of some of the lawyers as they spoke.

Daniel Webster had been holding forth for the better part of three hours, a truly magnificent performance and well worth traveling 500 miles to hear, as one New Hampshireman whispered. Young Webster's voice sounded a little hoarse now. He fell silent, apparently having finished his remarks. He stood before the court, and no one moved or said anything, though all eyes were on him. The only sound came from the stove, where a green pine log snapped and hissed.

Apparently as an afterthought, Webster turned back to the bench and fixed his gaze on the Chief Justice. "Sir," he said, his muted voice breaking with emotion. "You may destroy this little institution; it is weak; it is in your hands. I know it is one of the lesser lights on the literary horizon of our country." His voice barely audible, he paused, seeming at a loss for words. The Chief Justice and his associates leaned forward. "You may put it out," Webster whispered. "But if you do," he suddenly continued, gathering strength from somewhere, "you must carry through your work. You must extinguish, one after another, all those great lights of science which for more than a century have thrown their radiance over our land!" His voice trembled to a halt, and tears welled in his eyes. Clearing his throat, he resumed. "It is, Sir, as I have said, a small college. And yet, there are those who love it—" he shook his head, unable to continue, and shielding his eyes, went over to his chair and sat down. Observers noted that there were tears in the Chief Justice's eyes and in those of all the others on the bench.[36]

When passions had subsided and the justices had deliberated, their chief read a unanimous decision in favor of the college; and his definition of a corporation would become famous: "A corporation is an artificial being, invisible, intangible, and existing only in contemplation of law. It possesses only those properties which the charter of its creation confers upon it. . . . But it is no more a state instrument than a natural person, exercising the same powers, would be."[37] It was, concluded the Chief Justice, the "opinion of the Court, after mature deliberation, that this is a contract, the obligation of which cannot be impaired without violating the Constitution of the United States."[38]

The immediate result of this decision was that new corporations, whose stability, longevity, and efficiency the nation vitally needed, sprang up everywhere, confident that, having once been granted incorporation by a state government, they would not then face interference from that state, unless, of course, they broke the law. Long-term, this guarantee of the inviolability of a contract caused America's industrial base to develop far more rapidly and soundly than it might have otherwise.

Jefferson, no longer in the White House, became no less relentless in his drive to unhorse Marshall. In a letter to Governor William Plumer, he commented: "The idea that institutions, established for the use of the Nation, cannot be touched or modified . . . may, perhaps, be a salutary provision against the abuses of a monarch, but it is most absurd against a nation itself. Yet our lawyers and our priests generally inculcate this doctrine." Even then, thirty years after the horrors of the French Revolution, Jefferson saw any checks or restraints against the current popular will of the American people as "absurd."[39]

A scant few days later, the court heard an even more pivotal case: *McCulloch* v. *Maryland*. The Second Bank of the United States had established a branch at Baltimore and attempted to impose some limits to the fiscal irresponsibility practiced by the state banks. Naturally, friction resulted, and the state of Maryland had passed an act levying an annual tax of $15,000 on the local branch of the United States bank, which the latter refused to pay. The case came to the Supreme Court, for what was at issue here was "the supremacy of the National government, as against the dominance of State Governments."[40]

Daniel Webster opened on behalf of the bank, pointing out that if the state could tax the bank, it would be relatively easy for the state to put the Second Bank of the United States out of business, since the "power to tax involved . . . a power to destroy." In truth, when Maryland taxed the Baltimore branch of the national bank, it in effect taxed the national government itself.[41]

On March 6, 1819, the Chief Justice delivered the court's decision, beginning by pointing out that they could not "approach such a question without a deep sense of . . . the awful responsibility involved in its decision. But it must be decided peacefully, or remain a source of hostile legislation, perhaps of hostility of a still more serious nature."[42] The Chief Justice thus acknowledged his awareness that while the Court's earlier decisions may have gone largely unnoticed, this one had already elicited the rumblings of possible armed resistance, should the government try to enforce it. For no less a personage than Jefferson himself was again calling for people to be prepared to take up arms, and people listened.

Yet Marshall refused to back down. Speaking of the federal government's right to tax, as granted in the Constitution, he declared: "Throughout this vast republic, from the St. Croix to the Gulf of Mexico, from the Atlantic to the Pacific, revenue is to be collected and expended, armies are to be marched and supported."[43] The national government might withdraw from state taxation *any* taxable subject and not just those specifically withdrawn by the Constitution. He sustained this argument on "the great principle that the Constitution and the laws thereof are supreme; that they control the constitutions and laws of the respective States, and cannot be controlled by them."[44]

No wonder Jefferson and the states' rights advocates were up in arms! They correctly perceived that the Supreme Court's decision announced that, in principle, Congress had the power to intervene in the affairs of any state. That raised the prospect that Congress could ultimately "emancipate every slave in the United States," as John Randolph would declare five years later.[45] In this case, Marshall directly confronted the disunionist sentiment growing among sectors of southern slaveholders. No section of America could be allowed to dictate to the whole of America or decide for itself which laws it would obey and which it would ignore. For the government of the United States was "emphatically and truly a government of the people. In its form and substance, it emanates from them. Its powers are granted by them, and are to be exercised directly on them, and for their benefit."[46]

The Chief Justice had taken a clear and unequivocal stand for the American government as being a form of national covenant—a concept that went all the way back to the Pilgrims' arrival in 1620. Thirty-four years after this decision, another man, remarkably similar to Marshall in character, temperament, and vision, as well as physical appearance—and as deeply loved by all who knew him well—would reiterate the same principle at a windswept soldiers' cemetery at Gettysburg: "A government of the people, by the people, and for the people, shall not perish from this earth."

But opposition to the national covenant ideal grew. No sooner had the Supreme Court announced its decision in *McCulloch* v. *Maryland* than six states vehemently denounced it. Fortunately for the Court, at that moment in March 1819, the attention of both the House and the

Senate was caught up in the battle over the status of the Missouri Territory and whether she would be admitted to the Union as a slave or free state. As a result of such heated debates, one heard threats of civil war daily. Just at this crucial time, another case came before the court that would enable it to deliver a far-reaching decision for the concept of national covenant: *Cohens* v. *Virginia.*

The city of Washington had been incorporated by Congress and empowered to run a lottery to raise funds. The neighboring state of Virginia passed a law forbidding the sale of the "national lottery" tickets within its borders. Two men named Cohen were caught selling lottery tickets in the city of Norfolk, Virginia, and were fined. They appealed their case to the Supreme Court, and William Pinkney appeared as the principal counsel for the Cohens. In delivering the Court's decision, Marshall opened by addressing the question of whether the verdict of a state court in a criminal case could even be appealed to a higher national court. Give up the appellate jurisdiction of national courts, "from the decision of state tribunals," he declared, and "every other branch of federal authority might as well be surrendered. To part with this leaves the Union a mere league or confederacy."[47]

Never had Marshall delivered a stronger opinion than this, with the full knowledge that it would provoke the strongest reaction. Yet what would be the result, if he allowed the state of Virginia's position to stand? Nothing less than the prostration of the national government "at the feet of every State in the Union. . . . Each member will possess a veto on the will of the whole." Speaking of the power of the judiciary and the Constitution it was sworn to uphold, he declared: "The people made the Constitution, and the people can unmake it. It is the creature of their own will, and lives only by their will. But this supreme and irresistible power to make and unmake resides only in the whole body of the people, not in any subdivision of them. The attempt of any of the parts to exercise it is usurpation."[48]

As Marshall's biographer, Albert J. Beveridge, put it, "In *Cohens* v. *Virginia,* John Marshall stamped upon the brow of Localism the brand of illegality."[49] And in case his point wasn't perfectly understood, Marshall added: "The constitution and laws of a state, so far as they are repugnant to the Constitution and laws of the United States, are absolutely void."[50]

For nearly twenty years, John Marshall had been headed in this direction, and from his first decision on the bench, his course had never swerved. Over the years, the Supreme Court had erected the republic we know today, decision by decision. Granted, none had been so bluntly explicit concerning the subordinate status of the states, but never had the regional conflict been so precipitous. There was no ignoring the court's position now. Marshall's lifework and the future of America hung in the balance. In a rage, Jefferson took up the gauge: "If Congress fails to shield the States from dangers so palpable and so imminent, the States must shield themselves, and meet the invader foot to foot. . . ."[51]

One of the Founding Fathers was calling for armed rebellion. While he would not come out and openly attack his cousin, he encouraged his closest associates to do so, using all his influence to get anti-Marshall diatribes published far and wide. Spencer Roane wrote, under the *nom de plume* Algernon Sidney, that national judges have "no interest in the government or laws of any state but that of which they are citizens. [To any other state] they are completely aliens and foreigners. Virginia is as much a foreign nation as Russia, so far as jurisdiction of the Supreme Court over the judgments of State courts is concerned."[52]

Marshall would not respond publicly, but he privately wrote his friend Joseph Story: "I think for coarseness and malignity of invention, 'Algernon Sidney' surpasses all party writers who have ever made pretensions to any decency of character. . . . He will be supposed to be the champion of States Rights, instead of being what he really is, the champion of dismemberment."[53]

In all the years Jefferson had been trying to unseat Marshall, the Chief Justice had held his tongue where his attacker was concerned. But now, when he learned that Jefferson had condemned the Supreme Court's right of judicial review as "a very dangerous doctrine indeed, and one which would place us under the despotism of an oligarchy,"[54] he broke his self-imposed rule of silence. To Story, he confided:

> For Mr. Jefferson's opinion as respects this department, it is not difficult to assign the cause. He is among the most ambitious, and, I suspect, among the most unforgiving of men. His great power is over the mass of the people, and this power is chiefly acquired by professions of democracy. Every check on the wild impulse of the moment is a check on his own power, and he is unfriendly to the source from which it flows. He looks with ill at an independent judiciary. . . . There is some reason to believe

> that the essays written [by Roane] against the Supreme Court were, in a degree at least, stimulated by this gentleman.[55]

Story was able to confirm that Jefferson had indeed requested that Roane's articles be reprinted, and he replied to Marshall: "For this, he has several motives, and it is not among the weakest that the [judicial] department would never lend itself as a tool to work for his political power."[56]

Marshall responded with as great prophetic discernment as he had ever manifested: "A deep design to convert our government into a mere league of states has taken strong hold of a powerful and violent party in Virginia. The attack upon the judiciary is, in fact, an attack upon the Union . . . a masked battery, aimed at the government itself. . . . The whole attack, if not originating with Jefferson, is obviously approved and guided by him."[57]

Had Marshall chosen to fight his cousin with the same underhanded weapons used against him . . . but that was not his style. As always, he stood mute before his accusers, refusing to defend himself or answer in kind. History has answered for him, and it falls to Justice Story to deliver the summation: "He would have been deemed a great man in any age, and of all ages. He was one of those to whom centuries alone give birth—standing out like beacon lights on the loftiest eminences, to guide, to admonish, and instruct future generations, as well as the present."[58]

John Marshall had raised up the light of the original vision for all Americans to see—a covenanted people, committed to living together as a national family, one nation under God. The gathering storm would threaten to extinguish this flame, but its survival would be due in no small measure to this gentle warrior for the American vision.

Such men does God raise up when they are most needed. . . .

Pertaining to his death in 1835, there is a story that has become legend: it is said of the Liberty Bell that it received its crack as it tolled in mourning for the passage of the Chief Justice.

10

A House Dividing

Outside the windows of the Senate chamber, fat flakes of snow drifted down from on high—icy manna from heaven, on that chill February morning in 1820. Inside, no one needed Ben Franklin's ingenious firebox to warm the air—the doors to the furnace of hell were flung open and heating the rhetoric to an unheard of pitch. The tumult and the shouting were over the Missouri Territory: would it enter the Union as a slave state or free? On the surface, at issue stood the precarious balance between northern and southern states in the Senate. (The House was already the North's, despite the three-fifths slave allowance, and the flood tide of Irish, German and Scandinavian immigration increased the North's population 25 percent faster than the South's.)[1] But slavery threatened to split the Union; the leviathan moving through the deeps had suddenly broached. Until now, a gentlemen's agreement kept it from the floor, but never again would it submerge for long, and never had tempers run so hot.

James Barbour of Virginia stood, taking a poll of the members from the nonslaveholding states as to the advisability of calling a convention to dissolve the Union and agree on the terms of a separation. Freeman Walker of Georgia seemed to peer into the future, where he saw "intestine feuds, civil wars . . . the father armed against the son, and the son against the father . . . a brother's sword crimsoned with a brother's blood . . . our houses wrapt in flames, and our wives and infant children driven from their homes."[2] America was in peril, a house dividing; whether it could survive even a day, let alone a week or a year, seemed a moot point.

Slavery—the seeds of darkness. John Quincy Adams had discerned it to be "the great and foul stain upon the North American Union, and it is a contemplation worthy of the most exalted soul, whether its total abolition is or is not practicable. . . ."[3] With typical precision, the Secretary of State had laid bare the pivotal question, not only of 1820, but of the next forty-five years. Two generations later, 600,000 men would give their lives to find a solution in blood—more Americans than in all her other wars combined, before and after—and the nation would be nearly irreparably torn asunder, barely fourscore and seven years after its birth. Why?

What do we really *know* of the American experience of slavery, beyond the universal prejudices we assimilated in school? Beyond the images of *Gone with the Wind, Roots,* and other popular fictional treatments of the subject? Mention slavery, and people think of gingham-clad blacks bent over, harvesting cotton bolls under the broiling sun and the hard-eyed scrutiny of a mounted overseer . . . of breathtakingly beautiful antebellum mansions with tall-columned porticos, shaded by oaks or willows or magnolias . . . of dirt-floor shanties out back, where the evening hours knew only exhaustion, despair, and apathy . . . while in the big house, crystal chandeliers illumined cream-skinned ladies in hoops and crinolines, dancing reels with handsome escorts as, out on the curved drive in front, liveried coachmen waited alongside gleaming mahogany coaches. . . .

We could appreciate the intrinsic evil of slavery—of tearing a man away from his family and home, holding him against his will, and forcing him to do yours. We could see how men would go to war to put a stop to such practice and how other men would give their lives in defense of their homeland and families and way of life. But who of us bothered to look beneath the surface—to question how slavery could have gotten such a foothold in a country whose founders had declared all men to be created equal? What was slavery *really* like, once one cleared away the clutter of stereotypes? Ultimately, what about slavery could so corrode the souls of slaveholders that they could actually believe that God approved of it and wanted it perpetuated?

To find satisfactory answers to such questions would mean delving into first-person accounts, wherever possible. Fortunately, back in the 1930s, to help during the Depression, the government had hired a number of out-of-work authors to seek out and interview blacks who had been slaves. Going through the accounts, one is surprised to discover that many slaves genuinely loved their masters, often to the point of refusing to leave them, even after having been liberated by Union soldiers or after the Civil War was over and emancipation became the law of the land. According to their testimonies, a number of them had Christian masters who treated them with compassion. Moreover, these were unrehearsed, first-person accounts of ex-slaves—had we been misled all these years? If even a significant minority felt this way, then no wonder the abolitionists so polarized moderate, border southerners that they were fully prepared to go to war on the South's side, even if they didn't hold slaves or have any desire to.

Let the reader then sample some of the modern black historians, who point out that the slaves interviewed by the government project were in their eighties and nineties and that the mind has a way of blotting out painful memories. Some black historians point out that those interviews were taken in hard times; they reasoned that if the blacks told the white government representatives what they thought they wanted to hear—just like they used to do with the young massa—then maybe the government would help them out.[4]

Next, the reader should tackle some accounts of freed or runaway slaves—and discover that the horrors hitherto heard of paled in comparison to the reality of what actually transpired. Set aside the rabid extremists among the abolitionists and read just what the moderate antislavery publications printed—publications that strove to be dispassionate and scrupulously factual, because they knew their more strident colleagues alienated the very moderates whose opinions they wanted to sway. Without ranting or slanting, they simply presented the horrendous facts and testimonies and let them speak for themselves. Finally, read the journals of a few courageous southern women who risked cruel ostracism to record their testimony—Fanny Kemble, Anne Page, Kate Stone, Mary Chesnut, and the Grimké sisters.

In the end, the reader will have experienced something of the grief and injustice of both sides of the question and will have to ask himself: how would I have reacted, had I been born in the Deep South a century and a half ago, into a Christian plantation family with a tradition of treating its slaves uncommonly well. . . . If in my late twenties or early thirties, I had come into a personal knowledge of Jesus Christ as my living, risen Saviour and had begun to be convicted that slavery by its very nature was abhorrent to God. . . . If at the same time, radical northern abolitionists were calling my father and his friends scum and worse in their newspapers and imputing to them the lowest possible morals. . . . If northern agitators were distributing leaflets among those of my slaves who could read, encouraging them to take up arms and put us to death. . . . If, to protect inefficient northern manufacturers, a northern Congress had imposed a tariff that made me pay twice as much for farm and household goods as I would have paid to import them from England. . . . If northern bankers were flooding the South with worthless money that was wiping out the savings of countless less fortunate neighbors. . . . If, meanwhile, my closest friends, to whom I confided my thoughts of eventually freeing my slaves, looked at me as if I had gone daft, or worse, had turned traitor to our class. . . . *What would I do*?

At the end of such research, that would be a far more difficult question to answer than at the beginning. But let us return now to the Capitol a month later. The debate over Missouri continues unabated, while outside. . . .

The little column had been assembled less than an hour before, yet already it moved as a unit, bare feet raising small clouds of dust in the dry dirt road. It was only March, but no wind cooled the path, and the sun made it feel more like May. No one wasted energy in conversation; the only sound came from the *chinking* of the chains that bound them together. Actually, only the six males at the head of the column, or coffle as it was called, were chained, shackled to each other by the neck and wrist. The four females behind them, scantily clad, were joined by rope halters around their necks, and the four children, last in line, were not tethered at all, but followed under the watchful eye of the black driver. Like the blacks he herded, he walked, but his feet had shoes on them, and he carried a long switch with which he encouraged any who lagged or faltered. In back of them all, on a horse, came the white trader, a brace of pistols protruding from his belt and a loosely coiled blacksnake whip in his right hand.

Forward progress was slow, barely fast enough to avoid exasperating the driver, and they moved as one, accommodating one another as if they had been bound forever, instead of at the auction block, two miles away. The leader, tall and muscular, had been part of an illegal shipment of slaves smuggled ashore north of Norfolk. He managed to survive the voyage and learned quickly, keeping his thoughts and emotions to himself. The two men behind him were brothers, born and raised on a tobacco plantation outside Roanoke, which had fallen on hard times. Their master had wept at having been forced to sell them to a passing trader, and they had wept, too, for they left behind the only family and friends that they had ever known.

Next in the coffle line came a sullen hard case whose missing ear indicated theft or striking an overseer—probably the latter, judging from the striped scars on his back. There was no hiding such evidence; the trader would be fortunate to get $300 for him, come Missouri. But he could sell him, to one of the new, ruthless plantations that specialized in subduing rebellious and even criminal slaves. The next man in line was also likely to wind up on one of these: a troublemaker of a different sort, he had once been taught to read and write by some misguided white woman and now could not be trusted near a newspaper—or pen and ink, for that matter. His previous owner suspected him of having forged manumission papers for two other slaves who had suddenly disappeared.

The last man and first woman in the coffle were husband and wife, from Alexandria. "House niggers," they were trained in serving at table and running a home and a kitchen. They hoped to be sold as a pair and to be allowed to keep their son and daughter, who walked among the children at the back of the line; indeed, the man who had sold them to the trader had elicited a promise from him to make every effort to sell them as a family unit. But from what they observed of the trader since leaving Alexandria, only the mercy of God would enable them to stay together. For the trader would say anything that slave owners wanted to hear, to ease their consciences, and then would mock them out loud, as soon as the coffle had moved out of earshot. The other three women in line were still young enough for field work and broad enough in the hips to make good "breeders," an important feature on a new plantation, which would need all the new help it could get. The other two children belonged to them and would probably stay with them, until they were ten and old enough to do a half day's work.

On they trudged, while up ahead on the left, atop the last hill before the Potomac, loomed the magnificent white marble Capitol building—many times larger than any building they had ever seen, with endless long white steps, like a waterfall of marble. In a minute they would pass close by it, and the trader, wanting his wares to make a good impression, muttered something to the driver, who hollered at the slaves to start singing. When they did not respond, the driver began laying on the switch. They began to sing, and while they had not been on the same plantation, the spiritual they sang was known to them all, and they sang it to the tempo of their hobbled gait. Their words may have been unintelligible, but the sense of the spiritual was heart-searingly articulate. It spoke of families suddenly, capriciously torn apart, of loved ones tortured and beaten, of men degraded and forced to grovel, of women used for the gratification of lust and turned into breeding livestock. It told of a life in which there existed no justice, no recourse, not even hope—a life from which death was a welcome release, because at last they could go home to be with their Lord, the only One whose love they could trust.

As they drew near the gleaming terraces and steps, their eyes fastened on the dusty heels in front of them. They did not notice the Congressmen in their brocaded waistcoats, out taking the air during a brief recess in their proceedings, or the elegant ladies of fashion who had packed the visitors' gallery. But they, in turn, were noticed by those above them on the steps and terraces; they could hardly not be, as their mournful singing filled the morning air. All conversation died away; here before them, almost as if by plan, was an example of the very subject which they had been debating so heatedly in the House of Representatives, just a few minutes before.

On the steps of the Capitol, ladies averted their eyes, scandalized at the sight of the black women who made little effort to properly cover themselves, while some of the men chuckled and made low observations among themselves. Other men also turned away and took a bit of snuff to soothe their offended sensibilities. A few men stood and watched the sad procession file past; they said nothing, but the knotted muscles of their jaws indicated that the scene was being etched indelibly into their memories.

The sergeant-at-arms came out and with a hand bell summoned the Congressmen back inside, where they resumed their seats. High above their heads, the visitors' gallery was crowded with the flower of Washington society; indeed, so many women had driven in by carriage from several miles around that the Vice-president, in a gallant gesture, invited some of the ladies to come down and occupy those seats on the main floor normally reserved for foreign dignitaries. Their presence gave the ongoing debate an almost festive air and inspired the masters of oratory to new flights of grandiloquence. For in addition to the ladies, journalists from most of the prominent papers of the day were present, as the Missouri question was more hotly contested than any issue which had come before that body in the nearly thirty-three years of its existence.

The population in the Missouri Territory, the first to apply for statehood in the huge trans-Mississippi tract, had trebled in the previous three years, and since the majority of its settlers were slaveholders, their application contained no clause restricting slavery. But slavery had grown increasingly unpopular up north, and one by one the northern states had passed ordinances banning it. The constitutions of the most recent additions to statehood, Illinois and Indiana, specifically forbade slavery. In fact, many families from back east were moving there, rather than further south, so that their children would not have to grow up in a state that practiced slavery. The Puritan legacy that had permeated New England to its core and traveled west with its migrating farmers held that man was put on earth to obey God, not to please himself. Part of obeying God meant heeding His commandment to love one's neighbor as oneself, regardless of his neighbor's color. To be sure, their faith often did not live up to the old Puritan code, and they honored that commandment as much in the breach as in the observance. Yet it remained God's Word, as many practicing Christians, whose hearts were open to the conviction of the Holy Spirit, could also attest. Moreover, as we have seen, another part of the Puritan legacy put a high value on hard work; they and their descendents believed the Lord meant what He said, when He instructed His disciples: "the labourer is worthy of his hire" (Luke 10:7).

Some modern historians note that these same Puritans and their descendents had legalized slavery in New England before Virginia did, and that more than a few seventeenth-century Yankees held slaves themselves. According to them, the severity of the northern winters, to which blacks from tropical Africa had difficulty adjusting and the comparative smallness of the northern farms, which grew produce only for regional consumption, mainly caused the decline of slavery in the North. But the evidence of countless Yankee sermons and letters indicates that Christian tradition in the North had long been opposed to slavery.

The Methodists nearly abolished slavery permanently in their denomination. The Presbyterians made a strong statement against slavery in their General Assembly of 1818. All evangelical denominations uniformly and vehemently spoke against it, and of them all, perhaps the most effective at reaching influential moderates were the Quakers. This group, which had once horrified the Puritans with its radical extremes, had settled into a quiet faith, until now, in their humility and selflessness, many of them reflected a spirit reminiscent of the original Pilgrims. From the first antislavery preaching of John Woolman half a century before, it was these souls, patiently practicing their art of "gentle persuasion," who were most responsible for the coalescing of antislavery opinion—as much by their personal example as by what they had to say.

In truth, it was impossible for any Christians not already imbued in slavery to think of slaves as somehow subhuman or "property," as a farmer might regard his cows or pigs. Loving one's neighbor meant loving him whether or not he knew God, and part of that love meant giving him the opportunity to receive the Light of Christ into his own life. And as we have seen, part of the fruit of the Second Great Awakening was the explosive formation of the first great missionary societies, which dispatched eager young Light bearers to all corners of the globe, including the Slave Coast of Africa. And once you had learned enough of a man's language to communicate the Good News of Jesus Christ, once you had seen the joyous light of realization break across his face as he comprehended the promise of the Cross and the Resurrection and gave his life to His Saviour, it was inconceivable to ever think of that person as not quite human. No, any man who could confess his sin and be forgiven became not only a neighbor but a brother in the Lord, regardless of the pigmentation of his skin or his lack of formal education. So there had long existed in the North a strong and widespread, albeit largely quiescent, loathing of slavery and a growing determination to limit its spread.

When Missouri applied for statehood with no restriction as to slavery, northern opposition began to come together. For the would-be state's northern border, defined by latitude 40° 35′, would legalize slavery as far north as Springfield or Indianapolis, Columbus or Pittsburgh. That prospect aroused all the varied antislavery forces, weak and disorganized as they were, and on February 13, 1819, the gauntlet was thrown down by James Tallmadge, Jr., of New York, who proposed the following amendment to Missouri's application:

> That the further introduction of slavery or involuntary servitude be prohibited, except for the punishment of crimes whereof the party shall have been duly convicted; and that the children of slaves, born within [Missouri] after admission thereof into the Union, shall be free, but may be held to service until the age of twenty-five years.[5]

It was a relatively mild proposal, considering that it did not demand the manumission of slaves already in the Missouri Territory and allowed slave owners to keep children of slaves for the duration of their prime hard-labor years, generally reckoned to be eighteen to twenty-five. But the slaveholding states wanted no part of it, for to accede to it meant acknowledging that Congress had the right to determine the slave or free status of all future states—a precedent that would only encourage the nascent abolitionists. Moreover, the South, ever resentful at having had to relinquish so many of its sovereign states' rights, already felt apprehensive that the North would soon attempt to dictate its very life-style. The House was lost, and the Supreme Court was totally under the sway of a unabashed Federalist.

Only in the Senate had they preserved the balance between slave and free states—eleven to eleven. Yet that was enough: no legislation could be passed into law if it could not get through the Senate. In the previous three years, four territories had received statehood—Indiana and Illinois, free, and Mississippi and Alabama, slave. The subject of slavery had not been openly raised, as both sides had assumed that the territories would naturally follow the inclinations of their settlers. Northern farmers had migrated west into the northern territories; southern cotton growers had flowed into the Gulf Coast territories. Missouri was the first territory to attract settlers from both the North and the South, and now it put the Senate's fragile parity in jeopardy.

Moderates on both sides might have wished Tallmadge had not made his proposal and had given slavery a chance to die out of its own accord, as it already had in every other Christian nation on earth. It had no place in an enlightened, progressive society and would surely be done away with here, as soon as a feasible and equitable means of doing so could be found. No less than the leading southern thinker, Thomas Jefferson, had penned the words, "We hold these truths to be self-evident: that all men are created equal, that they are endowed by their Creator with certain inalienable rights, that among these are Life, Liberty, and the pursuit of Happiness" for the Declaration of Independence. Well aware of the disparity between their noble intent and the realities of slavery, to his fellow slaveholders, Jefferson warned: The Almighty has no attribute which can take side with us in such a contest."[6] But a card laid was a card played, and once that Pandora's box was opened, could never again be closeed. From now on, slavery would be the ultimate ground on which practically every battle in the House and Senate would be fought.

For now, the barrages remained oratorical, and as in so many things, it appeared that the South had all the heavy artillery—Calhoun, Randolph, Pinckney, Cobb, the roster went on and on—and if it were up to the gallery to decide, the South would have won every exchange, hands down. John Scott, for instance, speaking on behalf of his fellow slaveholding settlers in Missouri, declared that they "knew their own rights" and that the "spirit of freedom burned in the bosoms of the freemen of Missouri, and if admitted into the national family, they would be equal [with those allowed to hold slaves elsewhere] or not come at all!"[7]

Speaker of the House Henry Clay had then called a recess, to let things cool down a bit, and Congressmen and observers had gone out on the terraces of the Capitol, into the warm March air—and watched the coffle pass by and heard its mournful song. Yet as the 185 members of the Fifteenth Congress returned to their seats, the atmosphere seemed no less electric than when they had adjourned. No sooner had Clay reopened the House than Thomas Cobb of Georgia was on his feet. If the restrictionists persisted, he exclaimed, the Union would indeed be dissolved. Then, pointing at Tallmadge, he accused him of having "kindled a fire which all the waters of the ocean cannot put out, which seas of blood can only extinguish!"[8]

As Clay gaveled for order, Tallmadge jumped to his feet. "If blood is necessary to extinguish any fire I have assisted to kindle, I assure you, gentlemen, while I regret the necessity, I shall not forbear to contribute my mite!" Pausing to get his emotions under control, he went on to declare that, if slavery extended over the West, "you prepare its dissolution. You turn its accumulated strength into positive weakness, you cherish a canker in your breast . . . you place a vulture on your heart." He looked up at the gallery. "Nay, you whet the dagger and place it in the hands of a portion of your population stimulated to use it by every tie, human and divine."

There was absolute silence in the House now, for Tallmadge had touched the deepest fear in slaveholders' hearts: the possibility of an armed uprising among the blacks. He pointed to the tall windows through which the afternoon sun streamed and recalled the scene they had all witnessed, a few minutes before: "A slave driver, a trafficker in human flesh, as if sent by Providence, has passed the door of your Capitol, on his way to the West, driving before him about fifteen of these wretched victims of his power. The males, who might raise the arm of vengeance and retaliate for their wrongs, were handcuffed and chained to each other, while the females and children were marched in the rear, under the guidance of the driver's whip." He fixed the Speaker with his gaze. "Yes, sir, such has been the scene witnessed from the windows of Congress Hall, and viewed by members who compose the legislative councils of Republican America!"[9]

There were more exchanges of similar nature, and when at last the batteries fell silent, Selma Hale of New Hampshire put into words the sense of loss that moderates of all persuasions felt, when he wrote: "It was a painful scene, and I hope a similar discussion will never again take place in our walls."[10] His hopes were in vain. The debate had only begun, and it grew progressively more acrimonious, until phrases like "the dissolution of the Union" and "bloody civil war" scarcely raised an eyebrow. Hearts hardened, and so did positions. But mercifully, summer recess intervened, and everyone went home and became preoccupied with getting re-elected in the fall. They were no closer to a solution than when Tallmadge first proposed his amendment, but at least they had a summer and fall for their passions to cool off.

With Congress adjourned, it seems an appropriate moment to take a brief look at how it all happened. . . .

In 1619, the settlement at Jamestown, once abandoned and still ravaged by fever and periodic Indian uprisings, remained the seat of government in the Virginia colony. Early one morning, a trading ship loomed out of the mist that blanketed the James River and brought everybody running, for there might be extra food on board. But this one was unexpected; moreover she was not British. By her lines, she was a Dutch merchantman, yet the swarthy, bearded captain who strode down her gangplank was not Dutch, nor was his accent as he asked in broken English for the head man.

Quickly they summoned Governor John Rolfe. According to the captain, who gave his name as Jope, they had been blown far north of their projected landfall in the West Indies, and after a prolonged bout with heavy weather, they were desperately short of provisions. Could the governor possibly spare then some corn and flour and a keg or two of beer? They had no money, but they did have a valuable cargo, which they were willing to exchange for victuals. Rolfe, highly suspicious of their story, nonetheless granted their request, and the first black slaves, twenty of them, set foot on the shores of North America. The trade completed, the mystery ship cast off and disappeared into the morning mist, never to be seen or heard of again. In all probability, she was manned by pirates, who had stolen their cargo off of a Spanish ship, since the Africans had been given Spanish names—Isabella, Antony, Pedro. Obviously, they could not take their cargo to the Spanish-controlled Caribbean, where they would be instantly hanged as pirates, so they thought up the ruse to try on the obscure English colony on the coast to the north, and it had worked.[11]

At first, some of the slaves were treated as indentured servants and given written contracts that guaranteed them their freedom after four or five years' labor, the same as voluntary white workers from England. The crop they worked with was tobacco, a weed that did not require particular skill to grow, but did require constant attention. This the Africans were able to give it, and they fared far better in the steamy, near-tropical summers than did the whites. Even so, the colonists of Jamestown were reluctant to add to their number; by 1650, only 300 blacks lived in Virginia.[12]

But the popularity of tobacco in Europe continued to grow, and soon Virginia farmers found it six times more profitable to grow tobacco than any other crop. Consequently they planted tobacco on every square foot of cleared ground; at one point even the streets of Jamestown were plowed up and planted.[13] The trouble was, the "sot weed" soon leeched the nutrients out of even the exceptionally rich soil of Virginia and left it exhausted and worthless for any other crop. This meant they constantly needed to clear new land for more tobacco, and now the demand for labor soared. Enough unemployed workers in England existed to fill the requirements, but obviously, if any such workers could scrape together enough money for passage over, they preferred to buy their own land rather than work for wages on someone else's. If they had no money, they obviously could not afford passage, let alone the supplies they would need for the first growing season. So a system of indenture was worked out, whereby the laborer's way over was prepaid by the planter, in exchange for four or five years' work. The only trouble was, a planter kept having to replace his work force with raw newcomers untrained and unacclimated to the debilitating mid-summer humidity. A much better investment was illiterate black laborers—especially when they could stretch the terms of their indenture. Before long, phrases like "servants for life" and "perpetual servants" began to appear in their contracts, and in 1661, Virginia officially recognized the institution of slavery. Less than a century later, there were 120,000 blacks in the colony, to 173,000 whites.[14]

The extremely lucrative slave trade fueled this phenomenal growth. The slaving had been begun by the Spanish, who were the first to start plantation farming when they introduced a luxury commodity, sugar, to the West Indies. By the dawn of the seventeenth century, the production of raw sugar had become the largest industry in the world, requiring vast armies of captured blacks taken from the coastal tribes of West Africa. Soon the English were colonizing the British West Indies and developing sugar plantations of their own—and supplying them with slaves. Ever an industrious, seafaring mercantile nation, Britain shifted her slave trade into high gear with the formation of the British

Royal African Company, which dominated the market for half a century and viewed the English colonies as a logical market for its wares.[15] But slavery proved so immensely profitable—many investors doubled their money, after sharing with the captain and his crew—that they could not keep the Yankee traders out. As Congressman John Brown of Providence had exclaimed as early as 1800: "We want money, we want a navy; we ought, therefore, to use the means to obtain it. . . . Why should we see Great Britain getting all the slave trade to themselves?"[16] So the sons of New Bedford and Boston and New Haven Puritans entered the slave trade, and if there were any ruffled consciences, they were soon allayed by profits that saw their cargo often worth more than the ship itself!

The Yankee slave traders' role became more prominent with the establishment of the legendary "triangular trade." The Slave Coast of Africa, as it came to be known, was soon controlled by black tribes who specialized in raiding other tribal villages inland, rounding up their inhabitants and marching them to the sea, where they kept them in pens, to facilitate rapid loading. Sometimes the captured tribes were betrayed by their own chiefs; sometimes they were simply overwhelmed in surprise attacks. Either way, the whites purchased them with rum, which the slave traders found had a much higher value than the dry goods or glass beads they originally offered. With the slaves packed aboard in the space previously occupied by casks of rum, they set sail for the West Indies on the dread six to ten week "middle passage." There they sold the bulk of their slaves, took on a cargo of molasses, and headed for North America. On the southern coast, they sold the remainder of their slaves for pure profit and made their way to New England, where they exchanged the molasses for its end product—more rum, with which they returned to Africa.[17] Fortunes were made almost overnight as ships were now built specifically for the slave trade, with decks having no more than eighteen inches between them, so that the slaves were forced to lie flat, side by side, manacled to one another for the entire voyage, in "not so much room as a man had in his coffin, either in length or breadth," as one captain reported.[18]

In the annals of history, other than instances of deliberate torture, one cannot find a more shocking example of man's inhumanity to man. Not only were the slaves unable to change position, even for the most rudimentary acts of nature, during a storm seamen covered all gratings and battened down all hatches, with the result that the vast hold with its cargo of more than three hundred natives in their narrow decks became airtight. Within minutes the temperature would rise well above 100°, and the air grew progressively fouler as slaves became sick and began to die. The stench became overpowering, as fever and the "bloody flux" raged through the ship. Soon the decks were slippery with mucus and excrement—and blood, for during the unbroken ordeal, "the sense of misery and suffocation was so terrible in the 'tween-decks," reported one observer, "that the slaves not infrequently would go mad before dying or suffocating. In their frenzy some killed others in the hope of procuring more room to breathe. Men strangled those next to them, and women drove nails into each other's brains."[19]

If a black tore himself free, he desperately strove to throw himself overboard, preferring the sharks that followed the slavers to another moment of the hell between decks. But the captains strung nets around their ships to keep from losing any valuable cargo. Even so, the death rate on such crossings was 50 percent or greater—and *still* the trade was so profitable that each captain tried to cram even more slaves on board on his next voyage. The hell continued as children fell into the tubs of offal and suffocated, and "the shrieks of the women and the groans of the dying, rendered the whole scene of horror almost inconceivable."[20]

Gradually, slavery began to spread throughout the South, wherever field hands were needed—in the rice swamps of Georgia, growing hemp in the Carolinas, indigo along the coast, cotton on Sea Island. Today, in this age of ubiquitous air-conditioning, without which many a southern metropolis would become an instant ghost city, it is hard to imagine what hard labor in tedious heat, twenty degrees hotter than in the North,[21] would be like. To work hard in such humidity, bent over under the unrelenting sun hour after hour without respite. . . . Although the captured blacks had no more desire to work under such conditions than whites did, they *were* more acclimated to them.[22] Therein lay one of the great temptations to utilize slave labor.

After one's initial investment, slave labor was free—and with a good slave and a cash crop, the slaveholder was likely to earn back his initial investment in three years' time. Moreover, the Royal African Company worked hard to create a market for its slaves in the American colonies and especially in South Carolina, where four of its directors were proprietors of the colony. In 1663, they began offering potential settlers twenty acres of land free for each male slave they brought into the colony, and ten acres for each female. As a result, a century later the black population in South Carolina reached 90,000, to 40,000 whites. All told, when the figures of the first national census (taken in 1790 to establish representation in Congress) were tabulated, the five South Atlantic states (Maryland, Virginia, the Carolinas, and Georgia) had a black population of 641,700, with Virginia having the greatest number: 304,000, to 443,000 whites.[23]

Despite these figures, it appeared to most thinking men, as it had to the framers of the Constitution, that slavery was on its way out and would soon end. In more and more instances, it was proving economically infeasible, and distaste for it was as strong in most of the South as it was in the North. Indeed, some areas of the South eschewed it entirely; in the Piedmont regions of North Carolina, English, Germans, and Scotch-Irish Presbyterians preferred to do their own farming, and the Moravians spoke out against slavery. For that matter, the majority of the antislavery societies existed *below* the Mason-Dixon line (although there were comparatively few in the Deep South).

In 1793, a single event reversed that trend. A merchantman with a cargo of New England manufactured goods—nails, tools, shoes, barrels, plows—embarked from the port of New Haven and set sail for the southernmost state of the newly founded Union. Standing at the rail was the sprightly widow of General Nathanael Greene, the Revolutionary War hero who didn't know the meaning of the word *concede.* "We fight, get beat, and rise and fight again!" he had once exclaimed, as he harassed, disrupted and finally stymied the British campaign in the South. Out of gratitude the Commonwealth of Georgia had presented him with a rice plantation, and his widow, who had named it "Mulberry Grove," possessed the same spirit. She made it her home after his death, and now in the late fall of 1792, as the first frost was beginning to appear in the field, she was returning to its warmer climes for the winter. Gifted with an inquiring mind, Catherine Littleton Greene enjoyed meeting people, and while she had scandalized some of her friends up north, in Savannah she had earned a reputation as one of the South's most gracious hostesses.

Naturally and perhaps inevitably she struck up a conversation with the young man who stood beside her at the rail. She learned that he had just graduated from Yale College, and while he had once earned his living as a mechanic, now that he had completed his formal education he looked forward to filling the position of tutor to the children of one of Savannah's prominent families. As the ship plied its leisurely way south, their acquaintance grew into friendship; thus when they arrived and Eli Whitney discovered that his tutoring position had already been filled, Catherine Greene offered him the hospitality of Mulberry Grove, until something should turn up.

But nothing did turn up, and as the days turned into weeks with no way of his earning return passage, Whitney grew increasingly frustrated. The Greene children already had a tutor, Phineas Miller, who made no secret of his desire for a closer relationship with the children's mother—which was not surprising, since the widow Greene was comely enough to attract the attentions of several cotton-growing bachelors from upriver. These gentlemen were frequent visitors at Mulberry Grove, and during the course of an evening were given to discussing crops and season, produce and prices—and the problems they had with the short-staple, upland cotton. If only someone would invent a way of ginning it—of mechanically separating the lint from the seeds. . . .

Miller, familiar with Whitney's tinkering ability, urged him to have a try at it, and when the latter despaired of being able to afford even the rudimentary tools and equipment necessary to begin, Miller offered to go into partnership with him and take care of all his expenses from the money he had saved tutoring. Whitney agreed, and in early 1793 he developed his first working model of a gin. His solution was ingenious: a cylinder, bristling with fine wire spikes like the back of a porcupine and turned by a hand crank. The spikes reached down through the metal slots and into the raw cotton underneath. As the cylinder turned, the spikes brought up cotton lint, while the seeds, too thick to pass through the narrow slots, were prevented from following. Simultaneously, another turning cylinder, mounted with brushes, removed the lint that the tips of the spikes brought up.[24]

It was so simple, it seemed surprising that no one had thought of it before. Yet one wonders how long it might have gone uninvented had Whitney not been stranded at Mulberry Grove. . . . Long enough for slavery to have died out? Probably not, for in the Deep South, slavery had become more entrenched than casual observers of the day (or many historians of today) realized. In the last analysis, slavery's deepest hook was not acclimatic or economic; it was psychological. Slaveholding had a narcotic effect—its subtle but powerful addiction attacked the soul in unsuspected ways. Had the demand for slaves continued to diminish at the pre-gin rate, it is entirely possible that Maryland, Virginia and North Carolina might have eventually banished it, as their northern neighbors had. Without them, the proslavery forces would have been vastly diminished, when the volleys finally turned from words to lead.

No one questions Eli Whitney's genius—that of a man years ahead of his time—so the question of the timing of the gin remains moot. Was God's hand in the series of coincidences that wound up with him nearly a thousand miles south of his home, being given the challenge, the time, and the wherewithal to invent the gin? In light of the immediate result, one's first response would be an emphatic negative: overnight cotton became the South's number-one cash crop, surpassing even tobacco. Coincidentally, England, having just undergone an industrial revolution, had huge mills that could now process all the raw cotton the South could send her—and pay top dollar for it. Cotton needed two things: warmth and rich soil, and the richest soil in America lay waiting along the Gulf Coast. Cotton fever and land fever combined to produce a westward migration that equaled the North's, for a handful of alluvial delta soil felt black and moist, compared to the thin dusty stuff that covered New England's rocks. A New England farmer could grow enough food for himself and his neighbors, but that was about it.

But down South, they planted for the whole world. The only trouble was, that the other producers of cotton (India), sugar (the West Indies and Central America), tobacco (Cuba and Turkey), rice (southeast Asia), and hemp (China and Chile) were bare subsistence areas themselves. Their labor cost so little that the slave system alone could compete with it. One of the greatest ironies in American history is that as a result of a Yankee intervention, in less than a generation, the question of containing slavery, let alone abolishing it, became academic. And this was true of the upper South, as well. For Virginia, her soil leeched out by tobacco and too cold for cotton, had found a new, more lucrative cash crop: she began exporting slaves south and intensively breeding them to replenish the dwindling supply. This effort was redoubled in 1807, when the importing of slaves was finally abolished.

But while Congress may have outlawed the external slave trade, that hardly put a stop to it; with the price of a male slave in his prime having trebled, smuggling was worth the risk, and slavers who managed to slip past the American and British navies produced immense profits. But the captains of the slavers were hunted down like pirates, and as a result, they now doffed like an unwanted cloak any vestige of humanity that might have lingered with them. With an American or British frigate in pursuit, the only chance of escape was to lighten ship, and the quickest way to do that was simply to hurl the cargo overboard *en masse,* which generally created a feeding frenzy among the following sharks.

But—what if Whitney had not invented the cotton gin until, say, after the War of 1812? For one thing, the South would have felt considerably less pressure to bring Florida into the Union—or Texas, either, for that matter. And without the land and cotton booms that drew southern Americans west like a magnet, the national will might not have been concerted enough to deny the British New Orleans—or the Mississippi, for that matter. Without the sudden accelerated, post-gin development of the Deep South, it seems quite likely that the geographical boundaries of America might have been radically different from those we know.

The slave population of the South continued to grow, until by the time of the Missouri debates, the number of blacks in the South had risen to above 1.5 million, which meant that there was now one black for every two southern whites. With the exception of Maryland and North Carolina, the South had become dependent upon slavery for its economic viability; in short, while everyone still paid lip service to the fact that it was a deplorable evil, it had become a very necessary one. Which was why the South was profoundly shaken and responded with so much passion when, for the first time in the halls of Congress, others proposed that such an evil should not be allowed to expand.

America, following the ongoing debate in its newspapers and periodicals, was taken aback at the vehemence and deep emotions that had surfaced over the question of slavery—and alarmed to see just how deep a rift had grown between North and South and apparently had existed for some time. Sun, soil, and slavery do not go far enough to explain the division. As we have seen, the North's agriculturally unconducive climate played a key role in turning its inhabitants to trades, to shipping, and ultimately to manufacturing, for factories could work the year around, as long as the rivers didn't freeze so tight that the water ceased flowing through the mill races. Because of this orientation toward shops and artisanship and shipyards and industry, the northern tradition of urbanization continued and intensified—while further ruralization took place in the South. With ever larger plantations being formed, the white population became increasingly scattered to the point where, given the abysmal status of both roads and mails, nine out of ten southerners lived in almost total isolation.[25] In fact, other than church, the only social activities that brought people together were weddings, funerals, court proceedings, and "court days," in which they would journey to the county seat to hear candidates for election expound their views.

An additional explanation for the South's ruralism tends to get overlooked. For the North's townward orientation derived not just from its industrialization but also from its Puritan covenant legacy, and since the evangelical churches of the North were also the established churches, the dynamic energies of the newly regenerate were regularly funneled into all the areas of social concern embraced by the Church and endorsed by the establishment. In short, they *were* their brother's keepers, and each covenanted church functioned as a spiritual family, with the individuals truly caring for one another, to the point where they willingly became involved in one another's lives. In the North, as we have seen, this resulted in numerous movements for social reform.

In the South, the old-line establishment churches wanted nothing to do with revivals, camp meetings, or emotional "born again" experiences, so the New Wine went into new wineskins—dissenter churches, made up mainly of Baptists and Methodists. And these new Christians, having been forced to dissent from society in order to find Christ, were hardly in a position to reform it.

They continued to live and work apart, and what fellowship they did have they shared with their fellow dissenters. Christianity among these individuals was predominantly personal as they sought to amend their ways by foreswearing the personal sins that obviously alienated them from God—drinking, gambling, swearing, lusting, dueling, and so on. Many treated their slaves far differently, and some, under the powerful conviction of the Holy Spirit, freed them. But despite the early prevalence of polite antislavery societies, southern evangelicals never experienced a collective impulse to abolish slavery.

Slavery—why is it so necessary that we look the horror of it squarely in the eye? Because every concerned American should have an intimate knowledge of the evil that came so close to permanently wrecking this country. We need to understand the dark things in Americans—in *all* Americans, northern and southern, evangelical or otherwise—that allowed it to happen in a civilized, Christian nation so proud of its ideals. Because those same things reside within us today and a personal relationship with Christ is no guarantee of immunity. There were more than enough committed Christians on both sides of the Mason-Dixon line to have put a stop to slavery.

We have seen how slavery got started and what sustained it. We have recoiled at the horrors committed by the slave traders. We must now look at slavery as it *was* and what it did to human beings who, because they committed the sin of being born with black skins, were sentenced to life imprisonment at hard labor, sometimes under unbelievably sadistic wardens. We also need to see what slavery did to the whites who practiced it—in many ways an even more tragic history.

That is why we must look into the very heart of darkness, for in our fallen nature and our penchant for soothing self-deception, we have it within us to allow such things to happen again. If we forget that as a Christian people we were capable of cruelty to slaves so monstrous that it rivals in infamy the treatment of the Jews in the concentration camps, then we put ourselves in the same jeopardy as other peoples who have chosen to forget the dark chapters of their past—and are condemned to repeat them.

11

"A Fire Bell in the Night"

The black whip whistled through the air and slashed the naked back with such force that it sent out a spray of blood. The victim's body arched taut, her wrists straining at the thongs that bound her to the post. But not a sound passed her lips. Furious, her mistress, standing beside the overseer, whispered for him to make her beg for mercy, for by her silence, her personal slave was winning again.

The overseer scarcely bothered to acknowledge the request. She would cry out soon enough; he had seen them try to hold back the screams before. But after four or five of his best strokes, her will would start to crumble, and she would be shrieking for mercy loud enough to be heard halfway across the county. In the meantime, as long as she was determined not to give them the satisfaction of hearing her cry out, he would enjoy the contest. He aimed his second lash lower, where she would not expect it. From long experience he had learned that slaves who had not been whipped before invariably assumed that the lightning would strike in the same place, like spanking a child, and they would steel themselves to receive a second blow directly on top of the first.

So the overseer liked to surprise them. If there were to be more than a dozen or so lashes, he would open fresh wounds wherever possible. Such was his skill that he could not only make the whip either cut or merely raise welts, but he could lay a pattern of a dozen stripes without ever repeating. Between each blow—especially in the beginning, when the game was fresh, before it became tedious—he would pause between strokes, to build the suspense and let the victim have a little extra time to think about the next searing fire and try to anticipate where it would fall. After eight or nine lashes on untouched flesh, the earliest wounds would have begun to calm down and start to close. Suddenly he would return to them and reopen them one by one, and the shock and pain would feel worse than anything which had gone before. Such accuracy took exceptional aim, and the overseer prided himself on that.

After four lashes, the slave girl's body began to tremble, in spite of her iron determination that it should not, and the overseer could see her biting her lip to keep from crying out. It would not be long now. He glanced to his left, at the other slaves who had been assembled to witness this punishment, especially at the girl's brother. Now that was one slave whom he had been looking forward to humbling for a long time. But because he was the brother of the mistress's favorite slave, the overseer had been prohibited from whipping him and had had to endure the boy's silent contempt for many months. But soon his sister would become hysterical, and then the boy would lose control and would try something. The overseer would blow him to kingdom come. He smiled and fingered the butt of the pistol that protruded from his belt. Where aim was concerned, he was as deadly with a pistol or rifle as he was with a whip.

The brother stood still, hands clenched into fists at his side. He knew the overseer's thought, knew he would be dead before he took three steps towards him, let alone got his hands around that throat. Still, it was the hardest thing he ever had to do in his life—not to do anything. So he stood there, shaking with the effort, as the whip fell again and again.

The slave girl proved tougher than the overseer had anticipated. Nine strokes fell before the first involuntary moan escaped her lips. But that sound had the effect of a breach in a tidal dike. Her resolve collapsed, and with it caved in the last vestiges of pride and self-respect. She was screaming now and pleading with her brother to save her. Yet he stood without moving, tears coursing down his own cheeks. The overseer watched him closely now; there was one more thing he could do to get him to break. And aiming carefully, he reopened the lowest slash. At that, her brother screamed louder than she did, and his left foot came forward.

The mistress unwittingly saved them both. Clapping a hand over her mouth in a vain effort to keep from bringing up her breakfast, she waved to the overseer to stop, and turned from them, running toward the mansion.

The incident we have just dramatized is not fiction; it comes from the testimony of a former slave, Austin Stewart,[1] and it is frighteningly similar to hundreds of other recorded accounts. Reading them, one becomes increasingly appalled at the magnitude of this dark specter that had crept across the land. One's horror is amplified by the uniformly straightforward, unadorned, and almost dispassionate quality of these testimonies. The authors (and their publishers) obviously felt that their ordeals spoke for themselves—which they most movingly did. Yet after the fourteenth or twenty-seventh account, one's senses begin to numb; we start to lose the capacity to react with the moral outrage that such atrocities deserve. As with the modern horrors of Auschwitz and Dachau and Treblinka, we acknowledge gruesome reality and know that it is wrong to feel the slightest degree of indifference, but. . . . Confronted with the full enormity of the Holocaust or the torture in Communist prison camps or slavery, it is understandable that our senses would shut down; it is a defense mechanism of the psyche. Yet we should accept the reminders. It happened in America.

The wake-up horn sounded between 3:00 and 4:00 in the morning, depending on the season, to get the slaves into the fields by the first predawn light. Groaning, the six men and four women who occupied cabin 14 rolled off of their straw pallets and groped in the darkness for their field clothes. Several yawned widely, as if somehow that might dispel the bone-deep fatigue that dragged at their bodies. One, on whom the rest depended for his gift of humor, commented, "This old back is *convinced* that it is still yesterday!" They chuckled at the old joke, grateful for anything to laugh at. In the darkness of the cabin, they fumbled with shoes—those who still had them—and the women grabbed up hoecakes they had baked the night before, tied them into bandannas, and filled drinking gourds with water. For whatever they ate that day—and there would be only one meal before finishing their work that night—would be their own responsibility.

The eastern sky already showed streaks of pinks and grays when the last of them ran to the field, frantically tucking in the shirt he had been unable to find. The overseer waited, slapping the butt of his whip in his hand. "Jethro," he said wearily, "You're late again. Step forward." The slave did as he was bidden, and the overseer gave him about a couple dozen lashes—hard enough to make it worth his while not to be late again, but not hard enough so that he could not do a full day's work. As the lash fell, the boy hollered at the top of his lungs, but he and the overseer and the other slaves all knew that he exaggerated. It did not change the degree of punishment, but it made him feel better.

At this same hour, thousands of plantations large and small throughout the Deep South reenacted this scene. On older plantations, their huts were of frame and clapboard, yet had no windows or floors. They measured either eight feet by ten or ten by twelve, with anywhere from seven to twelve people in each and no thought of family relationships or separating people of the opposite sex. The beds were little more than boxes of straw along the walls, and some had not even that. On the newer plantations to the south, thatched palmetto leaves made up the huts, and farther west they were of logs, but the dimensions and the overcrowding remained the same. When it came to letting smoke out, ventilation was almost nonexistent, although come winter, there seemed to be plenty of chinks to let in fresh snow and icy wind.[2]

As for clothing, slaves were annually issued "a pair of tow and linen pants, and two shirts of the same material. For winter, they would receive a pair of shoes, a pair of woolsey pants and a round jacket."[3] An Englishman figured up the cost of this clothing to the planter at one pound, three shillings. Add another seven shillings for a blanket and two caps, and the total cost of outfitting a slave for a year was one pound, ten. Add to that the cost of victualing him with thirteen bushels of cornmeal and a hundred pounds of pork, and the amount the owner spent a year became two pounds, six. This Englishman valued the average slave's labor at around twenty pounds a year (a substantial sum in those days), which meant that the owner recompensed the slave a little over a tenth of what he deserved, had he worked for pay. That, he observed, did not square too well with Jeremiah 22:13 (RSV), "Woe unto him who builds his house by unrighteousness, and his upper rooms by injustice; who makes his neighbor serve him for nothing, and does not give him his wages." And he went on to cite James 5:4 (RSV), "Behold, the wages of the laborers who mowed your fields, which you kept back by fraud, cry out; and the cries of the harvesters have reached the ears of the Lord of Hosts."[4]

As soon as it was light enough to see by, the work began, and with the exception of a fifteen-minute break to eat what they had brought with them, it continued until there was no more light. Then they would bring their baskets of cotton to the gin, where it would be weighed and ginned. Each slave received a quota of how much cotton he or she was to have picked during the day—130 to 150 pounds, no matter how young or how old, how weak or how strong. The overseer set the quotas, and if perchance a new slave brought in ten or fifteen pounds more than his quota, instead of being rewarded for such industry, he might well find his quota revised upward for the following day; for slavery was a system utterly devoid of incentive.

On some of the smaller, older plantations, where the owners were practicing Christians and looked after their slaves with genuine compassion, the slaves responded in kind. But in the vast majority of cases, fear was the only motivation that slaves knew, and their existence became a lifelong contest of wills between master and slave, with the former suspecting the latter of deliberately slowing down, but never quite able to prove it. For that reason, quotas were seldom, if ever, revised lower, and heaven help the slave who did not meet his or hers, for severe floggings were administered on the spot, regardless of the excuse. If a man felt sick, he had better be so obviously sick that he could not stand up, or he would be whipped for malingering.

"No matter how fatigued and weary he may be," reported ex-slave Solomon Northrup, "no matter how much he longs for sleep and rest, a slave never approaches the gin-house with his basket of cotton but with fear. If it falls short in weight . . . he knows that he must suffer. . . . Most frequently they have too little, and therefore are not anxious to leave the field. For after weighing, follow the whippings."[5] Then came chores and the cooking of supper. Each slave received a quart of cornmeal a day and on wealthier plantations, possibly some bacon. What they didn't eat in the evening, they took with them into the fields, for their daytime meal. It wasn't nearly enough food for their massive hard labor, so they would augment it anyway they could—either with fish they had caught on Sundays or rabbit or 'possum they had trapped . . . or with a pig or chicken stolen from the plantation's supply and barbecued in the woods or swamp, where they would not be caught. And after supper, at last they fell into their beds; but even as they dropped off to sleep, fear would haunt them—fear that they would oversleep the following morning, an offense that "would certainly be attended by not less than twenty lashes."[6]

Fatigue and exhaustion were their constant companions, for not even Saturday afternoon and all day Sunday allowed sufficient time to recuperate from the numbing weariness. In fact, the only time they really began to feel good was at the end of the three to five days off they received each Christmas and toward which they looked forward all year long. In the meantime they did everything possible to conserve energy, doing no more than the absolute minimum necessary to fulfill their quotas. They watched the overseer and drivers in the fields, and the moment their backs were turned, would slow almost to a standstill. In the words of Frederick Law Olmstead, the northern architect (he designed Central Park in New York) whose carefully reasoned and dispassionate book *The Cotton Kingdom* had a profound influence on the British attitude toward slavery, "As often as [the overseer] visited one end of the line of operations, the field hands at the other end would discontinue their labor, until he turned to ride towards them again."[7] Slaves soon became adept at avoiding or delaying projects, even to assuming the semblance of simpletons, incapable of comprehending the most basic instructions. Tragically, many did suffer from arrested mental development, due to the severe malnutrition suffered by their mothers.

Their owners called it laziness and stupidity, but in truth it was deliberate—a combination of resistance and survival. Anyone who has not done hard physical labor in ninety degree weather with 80 percent humidity for hours on end with no respite cannot comprehend what field hands were subjected to. The planters themselves were well aware of this; the legislatures of Maryland, Virginia, and Georgia had passed laws limiting the amount of physical labor to be required of prison convicts to no more than ten hours in the summer and eight hours in the winter. By comparison, the slaves were worked fifteen hours in the summer and eight in the winter.[8]

No wonder the average life expectancy for a slave in good health joining a Deep South plantation was drastically foreshortened, particularly in light of the fact that the slaveholders' general policy did not involve conserving the slaves, but burning them out and replacing them. Indeed, under this regimen, they aged so prematurely that any slave who somehow managed to survive to his late forties was invariably called Old Joe or Old Rastus. The Reverend Dr. Reed of London made this report upon returning home: "Recently at a meeting of planters in South Carolina, the question was seriously discussed, whether the slave was more profitable to the owner if well-fed, well-clothed, and worked lightly, or if made the most of at once, and exhausted in some eight years. The decision was in favor of the latter alternative."[9] Reverend John Choules, pastor of a Baptist church in New Bedford, Massachusetts, had the following conversation while attending the Baptist triennial convention of 1835 in Richmond, Virginia. As a delegate from Massachusetts, he was a guest in the home of an officer of the Baptist Church in Richmond.

> I asked my host if he did not apprehend [fear] that the slaves would eventually rise and exterminate their masters.
>
> "Why," said the gentleman, "I used to apprehend such a catastrophe, but God has made a providential opening, a merciful safety valve, and now I do not feel alarmed at the prospect of what is coming."
>
> "What do you mean by Providence opening a merciful safety valve?"
>
> "The slave traders come up from the cotton and sugar plantations of the South, and are willing to buy up more slaves than we can part with. We must keep a stock for the purpose of rearing slaves, but we part with the most valuable, and at the same time the most dangerous. The demand is very constant, and likely to be so, for when they go to the southern states, the average existence is only five years."[10]

One might feel surprised to find such hardened hearts among professing Christians, but the more slave testimonies one reads, the more one finds that the slaves themselves preferred non-Christian masters. The sporting types, given to drinking and gambling, stayed in bed as long as they could in the morning, and when they did get up, they were usually so hung over that they could not focus on anything beyond how awful they felt. But after breakfast, and a couple of pick-me-ups, their mood began to regain its mellowness—which they sought to prolong with juleps for the remainder of the day.

Christians, on the other hand, having foresworn demon rum and the vile sot weed and the dusky pleasures that awaited in the slave quarters, became intent upon reforming their slaves' lives. Some truly did care about their conditions, but for too many others, reforming slaves' lives meant starting with their attitudes, especially when it came to giving an honest day's work (for an honest day's pay?) and respecting the authority that God (?) had placed over them. When this respect was not forthcoming, when in its place there appeared to be silent contempt, when the owner's will was crossed, or he suspected that he was losing a contest of wills, then God or no God, his vindictiveness would know no bounds. Perhaps the fundamental hypocrisy and unreality slavery forced upon all who embraced it caused such an attitude, but darkness appeared increasingly as light, and light, darkness. While a Christian wife in many cases became the one alleviating factor in an unbroken tapestry of plantation misery, not infrequently the wives were even worse than their slaveholder husbands.

Yet a handful of these women had the courage to risk certain ostracism and speak out against slavery and what it did to blacks—and whites. Their testimony stands as an unassailable indictment of the entire system. They did so at great cost, for they were regarded as the worst kind of betrayers, exposing as a cruel and pathetic sham the fragile fantasy ("our way of life") that the South had tacitly agreed to share. Two such witnesses were daughters of a justice of the South Carolina Supreme Court, and as such they were members of the uppermost strata of society in the South's most cosmopolitan city. The following is the written testimony of Angelina Grimké, concerning a Christian acquaintance of hers.

> A woman of the highest respectability—one who was foremost in every benevolent enterprise, and stood for many years at the head of the fashionable elite of the city of Charleston, and afterwards at the head of the moral and religious society there. It was after she had made a profession of religion and retired from the fashionable world that I knew her; therefore, I will present her in her religious character.
>
> This lady used to keep cowhides [whips] or small paddles called "pancake sticks" in four different apartments in her house, so that when she wished to punish, or have punished, any of her slaves, she might not have the trouble of sending for an instrument of torture. For many years, one or other, and often more, of her slaves, were flogged every day, particularly the young slaves about the house, whose faces were slapped or their hands were beaten with the pancake stick for every trifling offense—and often for no fault at all. . . .
>
> After the revival in Charleston in 1825, she opened her house to social prayer-meetings. The room in which they were held in

the evening, and where the voice of prayer was heard around the family altar, and where she herself retired for private devotion thrice each day, was the very place in which, when her slaves were to be whipped with the cowhide, they were taken to receive the infliction. And the wail of the sufferer would be heard, where, perhaps only a few hours previous, rose the voices of prayer and praise. . . .

It was common for her to order brothers to whip their own sisters, and sisters their own brothers, and yet no woman visited among the poor more than she did, or gave more liberally to their wants.[11]

Angelina Grimké's sister Sarah was no less outspoken. Her testimony puts the lie to the belief that Christian/high-born southerners of wealth and tradition treated their slaves more moderately than the frontier plantation *parvenus* who cared only for making the biggest possible profits in the shortest possible time:

A handsome mulatto woman, about eighteen or twenty years of age . . . was in the habit of running away. For this offense she had been repeatedly sent by her master and mistress to be whipped by the keeper of the Charleston work-house. This had been done with such inhuman severity that a finger could not be laid between the cuts . . . a heavy iron collar with three prongs projecting from it, was placed around her neck, and a strong and sound front tooth was extracted, to serve as a mark to describe her, in case of escape . . . These outrages were committed in a family where the mistress daily read the Scriptures, and assembled her children for family worship.[12]

This practice of deliberately mutilating slaves in order to facilitate their recapture and return, was widespread throughout the South. A random sampling of advertisements of the sort that crowded southern newspapers, major and minor, in a typical one-year period, gives ample evidence of the sort of thing that was universally done to potential runaways:

TEN DOLLAR REWARD—Julia, a negress, eighteen or twenty years old. She has lost her upper front teeth, and all her under ones are broken. Said reward will be paid to whoever will bring her to her master at 172 Barracks Street, or lodge her in the jail.—New Orleans *Bee*, May 31, 1837

TWENTY DOLLARS REWARD. Ranaway from the subscriber, a negro woman and two children. The woman is tall and

> black, and a few days before she went off, I burnt her with a hot iron on the left side of her face; I tried to make the letter M. She kept a cloth over her head and face and a fly bonnet on her head, so as to hide the burn. Her children are both boys; the oldest, in his seventh year, is a mulatto and has blue eyes. The woman's name is Betty, commonly called Bet.—Placed by Micajah Ricks, North Carolina *Standard,* July 18, 1838
>
> Ranaway, a negro girl called Mary; has a small scar over her eye, a good many teeth missing, the letter A is branded on her cheek and forehead.—Placed by Mr. J. P. Ashford of the Adams Co. in the Natchez *Courier,* August 24, 1838.[13]

To continue Sarah Grimké's testimony, she tells of being a guest at a plantation in North Carolina. Walking one day, she discovered an old white-haired slave with a gaping, untreated sore in his side, who was dying. He had been left in a windy shack in the middle of winter, with only a few boards for a bed and no one to care for him. When she asked him about this, he said that the other slaves

> "Often steal time to run and see me and fetch me something to eat; if they did not, I might starve." The master and mistress of this man, who had been worn out in their service, were remarkable for their intelligence, and their hospitality knew no bounds towards those who were of their own grade in society. The master had for some time held the highest military office in North Carolina, and not long previous to the time of which I speak, was the Governor of that state.[14]

Was there no legal recourse at all? Did not the states pass such legislation that would ensure at least the minimal humanitarian treatment of slaves, that was accorded to livestock? No, they did not. Animal protection societies had successfully lobbied for legal penalties against those who would mistreat their horses or other domestic animals, but slaves had no one to lobby for them. There were laws against torture and murder, of course, but where slaves were concerned they were unenforceable, because a black man could not give testimony against a white man. In addition, a dual standard in the laws themselves persisted: in South Carolina, for instance, the punishment for killing a slave "in a sudden heat or passion" was a fine of $500 and imprisonment "not to exceed six months"—provided, of course, that some white man could be found to give testimony against the killer. For plain assault and battery, that state's supreme court had given a clear ruling: "There can be no offense against the state for a mere beating of a slave. . . . The peace of the state is not thereby broken, for a slave is not generally regarded as legally capable of being within the peace of the state. He is not a citizen, and he is not in that character entitled to her protection."[15]

The legislature of North Carolina, on the other hand, anxious to demonstrate that it was more civilized than the other Carolina and "perceiving that Christendom would before long rank them with barbarians if they so cheapened human life," passed a law that declared: "he who is guilty of willfully and maliciously killing a slave shall suffer the same punishment as if he had killed a freeman."[16] Lest the reader lend approbation too quickly, however, there was a proviso tacked on to the end of that noble legislation: "Provided, always, this act shall not extend to the person killing a slave outlawed by virtue of any act of Assembly of this state; or to any slave in the act of resistance to his lawful overseer or master, or to any slave dying under their moderate correction."

Closer examination of this proviso reveals the consummate hypocrisy, not only of North Carolina, but of all the slave states. It gave free license to kill: 1. *Outlawed* slaves, which by definition would be any slave who ran away, or hid, or killed one of the master's hogs or chickens to keep from starving; 2. Any slave who *resisted*—by thrusting aside the branding iron, or grabbing the whip that was being used on him, or struggling to keep on his clothes when his master was trying to strip him, or trying to protect his wife or daughter from his master's assaults. In effect, under any such circumstances the proviso authorized the master to kill the slave on the spot. As for a slave dying under "moderate" correction, it is difficult to conceive of any correction as moderate, if it happens to cause the death of the correctee in the process.[17]

With no legal recourse, the only possible safeguard remaining to the slaves was the strength of public opinion, and many southerners did claim that this sufficiently held the more ruthless and sadistic among them in check. In theory, no planter would risk social ostracism by wantonly abusing or flagrantly mistreating his slaves. But in actual practice, as the Grimké sisters have testified, so many of those who influenced social opinion were themselves guilty of, or at the least indifferent to, the most wanton cruelty that they were not about to risk ostracism themselves by condemning the cruelty of their neighbors. Moreover, one doubts that it would even occur to them to do so, as ads for runaway slaves filled southern newspapers every day; if public knowledge of cruelty bore with it social stigma or disapproval, would the owners have so readily advertised their misdeeds? All evidence indicates that public opinion saw what was being done—and remained indifferent to it, regarding it as one of the unpleasant necessities associated with the necessary evil of slavery.

In all this unending agony of suffering and degradation, a slave had two sources of consolation—family and religion. Tragically, the former often hid within its warm folds the most cruel torture of all. No such thing as marriage existed between slaves, for to have granted them civil recognition and a religious ceremony would have been to acknowledge that they were people and not property. Instead, the slave owner simply informed Mattie that Tom was her new "husband," put him in her shack, and let nature take its course, hopefully providing the plantation with valuable progeny, which in a few years could be put to work or sold. Sometimes, as an act of rebellion, Tom and Mattie would refuse to cooperate, and Mattie would go childless. But if no offspring came after a year or two, quite often the owner would present Mattie with a new husband of proven stud capability and threaten her with severe punishment or the prospect of being "sold South," if she didn't start producing children.

In most cases, given no other option, Tom and Mattie did get "married," and if there were no lay preacher among them to say the right words before them, they would symbolically jump over a broomstick. If they had as their master a kind man, happy in his own marriage, he would let them live together in peace, perhaps even providing them with a little cabin of their own as the children started to come. But if he were not a kind man, and Mattie had the curse of beauty, he might at any time "forget" the marital arrangement he had made and take advantage of her—and Tom or anyone else could do nothing to prevent him. But presuming that Mattie was not beautiful, the chances became reasonably good that she and Tom would be allowed to raise a family. Indeed, many of the older plantations encouraged such relationships, because they tended to stabilize the slave population. A boy was not likely to run off and leave his beloved mama, or a man his wife and children. So the family would grow up together and support one another, especially when the going got tough or one of their members fell sick. No matter how bad it got with the overseer, no matter how much he seemed to have it in for you, your family always could comfort you and soothe your wounds.

But that was a lie: there *wasn't* always the family—and therein lay a cruelty that cut deeper than any whip. For a slave was property, without any rights or appeal. If, after a bad night at the card table, the master found himself a few hundred dollars short and for the sake of his honor had to settle up promptly, he might just have to sell that oldest boy, after all, despite the promise that he'd made to the boy's mother. There was nothing that Mattie, or anyone else could do, but grieve. The sadness of such tearing separations (far worse than any torn flesh, for flesh could heal) was made worse by the near certainty that none of the separated members would be able to keep track of one another, let alone ever see each other again. On rare occasion, there would be an exception, as in the case of Maria Perkins, a slave in Charlottesville, who, knowing how to read and write, urgently penned this letter to her husband Richard, who had been previously sold away, to tell him of the sale of their son.[18]

> Dear Husband,
>
> I write you a letter to let you know my distress. My master has sold Albert to a trader on Monday court day, and myself and our [other] child is for sale also. . . . Tell Dr. Hamilton and your master that if either will buy me, they can attend to it now, and I can go afterwards. I don't want a trader to get me. . . . A man by the name of Brady bought Albert and is gone, I don't know where. They say he lives in Scottsville. . . . I am quite heartsick—nothing more—I am and ever will be, your kind wife,
>
> MARIA PERKINS

But in most cases, the parting was as permanent as it was painful. Thomas Jones was a slave on a plantation in Hanover County, North Carolina. At nine years of age, he was sold to a Mr. Jones, of Wilmington, North Carolina, who sent his driver, Abraham, to fetch him.

> I was at home with my mother, when he came. He looked in at the door and called to me: "Tom, you must come with me." His looks were ugly, and his voice savage. I was very much afraid and began to cry, holding on to my mother's clothes and begging

> her to protect me, and not let the man take me away. Mother wept bitterly, and in the midst of her loud sobbings, cried out in broken words, "I can't save you, Tommy! Master has sold you; you must go!"
>
> She threw her arms around me, and while her hot tears fell on my face, she strained me to her heart. There she held me, sobbing and mourning, till the brutal Abraham came in, snatched me away, and hurried me out of the house where I was born.... She followed him, imploring a moment's delay and weeping aloud, to the road, where he turned around and, striking at her with his heavy cowhide, fiercely ordered her to stop bawling and go back to the house.[19]

For a slave family, the auction block signified the very pit of hell. Of the countless horrors that could here be included, one will suffice. What follows is the personal account of Josiah Henson, an escaped slave who became a famous preacher and may have been part of the inspiration for Harriet Beecher Stowe's *Uncle Tom's Cabin.* He was five years old when his master suddenly died, drowning in a stream on his way home from a night's revel. His estate, including his slaves, was to be sold and the proceeds divided among the heirs. (Even if a master had freed his slaves in his will, if his estate had incurred debts that could be satisfied no other way, his will would be set aside and the slaves sold.)[20] The auctioneer set up his stand, and after prospective buyers completed their examination of teeth and muscle, the auction began.

> My brothers and sisters were bid off first, one by one, while my mother, paralyzed by grief, held me by the hand. Her turn came, and she was bought by Isaac Riley of Montgomery County [Maryland]. Then I was offered to the assembled purchasers. My mother, half distracted with the thought of parting forever from all her children, pushed through the crowd while the bidding for me was still going on, to the spot where Riley was standing. She fell at his feet and clung to his knees, entreating him in tones that only a mother could command, to buy her baby as well as herself, and spare her one, at least, of her little ones.... This man disengaged himself from her with such violent blows and kicks, as to reduce her to the necessity of creeping out of his reach.... As she crawled away, I heard her sob out, "Oh, Lord Jesus, how long, how long shall I suffer this way?"[21]

The Lord Jesus was the slaves' other consolation, and this One never let them down. Ever since Christ Himself suffered and died on the Cross for all men, faith in Him has been strengthened rather than weakened by adversity. It seems that the more a believer in Christ is persecuted, the stronger his faith grows, and it should be no surprise that in the previous century some of the strongest faith on earth could be found among the slaves of North America. Meeting in secret arbors in the woods, singing hymns together at a whisper, undergoing fearful retribution when discovered, yet able to forgive their persecutors—there are startling parallels between the black church of the nineteenth century, and the Church behind the Iron Curtain today. Indeed, more martyrs came out of the ranks of American slavery than perhaps from any other group since the early Church. And God only knows the spiritual battleground won and paid for by their blood. For the power of the shed blood of martyrs is a holy mystery, not given to men to fathom. Yet in some way the fact that America today is "one nation under God, indivisible, with liberty and justice for all" could be in no small measure due to the price that they were willing to pay.

Why was the black church so persecuted, when Christianity was so demonstrably a calming, stabilizing influence? One would expect the planters, if anything, to encourage it, out of the same cynical self-interest that motivated the Spanish grandees of the New World to support the work of missionaries on the untamed frontier, where they used to joke that when it came to pacifying the savages one priest was worth a regiment of soldiers. Later, the more enlightened planters did encourage worship among their slaves, even providing them preachers (white preachers who dwelled heavily on the evils of stealing and endlessly on Ephesians 6:5, "Slaves, be obedient to those who are your earthly masters . . . " RSV).

The initial view that Christianity and slavery were incompatible institutions began to change when Christian leaders of the eighteenth century followed George Whitefield's lead and called for a strong missionary effort among the slave population—and among their owners. In 1739, America's first evangelist wrote an open letter to the slaveholders of Maryland, Virginia, the Carolinas, and Georgia:

> As I lately passed through your provinces on my way hither, I was sensibly touched with a fellow-feeling of the miseries of the poor negroes. Sure I am, it is sinful to use them as bad, nay

> worse than if they were brutes [beasts of burden]. And whatever particular exceptions there may be, (as I would charitably hope there are some), I fear that the generality of you who own negroes are liable to such a charge. Not to mention what numbers have been given up to the inhuman usage of cruel taskmasters, who by their unrelenting scourges have ploughed their backs and made long furrows, and at length brought them to the grave! . . . The blood of them, spilt for these many years in your respective provinces, will ascend up to heaven against you![22]

But even then resistance to the introduction of Christianity on either side of the master-slave equation surfaced, and a decade later a Swedish traveler in America, named Peter Kalm, put his finger on why. Speaking of the slave owners, he wrote:

> There are even some who would be very ill-pleased at, and would by all means hinder, their negroes from being instructed in the disciplines of Christianity. To this they are partly led . . . by thinking that they should not be able to keep their negroes so meanly afterwards; and partly through fear of the negroes growing too proud, on seeing themselves upon a level with their masters in religious matters.[23]

The concern that Christianity would promote egalitarianism among the slaves, "making them saucy and giving them ideas that they were as good as white folks," would prevail for more than a century. Back in 1740, Bishop Thomas Secker summed it up when he declared that some planters had been "averse to their slaves becoming Christians, because after that no pretense will remain for not treating them like men."[24]

So the black church was forced to go underground. The slaves developed a code to signal one another when there was to be a secret prayer meeting or worship service. Their overseers liked to hear them singing, for a singing slave was not a brooding slave, and singing, they early recognized, was a harmless safety valve. They would make their slaves sing, but they seldom understood the words—and never guessed that the spiritual "Stealing Away to Jesus" was the signal for a nocturnal gathering.

When the slaves gathered, after they had prayed for the sick and the old and the hurting, invariably their prayers would turn to freedom—and it was a testimony to their faith that they never lost hope that somehow, someday, the Lord *would* deliver them. They identified strongly with the Israelites in Egypt and knew just as surely that they would live to see the day when all slaves would be delivered from bondage.

In the meantime, some managed to escape north and others were manumitted. But as long as the institution itself remained and their skin was black, they were never truly safe. Unscrupulous traders or patrols of white peace keepers took thousands of freed slaves prisoner, and all their subsequent protestations were in vain. "But I've been *freed,* I tell you! When Master Beau died, it said in his will that all his slaves were free. Look, I'll show you: here's the paper that the man from the bank gave to each of us."

"How do I know you didn't write this yourself? You bespeak yourself pretty highfalutin for a nigger. Sure looks like a forgery to me. Clem, you can read, what do you think? Yup, 'spected as much. Well, I reckon we'll just tear up this here forgery, and I don't want to hear any more about it, you hear me, boy?" It was amazing how discerning a white man could be, when a thousand easy dollars were in the offing at the next auction block.

So they prayed for *real* freedom—the kind no one could wrest away from them. For their bondage was intolerable, and nothing less than complete freedom could assuage it. Jacob Stroyer recalled how his father had prayed one evening after Jacob had been beaten: "Lord, hasten the time when these children shall be their own free men and women." Josiah Henson asserted that "from my earliest recollection, freedom had been the object of my ambition, a constant motive to exertion, an ever-present stimulus to gain and save." Lunsford Lane underscored the paradox: "I saw no prospect that my condition would ever be changed. Yet I used to plan in my mind from day to day, and from night to night, how I might be free."[25] Some of the younger ones, like Jermain Longuen, could not muster the faith. "No day dawns for the slave," he acknowledged, "nor is it looked for. It is all night—night forever."[26] But many of the older slaves never ceased to look to Jesus, not only for their deliverance, but for their consolation and comfort and strength—though it sometimes drove their owners into a rage.

Why it affected some owners this way is difficult to say; perhaps they reacted to the convicting power of the Holy Spirit, for ever since Jesus walked by the Sea of Galilee, nonbelievers have been either threatened or drawn by the faith of believers. It could have been fear, for if there *was* a God, and He *was* heeding the prayers of the mistreated who were crying out Him—then what lay in store for their tormentors? It might even have been subconscious jealousy, for the master had assumed the role of absolute deity in the slave's life, decreeing everything that befell him and holding the power of life and death over him. How can that master react, when he discovers that the slave no longer fears him, or even death, for that matter? That he has given his unswerving allegiance to Another, whom he obviously believes is infinitely more worthy?

Regardless of the reasons, slave owners frequently overreacted to the Christianity of their slaves. Thomas Jones did not yet know his Saviour, but ardently sought Him, and prayed to Him often, even though his master "swore terribly at me and said he would whip me, if I did not give over praying. He said there was no heaven and no hell, and that Christians were all hypocrites, and that there was nothing after this life, and that he would not permit me moping around, praying and going to meetings. I told him I could not help praying, and then he cursed me in a great passion and declared he would whip me, if he knew of my going on any more in that foolish way."

There was a meeting the following night, and Thomas Jones went. His master found out and confronted him. "Didn't I tell you, I would whip you if you went nigh these meetings, and didn't I tell you to stop this foolish praying?" Thomas told him that he could not stop praying because he wanted to be good and go to heaven when he died. This reply infuriated his master, who beat him savagely and again forbade him. There was another meeting on Sunday, and again Thomas went. Someone told his master, and now his master was in a rage, stripping and whipping the slave, till his back was torn open in a dozen places and oozing blood. Finally, his owner paused to rest and catch his breath and asked him if now he would mind him and stop praying. "I told him I could not promise him not to pray anymore, for I felt that I must and should pray for as long as I lived. 'Well, then, Tom,' he said, 'I swear that I will whip you to death'. . . . He then began to whip me the second time but soon stopped, threw down the bloody cowhide, and told me . . . if I was determined to be a fool, why, I must be one."

It took a number of days for Thomas's back to heal from this beating, but it did not deter him from continuing his quest for salvation. At his next prayer meeting, he at last came into the born-again experience he had so longed for.

> While Jacob Gammon was praying for me, and for those who knelt by my side, my burden of sorrow which had so long weighed me down, was removed. I felt the glory of God's love warming my heart and making me very happy. I shouted aloud for joy, and tried to tell all my poor slave brothers and sisters who were in the house, what a dear Saviour I had found, and how happy I felt in His precious love. Binney Pennison asked me if I could forgive my master. I told him I could, and did, and that I could pray God to forgive him, too, and make him a good man. He asked me if I could tell my master of the change in my feelings. I told him I should tell him in the morning. "And what," he said, "will you do, if he whips you still for praying and going to meeting?" I said I would ask Jesus to help me to bear the pain, and to forgive my master for being so wicked. He then said, "Well, then, Brother Jones, I believe that you are a Christian."

Thomas Jones was as good as his word and told his master on the following morning. Down came the cowhide from where it hung on the wall, and with a sigh Thomas began to remove his clothing. "You crazy fool!" His master cried, "You keep your clothes on till I tell you to take them off!" And with that he proceeded to whip Thomas over his jacket. Thomas enjoyed such peace of mind in the Lord, that he scarcely felt the cowhide, and that was the last beating he ever received.[27]

Not all the testimonies of slaves being beaten for righteousness' sake have such happy endings. Sarah Grimké recounts this incident, related to her by a close friend whose husband was a plantation owner. On the adjacent plantation:

> There was a slave of pre-eminent piety. . . . A planter was one day dining with the owner of this slave, and in the course of conversation observed that all profession of religion among slaves was mere hypocrisy. His host asserted a contrary opinion, adding, "I have a slave, who I believe would rather die than deny his Saviour."
>
> This was ridiculed, and the master was urged to prove his assertion. He accordingly sent for this man of God, and peremptorily ordered him to deny his belief in the Lord Jesus Christ.

> The slave pleaded to be excused, constantly affirming that he would rather die than deny the Redeemer, whose blood was shed for him.
>
> His master, after vainly trying to induce obedience by threats, had him terribly whipped. The fortitude of the sufferer was not to be shaken; he nobly rejected the offer of exemption from further chastisement at the expense of destroying his soul, and this blessed martyr died in consequence of this severe affliction.[28]

As Lord Acton once observed to his friend Bishop Creighton, "Power tends to corrupt; absolute power corrupts absolutely." It is hard to imagine power more absolute than that which a master wields over a slave. As we have begun to see, the hideous thing about absolute power is that the one possessing it remains unaware of the corrosive effect of it on his soul. The slaveholders whom the Grimké sisters have described would have been shocked at their (and our) reaction to them. For more than a few southern planters, the power they wielded dehumanized them, without their realizing it.

We have seen what it was like on the receiving end of the lash. In many ways, even more tragedy befell the hand that held the whip. For like heroin or alcohol or any highly addictive narcotic, slavery has a way of enslaving those who practice it—to the point where they cannot give it up, even if they want to. In fact, they often have no more desire to, having become totally blind to its evil and what it has done to them. We need to look at what slavery did to the leadership of the South—indeed, what it did to the entire fabric of southern society.

What causes a man to take another man into bondage and keep him there against his will? Greed, basically—the sin in which, of all those in his arsenal, Satan had the greatest confidence. If any corporate sin could divert, deflect, and ultimately disrupt God's plan for America, it would be greed—the polar opposite of the selflessness of His peerless Son. Again and again, it had already worked—distracting Columbus with gold and the promise of money, position, and power; bringing the bloodthirsty conquistadors to the New World; causing the Pilgrims and Puritans to forget their calling. Greed caused George III and his ministers to squeeze his American colonies till they could hardly breathe. And greed had brought on the economic chaos that threatened to bankrupt the embryonic nation. But never had the wedge of greed been driven so close to the heart of America as it was with slavery.

Why work for yourself, when you could force others to work for you? As the Virginia planters who had introduced slavery to America soon came to realize, why pay wages when you can make them work for nothing? Of course, it eased the conscience a bit if one could think of one's slaves as slightly less than human—a trick of the mind that the British, always sticklers for moral principle, mastered for the administration of their West Indian sugar plantations, long before Nietzsche developed his concept of *ubermenschen,* the forerunner of the Nazi's super race. According to this theory, it was the birthright of some to be overlords, and the birthright of others to be their servants. . . .

It may seem strange in this enlightened age, but many American planters actually believed that God put blacks on earth to serve whites, that they were, in fact, descendents of Cain, cursed with his mark in the dark pigmentation of their skin. The slaveholders considered themselves the ruling class, and a number of them trained their children to think this way from the earliest possible age, even to the point of giving them whips and teaching them to beat any slave who gave them the slightest cause for displeasure. One observer, named Hall, noted "a remarkable instance of tyranny, exhibited by a boy not more than eight years old. . . . This youngster would swear at the slaves and exert all the strength he possessed, to flog or beat them with whatever instrument or weapon he could lay hands on, provided they did not obey him instanter. He was encouraged in this by his father, the master of the slaves."[29] Obviously, not all southern children were raised in this fashion; many decent families would have found such behavior repugnant in the extreme. But it was sufficiently prevalent to be noted in a number of different diaries and journals, such as this observation by Lewis Clarke: "I have seen a child, before he could talk a word, have a stick put into his hand, and he was permitted to whip a slave, in order to quiet him. From the time they are born, till they die, they live by whipping and abusing the slave."[30]

A few farsighted leaders could see what slavery was doing to America, and none saw it more clearly than Thomas Jefferson. Indeed, he could hardly avoid its ugly realities, so directly opposite were they to his lofty idealism. They existed at his own beloved Monticello and remained daily before his eyes. There would be the tragic episode of his alcoholic nephew, Liliburne Lewis, who, enraged at a slave boy for dropping a vase, slowly dismembered him with a hatchet.[31] Jefferson loved America and hated the institution that put the lie to the words he had penned into the Declaration of Independence, and to America's boast of holding up the torch of freedom to the rest of the world. "Can the liberties of a nation be thought secure, when we have removed their only firm basis, a conviction in the minds of the people that they are a gift of God? Indeed, I tremble for my countrymen, when I reflect that God is just, that His justice cannot sleep forever."[32]

Even more, he had a keen appreciation of the corrupting effect slavery had on white masters.

> There must doubtless be an unhappy influence on the manners of our people produced by the existence of slavery among us. The whole commerce between master and slave is a perpetual exercise of the most boisterous passions, the most unremitting despotism on the one part, and degrading submission on the other. Our children see this and learn to imitate it. . . . The parent storms, the child looks on, catches the lineaments of wrath, puts on the same airs in the circle of smaller slaves, gives a loose rein to his worst passions, and thus nursed, educated, and daily exercised in tyranny, cannot but be stamped by it with odious peculiarities.[33]

We have seen the wanton cruelty and even sadism that slavery elicits; we have seen normally decent people and even pillars of society fly into rages and exact vengeful punishment. Other writers have dwelt at more than sufficient length on the temptations of lust that unmitigated power gave to the white planters. Travelers and historians have noted the prevalence of mulatto children that seemed to populate every large plantation. On that subject, let the diary of Mary Chesnut, whose United States Senator husband owned one of the largest plantations in South Carolina, have the final word:

> God forgive us, but ours is a monstrous system and wrong and iniquity. . . . Like the patriarchs of old, our men live all in one house with their wives and concubines, and the mulattoes one sees in every family exactly resemble the white children—and every lady tells you who is the father of all the mulatto children in everybody's household, but those in her own she seems to think drop from the clouds."[34]

We have seen the caste system that slavery engendered with even the poor whites, many of them living in conditions as bad or worse than the slaves', nevertheless considering themselves infinitely superior to the latter simply because their skin happened to be white. They might be looked down upon as "poor white trash" by other, better-off whites, but at least they could humiliate or even kick or whip any passing black they chose to.[35]

What we have not yet looked at is the gradual economic and societal regression back to the equivalent of the feudal states of medieval England, such that a true southern gentleman did not work with his hands and despised his northern counterparts for being so commercially oriented. In this, rich men and poor men in the South bonded together: the mark of a man was how well he could ride and shoot and hunt, not how much money he could make. Certainly it was not in how well he could shoe a horse or make a wagon or mend a fence—that was "nigger" work. If a fence did need mending and the man who owned it also owned slaves, he would spend two hours hunting up two slaves and getting them to fix it, rather than taking half that time to do it himself. Slavery robbed white, as well as black, of initiative. As one visitor observed:

> The whites stand with their hands in their pockets, and the blacks are helping them do nothing. Fences are down, doors ajar, filth in the streets, foul odors in the air, confusion and neglect are everywhere. Go into a [planter's] house late at night, and they are all lounging about, too lazy to go to bed. Go in the morning, they are all yawning in bed, too lazy to get up. No one has his prescribed duties—the master scolds and drives, the slave dawdles and shirks."[36]

In the contest of wills between master and slave, the slave actually won many of the battles, if not the war. For unless the task was picking cotton, which would be weighed at the end of the day, the slaves ultimately set the pace for accomplishing a given job, regardless of how much slower their pace might be than their master desired. As a result, masters shared an opinion that became almost universal among slaveholders: slaves were unbelievably lazy and shiftless and so stupid one might rate their intelligence just slightly above that of four-footed livestock. (Ah, but if it were *their* cotton field, and *their* life savings in the land, and *their* mule. . . .) If any master was smart enough to suspect that his slaves were not nearly so stupid as they appeared, and that they were, in fact, adeptly conning their owner, he had no way on earth of proving it. Nevertheless, the slave would indulge in an extremely painful victory, for the realization could drive the master into a white-hot frenzy of retaliation.

Slavery was, in truth, a no-win situation, with both sides locked in, the whites bound as tightly by economic chains, as the blacks were by iron ones. In the Deep South, it was pointless to talk of "gradual emancipation," the nice-sounding phrase that Virginia's gentlemen farmers liked to use; cotton could not be grown without slaves, and almost everyone planted it now. The world market for cotton goods was expanding, the appetite of English mills appeared insatiable, and the supply of raw cotton would never outstrip the demand. A land rush was on and, treating the older land as they did the slaves, no one thought of conserving it or even bothering with the simple rotation of corn for cotton. When the land was used up it was abandoned. You could always buy more further west.

The trouble was, the planters had absolutely no control over the market. The mills in England set the price, and with more and more cotton being grown, that price dropped. After the first few boom years, the price fell to the point where the largest plantations barely broke even, and the smaller ones went further and further into debt. All planters, large and small, were at the mercy of their factors in the port cities of Charleston, Savannah, Mobile, and New Orleans—cotton brokers who sold the cotton for a 2.5 percent commission, loaned the planters the money they needed for the next crop at 8 to 12 percent, and for that service sometimes added a brokerage fee of .5 to 2.5 percent. In addition, for many of the planters these brokers acted as agents, purchasing their supplies for them—for a commission of 2.5 percent. When the price of cotton fell two years in a row, many of the smaller planters found themselves so in debt to their factors that they would have to use all of the next year's crop to pay for that year's loans. If the price continued to fall, not even that would be enough. . . . As many a farmer knows, when the debt spiral starts, it is almost impossible to come out of it. In perhaps the strangest irony of all, the entire southern factorage system itself operated as agent for American or European financial interests, based in New York City.[37]

Needless to say, with all but the richest planters so in debt that their future crops were mortgaged, their slaves representing their entire wealth, any holier-than-thou northerner who suggested that they emancipate their slaves without compensation, out of the goodness of their hearts, was hardly likely to receive a sympathetic hearing. The system held the whites in bondage as much as the blacks. All must try to live within it and make the best of it. As observed by John Bernard, manager of the Federal Street Theatre in Philadelphia, having traveled widely in the South:

> In nine cases out of ten, the supporters of the system [slavery] have been its greatest victims. I do not hesitate to say they have been its sincerest detesters. . . . I do not remember a single instance of a planter defending the origin of his possessions, or who defended the continuance of slavery by other than this single argument: that human agency is required in the cultivation of Southern soil."[38]

Writing in a more sardonic vein, Bernard's description of a day in the life of a southern plantation owner, though scathingly parodic, says a good deal about how heavily the hours must have hung.

> During the summer he used to rise about nine, when he exerted himself to walk as far as his stables to look at the stud which he kept for the races. At ten, he breakfasted on coffee, eggs, and hoe-cake, concluding it with the commencement of his diurnal potions—a stiff glass of mint-sling [julep]—a disorder peculiar to the South. He then sought the coolest room and stretched himself on a pallet in his shirt and trousers, with a negress at his head and another at his feet to keep off the flies and promote reflection. Between twelve and one, he would sip half a pint of some mystery termed bumbo, apple-toddy, or pumpkin flip. He then mounted a pony and with an umbrella over his head, rode gently around his estate to converse with his overseers. At three, he dined and drank everything—brandy, claret, cider, Madeira, punch, and sangaree, then resumed his pallet with his negresses, and meditated until teatime.[39]

With all the indolence, moral corruption, and resultant cruelty inherent for whites caught in the system, there was bound to be guilt—

and there was, though it often did not surface until the slave owner was literally at death's door. Surprising numbers of accounts tell of what seemed a fairly common occurrence: a planter on his deathbed, growing fearful that there might indeed be a Day of Judgment and summoning his slaves around the bedside to beg their forgiveness. Some were even given a glimpse of the eternity that lay before them. Sarah Grimké records one such passage.

> A punishment dreaded more by slaves than whipping, unless it is unusually severe, is one which was invented by a female acquaintance of mine in Charleston—I heard her say so with much satisfaction. It is standing on one foot and holding the other in one's hand. Afterwards, it was improved upon; a strap was contrived to fasten around the ankle and pass around the neck so that the least weight of the foot resting on the strap would choke the person. The pain occasioned by this unnatural position was great, and when continued, as it sometimes was for an hour or more, it produced intense agony.
>
> Her husband was less inhuman than his wife, but he was often goaded by her to acts of great severity. In his last illness, I was sent for, and I watched beside his death couch. The girl on whom he had so often inflicted punishment haunted his dying hours. And when at length the king of terrors approached, he shrieked in utter agony of spirit: "Oh, the blackness of darkness! The black imps, I see them all about me—*take them away!*" And amid such exclamations, he expired. These persons were one of the first families of Charleston.[40]

Similar testimony is offered by an ex-slave named John Brown, who belonged to a master named Thomas Stevens. Toward the end of his life, Stevens suffered several grave seizures from which he did not expect to recover. "In his fright, he sent for us," Brown recorded, "and asked us to forgive him. . . . I remember his calling old Aunt Sally and begging and praying of her to get the devil away from behind the door." Speaking for his fellow slaves, Brown added, "It is a common belief among us that all the masters die in an awful fright, for it is usual for the slaves to be called on such occasions, in order for us to say we forgive them for what they have done. So we come to think that their minds must be dreadful uneasy about holding slaves."[41]

Not only on the deathbed did southern slaveholders experience soul-shaking fear. For they now held more than 3 million blacks. What if it ever got into their slaves' heads to say, "Enough!" and grab the arm that held the whip? What if just 10 percent of their number rose en masse and took up arms? What if they ever started to pay back what they had been given for so long? Laws were passed, forbidding more than seven Negroes to ever congregate without a white present, and white "patrols" went abroad at night to make sure Negroes remained in their cabins. Nevertheless, there had been just enough minor uprisings and uncovered conspiracies to keep the rumors rife, and countless thousands of southern women forgot the meaning of a peaceful night's sleep. None could forget what happened in South Carolina in 1739. The Cato Conspiracy began on a plantation twenty miles west of Charleston, when slaves there killed two guards in a warehouse, stole arms, and began a march toward Florida. All along the way, other blacks joined them, and the rapidly swelling band killed every white person in their path. The whites quickly retaliated. Raising their own force, they went in pursuit. Several pitched battles were fought, and in the end, only ten slaves made it to freedom. Twenty-four others were killed, but thirty whites also paid with their lives.[42]

Then, within their lifetimes, an insurrection had occurred on Haiti of such magnitude that it might well have given the entire South nightmares. French planters had imported black slaves to that island to work on their sugar plantations and, under the leadership of the brilliant and charismatic Toussaint L'Ouverture, these blacks suddenly rose up and overthrew their masters, proclaiming themselves an independent nation. This did not sit well with Napoleon, who promptly dispatched an invasion force of 25,000 troops under his brother-in-law. Incredibly, they were unable to restore the island dominion to Napoleon's empire; on the contrary, the former slaves defended their new nation so staunchly that eventually the French gave up and acknowledged it.

No southerner lost sight of the fact that what had taken place a few days' sail to the south, scarcely a generation earlier, could happen here. Fear became a key factor in southern life—never acknowledged, but never forgotten—like the glimpse of an ominous dark form just beneath the placid surface of a sunlit cove.

In large measure, this fear grew out of guilt, for whether or not they acknowledged it, many southern consciences still felt some pain. Southern clergyman John Dixon Long declared that one of the major evils of slavery was "the guilt contracted and the remorse endured by those who hold, breed, and sell slaves for the market."[43] In Louisiana, Kate Stone spoke for many of her sisters when she asserted that her first recollection of slavery was "of pity for the negroes, and a desire to help them. . . . Always I felt the moral guilt of it, felt how impossible it must be for an owner of slaves to win his way to heaven."[44] But the most direct comment of all came from a devout and courageous slave owner in Virginia named Anne Meade Page. Concerning the evils of slavery, she wrote: "They cannot be seen by human powers. They form a part of those hidden things of darkness, which are linked by a chain which reaches into the dominion of Satan, not only here on earth, but into his more complete dominion in the realms of deepest hell."[45] Having so said and having prayed, she manumitted her slaves.

We begin to comprehend what slavery did to those who wanted something for nothing and were willing to force others to grow it or make it or fetch it or fix it for them. It was a bargain struck with the devil. Regardless of its initial rewards, in the end no one, not even Daniel Webster, beats the devil at his own game. Speaking of Daniel Webster, this wise Yankee statesman declared that the northern people should assure the South that "we consider slavery as your calamity not your crime, and we will share with you the burden of putting an end to it." Had that inspired attitude caught on, the nation might have averted disaster. But hardly any northerners agreed with him, for to do so would eventually mean compensating southern slaveholders for huge losses in capital and income. And the northern states would have to bear the brunt of the burden, since the southern states were practically broke. The northern attitude resolutely—and ominously—remained: "It's their problem; let them deal with it." Two locomotives continued to rumble through the night, down the single track. They were still miles apart, but the distance was rapidly closing.

So—what would the modern reader do, if he or she were born into a plantation family? Suppose that one had enjoyed all its benefits for all his life; given Christian convictions, what would he do? As it happened, that question was answered in the person of one Jeremiah Jeter. A young preacher who had been born and raised in western Virginia, where masters treated slaves with "great severity," Jeter determined never to own a slave. But he moved to eastern Virginia where they treated slaves more leniently, and there he met and fell in love with a girl who had inherited slaves from her parents. They married, and in accordance with his convictions, she agreed that he could do whatever he felt was right concerning the slaves. The answer was not as easy as he had once supposed.

> I could not free them, for the laws of the State forbade it. Yet even if they had not forbidden it, the slaves in my possession were in no condition to support themselves. It was simple cruelty to free a mother with dependent children. Observation, too, had satisfied me that the free negroes were, in general, in a worse condition than the slaves. The manumission of my slaves to remain in the State was not to be thought of. Should I send them to Liberia? Some of them were in a condition to go, but none of them desired to. If sent, they [would] be forced to leave wives and children belonging to other masters [on nearby plantations], to dwell in a strange land. Besides, to send away the men who could support themselves and aid in the support of others, and retain the women and children to be supported by my own labors, was stretching my humanity quite beyond its power of endurance. They could not go to Africa. The same unsuperable difficulties lay in the way of sending them north. Parents and children, husbands and wives [would have to be] separated, and many of them sent forth to certain starvation, unless they should find charitable hands to support them.

Finally, after much prayer and deliberation, Reverend Jeter determined to sell or give them away. But the slaves themselves objected to this and begged him to keep them. He did just that. "It was not only allowable for me, but my solemn obligation. . . . I should have been recreant to my duty and guilty of inhumanity if, under the circumstances, I had not assumed the relation of master and endeavored to meet the responsibilities arising from it."[46] For Jeremiah Jeter, to sacrifice the well-being of the slaves for the sake of principle was simply not the loving Christian thing to do. And therein lay the dilemma that thousands of southern Christian slaveholders faced, and that rabid northern idealists could never comprehend.

In 1820 the halls of Congress continued to ring with phrases like "civil war" and "disunion." The summer recess and fall elections had done nothing to cool tempers regarding the Missouri question; if anything, after communing at length with their constituents, the lawmakers returned more confirmed than ever in their regional biases. And observers began to wonder aloud if they were witnessing the beginning of the end of the United States of America. Those who still loved the republic enough to put her interests first felt a deep grief and sadness at what was taking place. John Tyler demanded to know if the North expected the South to join her in forcibly putting down Missouri's resistance to a slavery restriction. "Do you believe that Southern bayonets will ever be plunged into Southern hearts?"[47] Henry Clay, William Lowndes, and Philip Barbour declared that if the North had its way they would leave Congress and consult back home to see if they should ever return. Clay even went so far as to predict that within five years there would be three separate confederacies.

Of all the disunionists, John Randolph of Roanoke was the most conspicuous. Once the most charismatic of all the southern orators, Randolph would stride into Congress as if fresh from a fox hunt, sporting English riding breeches and boots and a riding crop; on one occasion he even brought in a brace of hunting dogs. But as the years passed his speeches became noted more for their wry, sardonic style than for the careful reasoning of their content. After listening to him for several hours, John Quincy Adams concluded: "Egotism, Virginian aristocracy, slave-scourging liberty, religion, literature, science, wit, fancy, generous feelings, and malignant passions constitute a chaos in his mind, from which nothing orderly can ever flow."[48]

Randolph's passion was certainly at the boil as he made it clear that he, for one, stood ready to rally round the flag of the Old Dominion and with bared steel repel the invader, exclaiming: "God has given us Missouri, and the devil shall not take it from us!"[49]

But all swords would remain in their scabbards in 1820. For the vision of the Founding Fathers—of one nation under God—yet shone brightly enough in the breasts of a few key men for them to put it ahead of their own region's interest. Maneuvering with such parliamentary skill that he would receive the sobriquet the Great Compromiser, Speaker of the House Henry Clay, in his finest hour, used every procedural trick in the bag (and several that weren't) to bluff, browbeat, and bludgeon the moderates on both sides into accepting a compromise. In exchange for the North's admitting Missouri to statehood without restriction as to slavery, the South withdrew its refusal to admit Maine as a free state. In exchange for the North's accepting slavery as far north as 40° 35′ (Missouri's northern border), the South agreed slavery could be excluded above the new state's southern border (36° 30′) in the remainder of the Louisiana Purchase.

In the words of the young journalist Horace Greeley, it was "an offer from the milder opponents of Slavery Restriction to the more moderate and flexible advocates of that Restriction: 'Let us have slavery in Missouri, and we will unite with you in excluding it from all the uninhabited territories north and west of that State.' "[50] At the time, that seemed a modest concession indeed, for most held with the prevailing opinion that the territories in question were uninhabitable—"the Great American Desert."

So, America struck the Missouri Compromise. For the future of the American vision, it was a good thing, for the North's will was far less resolved than the South's, and the South had by far the best warriors, officers, and men. The North would never have had the stomach to persevere beyond the first shock of battle.

The whole nation exhaled a sigh of relief. Neither side was happy with the compromise, but enough men on both sides felt they could vote for it without impugning their honor or integrity. For now, the fiery oratorical arrows were returned to their quivers, and the blazes that they had started began to burn out. Or so it seemed. . . .

But as anyone who has been camping in the wilderness in the company of an experienced guide knows, campfires tend to smolder on underground, undetected. That's why, when the forest is dry, a guide will douse the site of a campfire twice, kicking the ground with his boot to make sure that the wetting has gotten well below the surface. For in the deep decay of virginal timberland, a "dead" fire can travel for days underground, before it suddenly flares up and ignites the surface.

The great statesmen who put this nation together were much like woodsmen who loved their forest. Sometimes they saw things untrained eyes might overlook. It behooved the tenderfoot to heed their warnings, even if he disagreed with their politics. Two such men, implacable opponents in the political arena, with diametrically opposed beliefs, reconciled and became close friends in the waning years of their lives. What drew them together was the vision they still shared—a vision so powerful and captivating that they had been willing to risk all for it when they affixed their signatures to a declaration of independence that would see them swinging from the end of a rope, if God did not prosper their cause. One of them penned that document in noble words, soon chiseled in marble and etched in steel for centuries to come. The other summed up the vision in equally moving words: "I am well aware of the toil and blood and treasure that it will cost us to maintain this declaration, and support and defend these States. Yet through all the gloom, I can see rays of ravishing light and glory. I can see that the end is worth more than all the means."[51]

On July 4, 1826, fifty years to the day that they had signed that Declaration, John Adams and Thomas Jefferson both died. Millions of Americans saw God's hand in that "coincidence," and took heart in the idea that if these two champions of the North and the South could be reconciled at the end of their lives, perhaps hope remained that the regions themselves might dwell in peace within the Union. Yet few heeded what these two had to say about the dark cloud on the horizon, which had already grown far larger than a man's hand. As early as 1810, John Adams had written:

> Slavery in this country, I have seen hanging over it like a black cloud for half a century. If I were as drunk with enthusiasm as Swedenborg or Wesley, I might probably say I had seen armies of negroes marching and counter-marching in the air, shining in armor. I have been so terrified of this phenomenon that I constantly said in former times to the Southern gentlemen: "I cannot comprehend this object; I must leave it to you. I will vote . . . no measure against your judgments. What we are to see, God knows—and I leave it to Him, and His agents in posterity.[52]

Jefferson, who had consistently spoken out against slavery and arranged for the manumission of his slaves upon his death, now saw the situation with a clarity that often comes at the end of life. Profoundly troubled by the depth of passions stirred by the Missouri controversy, in a letter to antislavery crusader John Holmes, he called it:

> A fire bell in the night, which awakened me and filled me with terror. I considered it at once the [death] knell of the Union. It is hushed, indeed, for the moment. But this is a reprieve only, not a final sentence. A geographical line [latitude 36° 30′], coinciding with a marked principle, moral and political, once conceived and held up to the angry passions of men, will never be obliterated; and every new irritation will mark it deeper and deeper. I can say . . . that there is not a man on earth who would sacrifice more than I would to relive us from this heavy reproach in any practicable way. . . . But as it is, we have a wolf by the ears, and

> we can neither hold him, nor safely let him go. Justice is in one scale, and self-preservation in the other.[53]

In the end, he became convinced that the Missouri question had inflamed and polarized public opinion to such a degree that disunion was inevitable. "I regret that I am now to die in the belief that the useless sacrifice of themselves by the generation of 1776, to acquire self-government and happiness to their country, is to be thrown away by the unwise and unworthy passions of their sons. My only consolation is that I will not be alive to weep over it."[54]

12

Old Hickory

The lone walker paused at the top of the mountain pass and turned to gaze at the late afternoon sun, low on the horizon behind him. The mountains and the foothills to the west seemed bathed in a golden haze, their ridges limned and almost iridescent, while their eastern slopes already slept deep in shadow. Above, a hawk circled in the clear sky, its wings bronzed by the sun's rays, while far below in a wooded valley a deer and her fawn timidly approached a sheltered pond. Stretching his arms and shoulders, the walker shifted the old army pack and turned to start down the eastern slope when a movement caught his eye. Coming up the winding track he had just climbed was a farm wagon pulled by two horses. A man and a woman, evidently husband and wife, shared the seat on the wagon which appeared to be lightly loaded. Suddenly he realized how tired he was and sat down on a boulder.

As the wagon reached the top of the pass, the farmer at the reins called out to him: "You going to see Old Hickory get sworn in?"

The walker grinned. "Sure am."

"Well, so are we; climb aboard!" And as the man got up and approached the wagon, the farmer added, "You serve with him?"

"Yup," the other replied, throwing his pack in the back and climbing in after it. "Down in New Orleans."

"You don't say!" The farmer exclaimed. "Missed that one myself. The missus was carrying our third child and was sick. . . ."

That night they joined the campfire of two other wagons headed for Washington. All over eastern America the scene was being repeated; indeed, it seemed almost as if someone had announced a national camp meeting there. Such old-fashioned neighborliness was rare these days, though it had once been a common denominator of American life. At one time neighbors felt close. They worshiped together, in churches that often formed the hub around which the life of the community revolved. They had built barns together and had shared problems and solutions. Sometimes, on the frontier, their very survival depended on one another. But the old soil played out, and the new cheap land beckoned westward.

A profound change had come to young America. There was a "go ahead" fever in the land, an impatience to get on with the next chapter of America's destiny. People became restless, leaving towns where their roots had been down for generations. They moved to bigger spreads with better land and made more money. The only trouble was, those untouched by the Second Great Awakening often ended up with not so many friends, certainly none as close as those they'd left behind. They also lacked a church to draw a community together and give it purpose—no sense of living for God and others, instead of for oneself. Precious little antidote existed to kill off the greed enveloping the country—and not just in the West, where the land came as cheap as buffalo chips or the South, where they began to crown cotton king. Back East, establishment bankers and brokers and businessmen were making overnight fortunes—often at the expense of their more gullible and naive but equally greedy compatriots. Too many banks had failed, too many others refused to honor paper money—even that which they themselves had printed. From what one read in the papers, it appeared that the government and the politicians were in league with them, hand in glove. Scarcely a day went by without news of yet another scandal involving public servants betraying the public's trust.

The sledgehammer blows on the wedge of slavery may have ceased for the moment, but the nation became no less divided. The three confederacies Clay had predicted if his compromise wasn't accepted might yet come to pass. New England had already flirted with secession, in the middle of the second war with England. Before that, all the way back to the Constitutional Convention, delegates from the South had made it clear that their states would not ratify the Constitution if slavery was made an issue. As for westerners, they united in their suspicion of all bankers or businessmen east of the Ohio. In many cases, the attitude of such men justified such doubts, for easterners generally considered themselves a cut above the pioneers and the frontiersmen, socially, financially, and every other way, and any real concern for western problems stopped at the Blue Ridge Mountains. Yet westerners felt no great concern, confident they could make it on their own.

The rifts cut into the earth of America so deeply that nothing short of a cataclysmic upheaval could close them—and at this point in time, the country could not have survived the shaking. She desperately needed time—time for the underlying ties that did bind the land together to strengthen and mature. The one thing that could do this was a leader behind whom all sections of the nation could unite—a leader so strong that no individual or group or section could manipulate him and so selfless that he would put the founding vision for America above all else. Such a man America had chosen as President. From now on, things would be different. And so, they converged on Washington, this amiable army of farmers and rivermen, hired hands and freed slaves, former soldiers and soldiers of fortune, in that early spring of 1829. Some of them had stood on the ramparts with him outside New Orleans or had followed him through the steaming Florida wilderness, in pursuit of the Spaniards. Many had named sons after him, and now they wanted to be there when General Andy Jackson raised his right hand. The majority of them had never clapped eyes on him. But they liked what they read about him in the papers, and liked what he had to say when his speeches were reprinted. They even liked him because of the enemies he had made and what his detractors said about him. They liked him because he sounded like—one of them.

It had been a long time. The fifty-three-year-old nation had had an unbroken succession of eastern aristocrats in the White House. The Declaration of Independence stated that all men were created equal, but how could there be equality when that gentlemen's club ran things? The longer they stayed in, the more they abused the power handed down to them. It got so you didn't even want to open the paper anymore! What had happened to honor and morality in this country? Andrew Jackson was asking the same questions, in anger. So they voted for him. Now, thousands of them trekked to Washington, to cheer him on as he launched his great reformation.

On that bright March 4 morning, upwards of 20,000 of them, from every one of the twenty-four states, gathered on the mall below the Capitol and waited. Washington society had never seen anything like it, and was alarmed at the invasion of this barbarous horde. Their coming even took the politicians by surprise. Daniel Webster noted: "I never saw such a crowd here before . . . they really seem to think that the country is rescued from some dreadful danger."[1]

They waited in silence, squinting up at the portico, which seemed to shine a soft white in the watery sunlight. At last, the official party emerged from between the enormous, high columns—Chief Justice Marshall first, frail and bent with age, and behind him the tall, gaunt figure they all waited for. A thunderous roar arose from the multitude, startling those in lace bodices up among the special guests and seeming to shake the very ground they stood on. But it was a cry of triumph, and as thousands of hats were doffed, they revealed broad smiles on upturned faces. Jackson's inaugural address was brief and to the point, and Margaret Bayard Smith, the wife of one of Maryland's Senators, noted at its conclusion that the new President "bowed . . . to the people—yes, to the people in all their majesty."[2]

That graceful, unprecedented act of recognition summed up Jackson's attitude toward the American public: the country belonged to them, not to the ruffled-shirt, bemused gentry who surrounded him, and he intended to give it back to them and to serve them to the utmost of his ability. The people sensed this, which was why they had come so far to be there when he solemnly swore to uphold the Constitution.

The inauguration over, the President made his way with difficulty through the throngs that pressed forward to touch him or just see him up close. "Hey, Andy! Remember me? Pensacola, in '14! Good luck, hear?" No President had ever been regarded so familiarly, and no President had ever realized with such clarity that these same people had put him in office. At the bottom of the steps an aid held his horse, but the wall of people in front of it was almost impenetrable. While men attempted to make a path for him, he smiled and waved—and nearly got mobbed. Indeed, he barely made it to the White House ahead of his supporters, bent on celebrating the day with him.

That afternoon, a formal reception was scheduled to be held there for foreign dignitaries and the most prominent members of Washington society, which included Margaret Bayard Smith. When she finally made her way to the White House, she discovered that the President had already "retreated through the back way and escaped to his lodgings" nearby. She found herself surrounded by

> A rabble, a mob of boys, negroes, women, children, scrambling, fighting, romping . . . the whole house had been inundated. . . .

> Ladies fainted, men were seen with bloody noses, and such a scene of confusion took place as is impossible to describe—those who got in could not get out by the door again but had to scramble out of the windows. . . . But it was the People's day and the People's President, and the People would rule. . . . The noisy and disorderly rabble in the President's house brought to my mind the descriptions I had read of the mobs in the Tuileries and at Versailles.[3]

Newspapers describing the event would call it a riot, and upper-class Americans, reading lurid accounts of the destruction and chaos, feared that the "people" had begun to march, under the banner of Jackson and democracy, and soon the well-bred and well-educated would not be safe in their beds. But in actuality, it was just a bunch (a huge, swarming bunch) of happy Americans with good cause to celebrate, looking for a good time. Their candidate would live in the White House, and they just expressed their natural curiousity in seeing it. Rum punch filled those big silver bowls—things just got a little out of hand, that was all. Happened all the time, out west. Sure, they should have taken off their muddy boots and left them outside, but in that crowd they would never have found them again. As for taking souvenirs, well, a silver spoon from the White House was a thing to treasure and pass down to one's grandchildren, and after all, it wasn't as if it really belonged to Andy. . . .

To save the remaining silver—and the yet unbroken china and cut crystal—the White House staff moved the silver bowls and all the other refreshments out onto the lawn. That was when the traffic jam occurred. Those inside now found the doorways blocked by hundreds more behind them, pressing in to get their own look-see. There was only one thing to do; they pulled sofas under the windows and clambered out over them, muddy boots and all, pulling down the draperies in the process. Since they'd already gotten torn, there didn't seem any harm in cutting off a swatch to show the wife and kids back home.

Washington aristocracy observed all these goings on with the morbid certainty that they were witnessing the equivalent of the sacking of Rome. Why didn't the President do something? He was the only one who could put a stop to it. Was it because he was of like mind? Was the country in for four years of Attila the Hun?

If Jackson, watching the scene out the window of one of the rooms he had been renting, suspected such a reaction, he only smiled. Those who regarded themselves as the top level of eastern society had consistently misunderstood him—because they consistently misunderstood the heart of the people, a heart Jackson did understand, which was why he had beaten them so badly. For that reason, too, he would change the country, when so many others had promised to and done nothing.

He had traveled a long road to the White House, but that was where the road had been leading from the very beginning. Had the sachems of the old order, no fools themselves, been present at a glade in a certain poplar forest on the banks of the Red River north of Nashville, some twenty-three years before, they would have discerned the key to Jackson's character and never underestimated him again. On that still, early morning in May the first shafts of the rising sun began to pierce through the tall trees. In this timeless silence, three dismounted riders stood by their horses and waited. One checked his watch, while the principle just gazed at the treetops, a faint smile on his lips. Of the three, that young lawyer from Nashville acted the most relaxed and had the least reason to be. Soon, he would toe the mark and face the man whose wife's honor he had slurred. But Charles Dickinson was known as the best marksman in Tennessee, a reputation earned on just such dueling grounds as these, and his seconds felt no concern for him.[4] They looked up and to the west; in the distance, horses approached.

Three horsemen came on at a slow but deliberate pace. In their lead was the tallest, Andrew Jackson, the challenger. Well aware of his opponent's skill, he confided to his friend John Overton, who acted as his second, and his surgeon: "He's sure to fire first. The chances are nine out of ten he'll hit me—but that won't matter. I'll take my time, aim deliberately, and kill him, if it's the last thing that I do."[5]

The second party arrived at the glade and dismounted. Greetings were brief, courteous, and subdued. In the middle of the clearing, two stakes were driven into the ground, exactly twenty-four feet apart. The two duelists would stand at these marks and face each other, their loaded pistols pointing straight down. At the command to fire, they would take aim and fire at their discretion. No one saw reason to delay, and Dickinson, wearing a short blue coat and gray trousers, stepped confidently to his mark. Jackson, his spare frame covered by a bulky, loose-fitting frock coat, followed. The men assumed their positions—

Dickinson, smiling and impatient; Jackson erect and concentrating intently. Again silence closed over the glade.

"Gentlemen," called out Overton. "Are you ready?" Both answered in the affirmative.

"Fire!"

At the command, Dickinson, lightning fast, raised his gun and fired, and a puff of dust rose from Jackson's coat, just to the left of the center button on his chest. The lean body shuddered, and his left arm flew to his chest. Then he straightened and slowly raised his pistol. Dickinson, dumbfounded, stepped backward. "My God!" he cried, "Have I missed him?"

"Back to the mark, sir!" Overton cried, his own pistol now raised and leveled on Dickinson, ready to shoot him, as the duelists' code required, should the latter not obey. Dickinson, becoming aware that he had stepped away from the stake, returned to it and folded his arms casually across his chest. He watched as Jackson, wavering slightly and still holding his chest with his left hand, took careful aim.

Slowly he exerted pressure on the hair trigger, and a second report shattered the silence. The ball tore through Dickinson's side, just below his folded arms. He paled and toppled forward, blood gushing from his wound. His surgeon rushed to him, but little could be done, as the bullet had ripped through the intestines.

Jackson turned and walked away stiffly, his party joining him. He had Overton take a bottle of wine to Dickinson, only to learn on his return that his adversary's surgeon said it would be of no use. Then Overton noticed that Jackson's left shoe was full of blood. Shocked, he and the surgeon eased Jackson to the ground and gently removed his coat, to discover that he had indeed been hit. The bullet, deflected by his breastbone, broke two ribs and lodged in the chest cavity. Overton commented that the set of Jackson's loose-fitting coat had probably saved his life. Had he not worn it, Dickinson's bullet would surely have hit his heart, instead of missing it by an inch. When he said as much, Jackson replied through clenched teeth: "I'd have hit him, if he'd shot me through the brain!"[6]

Jackson paid a severe price for that victory. Doctors soon ascertained that Dickinson's bullet lay too close to his heart to risk removing it. He would carry it for the rest of his life, and it impinged upon his left lung, so that a pulmonary abcess formed. Over the years, one respiratory infection followed another, and coughing became incessant. During the worst spasms, he brought up blood. Nor was this the only bullet in his body. He received the second in another affair of honor, this one a gunfight with Thomas Hart Benton and his brother Jesse. The bullet lodged in his left arm, just below the shoulder, and it was a long time before he could raise it enough to dress himself without great difficulty and discomfort. The inflammation connected with this latter wound never did subside, and eventually osteomyelitis set in.

Either of these two wounds would have been enough to keep him in constant, lifelong pain, but he suffered more—much more. During his campaign against the Creeks, he contracted both dysentery and malaria, and these, too, would never leave him. If these afflictions were not enough, he suffered from a worsening condition of acute rheumatism and repetitive toothaches, so severe that they frequently robbed him of all sleep and ultimately tormented him so much that in 1828, at the age of sixty-one, he had every one of his teeth extracted. In sum, Andrew Jackson suffered acute pain of one sort or another for the last twenty-four years of his life—pain so severe and unrelenting that it might have caused another man to wish for death. As it was, he overcame these fiery thorns in the flesh by the sheer strength of his indomitable will.[7]

As Jackson grew older and became less able to tolerate the suffering with equanimity, he would lash out at his enemies with such vehemence that it would startle even his closest friends. The great ameliorating and soothing influence in his life was his wife, Rachel. Plain and heavy-set, she had no social ambitions and felt quite content to remain in the background. For all that, she was well-liked by those who knew her and possessed a spirit both cheerful and devout. Jackson adored her. He thus became all the more enraged when his opponents attempted to make political hay out of the fact that he and his wife inadvertently married before the divorce of the man who had deserted her became final. Dickinson was hardly the last man to receive a challenge to the field of honor, though by now Jackson's own reputation had grown so that hardly any man would be foolhardy enough to accept it.

While Jackson did not seem to share her deep personal commitment to Christ, he greatly respected Rachel's faith and would say or do nothing that might offend it. Indeed, he valued his personal morality second only to his honor, and while he had resisted the desire of his mother, a devout Presbyterian like his wife, that he go into the ministry, he appeared to have a mounting religious conviction in his later years, culminating in his formally joining the Presbyterian Church. And before his presidency, when he was away serving in Washington, and Rachel stayed at home, he went to church every Sunday and reported this fact in letters home, knowing how much it would please her.

> I trust that the God of Isaac and of Jacob will protect you, and give you health in my absence. In Him alone we ought to trust; He alone can preserve and guide us through this troublesome world, and I am sure He will hear your prayers. We are told that the prayers of the righteous prevaileth much, and I add mine for your health and preservation until we meet again.[8]

The Lord would continue to preserve and guide the President as well; we have seen the bullets that narrowly missed finding their mark, in national and personal combat. But none would rival what occurred on January 30, 1835. Having attended the funeral service of South Carolina Congressman Warren Davis, in the House of Representatives, Jackson started to leave through the east entrance of the Capitol when a bearded man stepped out from behind one of the columns, drew a pistol, and fired at close range at the President. As the report rang off the surrounding stones, Jackson raised his walking stick and rushed his assailant, who now drew another pistol and fired it, too, this time at point-blank range. Jackson's naval attaché hurled the bearded man to the ground, while others went to the President's aid.

"Let me go, gentlemen!" Old Hickory bellowed, still determined to get at his attacker. "I am not afraid—they can't kill me—I can protect myself!"

Examination of the two pistols revealed that while their percussion caps had indeed detonated, for some reason neither charge had been ignited. The next day, at the Navy Department, fresh percussion caps were put on the weapons, and they were fired again. Both discharged perfectly![9]

Not only did Jackson firmly believe in God's providential care, but at no time would he brook anyone speaking derogatorily of Christianity. Peter Cartwright, who had noted Jackson in his congregation on more than one occasion, was once invited to the Jacksons' for Sunday lunch. Other guests at the table included several ladies and gentlemen, among them a clever young lawyer from Nashville, who started baiting the Methodist circuit rider about his Christian beliefs. Out of politeness, Cartwright ignored the taunts until finally in a pause in the conversation the lawyer, oblivious to the fact that his host's steely blue eyes had narrowed and centered on him, confronted the preacher: "Mr. Cartwright, do you believe there is any such place as hell, a place of torment?"

"Yes, I do," replied Cartwright gravely.

"Well," the lawyer laughed at him, "I thank God I have too much sense to believe in such a thing!"

Jackson could keep silent no longer. "Well, sir," he stormed, "I thank God that there is such a place of torment as hell!"

"Why, General Jackson," blurted the astonished lawyer, "what do you want with such a place as hell?"

"To put such damned rascals as you are in, that oppose and villify the Christian religion!" Jackson thundered, and the young man gasped and fled the room.[10]

After his vindication in the taking of Florida, Jackson had retired to his beloved Hermitage, content to spend the remainder of his days there with Rachel, farming and raising his family and occasionally racing his horses. But with the passage of time, the popularity of the hero of New Orleans had grown, not declined. Without his consent, two would-be political kingmakers put his name forward as a candidate for United States Senator from Tennessee. Though he won handily and acquitted himself well in office, he still had no real taste for politics—until he found himself being seriously considered as a dark horse candidate in the forthcoming 1824 presidential election.

At that time, the two-party system had yet to evolve, and thus the dominant National Republicans, as the Democratic Republicans had come to be known, could usually deliver the election to whomever they nominated. Because of this it is not difficult to see how the presidency passed down so smoothly to the Secretary of State, as soon as the incumbent had served his terms. But this election would be different. While the Secretary of State certainly deserved the position, having served with distinction under every President since Washington and being universally respected, John Quincy Adams lacked popular appeal and was most assuredly not a National Republican. Secretary of War John C. Calhoun, on the other hand, had more than his share of charisma, yet he had aligned himself as a states' rightist who stood against expending federal funds on such internal improvements as systems of roads and canals. As such, he contented himself with running for Vice-president (which position was not yet yoked with the Presidency). As for the Virginia dynasty, they obviously preferred Secretary of the Treasury William Crawford, a canny and resourceful politician from Georgia. Rounding out the field and coming up fast was Speaker of the House Henry Clay, who had cast himself as the champion of the West—until Jackson was observed to be in the race, as well.

Crawford clearly had the inside track, until the obese Georgian suffered a paralyzing stroke. He did partially recover, but suddenly the race became a wide-open contest. To no one's surprise, the popular vote went to Jackson, with 153,000 votes, and he received majorities everywhere but in New England. To everyone's surprise, Adams did much better than expected, winning 114,000 votes despite virtually no support in the West. Clay and Crawford each won roughly 47,000, and Calhoun was a shoo-in for the vice-presidency.[11] The electoral college returns generally reflected the popular vote, although Jackson wound up just short of the necessary majority. This meant that the final decision would go to the House of Representatives, who would decide between the three candidates with the most electoral-college votes.

Such was Clay's power there that, had Crawford edged him out in electoral votes, he might have been able to swing the election in his own direction. As it was, he was clearly in the role of kingmaker and relishing it. To whom would he throw his support, Jackson or Adams? Could he really deliver Kentucky, Ohio, Missouri, and Illinois? Both sides courted him indirectly, but Jackson steadfastly refused to offer him any guarantee of a position in his cabinet, specifically Secretary of State, which would cast him as Jackson's successor. Jealous of the general's rising popularity in what had been his exclusive domain, Clay bitterly attacked Jackson over the Florida campaign. On the other hand, considering Adams, Clay had served with him on the Ghent Peace Treaty commission and felt that the two of them could work together; most important, Clay could count on Adams making him Secretary of State, and Henry Clay wanted to become President more than any man in America.

So blinded by ambition that he failed to see that he was committing political suicide, Clay threw his full support behind Adams. He instructed the Kentucky congressmen to vote for Adams, and they did, ignoring the fact that Adams had not received a single vote in their state and that they had just received instructions from their state legislature back home to vote for Jackson. Ohio, too, shifted from Jackson to Adams, and Clay also claimed credit for bringing Louisiana into the fold.

Even so, it appeared that several key states might wind up deadlocked, their representatives unable to reach a majority decision, which could possibly have swung the election to Crawford. New York was one such, and in his autobiography years later Martin Van Buren reported an extraordinary happening. Adams was one vote shy of winning the necessary majority, and none of the New York congressmen appeared ready to budge, save one: the former major general Stephen Van Rensselaer, nicknamed "the Patroon."

On his way to the House that morning, Van Rensselaer had been waylaid by Clay and Webster, who had exhorted him to vote for Adams for the good of the country. Yet previously he had promised Van Buren he would vote for anyone *but* Adams. Now he felt torn by indecision, as from all sides friends and advisors put increasing pressure on him. Tears came to his eyes, and he was heard to murmur that the vote of New York depended on him, and if he gave his vote to Adams, the latter would probably win on the first ballot. A devoutly religious man, in this desperate moment he lowered his head to the edge of his desk and prayed. As his turn came to vote, he slowly lifted his head—and there, lying on the floor next to his desk, he saw a ballot marked with a single name: John Quincy Adams. Convinced that God had answered his prayer, he picked up the ballot and cast it into the box, thus giving New York to Adams—and with it a majority of the states. John Quincy Adams would be the sixth President of the United States.[12]

Andrew Jackson and his supporters were enraged. The election which they had fairly won had been stolen from them. But in light of the pivotal Van Rensselaer episode, it seems right to pause and at least consider that perhaps it *was* God's will for Adams—not Jackson—to become President at that point. Terrible corruption in high places and abuses of the public trust existed, and this would continue to a lesser degree under Adams's administration, though his own integrity remained beyond reproach. But for all Jackson's popularity and natural leadership, the forces then aligned against him were so powerful that they could have blocked and thwarted his administration at every turn and rendered him ineffectual. To do what he wanted to do would require an indisputable, overwhelming mandate, and that he clearly did not have. The American people would have to get a little more sickened at the way things were, before they would readily give Jackson their unequivocal support. In addition, Jackson yet lacked one thing Adams had and that the United States would shortly have great need of: a strong, clear vision of what the Union could and should become. For in 1824, Jackson was still a Tennessee general, his horizons for the most part narrowed to regional and personal interests. He did care for the people, but he did not care for them above all else—not yet. That was coming. In the meantime, God honored the obedience of a selfless, faithful servant of the people by rewarding him with the highest position the country could bestow.

The next four years passed slowly and frustratingly for Jackson, a general with no war to fight and plenty of fight left in him. Everyone he knew urged him to run again, and he was inclined to agree. By rights, the presidency should have been his; now he set his implacable will toward attaining it—not for himself, but for the country. Earlier, when it first began to look like political maneuvering might negate the results of the 1824 general election, Jackson had declared: "The people are the safeguards of their own liberties, and I rely wholly on them to guard themselves. They will correct any outrage upon political purity by Congress; if they do not, now and ever, then they will become the slaves of Congress and its political corruption."[13] That outrage had taken place, and the people might apply the corrective through the next general election. If they did, "they may preserve and perpetuate the liberty of our happy country. If they do not, in less than 25 years, we will become the slaves, not of a military chieftain, but of such ambitious demagogues as Henry Clay."[14]

The people were ready to apply the corrective. For the most part, they felt dismayed, if no longer shocked, by the manipulations which had taken place during the election, and more than ever their sympathies lay with Jackson. And now the grass-roots, go-ahead Americans demanded a candidate of their own. The trickle of politicians and friends, fair-weather and foul, calling at the Hermitage became a steady stream. Jackson now subscribed to twenty newspapers and avidly followed the news around the entire country. His hatred of the vested interests that were taking advantage of common folk now distilled and focused into a nationwide call for reform—a reform that would cleanse this government from stem to stern and return it to the people for whom it was originally created. He planned and fumed and waited, and his reform policy took shape as he wrote to friends like John Coffee:

> The patronage of the government for the last three years has been wielded to corrupt everything that comes within its influence and was capable of being corrupted, and it would seem that virtue and truth has fled from its embrace. The administration of the government has stained our national character, and it rests with the people to work it out, by a full expression of their disapprobation. The present is a contest between the virtue of the people, and the influence of patronage. . . . I hope the virtue of the people may prevail, and all may be well.[15]

By the time of the campaign of 1828, he no longer just had the outlook of a Tennessee general. The scope of his vision had expanded to include the whole of the nation—from Maine to Florida to Missouri. Most important of all, he saw not three distinct regions, but one country—a country he passionately wanted to save and to serve.

Needless to say, those in power wanted with equal passion to keep him out, since obviously nothing less than a peaceful revolution was underfoot, with Jackson as its leader. If he got in, he would thrust out those who had held power for so long. For the first time, America got a taste of gutter politics at its worst; the campaign of 1828 would go down as one of the ugliest in history. Jackson's opponents dredged up the brief, unwitting bigamy between him and Rachel and then attacked his parentage with the most ridiculous slander, apparently convinced people would believe anything, as long as it appeared in print:

> General Jackson's mother was a COMMON PROSTITUTE, brought to this country by the British soldiers! She afterward married a MULATTO MAN, with whom she had several children, of which number General JACKSON IS ONE!!![16]

Rachel found him one afternoon, holding the crumpled newspaper that contained the above article, tears streaming down his face. "I can defend myself; you I can defend. But now they have assailed even the memory of my mother." Rachel, too, was grief stricken, because for once she could do nothing to help him. Jackson's advisors strongly counseled him not to respond personally to these attacks, but to leave it to his friends to remind people that his parents had emigrated from Ireland. This they did and then proceeded to attack Adams and Clay in equally wild and libelous fashion. This ongoing mutual bombardment so polarized the nation politically into pro or con Jackson camps that when the guns finally fell silent, the two-party system had emerged.

In the end, the newly formed Democrats, led by Jackson and Calhoun, soundly defeated the National Republicans, gaining 56 percent of the popular vote, and winning the electoral college contest 178 to 83—mandate enough to get the job done. But there was no joy at the Hermitage, no cause for celebration. For in winning the presidency, Jackson had lost the thing he held most dear on earth—his wife, Rachel. She had suffered with all the things said about her, praying for her slanderers and asking God to forgive them, but dreading the prospect of moving to the White House, in their very midst. More than once she was heard to say: "I would rather be a doorkeeper in the house of God, than to live in that palace in Washington."[17] Yet all the while she maintained a cheerful countenance during the campaign, making light of the attacks of bronchial asthma that were growing progressively more severe, and the heart palpitations now beginning to torment her. As soon as the news of the victory was received and her poor health would no longer burden or distract her husband, her own tenacious will to live relaxed, and she died of a massive heart attack.

Jackson was inconsolable; Washington and all its trappings he would have given up in an instant, if it could have recalled her to life. He grieved alone, in solitude, until Christmas Eve, the day of her funeral. Ten thousand people crowded around the mansion on that cold, wet, gray day, not only out of respect for the President-elect, but because "Aunt Rachel" was genuinely loved by all who knew her. When the funeral party emerged, Sam Houston led the pallbearers; the general, supported on both sides, followed the casket to the place in the garden where he and Rachel had long before agreed to be buried. Observers were stricken at the sight of his grief; several would later note that he seemed to have aged twenty years overnight. At her graveside, a slave who loved her, weeping and wailing, tried to throw herself into the grave to be buried with her. When others tried to quiet the woman, Jackson said, "Let that faithful servant weep for her best friend and loved mistress; she has the right and cause to mourn . . . her grief is sweet to me."[18]

Then Jackson himself wept openly for the first time since Rachel's death. Looking about him, he seemed embarrassed and explained: "I know it's unmanly, but these tears are due her virtues. She has shed many for me." He paused. "In the presence of this saint, I can and do forgive my enemies." And then his voice rose. "But those vile wretches who have slandered her must look to God for mercy!"[19]

Some of these recollections may have passed through his mind as he stood at the window of his Washington lodgings, watching the inaugural carryings-on over at the White House. He would move there tomorrow, without the mate who had been by his side for twenty-seven years. How he missed her cheerful smile and steadying hand. Well, there was much to be done. The country was so divided that his predecessor had despairingly predicted that the Union would not last five more years. The jaw muscles on Jackson's lean face tensed: the Union would not dissolve while *he* was President.

The strength of the Union would be tested sooner than anyone anticipated. As we have seen, the cessation of hostilities between Britain and America in 1815 suddenly threw open one of Europe's major export markets to receive manufactured goods—goods that had piled up for several years. Fleets of merchant ships loaded with manufactured items had sailed for the New World, where they dumped their products on the market at prices the New England factories could not possibly match. As a result, even though the European goods were often vastly inferior in quality, they were too cheap to resist, and American manufacturers soon found themselves facing bankruptcy. This was a serious situation because by 1824 some two million men and women took part in manufacturing—a tenfold increase in five years. That number now amounted to more than a fifth of the entire free population.

In desperation, New England's industrial interests had appealed to Congress for protective tariffs, and finally in 1826 the Senate and House approved them by the narrowest of margins, over the vehement objections of the South, which would now have to pay half again as much for the agricultural tools and supplies they needed. Of the objecting states, South Carolina was the most organized and articulate, the planters of Charleston claiming that they were, in effect, being personally taxed to support the mercantile interests of New England.

Two years later, a second round of tariffs was passed, which promptly became known as the Tariff of Abominations, and now the South engaged in open and widespread talk of secession. South Carolinians, under the guidance of Calhoun, who drew on the "precedents" of Jefferson's Kentucky and Virginia resolutions, began to develop a policy of nullification. The Constitution was merely a compact made by the states, and thus a state legislature could declare null and void a federal statute that directly impeded the vital interests of that state. Militants in the nullification ranks declared: "By all the principles of liberty, by the glorious achievements of our fathers in defending them, by their noble blood poured forth like the waters in maintaining them, by their lives in suffering and their deaths in honor and glory, our countrymen, we must resist!"[20]

The seams of the fabric of America, temporarily patched by the Missouri Compromise, once again threatened to pull apart. This time, the issue wasn't slavery; it was economics, hitting the pocketbook, instead of the heart. The South hung on in the hope that Jackson, the champion of the people against the vested interests of banking and business, would do something. Contrary to the earlier predictions of his opponents, however, Jackson was moving cautiously and conservatively, and for two years the Tariff of Abominations remained in place. At the beginning of 1830, the South saw its chance to sever the last tenuous strands holding the West to the Northeast and to bind it tightly in a new alliance with the South that would give the latter enough leverage to impose its will on the North, instead of vice versa. Beautifully simple, the gambit had a fair chance of succeeding.

For decades, New England had been losing enterprising and energetic citizens to the lure of the West. Now cotton growers poured into the lower regions of the Louisiana Territory at such a rate that the North feared a plethora of new slave states that would destroy the precarious balance then existing in the Senate. Therefore, on January 18, Senator Samuel Foot of Connecticut, proposed to shut down the sale of public lands, limiting them to those properties already on the market.

Instantly, Thomas Hart Benton of Missouri leaped to his feet, attacking the proposal on behalf of the West. The following day, at the behest of Vice-President Calhoun, the man masterminding the southern strategy, Robert Hayne of South Carolina, the South's finest debater, rose to confirm all Benton had said and to demonstrate how closely aligned in spirit the South was with the West. Adeptly Hayne condemned the miserly attitude of New England for wanting to hold its citizens captive, to work long hours in gloomy sweatshops, when the West beckoned them with limitless frontiers where a man could become anything he chose and could see the rapid fruit of his labors. By the time he finished, many heads were nodding at the points he made, and it did seem that South and West had a common cause.

But by one of those strange "coincidences" of fate that Christians claim are not coincidental at all, just as Hayne began to speak, Daniel Webster happened by the Senate chamber. At the time, the Senator from Massachusetts was deeply involved in arguing a case before the Supreme Court. He had not followed the Senate's debate, but as long as the Court had adjourned early that chilly afternoon, Webster decided to poke his head in, a sheaf of law papers still tucked under his arm. At first, he only half listened to Hayne, but it soon became apparent that the Senator from South Carolina had launched a deliberate attack upon New England. Listening intently now, Webster became alarmed. For he discerned what was going on beneath the surface, and it was a lot more serious than the pros and cons of public land sale.

Thus, when Hayne concluded and his friends urged him, as New England's champion, to take the floor in her defense, Daniel Webster readily assented. He rose and proposed an indefinite postponement of the measure, but in so doing, he defended New England's role in the development of the West. The battle was joined, and Benton of Missouri went for blood, attacking on behalf of the South as his colleague from South Carolina had spoken for the West.

"Slavery in the abstract," he insisted, "has few advocates or defenders in the slaveholding States, and . . . slavery as it is . . . would have fewer advocates among us than it has, if those who have nothing to do with the subject would only let us alone. . . . Christ saw all of this—the number of slaves—their hapless condition—and their white color which was the same as His own. Yet He said nothing against slavery; He preached no doctrines which led to insurrection and massacre."[21] Benton went on, presenting the arguments all had heard so many times before.

But Webster had said nothing of slavery and refused debate on it. To Benton's indignant consternation, he ignored him completely. (Why do battle with a yeoman armed with a battle-ax, when a more challenging adversary was in the offing, as skilled at the saber as he was himself?) Besides, slavery was not the issue here; the issue of nullifacation skulked behind the draperies, and although he was as unprepared as his opponents were well-prepared, Webster felt equal to the task. For the man from Massachusetts valued one thing above all else: the preservation of the Union.

Webster had the same vision of one nation under God that Washington had had, and John Quincy Adams, and Marshall, and Jackson. Each of the men to whom God had entrusted the vision of His plan for America would be called upon to preserve and protect that plan at a crucial juncture. Washington had made the whole thing possible, JQA had done his part in Belgium and as Secretary of State and President, and Marshall had guided the Supreme Court through the rocks and shoals of Jefferson's best efforts to break it and weaken the federal government. Now the Senate had become the arena, and the burden had fallen to Daniel Webster.

In the golden age of oratory, many would argue that the Webster-Hayne debate was its finest moment. Hayne had attacked the whole "American system" of roads and canals—an ambitious program of internal improvements launched by the federal government. What possible interest, he had asked, could South Carolina have in a canal in Ohio? Lasting the better part of two days, his speech reflected the care and concentration that had gone into its preparation. As the Senate adjourned on January 25, all agreed Hayne had made one of the greatest speeches ever heard in that chamber, and aside from his magnificent delivery, the logic and progression of his reasoning most impressed nonpartisan observers; Webster would have to come up with the finest effort of his career the next day, just to hold even.

That evening, gloom descended on Webster's supporters. Not only had Hayne surpassed himself in delivery and preparation, but there was no time to prepare a rebuttal. Even so, his friends seemed far more anxious than Webster himself. "Did you take notes, Mr. Webster?" Edward Everett asked him.

The Senator frowned as he fished in one vest pocket after another. Then with a smile, he extracted a small piece of paper with a scribbled note on it: "I have it." Supreme Court Justice Joseph Story stopped by to express his own concern, offering to be of whatever assistance he could that night. But Webster smiled and shook his head. "Give yourself no uneasiness, Judge Story; I will grind him as fine as a pinch of snuff." It was not bravado; by coincidence, Webster had already prepared to debate on that very subject for another purpose, and as he would later remark: "If Hayne had tried to make a speech to fit my notes, he could not have hit it any better."[22]

The next morning, long before the Senate would begin its session, onlookers so jammed the chamber that even shifting one's position proved impossible. Some gallant Senators had given up their own seats to ladies, and the latter's gaily colored bonnets added a festive air to the usually solemn surroundings. Practically everyone who was anyone in Washington had come; even Congressmen had stolen away from their proceedings in the adjacent House of Representatives and slipped into the Senate.

When Webster rose, a hush fell over the assembly. Calmly and with great strength, he began to speak. Observers noted that "a deep-seated conviction of the extraordinary character of the emergency, and of his ability to control it, seemed to possess him wholly."[23] Those listeners familiar with the Bible must have been struck by the similarity between Webster's defense of the Union and the Apostle Paul's plea to the believers in Corinth for unity in the body of Christ—"For just as the body is one and has many members, and all the members of the body, though many, are one body. . . . If one member suffers, all suffer together; if one member is honored, all rejoice together" (1 Corinthians 12:12, 26 RSV).

> Sir, we narrow-minded people of New England do not reason thus. Our notion of things is entirely different. We look upon the States, not as separated, but as united. We love to dwell on that union and on the mutual happiness which it has so much promoted, and the common renown which it has so greatly contributed to acquire. In our contemplation, Carolina and Ohio are parts of the same country—States united under the same general government, having interests, common, associated, intermingled. In whatever is within the proper sphere of the constitutional power of this government, we look upon the States as one; we do not impose geographical limits to our patriotic feeling or regard. . . ."[24]

Now Webster must deal with Hayne's most dangerous thrust. Hayne had concluded his two-day speech by attacking the very position into which Webster, in his initial remarks, had led him: "As to the doctrine that the Federal Government is the exclusive judge of the extent, as well as the limitations, of its powers, it seems to me utterly subversive of the sovereignty and independence of the States. It makes but little difference, in my estimation, whether Congress or the Supreme Court are invested with this power."[25]

All the dueling of the previous five days, the feints and parries, lunges and ripostes, came down to this end game. There was no more maneuvering room, the swordsmen stood alone on a narrow stairway. With renewed energy, Webster pressed home his attack, his concentration and focus never more awesome.

> The great question is: Whose prerogative is it to decide on the constitutionality or unconstitutionality of the laws? On that, the main debate hinges. The proposition that, in case of a supposed violation of the Constitution by Congress, the States have a constitutional right to interfere and annul the law of Congress—I do not admit it. If the gentleman had intended no more than to assert the right of revolution for justifiable cause, he would have said only what all agree to. But I cannot conceive that there can be a middle course between submission to the laws, when regularly pronounced constitutional, on the one hand, and open resistance, which is revolution or rebellion, on the other.[26]

All of Hayne's (and Calhoun's) quasilegal moves had been deftly countered, and it had come down to this: submit or rebel. With lightning swiftness, Webster pressed in.

> This leads us to inquire into the origin of this government and the source of its power. Whose agent is it? Is it the creature of the State legislatures, or the creature of the people? If the government of the United States be the agent of the State governments, then they may control it—provided they can agree in the manner of controlling it. If it be the agent of the people, then the people *alone* can control it, restrain it, modify or reform it. . . . If there be no power to settle [the constitutionality of the 1828 tariff which South Carolina rejected and Pennsylvania affirmed] independent of either of the States, is not the whole Union a rope of sand? Are we not thrown back again, precisely, upon the old Confederation?

The clash of verbal steel rang in the chamber as Webster prepared to end the refrain.

> I hold [the United States of America] to be a popular government, erected by the people.... It is not the creature of State legislatures; nay more, if the whole truth must be told, the people brought it into existence, established it, and have hitherto supported it for the very purpose, among others, of imposing certain salutary restraints on State sovereignties.... And, sir, if we look to the general nature of the case, could anything have been more preposterous than to make a government for the whole Union, and yet leave its powers subject, not to one interpretation, but to thirteen or twenty-four interpretations?... Shall constitutional questions be left to four-and-twenty popular bodies, each at liberty to decide for itself, and none bound to respect the decisions of others; and each at liberty, too, to give a new construction on every election of its own members?

And now he thrust home.

> I profess, sir, in my career hitherto, to have kept steadily in view the prosperity and honor of the whole country, and the preservation of our Federal Union. It is to that Union we owe our safety at home, and our consideration and dignity abroad. It is to that Union that we are chiefly indebted for whatever makes us most proud of our country.... It has been to us all a copious fountain of national, social, and personal happiness ... I have not allowed myself, sir, to look beyond the Union, to see what might lie hidden in the dark recess behind. I have not coolly weighed the chances of preserving liberty when the bonds that unite us together shall be broken asunder. I have not accustomed myself to hang over the precipice of disunion, to see whether, with my short sight, I can fathom the abyss below ... while the Union lasts, we have high, exciting, gratifying prospects spread out before us.... God grant that, in my day at least, that curtain may not rise.

As he closed, Webster paused, and turned to look at the flag.

> Behold the gorgeous ensign of the republic, now known and honored throughout the earth, still full high advanced, its arms and trophies streaming in their original lustre, not a stripe erased or polluted, nor a single star obscured.... [It does not bear for its motto the] words of delusion and folly, "Liberty first and Union afterwards"; but everywhere, spread all over in characters of living light, blazing on all its ample folds, as they float over the sea and over the land, and in every wind under the whole heavens, that other sentiment, dear to every true Ameri-

> can heart—Liberty *and* Union, now and forever, one and inseparable!

As Webster sat down, there was no applause, no acclaim. All remained silent, listening to the echo of his words. One of those present noted: "The feeling was too overpowering to allow expression by voice or hand. It was as if one was in a trance, all motion paralyzed."[27] Then the speaker's gavel fell and broke the spell, and there was a long-drawn, deep breath on the part of the audience.

Webster's speech was published far and wide, and throughout the land schoolchildren labored to memorize its stirring conclusion. The proponents of States Rights and nullification had received a staggering blow. But they remained confident they had an ace up their sleeve that could yet turn the game: Andrew Jackson. Throughout the Webster-Hayne debate and the wrangles over nullification which followed it, the President had maintained scrupulous silence. But surely they could count on Old Hickory, the champion of the downtrodden, to throw his weight against the eastern industrialists who had sought the tariffs. So certain of his support were they that they engineered a stratagem that would at last bring him out in the open—on their side.

On April 13, the birthday of Thomas Jefferson, a dinner would be held to honor his memory—and revive his doctrines. The President and all his cabinet received invitations, along with noted political figures from each of the twenty-four states. In those days, toasting had none of the spontaneity of today. The order of toasts at the Jefferson Day dinner—what would be toasted and by whom—had as much organization as a young lady's dance card at a cotillion. One spokesman from each state would give a toast. Starting with Jefferson's Resolutions, these were orchestrated to gradually bring out the historic precedents for states' rights. Hayne was the featured speaker, and although hidden at the outset, gradually a direct challenge to federal authority emerged.

As the evening progressed it became obvious to Jackson that he had been set up. He heard toasts tantamount to treason. Nonetheless, he masked his anger as shrewdly as the expert card player that he was. Finally, his turn came, and all eyes turned expectantly to him. He stood and looked at the faces beaming up at him. Unsmiling, his blue-gray eyes as icy as they had been on the dueling grounds years before, he slowly raised his glass and extended it, as if he were taking aim: "Our *Federal* Union. It *must* be preserved."

The assembled body sat as stunned as if it had just received a seventy-caliber ball in the chest. For a long moment, no one moved. Then all eyes turned to the Vice-president, as Calhoun, his hand trembling so that the contents of his glass slipped over the rim, rose to his feet. In shaken tones, he attempted a riposte: "The Union. Next to our liberties, the most dear. . . ."[28]

News of Jackson's toast swept through the nation and clearly revealed his determination to preserve the Union. Across the country, support began to rally behind him. Any lingering doubt as to the depth of the President's commitment to his present course dispelled when a South Carolina Congressman paid a call on him and asked him if he wished the Congressman to convey any message to his friends in South Carolina. "Tell them from me," Old Hickory declared, "that they can talk and write resolutions and print threats to their hearts' content. But if one drop of blood be shed there in defiance of the laws of the United States, I will hang the first man of them I can get my hands on to the first tree I can find."[29]

The rift between the President and the Vice-president widened to an uncloseable chasm and would eventually see Calhoun retire after his term in the vice-presidency, to devote his full energies to promoting nullification. That policy, despite Webster's historic speech and the President's resolute and unequivocal opposition, continued to gather momentum. Now James Madison, whose modified version of Jefferson's resolves had become the Virginia Resolutions on which Calhoun partially based his doctrine, issued a sharp rebuke. In his promulgated statement, nullification "has the effect of putting powder under the Constitution and the Union, and a match in the hand of every party to blow them up at pleasure."[30]

But South Carolina proceeded relentlessly on its determined course, even though in 1832 new, milder tariffs replaced the detested Tariff of Abominations. In one of those footnotes to history that remind one that God is in charge, the amended tariffs were proposed by the freshman Congressman from Plymouth, John Quincy Adams. The former President, who had left the White House so deeply hurt that he wished for death, had discovered that God was not finished with him yet. On the contrary, what lay ahead for him years later would prove as crucial to the future of America as anything he had hitherto accomplished. Others urged him to run for Congress, and after much prayer he assented—and was elected by a wide margin, in the proudest moment of his life. Men who once politicked against him viciously now lined up to greet him and welcome him to Congress; indeed, it seemed that for the first time in his long career, he had no enemies, only friends and admirers. Feeling younger than he had in years, JQA rolled up his sleeves and got to work. He saw the effect of the protective tariffs on the fabric of the country and soon became instrumental in modifying them; the Adams amendment to the new tariff bill did much to take the sting out of it.

But the nullification movement now seemed to have a momentum of its own, even though a great many South Carolinians adamantly opposed it. Finally, on November 24, 1832, the legislature of the State of South Carolina proclaimed the tariff acts of 1828 and 1832 null and void, "and further declared [it] to be unlawful for any of the constituted authorities of the State or of the United States to enforce payment of the duties." The proclamation directed that no appeal to the United States Supreme Court would be allowed, and in the event of any effort by the United States to enforce the collection of the tariffs in question, the people of South Carolina would "thenceforth hold themselves absolved from all further obligation to maintain or preserve their political connection with the people of the other States, and will forthwith proceed to organize a separate government."[31] There it was—the ultimate threat: secession.

We have often marveled at the miracle of God's handiwork—the right man being in the right place at the right time. America was profoundly fortunate to have as her chief executive a military commander with the rare ability to make the quick, bold decisions that often turn the tide of battle. No temporizing, no paralyzing indecision or agonizing self-recrimination delayed action, while President and cabinet lost precious days, wrestling in seclusion over pros and cons. Before the cement of the South Carolina proclamation could harden into accepted fact, the President drafted a proclamation of his own, addressed to the people of South Carolina: Nullification was "incompatible with the existence of the Union, contradicted expressly by . . . the Constitution, unauthorized by its spirit, inconsistent with every principle on which it was founded, and destructive of the great object for which it was formed. . . . To say that any State may at pleasure secede from the Union is to say that the United States is not a nation." And then, he turned from wrath to appeal: "Fellow citizens of my native State, let me not only admonish you as the First Magistrate of our common country, not to incur the penalty of its laws, but use the influence that a father would over his children, whom he saw rushing to certain ruin. . . . Disunion by armed force is *treason.* Are you ready to incur its guilt?"[32]

Jackson's proclamation made it absolutely clear that he intended to uphold the Constitution, even if it meant resorting to force; yet at the same time he appealed to whatever national spirit remained, and he afterward pledged himself to obtain a further reduction in the hated tariffs. Indeed, such a bill did go through Congress in a matter of days, but it was not enough; the nullifiers, riding high, determined to stay their course.

They left the President with no choice but to go to Congress and request a bill that would permit him to enforce the collection of duties by whatever measures were necessary. The Force Bill, as it became known, set off a new round of debate, with Calhoun, back in Washington now as a Senator from South Carolina, offering the primary oration against it, and appealing to every southerner to stand with him now and be counted for the southern cause.

Once again, the unanimous choice to defend the Union was Daniel Webster. And once again, by the grace and anointing of God, he spelled it out as no one else could, so clearly that none could equivocate or misunderstand. Nullification, Webster had summed up, struck "a deadly blow at the vital principle of the whole Union." To claim that it did not necessarily lead to secession and to "the dismemberment of the Union and general revolution" was like believing that one could take the plunge over Niagara Falls, "and cry out that he would stop half-way down."

He concluded: "Sir, the world will scarcely believe that this whole controversy has no other foundation than a difference of opinion . . . between a majority of the people of South Carolina, on the one side, and a vast majority of the whole people of the United States on the other. . . . [To the world, it must seem] incredible and inconceivable that a single State should rush into conflict with all the rest . . . and thus break up and destroy the world's last hope."[33]

He sat down, and was greeted not by silence this time, but by thunderous and sustained applause. It continued as Calhoun and his supporters stalked out of the chamber. In their absence, the Force Bill passed 32 to 1. Over in the Supreme Court, Chief Justice Marshall, nearing the end of his life, felt tremendously encouraged by the turn events had taken, and his optimism for the future of America was restored. In the White House, Andrew Jackson felt confirmed in his action. Looking back, he would later confide: "I thought I would have to hang some of them and would have done it." But he had no illusions that this ended it and, anticipating their next move, added: "The nullifiers in the South intend to blow up a storm on the slavery question . . . for be assured, these men would do any act to destroy this Union and form a Southern Confederacy, bounded, north, by the Potomac River."[34]

But for the moment, down in South Carolina, certain fire-eaters began to have second thoughts. For even as they created secret stockpiles of arms, in the event that they would have to defend their native soil against federal troops, they learned that many of their fellow Carolinians were also gathering arms—not to fight the United States Army, but to fight *them*. In fact, a large, pro-Union rally was being organized to take place as soon as everyone finished the spring planting, and pro-Union companies were being formed to take on the nullifiers, wherever they might showed themselves. One Unionist described the latter as "all the idlers, loafers, vagabonds and dandies who inhabit the cities and live by their wits."[35]

In short, it appeared that, should the nullifiers persist in their present course, civil war would result *within* the state, and there was every chance that they would experience defeat before the federal troops could even get there. Even more deflating, not one other southern state elected to stand with them; on the contrary, several condemned them, and the general feeling was that Calhoun, his perception distorted by his own frustrated ambition to become President, had pushed the whole thing too far. After due consideration and debate, the nullifiers voted to rescind their proclamation. The great secession crisis was ended—for the moment.

God had preserved His plan through three pillars of the Union—Marshall, Jackson, and Webster, each in his respective branch of government—who had stood strong. Now He was about to add a new spiritual soldier to the ranks of Whitefield, Edwards, Dwight, Asbury, Cartwright, and Beecher.

13

New Wine, New Wineskins

All day long and into the night, the unbroken caravan of wagons rolled through Litchfield County, Connecticut, raising such clouds of dust that it coated everything that wasn't moving, and most of what was moving. To protect themselves the town people could only close their windows, even though the temperature was often sweltering. For Litchfield lay directly on the main westward migration route, and that summer of 1794, it seemed as if someone had pulled the plug and the entire state of Massachusetts had begun to drain out. Some wagons had a lowing cow or two tied behind; it had been too long since the last watering place. But the wagon drivers needed to hurry; every day spent on the road meant one less growing day when they reached Ohio or Pennsylvania or western New York, or whatever their destination was.

The men of Litchfield listened—to the creaking wagons and the cattle and the excited children—sounds of hope and optimism and confidence and courage, of men and women who had taken charge of their lives, for better or for worse. As they listened, they couldn't help thinking about their own lives—the failed farm and now the job in the livery stable or tenant farming someone else's spread, with the wife having to teach school to make ends meet. The men of Litchfield listened, and some had to live with the bitterness that *they* couldn't pioneer, *they* couldn't risk everything . . . because they'd probably just fail again.

Their wives came to them as they looked out at the dusty caravan. They tried to bring their husbands away from the window, but their gentle hands were shaken off. Finally, some of the Litchfield men could stand it no longer. They gathered up their families, sold everything they didn't absolutely need, bought wagons and implements, and joined the caravan. Better to be going ahead than to be ground down to nothing by circumstances.

One go-ahead family was named Finney, and in their wagon sat a two-year-old lad whom they'd named after the hero of a popular moral novel: Charles Grandison. Leaving his birthplace, Litchfield, could hardly disturb a boy too young to have any idea where Oneida County lay on the map of New York State's northwest frontier. But there his family headed, and there he would grow up. Neither of his parents were praying Christians, but God saw fit to bless them anyway—so much so that when young Finney reached his early twenties and would make the best use of a formal education, they were able to send him back to Connecticut. He studied hard and prepared to enter Yale, but his preceptor, a Yale graduate himself, advised that he could gain the same education studying on his own, in half the time. Patience never being one of young Finney's greater virtues, he elected the solo route, continuing his studies and teaching school for a season. When he informed his parents of his plans to go to Florida with his preceptor, to start a private school there, they abruptly fetched him home. Noting the dearth of well-trained lawyers on the frontier, they urged him to start reading law, for the legal profession was sufficiently varied and disciplined to challenge their son's quick and inquiring mind. Young Finney agreed and began his training in a law office in the small town of Adams. Within two years he had been admitted to the New York State bar.

During his studies, Finney had encountered numerous references to the Mosaic Institutes as the authority for many of the great principles of common law. Intrigued, he went out and purchased a Bible, believing, as a good lawyer, in going directly to the source. But in reading the Bible, he found more than he had bargained for, and Finney became interested in what it had to say about his personal condition, which he discerned to be unsaved. For although he attended the local Presbyterian church regularly and even sang in its choir, he was not a professing Christian, nor had he had any desire to become one. Little seemed to recommend this Christianity, even if he could have done anything to join the company of the saved, which the hyper-Calvinists insisted was totally beyond his control. But now he "became very restless. A little consideration convinced me that I was by no means in a state of mind to go to heaven, if I should die."[1] It began to seem increasingly important to him that he be saved. Finally, on a Sabbath evening in the autumn of 1821, at the age of twenty-nine, "I made up my mind that I would settle the question of my soul's salvation at once, that if it were possible, I would make my peace with God."[2]

Too proud to be caught studying the Bible, Finney would hide it under the law books on his desk when anyone came into the office. He felt determined to work this thing out on his own, and quickly; the only trouble was, his heart would not cooperate. "During Monday and Tuesday my convictions increased; but still it seemed as if my heart grew harder. I could not shed a tear; I could not pray."[3] Wednesday he started for the office as usual, but just before he got there, he stopped dead in the street. An inward voice asked him: "What are you waiting for? Did you not promise to give your heart to God? And what are you trying to do? Are you endeavoring to work out a righteousness of your own?" Finney reports:

> I think I then saw, as clearly as I ever have in my life, the reality and fullness of the atonement of Christ. I saw that His work was a finished work; and that instead of having, or needing, any righteousness of my own to recommend me to God, I had to submit myself to the righteousness of God through Christ. . . . After this distinct revelation had stood some little time before my mind, the question seemed to be put: "Will you accept it now, today?" I replied: "Yes, I will accept it to day, or I will die in the attempt."[4]

North of the village and over a hill lay a wood in which Finney was in the habit of walking in the summer. It was October now, and chilly, yet he turned from the direction of the office and headed for his favorite high stand of trees, fired a brilliant red and gold in the early morning sun. As he entered them, he said aloud: "I will give my heart to God before I ever come down again."

But when he reached the crown of the hill, he found that his heart would not pray. Several times, as he would get ready to, he would hear a rustling in the leaves and imagine someone coming. "Finally, I found myself verging fast to despair. I said to myself: 'I cannot pray. My heart is dead to God, and will not pray.' I then reproached myself for having promised to give my heart to God before I left the woods." Again he thought he heard someone approaching, and now abruptly became convicted of his overwhelming pride. "What!" he exclaimed, "such a degraded sinner as I am, on my knees confessing to the great and holy God; and ashamed to have any human being . . . find me on my knees endeavoring to make my peace with my offended God!" And he broke and wept.

At this point, a Scripture seemed to drop into his mind with a flood of light: "Then shall ye go and pray unto me, and I will hearken unto you. Then shall ye seek me and find me, when ye shall search for me with all your heart." Finney had intellectually believed the Bible before, "But never had the truth been in my mind that faith was a voluntary trust, instead of an intellectual state. . . . I knew that it was God's word, and God's voice, as it were, that spoke to me." Other promises now impressed themselves on him concerning the Lord Jesus Christ. "They did not seem so much to fall into my intellect as into my heart, to be put within the grasp of the voluntary powers of my mind; and I seized hold of them, appropriated them, and fastened upon them with the grasp of a drowning man."

Finney continued to pray and receive promises, until he lost all track of time. Finally, to his astonishment, he noted that the long shadows of the trees now lay in the opposite direction—he had been up there the entire day! He got up and as he descended the hill, he found that his mind "had become most wonderfully quiet and peaceful. . . . It seemed as if all nature listened." It was suppertime now, so he went home, but had no appetite and, being restless, went to the office. There, he took down his bass-viol and began to play and sing some pieces of sacred music. Immediately, "I began to weep. It seemed as if my heart was all liquid. . . . After trying in vain to suppress my tears, I put up my instrument and stopped singing." It should be noted that Charles Grandison Finney was a lean, hard rugged frontier lad who topped out at six foot two inches, in an age when the average man was five foot five inches. This was the first time in his life that his heart had ever thus melted, but it was only a precursor of what would transpire that evening.

Later, his employer came by the office to move some furniture and books, and after he had left Finney found his heart again turning to liquid. So overcome was he that he rushed into the back room to pray. There was no fire in the fireplace, and no light in the room:

> Nevertheless it appeared to me as if it were perfectly light. As I went in and shut the door after me, it seemed as if I met the Lord Jesus Christ face to face. . . . It seemed to me that I saw him as I would see any other man. He said nothing, but looked at me in

> such a manner as to break me right down at his feet. . . . I fell down at his feet and poured out my soul to him. I wept aloud like a child, and made such confessions as I could with my choked utterance. It seemed to me that I bathed his feet with my tears, and yet I had no distinct impression that I touched him, as I recollect.

Finney continued prostrate until the vision faded. Regaining his composure, he returned to the front office, where the fire he had built just before going into the back room had nearly burned out. He went to take a seat by the fire, to reflect on what had just happened, but the Lord was not yet finished with him.

> The Holy Spirit descended upon me in a manner that seemed to go through me, body and soul. I could feel the impression, like a wave of electricity, going through and through me. Indeed it seemed to come in waves of liquid love, for I could not express it any other way. It seemed like the very breath of God. I can recollect distinctly that it seemed to fan me, like immense wings.
>
> No words can express the wonderful love that was shed abroad in my heart. I wept aloud with joy and love . . . I literally bellowed out the unutterable gushings of my heart. These waves came over me, and over me, and over me, one after the other, until I recollect I cried out, "Lord, I shall die if these waves continue to pass over me!" Yet I had no fear of death.

Finney slept fitfully that night. Time after time he was tempted to doubt the experience, and each time he refused the doubt. When he awoke, the rising sun was pouring into his room.

> Words cannot express the impression that this sunlight made upon me. Instantly the baptism that I had received the night before, returned upon me in the same manner. I arose upon my knees in the bed and wept aloud with joy. . . . It seemed as if this morning's baptism was accompanied with a gentle reproof, and the Spirit seemed to say to me, "Will you doubt?" I cried, "No! I will not doubt! I cannot doubt!" He then cleared the subject up so much to my mind that it was in fact impossible for me to doubt that the Spirit of God had taken possession of my soul. . . . My sense of guilt was gone; my sins were gone. . . . I felt myself justified by faith. . . .[5]

Finney went to work that morning, and even in the law offices the waves of God's love continued to wash over him. He could not help speaking a few words about salvation to his employer, and while that gentleman made no reply he would learn later that his words had pierced his employer to the heart and continued to trouble him until he had committed his own life to the Lord.

Next into his office came one of his own clients, who happened to be a deacon in the church. With a lawsuit pending, he had retained Finney to represent him. Now as he entered his young attorney exclaimed: "Deacon, I have a retainer from the Lord Jesus Christ to plead His cause, and I cannot plead yours." And with that pronouncement, Charles Grandison Finney forthwith gave up the practice of law to devote himself full-time to preaching.

News of Finney's conversion traveled fast, and at that evening's church meeting practically the entire town turned out. Finney rose and narrated his experience, whereupon an old lawyer who had earlier in the day declared that the report of Finney's conversion was a hoax, now admitted: "He is in earnest, there is no mistake; but he is deranged, that is clear."[6]

Revival promptly broke out and spread throughout the town and into the surrounding communities. Almost all the young people with whom Finney had been associated were converted. Finney himself burned to get on with his calling, and that spring of 1822 he put himself under the care of the local presbytery (a group of Presbyterian ministers and elders) as a candidate for the Gospel ministry. "Some of the ministers urged me to go to Princeton, to study theology, but I declined." When they pressed him for his reasons, "I plainly told them that I would not put myself under such an influence as they had been under; that I was confident that they had been wrongly educated, and they were not ministers that met my ideal of what a minister of Christ should be. I told them this reluctantly, but I could not honestly withhold it."[7] Bluntly honest as usual, he did not exactly endear himself to his future fellow clergy. But he had spoken the truth: the doctrine of salvation only for a vague and undefined "elect" had spread throughout the ranks of Presbyterian clergy, and its fountainhead was Princeton.

In the end, they recommended that he put himself under his pastor, George Gale, whose library he could use and who would guide his course of theological training. Most of Finney's conversations with Mr. Gale wound up as debates, but the Lord used these conflicts to shape and temper His new preacher's beliefs. "Often when I left Mr. Gale, I would go to my room and spend a long time on my knees over my Bible. . . . beseeching the Lord to teach me His own mind on those points. I had nowhere to go but directly to the Bible. . . . and gradually formed views of my own."[8]

For Finney, ministers of the Gospel needed to study Scripture, not for gaining head knowledge, but to bring them into a closer relationship with the living God. In reading the Bible, Finney discovered:

> When Christ commissioned His apostles to go and preach, he told them to abide in Jerusalem till they were endued with power from on high. This power, as everyone knows, was the baptism of the Holy Ghost poured out upon them on the day of Pentecost. . . . The baptism itself was a divine purifying, an anointing bestowing on them a divine illumination, filling them with faith and love, with peace and power; so that their words were made sharp. . . . This is an indispensable qualification of a successful ministry; and I have often been surprised and pained that to this day so little stress is laid upon this qualification for preaching Christ to a sinful world.[9]

In spite of his theological differences with Mr. Gale and others of his peers, in March of 1824 the presbytery licensed him to preach. His first call came immediately: the Woman's Missionary Society of the Western District of New York commissioned him to work for three months in the northern part of Jefferson County.

And so it was that the tall, thirty-two-year-old attorney found himself in the tiny four corners known as Evans' Mills. It was a peaceful, rural setting, and the people were comfortable and set in their ways. On Sundays, their large stone schoolhouse doubled as a church, and there Finney preached his first sermon to a congregation—a little larger one than usual, as those who might have found excuses to stay home were curious about this young ex-lawyer whom the missionary society ladies had imported. He was an attractive young man who preached well, even if he did tend to get a bit carried away. The next Sunday most of them came back.

For several weeks, Charles Grandison Finney declaimed, exclaimed, and proclaimed—and nothing happened. So finally one night, he informed those who returned for the evening service that there was no point in his remaining in their town one day longer if they would not receive the Gospel. Would all who were ready to become Christians please rise? Those who were determined "not to accept Christ" should remain seated.

Stunned by the sudden exhortation, the congregation stayed on the school benches—just as the young preacher had anticipated. "Then you are committed!" Finney roared at them. "You have rejected Christ and his Gospel, and ye are witnesses one against the other, and God is witness against you all!"[10] The congregation now did come to its feet—furious. When Finney refused to offer explanation or speak further, they started to leave. At the last moment, he relented and told them he would preach once more, on the following night.

The whole town was in a state of consternation, and threats of violence against Finney were heard throughout the next day.[11] His behavior shocked and dismayed even the handful of committed Christians in the town—all except for one Baptist deacon who told Finney privately that he thought he had done exactly the right thing. That deacon proved to be a friend indeed; he met with Finney and together they prayed all afternoon that God would have His way in the meeting that night. For Finney, it was a long day's journey, but as anyone who has sought God's help in a time of great crisis knows, it was a journey of definite stages—from anxiety, doubt, and fear, to ultimate peace and the certain knowledge that God was with him and would speak through him.

That evening, a large number turned out, some curious, some still indignant and ready to bid the new preacher swift adieu, some prepared to accept his inevitable apology in the spirit of Christian forgiveness. To everyone's surprise, Finney's message remained as stern as it had been the night before. As they sat there, he looked upward and spoke to God, referring to them as a people who had hardened their hearts like rock against Him. Then:

> The Spirit of God came upon me with such power that it was like opening a battery [of heavy artillery] upon them. For more than an hour . . . the word of God came through me to them in a manner that I could see was carrying all before it. It was a fire and a hammer breaking the rock, and the sword that was piercing to the dividing asunder of soul and spirit. I saw that a general conviction was spreading over the whole congregation. Many of them could not hold up their heads.[12]

Finney had no leading to cut short what God was doing in their midst, so he issued no call to confession and repentance, no invitation to come forward for prayer to accept Christ, no absolution of any sort.

But he held out to them the hope of a service on Sunday. As the congregation departed, one woman was so overcome that two friends had to help her home. For sixteen hours she lay on her bed, literally speechless, and when her voice returned she declared that for eight years she had been a member of the church and thought she was a Christian, but in that meeting she saw that she had never known the true God, and the realization devastated her. Now, she was glad to announce, she had set her feet on the Solid Rock of Jesus Christ.

The tidings spread quickly, and revival broke out in Evans' Mills. Throughout the village, people either turned back to God or turned to Him for the first time. Most of the prominent men in that town were nominal Unitarians, vaguely believing in an impersonal God. For their benefit, on Sunday morning Finney preached a sermon in which he took them step by step through the tenets of Unitarianism and compared it to the Gospel of the Trinity. The Word of God convinced them, and all save one gave their lives to Christ.

The revival gained momentum. It began to spread now into the countryside, infecting neighboring villages and farms. But there was still a bastion of resistance:

> There was a man by the name of D——, who kept a low tavern in a corner of the village, whose house was the resort of all the opposers of the revival. The bar-room was a place of blasphemy; and he himself a most profane, ungodly, abusive man. He went railing about the streets respecting the revival; and would take particular pains to swear and blaspheme whenever he saw a Christian.

The converts added D—— to their prayer lists. . . . A few days later, he suddenly appeared at one of Finney's meetings. Such was his reputation that a number of those present, convinced that he had come to disrupt the proceedings, got up and left. But that was not at all D——'s intent. "He soon arose, and tremblingly asked me if he might say a few words. I told him that he might. He then proceeded to make one of the most heart-broken confessions that I almost ever heard. His confession seemed to cover the whole ground of his treatment of God, and of his treatment of Christians, and of the revival, and of everything good."[13] D—— was as good as his word, turning his bar room into a prayer room and holding nightly prayer meetings there. As word of this miraculous transformation spread, so did the revival, until it began to sweep through all of western New York.

In July, Finney's presbytery met to consider the advisability of ordaining him. They clearly felt uneasy about it, for he had not been seminary trained; thus the Bible was his only authority in theological discussions. Moreover, he seemed to condone and even encourage outbreaks of enthusiasm in his meetings and used "new measures" to reach his listeners. These included an "anxious seat" in the front of the gathering, to be occupied by those under conviction and contemplating repentance; holding meetings almost nightly and allowing them to go on until the small hours of the morning; permitting women to pray aloud in public; and praying out loud by name for prospective candidates for conversion. Most serious of all, the Gospel according to Finney completely swept aside what he called "cannot-ism," the perverted view of the old-school hyper-Calvinists, who claimed that people could do nothing to facilitate their conversion but "wait God's time."

In other words, Finney confronted the same old "damned if you do, and damned if you don't" theology that Timothy Dwight and Lyman Beecher had come up against in the previous generation. Despite the impact of the Second Great Awakening, it had never died out, and gradually, through seminaries like Princeton's, it had regained control of conservative ecclesiastical thinking. But now Finney defied the accepted mode of the old Presbyterian establishment: according to him, ministers who thought this way were lulling their flocks into complacency and dangerous passivity. He believed that a sinner stayed in his sin, not because he was stuck there by fate, but because he *chose* to remain there. As Finney himself summed it up: "I insisted upon the voluntary total moral depravity of the unregenerate and the unalterable necessity of a radical change of heart by the Holy Ghost, and by means of the truth."[14]

And what of the sinner who had had enough of sin? He could choose to confess his sins and repent of them and ask God to forgive him and give his life to Christ—and enter the Kingdom. None familiar with Finney's sermon "Sinners Bound to Change Their Own Hearts" could forget his likening the conversion of a sinner to standing at the brink of Niagara Falls, watching someone lost in thought approach the precipice. At the moment he is about to step over the edge, Finney says, "You lift your warning voice above the roar of the foaming waters, and cry out, *stop!* The voice pierces his ear and breaks the charm that binds him; he turns instantly upon his heel, all pale and aghast, and retires quivering from the verge of death." Likewise, said Finney, the preacher cries *stop,* but the Holy Spirit speaks to the sinner through the preacher's voice. So while it is God who turns people, the act of turning is the sinner's own act; in a sense, he has done it himself, albeit under the Spirit's influence.[15]

As much as the ministers of his presbytery might disapprove of this departure from hyper-Calvinism, every last one of them had seen the membership rolls of his own church significantly expanded by enthusiastic Christians converted under Finney's preaching. Nor could anyone deny that the accelerating revival was a sovereign work of God. They had no choice: they duly ordained Charles Grandison Finney.

Now God's new lightning storm broke in earnest, with Finney, like Whitefield a century before him, His itinerant lightning rod. He preached with more gravity than Whitefield and less self-deprecating humor—indeed, he was the prototype of the great nineteenth-century hammer-and-anvil preachers—but he generated an identical enthusiasm. Similar results also occurred: converts numbered in the scores, then the hundreds, then the thousands.

Once again, as in all great revivals, the fragmented, jealous, bickering Body of Christ became reunited in spirit. Soon after his ordination, Finney visited the town of De Kalb, where the Methodists and Presbyterians had not been on speaking terms since the time of the previous revival, which had broken out under the preaching of Methodist circuit riders. On that occasion, there had been several cases of people "falling under the power of God," which the Presbyterians had dismissed as blatantly self-induced emotionalism, warning everyone against the Methodists. The root of bitterness between them had grown deeper with each passing year.

Apprehension surrounded Finney's arrival, for many had been know to "fall under the power" during the course of *his* preaching. Undaunted, Finney began in typical style, and once more the lightning fell. So did a number of those listening to him—and the first to topple from his pew was a Presbyterian. What was more, it turned out that *all* who fell were Presbyterians! (Has anyone ever doubted that God has a sense of humor?) Red-faced Presbyterian leaders consulted with their Methodist counterparts, and through much "confessions and explanations" both sides effected a lasting reconciliation. When word spread of the ax that had been laid to that root of bitterness, it did as much to encourage the revival as anything Finney ever preached or did.

On and on the tall, lean preacher traveled, pushing himself relentlessly, through sickness and exhaustion, to the point where he coughed up blood. For he gave everything to his ministry for God, just as Whitefield and Asbury had before him. Everyone noted his penetrating gaze, and in existing portraits and daguerreotypes, his deep-set eyes are indeed arresting. Word of his solemn stare went before him, and one convert exclaimed that no man's soul had ever gazed out so through his face.

Once, when Finney was being shown through a textile mill not far from Utica, two girls, weaving at their looms, recognized him as the visiting evangelist whom everyone was talking about. They stopped work, pointed at him, and started giggling. When Finney saw them, he just looked at them. Their smiles vanished, and soon tears flowed, where laughter had reigned shortly before. He had not said a word. Other young women, working near these two, became similarly affected whereupon the proprietor, though not a Christian himself, ordered the superintendent to "stop the mill, and let the people attend to religion; for it is more important that our souls should be saved than that this factory run."[16] A revival meeting took place immediately, and before long almost the entire work force of the factory had given their lives to the Lord.

Utica now became the center of Finney's ministry, and revival reached out in all directions from it, like spokes running from a hub. Other ministers now traveled several days to be a part of it, carrying the work forward and eventually transporting it home. But not everyone who came to Utica did so for the purpose of helping. Attending Hamilton College at Clinton, New York, was a natural leader also dead set against the "new measures" revival everyone heard so much about. When he spoke against Finney, his fellow students listened, for in addition to his own persuasive eloquence, his father was a prominent New England clergyman. Thus, when Theodore Dwight Weld announced that he was going to spend the week down in Utica, visiting a favorite aunt, his comrades rubbed their hands in gleeful anticipation of his confronting Finney. Young Weld had no intention of crossing swords with the revivalist; indeed, such was his contempt that he sought to avoid meeting him. But his aunt, deeply concerned over his spiritual condition, had other ideas. On the Sabbath she took him to a service where someone other than Finney had been scheduled to preach and then arranged other relatives in the pew in such a fashion that her nephew could not leave, when he discovered that Finney would be preaching after all.

Finney, meanwhile, learning that a young but influential detractor would be in the congregation, chose for his sermon text: "One sinner destroyeth much good." Under a powerful anointing, he detailed how much harm a person could do in an influential position, and there was no mistaking to whom he was addressing his remarks. As Weld would record years later in his memoirs, "Finney toasted me on the prongs of his fork."[17] Twice Weld tried to leave, but each time his aunt leaned forward in silent prayer, blocking his way. Weld was livid, and the following day, when he happened to meet Finney by chance in a store on Genesee Street, he let him have it with both barrels. Never in Finney's life had anyone so berated him. On and on the lad went at or near the top of his lungs, so that clerks and customers in other stores came and crowded in. Finally, for want of breath, the stream of vituperation paused, whereupon Finney simply said: "Mr. Weld, are you the son of a minister of Christ? And is this the way for you to behave?"[18]

Stung, Weld immediately left the store, and within an hour he called at Finney's lodgings, asking forgiveness. The two shook hands and had a kindly conversation—ending with Finney having a brief word of prayer for Weld.

That evening, Weld's aunt asked him to lead her family's prayer time, which he did, though he was still in great consternation. All night long, Weld wrestled with his thoughts and conscience, and in the morning he seemed to hear a voice commanding him to repent—*now*. He did, and the next evening at Finney's meeting, he stood up and asked permission to address the assemblage. Finney nodded and Weld announced that he wanted to remove the stumbling block he had cast before the whole people, and he proceeded to make "a very humble, earnest, broken-hearted confession." From that time forth, Weld became one of Finney's most diligent helpers. A powerful speaker in his own right, he left college and devoted his full energies to the revival, working so hard that his health finally broke under the strain. He took some time off to recover, and in a few months he was back again, working as hard as ever.

Resistance to the revival did not die with Weld's repentance. The further its fame spread, the more some ministers resented it. While the Presbyterians were by now largely reconciled to it, this was not the case with the New England Congregationalists, the most influential ministers in the northern part of the country. They, too, had heard reports of excesses at the New York revival meetings and undoubtedly they had occurred; some young ministers in their zeal had added new measures of their own, beyond those subscribed to by Finney. Unfortunately, the old guard—in this case, Asahel Nettleton, Heman Humphrey, who had become president of Amherst College, and the most influential of them all, Dr. Lyman Beecher—chose to believe every report and rumor, without personally checking out any of them.

Thus does Satan continually seek to divide the Body of Christ, playing on the potent combination of jealousy and self-righteousness. "Did you hear about the crazy things XYZ ministry is doing?" Or, "Do you know who is in trouble with the IRS?" We listen, and inwardly thank God that we wouldn't do anything like that. Sadly we first listen, instead of refusing to pay any attention to malicious gossip, which can only tear down and destroy. Once we've heard, we often choose to believe, without checking or challenging, because we enjoy the feeling of righteous superiority that it gives us, and we pass on the rumor at the first opportunity. From the beginning, Satan has known exactly how to divide us; in fact, we make it easy for him.

To be fair, there *were* excesses in the new-measures revival, as young ministers, in their enthusiasm, frequently moved ahead of God and attempted to emulate the work of the Spirit in the arm of flesh. They tolerated disorder and excused wild emotionalism. Brash, young ministers, riding the crest of the revival, felt so sure of the rightness of their acts, that they would brook no correction and became positively arrogant in their self-assurance. Had they heeded the wisdom and learned from the humility of some of the older clergy, their growth toward maturity might have greatly accelerated, but they had no time for that. Sometimes unwittingly and more often uncaringly, they offended the very leaders who could have most helped them. In this case, however, the reaction of the old guard was particularly tragic, for they themselves had had to overcome almost identical resistance when they were in the eastern vanguard of the Second Great Awakening. Apparently age and respectability had caused them to forget how clean some new brooms tended to sweep. They seemed to regard Christianity as their exclusive club, and as directors, they envisioned it as their duty to uphold the club's standards by keeping such undesirable elements as Finney out.

The revival continued and inevitably the irresistible force came up against the immovable object. While Nettleton had fired most of the bullets, others had loaded his pistol, though Beecher had been careful to modulate his own public utterances. In the summer of 1827, Nettleton called for a conference between new-measures ministers and old-guard ministers, to settle differences. Finney agreed, and the conference was held in New Lebanon, New York, just west of the Massachusetts state line. One discreet observer described the atmosphere as "strained." Not wanting to give the proceedings the appearance of some kind of ecclesiastical trial in which he took the rode of defendant, Finney maintained an aloofness, while on their part his potential accusers became painfully aware that if one judged the new-measures tree by its fruit, they might well be advised to go out and do likewise.

For most of the convention, both sides skirted the issues; no one, not even Nettleton, actually brought charges against Finney. Finally, the New Englanders got down to business and proposed the censure of such "abuses" as audible groaning and public female prayer. Some of the New Yorkers went along and some abstained. The new-measures ministers countered by moving to condemn those who heeded and believed unfounded rumors and "lukewarm professors," while the old guard abstained.

All of this was done in good Christian conscience, with quantities of prayer on all sides. In the end, while neither side emerged as the victor, the conference was probably a good thing because everyone had a chance to blow off some steam—and to see that sober, responsible men existed on the other side. Thereafter, conservative criticism of the new measures muted considerably. Finney, of course, proceeded exactly as he had before, and Nettleton's influence, already on the wane, now became inconsequential. But the conference taught Finney one thing that would stand him in good stead, for it gave him a greater understanding of how jealousy and self-righteousness could divide the Body of Christ and block revival. He had seen new-measures ministers every bit as guilty as the old guard. The key was repentance on the part of *all* the Church's ordained and lay leaders.

> All must repent. God will never forgive them, nor will they ever enjoy His blessing on their preaching . . . till they repent. . . . There doubtless have been now, as there were then, faults on both sides. And there must be deep repentance and mutual confession of faults on both sides. . . .

> If they have in any way either directly or indirectly opposed the work, or have so behaved in their public performances or private conversation, as had prejudiced the minds of their people against the work, if hereafter they shall be convinced of the goodness and divinity of what they opposed, they ought by no means to palliate the matter and excuse themselves. . . . They who have laid great stumbling blocks in others' way by their open transgression, are bound to remove them by their open repentance. . . .
>
> Those who have been engaged in promoting the work must also repent. Whatever they have done that was wrong must be repented of, or revivals will not return as in days past. Whenever a wrong spirit has been manifested, or they have got irritated and provoked at the opposition and lost their temper, or mistaken Christian faithfulness for hard words and a wrong spirit, they must repent. Those who are opposed could never stop a revival alone, unless those who promote it get wrong. So we must repent, if we have said things that were censorious, or proud, or arrogant, or severe.[19]

The revival continued, and Finney became a national figure, now going into major cities to preach, where hitherto he had kept to rural areas. Because of his legal training and willingness to logically argue the case for Christ, he reached a stratum of society never touched by revival before. In Philadelphia, in New York, and even Boston, many professional men and their wives came to the Lord. But the series of revival meetings which would become his most famous occurred in Rochester, New York, in 1831. There, roughly one-tenth of the city's population was converted to Christ, and the impact on the life of Rochester was profound. "The moral atmosphere of the city was greatly changed. Grog shops were closed. Crime decreased, and for years afterward the jail was nearly empty. . . . A large number of men prominent in business and social life were brought into the churches. It was estimated that forty promising young men, who had been converted in that revival, entered the ministry."[20]

Similar results followed in Auburn, New York, and Buffalo, and Providence, Rhode Island. And he was invited to Boston and warmly greeted there by none other than Lyman Beecher, who, according to his memoirs, at the New Lebanon conference four years before had shouted: "Finney, I know your plan! You mean to come to Connecticut and carry a streak of fire to Boston. But if you attempt it, as the Lord liveth, I'll meet you at the state line and call out all the artillerymen, and fight you every inch of the way to Boston, and then I'll fight you there!"[21] But now any previous opposition on Beecher's part had obviously disappeared, and throughout the remainder of Finney's long and illustrious service for the Lord, his preaching would be attended with great success. One estimate of his ministry's impact says that he was instrumental in the salvation of 500,000 people![22]

The revival of Finney's time was not a separate or unique event, but rather a continuation of the great revival that opened the nineteenth century, for while the fires had grown so familiar that they no longer attracted front-page attention, they had hardly died out, as religious publications and church histories of that era attest.[23] In 1800, one out of every fifteen Americans was affiliated with a church. By 1835, that ratio had dropped to one in eight, and by 1850, it was one in seven.[24] In the same half-century, the ratio of people to churches went from 1,740 to 1, to 895 to 1.[25] Noted the late historian Perry Miller: "The steady burning of the Revival, sometimes smoldering, now blazing into flame, never quite extinguished (even in Boston) until the Civil War had been fought, was a central mode in this culture's search for national identity."[26]

The most important factor of this wave of revival was not the number of conversions it achieved, but the emphasis it placed on the reformation of society by the Spirit of Christ, operating through the newly regenerate. As *The Christian Spectator* modestly declared: "The grand result to which revivals are here tending, is the complete moral renovation of the world," which they mean to accomplish by elevating "the intellectual, spiritual, and social condition of men."[27] Finney himself urged new converts to get involved—in "abolition of slavery, temperance, moral reform, politics, business principles, physiological and dietetic reform."[28]

Once again, men learned that true Christianity required not just loving God with all one's heart, soul, mind, and strength; it meant also loving one's neighbor as oneself. And as before, when men and women experienced revival, charitable works abounded. Christians found they could not abdicate their responsibility for influencing the society in which God intended them to act as salt and leaven. As Bishop McIlvaine said in 1832, the more important objective of revival was not just the winning of new souls into the Kingdom, but "the quickening of the people of God to a spirit and walk becoming the Gospel."[29]

No longer could Christians consider themselves above the dirty traffic of politics, not deigning to sully the hems of their ethereal garments. "The time has come," exclaimed Finney, "that Christians must vote for honest men and take consistent ground in politics, or the Lord will curse them. . . . God cannot sustain this free and blessed country, which we love and pray for, unless the Church will take right ground. Politics are a part of religion in such a country as this, and Christians must do their duty to the country as a part of their duty to God."[30]

Indeed, it came to be looked upon as one's patriotic duty to spread revival in America, when and wherever possible. Farsighted spokesmen soon claimed that revivals were essential to the well-being and the future of the nation. In 1831, in Lyman Beecher's magazine, *The Spirit of the Pilgrims,* an article entitled "The Necessity of Revivals . . . to Our Civil and Religious Institutions" reflected the mind of the revivalists: "Unless some subduing, tranquilizing influence can be applied, superior to all which man can apply, our race as a nation is swift, and our destruction sure." Only the intervention of God, "in great and general Revivals of religion [will] reform the hearts of this people, and make the nation good and happy."[31]

In fact, the revivalists generally believed that, of all the great civilizations of history, America alone had a chance of avoiding the fate of Chaldea, Egypt, Greece, and Rome—because of her Christian foundation and heritage. Let the Christianity at the heart of America wither and die, and in a very short time the marble monuments on the Potomac would join the ruins on the hills of Rome and the banks of the Nile. From the moment that Jefferson had called for a de-emphasis of the church's influence on state, that became (and still is) the eternal American debate. Two years earlier, *The Christian Spectator* had grimly summed up the revivalists' position:

> What has religion to do with the State, you ask? In the form of ecclesiastical alliances, nothing. But in its operation as a controlling, purifying power in the consciences of the people, we answer, it has everything to do. It is the last hope of republics. And let it be remembered, if ever our ruin shall come, that the questions which agitate, the factions which distract, the convulsions which dissolve, will be but secondary causes. The true evil will lie back of these, in the moral debasement of the people. And no excellence of political institutions, no sagacity of human wisdom, which did not, like that of our Puritan fathers, begin and end with religion, could have averted the calamity.[32]

But in 1831, Beecher's *The Spirit of the Pilgrims* was more optimistic:

> The government of God is the only government which will hold society, against depravity within and temptation without; and this it must do by the force of its own law written upon the heart. This is that unity of the Spirit and that bond of peace which alone can perpetuate national purity and tranquility—that law of universal and impartial love by which alone nations can be kept back from ruin. There is no safety for republics but in self-government, under the influence of a holy heart, swayed by the government of God.[33]

America could lead the rest of the world into the Millennial Age—but would it? We had the foundation, and all the potential—mental, physical, and spiritual. All that was required was for revival to spread far enough and deep enough. . . . For that reason farsighted spiritual leaders put so much emphasis on our daily life in the nation. If we could just put our own house in order, God would use our example to show the way to all the other nations.

The challenge had been given before, but never with such urgency. For the pace of America's development had just increased by several notches, and her growth was about to outstrip all the best efforts of the denominations and home mission societies to keep up with it. Westward expansion had shifted from a trot to a canter to a gallop, and it remained to be seen whether God would continue to shed His grace, from sea to shining sea.

14

"From Sea to Shining Sea"

Sky-filling cumulonimbus formations towered 30,000 feet high as the thunderstorm swept across the Great Plains. The prairie grass ahead of it was flattened first by the wind, then by the rain. The combination of shrieking wind and stinging rain caused gophers to huddle deep in their holes and a herd of buffalo, caught in the open on the vast grasslands, stampeded madly, pounding this way and that in a frantic, hopeless effort to escape.

Ahead of the storm, however, the April sun continued to bake the rich soil, reaching into the earth to loosen the last of winter's iron grip, a foot beneath the surface. As the storm front reached the Missouri River the change in temperature became so acute that great streaks of lightning flashed among the dark, roiling clouds and explosions of thunder shook the earth below while tremendous updrafts lifted grass and dirt just ahead of the leading edge of the storm.

Taking advantage of these unusual thermals, two birds of prey circled upward in slow, ever-ascending spirals. Higher and higher they soared, the sun alternately glinting on their wings and outlining them against the lowering thunderheads that seemed to reach out for them. Already they were far above the normal hunting altitude of a hawk and were now approaching their ceiling, beyond which the air became too thin to support them. From that great height, not even their honed eyesight could discern the movement of a prairie dog. In fact, the covered wagons, clustered in three groups on the outskirts of the town, showed up as little more than white specks against the sere grass of the plains.

Down among the wagons, one pair of grey-blue eyes continued to follow the flight of the hawks, just ahead of the onrushing storm. Everyone else in the wagon train was in near panic, getting all their loose gear inside their wagons and lashing shut the flaps, facing the wagons into the wind, tethering their oxen, and trying to calm their horses. But

Jim Bridger had weathered many such prairie storms. He knew that rain would soon drench him and that there was precious little to be done about it. He also knew that the storm would pass, the sun would return, and they would be dry again and not much the worse for wear. While the greenhorns scurried about in panic, Bridger took pleasure in the joy of the hawks as they soared higher and still higher.

The place was Independence, Missouri, the jumping-off point of all the trails west. The year was 1843, as the Great Emigration was about to reach its peak. H. D. Thoreau summed up "the prevailing tendency of my countrymen. . . . Eastward, I go only by force, but westward I go free."[1] So strong had the westward compulsion become that a popular saying had arisen about it: "If hell lay to the west, Americans would cross heaven to get there." Word had come back that the land in the Willamette Valley of the Oregon Territory was unbelievably fertile, and a man could have a square mile (640 acres) just for the asking. Now came further word that the valleys of the Southern California region were so clement that a farmer could raise two crops a year there, possibly even three. Nor did these tales come from mountain men, notorious for their embroidery of the truth, for missionaries had already settled in the territory known as Oregon, whence they wrote glowing accounts of the Willamette Valley, the new Eden to which God had led them. "As far as its producing qualities are concerned, Oregon cannot be outdone in wheat, oats, rye, barley, buckwheat, peas, beans, potatoes, turnips, cabbages, onions, parsnips, carrots, beets, currants, gooseberries, strawberries, apples, peaches, pears, or fat and healthy babies."

While Yankee sea captains developed such a flourishing fur trade with the coastal Indians that those natives began calling all white men "Bostons," the missionaries opened Oregon for settlement. Because those back home knew these missionaries as sober and responsible believers, their accounts could be trusted, no matter how glowing. Those letters came as an answer to prayer for hundreds of families wiped out by the crash of 1837, or with played-out farms, or those simply caught up in the westward compulsion that had caught the spirit of the nation. Even though, according to treaty, the British and the Americans jointly owned Oregon, and California technically belonged to the Mexican Republic, it seemed manifestly self-evident to many that America was intended one day to stretch from the Atlantic to the Pacific.

Already three trains of close to a hundred wagons each were waiting till the prairie grass grew lush and ripe enough to support their livestock; more newcomers added themselves to their number every day. Leading them were mountain men like Jim Bridger, Old Bill Williams, Thomas "Broken Hand" Fitzpatrick, ex-Kentucky-brawler Mike Fink, and Kit Carson—names already legendary back East, thanks to the extravagant newspaper accounts that dramatized their exploits. These men had traveled to Oregon and back several times; indeed, Bridger even had a fort (or fortified trading post) named after him. They had crossed the vast, empty plains known back East as the Great American Desert—considered worthless and uninhabitable. But now that the impenetrable Rocky Mountains had been breeched and the Pacific Northwest had been found to be decidedly habitable, more and more pioneers put feet on their dreams of a promised land.

The storm reached them, lashed them, drenched them—and passed on. "Wagons, *ho!*" came the cry, and under the watchful eye of the wagon master, each wagon took its assigned place, and slowly a graceful line of white canvas uncoiled from the assembly camp and headed west along the south bank of the Kansas River. The sun came out again, and at last, after weeks of waiting and months of dreaming, they were underway! Some of the wagons were pulled by a team of eight or ten mules, but more often three or four pair of oxen put their massive shoulders to the yoke. Oxen cost about half the price of mules and were more tractable, but a good skinner could do amazing things with a mule team. Each animal had its staunch advocates, and many evenings those about the campfire debated their relative merits. The wagons themselves, many with a milk cow or saddle horse (and sometimes both) trailing along behind, bore the proud manufacturer's name *Studebaker* on the side. They were smaller and considerably lighter than the giant Conestogas that crossed the Cumberland Gap; they never would have survived the mountainous terrain ahead. Outfitting a family for pioneering did not come cheap. Depending on whether you had oxen or mules, and how many, it ran anywhere from $700 to $1500 [1834 dollars]. No wonder, then, that their owners stuffed the wagons chock-a-block full of possessions and provisions—so full, in fact, that cooking utensils, needed every day, festooned the outside of the wagon, and there was only room for the driver and his wife on the bench up front. In the mornings the children walked, or on such a beautiful day as this, scampered. The pace was slow enough for them to easily keep up—the greatest adventure of their lives, for parents as well as children, had begun.

The river they followed stretched west across a land that lay flat as far as the eye could see. The men who held the reins separated between their fingers, with their thumbs riding loosely on top to keep a constant feel for their team, squinted at the horizon in the distance. Up above, the sky turned a deeper blue than ever, decorated with billowing white clouds. It really *was* a big sky. And at night, waiting for sleep to come and lying on ground that might echo a distant herd of buffalo, you looked up at the stars, which seemed to hang so close that you could reach up and touch them. Such a huge sky never hung over the narrow ridges and valleys of Connecticut. At least about that, their predecessors had not exaggerated. The drivers shook their heads and encouraged their teams. Because of the fresh rain, the dust was down, and the wagons chinked and clanked merrily as swaying pots and pans created their own symphony in concert with the creaking wheels and the sound of oxen hooves and laughing children. They listened and smiled; they would face hard times ahead—unbelievably hard times—but this day, their first on the trail, seemed perfect.

Far ahead, at the point of the column, rode Jim Bridger, wearing the buckskin garments of the mountain men, with a long-barreled buffalo rifle balanced crosswise, just behind his saddle horn. These guides with their deeply tanned, weathered faces and eyes that seemed to have a superhuman ability to pick out minute details at immense distance, were a breed apart. They had forged ahead into the soaring, unforgiving Rockies, and conquered them. They had located the springs, found the passes, and opened the way. Now they showed others. But they were not the first. The curtain on Act I of the great drama of America's westward expansion had risen some forty years before. . . .

On the turn-of-the-century map of North America that President Jefferson's aide rolled out on the table before him, the features of the eastern seaboard were well detailed and easily recognizable. And moving inland from the coast, the configuration was still reasonably reliable—until one reached the Mississippi. What lay further to the west had more basis in the mapmaker's imagination than in reality. A great stretch of emptiness lay beyond that river and then a formidable barrier of mountains, vastly larger than the Appalachians. The outline of the Pacific coast, though far less precise than the Atlantic seaboard, was still recognizable, and progressively more so, as one's eye traveled south, approaching the ancient mission settlements of Southern California and the Baja. (Spanish cartographers were as skilled as their British counterparts and had had a century's more practice.) On closer examination of the wasteland west of the Mississippi, one might be surprised to discover a mountain of pure salt a mile high or a westward-flowing, navigable river whose headwaters practically intertwined with those of the Missouri—amounting to no less than the legendary Northwest Passage!

Jefferson's aide weighted down the corners of the map with silver candlesticks, and in the soft glow of their light, the third President and his Secretary of State, James Madison, stared at it in disbelief as they contemplated the enormity of the secret proposal just brought to them. To ensure the continuation of the free trade down the Mississippi, which was so vital to the burgeoning settlements of Kentucky, western Pennsylvania, and the Ohio Valley, Jefferson had sent James Monroe to Paris to offer to buy the port of New Orleans for $2 million. Napoleon had countered by offering to sell the entire Louisiana Territory—from the Mississippi west to the mountains, north to latitude 48°30′, which delineated British territory, and south to the Spanish territory known as Texas. The emperor's price was steep: ten times what the United States had been willing to put up for New Orleans. And it was an all-or-nothing deal, no parceling or subdividing.

Jefferson and Madison knew what lay behind the offer: for his conquest of Europe, Napoleon needed every Frenchman who could bear a musket. In the event of a move by the British from Canada down into the Louisiana Territory or a thrust at New Orleans from the sea, he could not afford to respond with a projection of military force into North America. Even if he *could* spare one regiment, he no longer had a reliable base. Santo Domingo (Haiti), the French colony in the Caribbean, had been torn apart by a slave revolution five years before. So rather than let his last holdings in the New World fall unopposed into British hands, why not ensure that they went to the Americans, who were in a position to defend them? For a price, of course—as much as the traffic would bear.

Jefferson traced the outline of the territory in question with his finger and shook his head. If he acted expediently, he could pull off a coup like none other in the history of the New World. With the stroke of a pen, he could literally double the size of the United States. . . . The trouble was, he would face vehement opposition from the Federalists in Congress. For once, they would be speaking for the majority: most Americans looked east, not west. On the Atlantic seaboard, from Maine to Georgia, merchants and farmers alike were concentrating on the European marketplace. How much would it cost to build and outfit another ship? How quickly could one fill her with timber and hides and cotton and dispatch her to Europe, and receive back a cargo of bolts of cloth and machinery that would more than pay for the cost of the ship itself? Even the frontier farmers looked east, relying on the Mississippi to get their goods to market in New Orleans, where they were transshipped around Florida and either up the East Coast or over to Europe. To them it seemed inconceivable that the British would ever be allowed to gain control of their river, let alone impose tariffs. What did they care about Northwest Passages?

But the man who stared at the unscrolled map was sufficiently suspicious of the British to believe that they *would* grab New Orleans if they thought they possibly could get away with it. For that reason he had sent Monroe to Paris in the first place. He did care about the Northwest Passage. For in addition to his well-known intellectual bent, Jefferson remained a bit of a dreamer and an unfulfilled adventurer himself. As early as 1787, while United States minister to Paris, he had conceived of a scheme to have a lone explorer cross Siberia, pick up a ride on a fishing ship to the northwest corner of North America—and walk home. He had even found a man willing to make the attempt, but then Catherine the Great reneged on her part of the bargain.[2] Four years later, back in America as Secretary of State, he had developed another scheme: to send a French botanist up the Mississippi and then overland to the Pacific. Unfortunately, the man he selected was an *agent provocateur* for the French government, and his real purpose was to stir up trouble between the new American republic and the long-established Spanish colonies to the south and west. But now that he was President, Jefferson could at last project his dream into some form of reality. With the right combination of favorable circumstances. . . .

Through a most extraordinary chain of coincidences, those circumstances, like the tumblers of a mighty bank vault, had suddenly fallen into alignment. Some would raise loud objections, of course, but enough other men of vision sat in Congress, who could appreciate the magnitude of the opportunity that now lay before them. He was hardly the only one who foresaw America one day stretching from ocean to ocean. Now if Monroe could get Napoleon to come down $5 million. . . .

To the surprise of the world and the consternation of Great Britain, America and France struck the deal for $15 million. The first thing the President did was to create America's first Corps of Discovery—a small scientific expedition charged with exploring the Missouri to its source and sending back samples of flora and fauna as well as making observations of the various Indian tribes and then finding an overland route to the Oregon territory (if indeed the convenient, westward-flowing river was a myth). Moreover, he had just the man to lead the expedition: his personal secretary, Meriwether Lewis. Young Lewis was of a fine old Virginia family, and his loyalty was beyond question. Moreover he had pestered his employer for the chance ever since he learned of the proposed formation of the corps. While at twenty-six he seemed a bit young, he had shown his mettle under fire at the Battle of Fallen Timbers, where he served with distinction under Anthony Wayne.

Lewis, in turn, requested that command of the corps be shared with his good friend and fellow combat officer William Clark. Jefferson had no objection; Clark also came from a good Virginia family. His elder brother was none other than Colonel George Rogers Clark, renowned as the Continental Army's ablest commander on the northwest frontier. All things considered, the prospects for the corps seemed brighter and brighter as the time for their departure approached. Indeed, seldom in the history of America, before or since, has an expeditionary force been so bountifully blessed.

The sun had scarcely risen behind them on the morning of May 14, 1804, when forty-three men in a fifty-five-foot, flat-bottomed keelboat and several smaller boats crossed the Mississippi and proceeded up the Missouri. Their company included a dozen men who would bring the keelboat back downriver in the fall, at the first sign of ice, plus fourteen regular army volunteers, nine Kentuckians recruited by Clark, and two of the intrepid French Canadian trapper-explorers known as *voyageurs,* who were skilled boat handlers and who could speak a variety of Indian dialects. Well fed and well rested, the men felt content under the leadership of two captains who, under fire, had already demonstrated their wisdom and maturity. They looked forward to a good trip.

While they were hampered by prevailing westerly headwinds and could often make no more than three or four miles a day upriver, nonetheless morale remained high. For they passed through magnificent, heart-filling country, and each day brought new marvels. Faithfully checking the temperature and soil characteristics and mapping the river and surrounding territory as they went, they recorded it all—the cottonwood, oak, black walnut, and hickory trees, the succulent plums and raspberries, the catfish teeming in the river beneath them, the deer on the plains, and the turkey and geese in the sky—for this was, first and foremost, a scientific expedition. The Kentucky riflemen in their number ensured that it was also a well-fed expedition.

Contrary to frontier rumor, the various tribes of Indians that they met were for the most part friendly. Lewis and Clark's instructions from their Commander in Chief on this point had been specific: "Treat them in the most friendly and conciliatory manner. . . . make them acquainted with the position, extent, character, peaceable and commercial dispositions of the United States, of our wish to be neighborly, friendly, and useful to them. . . ."[3] The Indians responded in kind—except for the Teton Sioux. The expedition quickly noticed that they were being shadowed on the riverbank by a party of fifty warriors, who, as it turned out, had never seen a craft larger than a dugout canoe. Using as interpreter one of the voyageurs who knew a few words of the Sioux language, Lewis and Clark invited the five chiefs among the party to come on board the keelboat.

Curiosity overcame caution, and the chiefs accepted the invitation and delightedly received the presents of glass beads and trinkets the expedition had brought with them for such a purpose. Then Lewis and Clark made their first mistake: they produced a bottle of whiskey and poured each of the chiefs a quarter of a glass. The chiefs consumed the potion in one gulp and, amazed at the result, suddenly grabbed the bottle away from their hosts. Tilting it to their lips, they passed it to one another until it was empty and obstreperously called for another. Sensing a potentially volatile situation, Clark managed to get the chiefs into one of the smaller boats and, with five of his men rowing, accompanied them to shore.

No sooner did the boat nose into the bank than three of the braves, waiting at the river's edge, grabbed the boat's bowline so that it could not return. Clark and his five men got out, and he described in his journal what happened next: "The second chief, who affected intoxication, then said that we should not go on, that they had not received presents enough from us."[4]

To the chief's demand for more presents and whiskey, Clark, now growing a bit heated himself, replied: "We are not squaws but warriors, sent by our great father, who could in a moment exterminate you!"[5] The chief responded that he, too, had warriors, and at that, Clark drew his sword and signaled the boat to prepare for action. Immediately the Indians put arrows to bowstrings and formed a circle around Clark, while on the keelboat, hammers drew back on rifles, targets were agreed upon, and the two swivel guns, loaded with grapeshot, were brought to bear on the mass of Indians. At the same time, twelve armed men swarmed into a small boat and headed for their beleaguered captain.

For the moment, all history seemed to hold its breath. With their swivel guns and rifles, the expedition could inflict heavy casualties and drive off their adversaries, but further progress would be impossible. Moreover, thousands of Sioux between there and Saint Louis would not rest until they avenged their fallen brothers. With the possibility of an ambush waiting around each bend, the river would become an interminable gauntlet, day and night, from which there would be no escape, until the last white man's scalp hung from a Sioux belt. The soldiers knew this and grimly settled their sights on the heads and hearts of the menacing natives.

The leading chief, Black Buffalo, noting their determination, raised his hand and signaled his men to draw back. Accustomed to having things their own way, the Sioux had never encountered such resistance before. This shift in circumstances allowed Clark to regain his poise, and he relaxed and held out his hand in an unmistakable gesture of friendship. Black Buffalo and his second chief spurned the hand and turned to leave, but for some unaccountable reason, turned back again and asked to come back aboard the keelboat. Again they were welcomed, stayed all night, and in the morning asked if their women and children might also visit the boat. Thus, by the grace of God a tragedy that would have poisoned relations for generations to come was averted by the narrowest of margins.

On the prairies, with no lakes or hills or woodlands to round the edges, changes in climate are abrupt and extreme. When it is hot, it swelters; when it is cold, it chills the bones. For several weeks, they had watched the level of mercury in their thermometer drop lower and lower; and providentially, just as it failed to rise above thirty-two of Professor Fahrenheit's degrees, even under the high noon sun, and the river began to ice over, they arrived at the main settlement of the Mandan, the first tribe they had met that lived more by what it could grow than what it could kill. Here they wintered over, constructing two barges to take the place of the keelboat, which they would dispatch back to civilization, come spring. Living with the Mandan were two *voyageurs,* one of whom had a wife with him—a sixteen-year-old Shoshoni named Sacajawea, who had been bought from the Minitarees, who had taken her during a raid on her people. She was a cheerful young woman who would soon figure into the expedition's plans far more than Lewis and Clark could ever imagine.

Each day, the expedition's log recorded that the sun rose a minute or two earlier, and almost imperceptibly the average of the mercury levels began to rise as well. At length, in April, it remained above thirty-two degrees long enough for the river to lose its sheath of ice. The keelboat, packed full of specimens of dried flora and stuffed fauna and accompanied by an escort of soldiers, returned to Saint Louis, while the expedition continued west, with Sacajawea and her *voyageur* husband now a part of it. As the Mandan had warned them, the river became progressively more difficult—frequently too shallow or rocky to paddle up or pole. Then, out would come the towropes and the men would double as pack mules. Even so, morale remained high, for the hunters, fanning out ahead of them, had no trouble taking elk, antelope, and buffalo. One animal did give them pause, however—an enormous bear that reared eight feet in the air when aroused and apparently had never encountered a natural enemy that it couldn't best. This was the giant grizzly, who would as soon charge a man as look at him and whom a man could stop only by a perfectly placed bullet in the heart or the brain. Anything less only infuriated him more, and not even the fabled Kentuckians remained cool enough to stand their ground when they felt the earth shaken by the rapid approach of half a ton of deeply perturbed bear.

Their surroundings never ceased to amaze them. In the middle of what is now Montana, they got their first glimpse of the Great Falls, which stood across the river like a roaring wall of water ninety feet tall. Lewis particularly was awestruck by "this truly magnificent and sublimely great object which has from the commencement of time been concealed from civilized man."[6] After a grueling, eighteen-mile portage around the falls, they continued poling and pulling day after day, until they passed through the "Gates of the Rockies"—perpendicular cliffs of black granite, towering some 1,200 feet above them. Now they were out of their barges and canoes more often than they were in them, as they began to ascend into the foothills of the majestic, snow-peaked mountains that lay ever before them.

On July 25, they reached the place where three tributaries joined to form the Missouri. They named these the Jefferson, the Madison, and the Gallatin. As the Jefferson seemed the largest, they pushed on up it—literally, for in places it was little more than a stream, plunging down rapids and over beaver dams. The going became torturous now; the river turned shallow and rapid, and dense cottonwood brush lined the banks, forcing the men to get out and haul their craft upriver through the shallows. On shore, the prickly pear bushes pierced their wet moccasins, and their feet became ulcerated and infected. In these higher elevations, downpours often carried hailstones that bruised and bloodied them, and now many of the men had stomach ailments and boils and blisters covered their skin.

Encouragment came only from the fact that Sacajawea was beginning to recognize landmarks. They were nearing Shoshoni country—the Shoshoni would have horses that they might be willing to sell—a good thing now that the river was almost impassable. In desperation, Lewis took three men and went ahead, traveling light and scouting for Indians. On August 12, 1805, he and his companions reached the top of the Continental Divide, the roof peak of the Rockies, 7,373 feet above sea level. Had it rained as they stood there and had they been facing north as it rained, the water that fell to their left would ultimately flow into the Pacific; that which fell on their right would join the Mississippi and go to the Gulf of Mexico. It might have been an auspicious moment—if they weren't so sick and tired and hungry.

They scarcely paused, clambering down the western slope, looking for Indians. They did catch a glimpse of some, but the natives fled long before the white men could get close enough to make their needs known. Lewis neared despair, but the next day the Lord had mercy on them: in their continuing descent, they came upon a party of squaws who did not run away. These took them to their village, where they were warmly welcomed; indeed, they were embraced by the warriors until "we were all caressed and besmeared with their grease and paint."[7] However, after several days, Clark and the main party failed to appear, and the Shoshoni became suspicious. Lewis and his companions began to fear that their lives might be in danger, when at last Clark and the others arrived. All was well: Sacajawea turned out to be the long-lost sister of the Shoshonis' chief! So great was the tribe's rejoicing that Lewis had no trouble striking a favorable bargain for the horses they needed so badly.

Their western odyssey resumed—days, weeks, slowly picking their way through the mountains, pushing north and mostly west. As September turned into October, they began encountering early blizzards. Game became scarce, and once again hunger was their constant companion. Eventually, they were reduced to less than half-rations, and the specter of starvation followed them as a silent beast of prey, stalking their trail. Barely able to continue, they finally stumbled upon the Columbia River—and some friendly Indians who gave them dried salmon. Making dugout canoes by burning out logs in Indian fashion, they started downriver. The Columbia was one rapids after another, and far stronger than any that they had experienced, but they survived, and on November 7, 1805, one year and a half after leaving Saint Louis, they caught their first view of the "South Sea."

"Ocean in view! Oh, the joy!" exclaimed Clark in his journal. That night he added: "Great joy in camp. We are in view of the ocean, this great Pacific Ocean which we have been so long anxious to see. And the roaring, or noise made by the waves breaking on the rocky shores, can be heard distinctly."[8] They had done it! They traveled an incredible 4,155 miles—an expedition that stands as a monument to the undaunted spirit of the American pioneers who stoically and routinely endured physical hardship and privation almost unknown today. Moreover, they demonstrated that, not only was it possible to travel overland to the Oregon territory, but well-prepared expeditions could forge a settlers' movement there and thus secure America's claim to that land.

When the explorers returned home safely, they were welcomed and feted as national heroes and the first act of the great drama of westward expansion drew to a close. While Lewis and Clark never did publicly acknowledge their debt to a superintending Providence, in the central park of Portland, Oregon, there stands today the statue of an Indian woman—Sacajawea, God's provision for America's first Corps of Discovery.

The central characters of Act II seemed larger than life, giants striding across the stage. Their names already household words back East, the mountain men stood ready to live up to their reputation as the most fearless, independent, resourceful breed of men ever seen on the face of the earth (which probably held little exaggeration). Only the strong survived, and the toughest were invariably the lone adventurers who drifted ever further west, keeping ahead of the edge of civilization. With the opening of Kentucky, they were the "roarers"—brawlers who would gouge out an eye or bite off a nose, if that was what it took to win a fight. With the opening of the Mississippi, it became the rivermen, who drank and gambled away a month's wages in any of the countless New Orleans saloons, ready to fight anyone who doubted (or even looked as if they might doubt) that they were the meanest men in the place.

But the mountain men *were* more. They had to be, to survive in a wilderness so barren that the nearest game might be days away, and the nearest white man three months to the east.[9] Instant death was just a shadow away—a misstep on a mountain cliff, an unguarded moment, stooping to drink from a spring in hostile Indian country, a bad-tempered grizzly who could shrug off the contents of your rifle and both pistols and with one swipe of his paw tear your face off and break your horse's back for good measure. Grizzlies so populated the land that you might count fifty or sixty in a single day—if you saw them first. You developed a sixth sense for imminent danger—a sound you heard that you shouldn't have or one you should have and didn't—and you learned to trust that sense and act instantly on it. For if you ever took time to think.... No wonder Thomas Farnham, writing in 1843, would describe the mountain men: "Habitual watchfulness destroys every frivolity of mind and action. They seldom smile; the expression of their countenances is watchful, solemn, and determined."[10]

Of all the hazards, Indians were the greatest. Many acted kindly toward strangers, but some became treacherous, and you couldn't tell which were which. Some, if they thought you might have something they wanted, would kill you to find out, even if it meant tracking you for several days. You only survived if you could beat them at their own game: you had to become better at tracking and living off the land than they were. You had to hear them or even smell them, before they got wind of you, and if cornered, you had to shoot better with a rifle than they did with a bow, and strike more quickly and fatally with a Bowie knife than they could with a tomahawk.

What drew these men into the mountains? "Brown gold"—the rich, warm, durable pelt of the beaver. In the early part of the nineteenth century, the fashion world had suddenly developed a passion for beaver hats—and not just hats, but coats and muffs, as well. Anyone of any standing in society (or anxious for that appearance) simply had to have them. Before they became fashionable, beaver skins were supplied by the Indians, who used them for barter. But as the demand increased and prices went up and up white adventurers quickly saw a good thing. Yankee ingenuity had come up with an iron trap that worked far more efficiently than the Indian's snare, and armed with these, the mountain men could trap enough beaver in a few weeks to support themselves for a year, provided they didn't get drunk and gamble it all away at the first opportunity, which they often did. No matter—there were plenty more beaver out there.

Back east, entrepreneurs with venture capital also quickly seized upon a good thing. John Jacob Astor and his friends decided to corner the burgeoning beaver market, if they could. To that end, they formed the American Fur Company, organized and dispatched parties of trappers, and began to take on the mighty Hudson's Bay Company at its own game. The Bay Company had the advantage of its long-established wilderness trading posts and good relations with the Indians, which went back many generations. To counter this, the American Fur Company devised a refinement that dramatically increased the rate at which beaver were trapped: the annual rendezvous. Rather than have the trappers bring their early spring and late fall pelts all the way back to Saint Louis, a company caravan, loaded with trading goods, camping supplies, and plenty of hard currency and whiskey, would in early summer make an annual trek upriver and into the foothills, to a prearranged site. Sometimes "it was beneath the red sandstone cliffs of the Wind River mountains, where the valleys of the Popo Agie or Wind rivers were bright with flaming wild flowers; sometimes along the shores of the meandering Bear River, where the grass was lush and tall; sometimes in Jackson's Hole or Pierre's Hole, where calm lakes reflected the naked peaks of America's most majestic mountains, the snow-dappled Grand Tetons."[11] Here, the company caravan would meet with the company's trappers as well as Mexicans from Santa Fe, French Canadian defectors from the Hudson's Bay Company, loners, Indians—anyone who had beaver pelts to sell. The rendezvous saved the trappers several months of travel time, while at the same time assuring Astor and company a virtual lock on the beaver trade.

These annual get-togethers were the most extraordinary gatherings of their kind in the nineteenth century. A city of tents would bloom on a field in the foothills, as down from the mountains came one character after another, usually leading a mule or two piled high with pelts. Indian women would greet them, and even some of the hardier white dance-hall girls. The traders offered every conceivable article that the trappers might take a fancy to, turning their wagons into miniature general stores. Whiskey would flow like water, leading to wild horse races and reckless gambling, and for music, there would be fiddles and perhaps even a spinet piano. . . . Everywhere a spirit of carnival and celebration reigned, for each year the price of beaver fur went higher than the year before.

Every mountain man worth his salt appeared there—men whose names were already famous and who would soon be immortalized by the dime novelists. The way they carried on, they seemed bent on enlarging their already ample reputations. "I'm a ring-tailed mountain cat, the meanest, orneriest, fastest. . . ," and if someone happened to be shouting the same thing at the other end of the long makeshift bar, it wouldn't be too long before fists and occasionally knives settled it. For these men had lived with fear on a daily basis for so long that they had overcome it. They had become as fearless as men could be, yet they bought it at a steep price: they had little respect for human life—their own, or anyone else's. They had seen too many men die and had grown protective calluses over their hearts, so that at such times they seemed downright indifferent. "Too bad about Old Joe; his luck plumb ran out on him. . . ."

Thus it was with Hugh Glass, when he was attacked and severely mauled by a grizzly, with arms, legs, and torso torn open. At first, his two companions, having tried and failed to stanch the flow of blood, promised to stay with him to the end. But the end took its time in coming, and after two days, when he finally slipped into a coma, they decided that there was no point in waiting until he was actually dead. Why leave his horse and favorite rifle for the Indians? So they took them and departed. Incredibly, Glass recovered consciousness. Finding himself alone, he got water from the spring which they had laid him next to and managed to scrounge a few wild berries. For ten days, he felt too weak to move, but finally he determined to leave. Too hurt to stand, he could still crawl, so on his knees, he started for Fort Kiowa—nearly a hundred miles away. To the dumbfoundment of those inside the fort, the day came when he crawled in through the front gate. But he didn't stay to rest. Taking nourishment and provisions, he continued to track the two men who had abandoned him and taken all his belongings, including his beloved rifle. He caught up with the younger one, Jim Bridger, on New Year's Eve and staggered into the fort's festivities, frightening everyone, for he looked more like an avenging ghost than a man. But he forgave Bridger, because of his youth—and then forgave the other companion, too, as soon as he got his rifle back, saying only: "Go, false man, and answer to your own conscience and to your God."[12]

With all the breathtaking natural beauty around them, most of it never seen by white men before their arrival, one would think that their resting thoughts might turn toward the Creator. Not so; from Lewis and Clark through Kit Carson, there is scant record of any spiritual predilection among them. In the words of one contemporary observer, "They had little fear of God, and none at all of the devil."[13]

There was one prominent exception, a man for whom the other mountain men had profound respect: Jedediah Smith. He came from a deeply religious pioneer family whose roots went back to New Hampshire and to whom he would write in the long quiet of winter encampment: "As it respects my spiritual welfare, I hardly darest speak. I find myself one of the most ungrateful, unthankful creatures imaginable . . . I have need of your prayers." And on another occasion: "Then let us come forward with faith, nothing doubting, and He will most unquestionably hear us. . . . Some, who have made a profession of Christianity, and have by their own negligence caused the Spirit to depart, think their day of grace is over. But where do they find such doctrine? I find our Saviour ever entreating and wooing us, using the most endearing language and endeavoring by every means without compelling (for that would destroy our free agency) to bring us to Him, that we may have life."[14]

A tall, silent man who never used tobacco or profanity or touched the Indian women and took a ceremonial drink only on formal occasions, Smith seemed out of place among the boisterous trappers. Yet his faith gave him leadership ability, coolness under fire, and a perseverence in the face of suffering and deprivation. Two incidents guaranteed his place in the chronicles of American heroism: he was with the first trapping expedition up the Missouri in 1822, when the party came under Indian attack. The others leapt into the river and swam for the boats, but Smith stood his ground, took careful aim, and dropped the lead Indian before tucking his rifle in his belt and following them. Hugh Glass was in that party, and he wrote the parents of one of the fallen trappers: "My painful duty it is to tell you of the death of your son, who befell at the hands of the Indians, 2nd of June in the early morning. . . Mr. Smith, a young man of our company, made a powerful prayer which moved us all greatly, and I am persuaded John died in peace."[15]

The second incident took place not long after as Smith led a trapping expedition. Coming through a thicket, he found himself face-to-face with a grizzly. Instantly the bear was on him, breaking his ribs with the blow of a paw and getting most of Smith's head in his mouth before the rest of the party could drive him off. Smith, his ear dangling off the side of his face and blood pouring out of the wound, nevertheless calmly directed his men to wash the wounds and stitch them up with needle and thread. Two men, who stayed behind to care for him, were killed by a band of marauding Indians, and Smith, hiding in the underbrush, barely escaped detection. The Indians made off with everything in sight—horses, saddles, blanket, even cooking utensils. All Smith had left was his rifle, his knife, a flint for making fire, and the Bible he always carried with him. Now he opened it and read, in Job 33: "He is chastened also with pain upon his bed, and the multitude of his bones with strong pain. . . . Yea, his soul draweth near unto the grave, and his life to the destroyers. . . . His flesh shall be fresher than a child's: he shall return to the days of his youth: He shall pray unto God, and He will be favorable unto him."

Taking that passage as a promise, Smith the next morning dragged himself from one beaver trap to the next, until he found a beaver, which he cooked. The next two days, he went without food, finding solace in his Bible. On the third he shot a fat buck who came to drink at the creek. Yet still he went without dressing for his wounds and grew steadily weaker. Again he opened his Bible, this time to the twenty-third Psalm: "Yea, though I walk through the valley of the shadow of death, I will fear no evil: for Thou art with me. . . ." He was nearly dead, three days later, when a party of trappers, led by a friend who had gone for help after the bear attack, found him.[16] Incredibly, in a few more days, he returned as the expedition's head, leading them into the wilderness.

Like the black-robed missionaries two centuries before him, Jedediah Smith's greatest earthly passion was exploration, and historians have belatedly placed his name beside Lewis and Clark's in this area of achievement. For Smith found the South Pass that truly opened up the Rockies. Smith was the first white man to travel overland to California from the interior, the first to traverse the Great Basin, and the first to reach Oregon by going up the coast of California. Other white men would find the southern pass across the Continental Divide, but Smith made it known to the countless missionaries and settlers who would follow. Of his journeys, he kept a journal filled with wonder at God's myriad creations—wood so baked by the sun that it resembled stone, a pricker tree that gave water to thirsty travelers, the illusion of a silvery lake that vanished as one rode toward it, and at last, the immense Pacific Ocean. When a man loved God, it seemed to magnify the glory of his natural surroundings—as if the Maker had put it there as a special gift to His children.

Jedediah Smith's greatest feat of exploration remained his 1826–27 trek to California, which began as a search for beaver and continued out of dire necessity. Smith and his party left the rendezvous in present-day Utah on August 16 and headed southwest through the valley of the Great Salt Lake, a sweltering land Smith described as "a country of starvation—sandy plains and rocky hills, and once in twenty, thirty, or forty miles, a little pond or spring."[17] The sand became red and the thorny vegetation increasingly scarce, little more than sagebrush and an occasional juniper. Since beaver required moving water and since there was obviously none of that around, the men became edgy and quarrelsome. Their supply of dried buffalo meat gave out. But God remained with them; Smith found some corn and pumpkins that Indians must have planted. It helped, but not for long; by the time they reached Mohave Indian country, they were walking, all their horses having given out. The final stretch took most of November, as they followed the old Indian trade route across the Mohave Desert, going all day without water, over a plain crusted with salt that reflected the sun with blinding intensity. At last, stumbling along beside the Mohave River, they came down out of the mountains and into the beautiful San Bernardino Valley, where sheep and horses grazed beside laughing streams. Even the most hardhearted among them were convinced they had reached the Promised Land!

Smith would surely have gained renown equal to Kit Carson and the others, were his life not tragically cut short at the age of thirty-two. On an expedition to Santa Fe in 1831, Smith's party had gone without water for three days. In desperation the men fanned out looking for water holes, and Smith came upon one. Perhaps his thirst dulled his sense of danger, but he rode up, unaware of a band of Comanche Indians hiding there, lying in wait for buffalo. In an instant, they surrounded him. He tried to parley with them, but they deliberately spooked his horse, and when it reared and wheeled, they shot him in the back. He turned and got one shot off, killing their chief before their lances went through him. But even in death, God may have had mercy on Smith, sparing him having to live through the twilight of the mountain men.

By 1834, the beaver trade had reached its high-water mark. More and more freebooters joined the ranks of the mountain men, forcing the trappers to go further and further into the Rockies, in search of mountain streams that had not already been trapped out. In just four more years, the catch so dwindled that the American Fur Company decided it could no longer afford to send out caravans, and they canceled the rendezvous. The trappers were shaken, but not the capitalists back east; they had already made their fortunes and now quickly noted that the ever-fickle taste of the fashion world was turning away from beaver hats, in favor of hats made of silk. Indeed, because of the sudden shift, even though beaver pelts were rapidly becoming a rarity, instead of rising, the going price for them plummeted. In two more years, no one wanted them at all—fortunately for the beaver, which as a species, had practically disappeared.

As had the mountain men. Cut off from their source of relatively easy financial reward, they had to find something else. Some drifted back east, some headed for the Pacific Coast, but the wisest and the most enterprising among them had already begun raising the curtain on the third act of the westward drama, even before Act II drew to a close. For they had a unique and now marketable talent: they could find their way through the wilderness. With westward migration burgeoning, more and more settlers who couldn't find their way willingly paid well for guides who could.

It all began in 1823 with an inspired schoolteacher (the man who introduced the blackboard into schoolrooms) named Hall Jackson Kelley. God had given him a vision, he said, of 3,000 New England farmers emigrating en masse to the banks of the Columbia River. "The word came expressly to me, to promote the propagation of Christianity in the dark and cruel places about the shores of the Pacific."[18] For the next ten years he labored to bring the vision to fruition, and by 1829 he had won enough followers to formally establish the American Society for Encouraging the Settlement of the Oregon Territory. Its mission: "planting, in the genial soil of those regions, the vine of Christianity, and the germ of civil freedom."[19]

One of the society's early members, Nat Wyeth, actually set out on his own at the head of a small company in 1832, and eight months later reached the Hudson's Bay Company post, Fort Vancouver. Wyeth made his way back to Boston and started out again in 1834 with another band of pioneers, which this time included a Methodist clergyman named Jason Lee, who had been powerfully moved (as would be several thousand Christians in his wake) by a letter that had been printed the year before in the *Christian Advocate and Journal.* The letter, written by a Wyandot Indian named William Walker, described his encounter with four Indians, three Nez Perces and one Flathead, who had traveled 3,000 miles to Saint Louis, because "the white people away toward the rising sun had been put in possession of the true mode of worshipping the Great Spirit; they had a book containing directions."[20] They had come to learn the contents of the Great Spirit's book, and so difficult had been their journey that two of them had died of sickness and exhaustion upon arriving. Although historical evidence indicates that shows Walker may never have actually met these Indians, nevertheless his letter had a sensational effect on American Christians. Ministers and religious publications began appealing for missionaries to respond to the plea of the poor heathen. So Lee and four like-minded Christian men had joined up with Wyeth's company and embarked to find the Flathead Indians. Their charge from the Methodist Church: "Live with them, learn their language, preach Christ to them, and, as the way opens, introduce schools, agriculture, and the arts of civilized life."[21]

At Fort Hall, Jason Lee preached the first American sermon west of the Rockies, to a combined congregation of trappers and Indians, who apparently were impressed, for they "sat on the ground like statues."[22] They reached their ultimate destination, Fort Vancouver, on the Pacific Ocean, on September 16, 1834, and were warmly greeted by the Hudson's Bay Company's director for the territory, Dr. John McLoughlin. He advised the eager missionaries that the Flathead Indians lived in dangerous country many days' travel from the fort and suggested that they settle instead in the nearby Willamette Valley. This they did, and soon Lee was planting crops, starting a school (with a blackboard), and writing the mission board back east to send families and teachers.

They had little trouble finding ready, willing, and able volunteers, for the letter in *The Christian Advocate* had galvanized many other Christians. One was a young doctor from upstate New York named Marcus Whitman, destined to accomplish more for the settlement of Oregon than any other person. Burning with zeal to serve the Lord, Dr. Whitman petitioned the American Board of Foreign Missions to send him to Oregon. Having already commissioned the Reverend Samuel Parker to explore the feasibility of missionary work in Oregon, they granted Whitman permission to accompany him. So the robust Whitman and the thin-lipped, overly starched preacher arrived in Saint Louis in April of 1835 and attached themselves to a rowdy caravan of trading wagons, heading into the mountains for their annual rendezvous with the mountain men, under the leadership of the famous Jim

Bridger. While Dr. Whitman threw his efforts into lashing down equipment, lifting wagons out of sinkholes, and treating a cholera epidemic among the men, Parker occupied himself with supervising others, criticizing Whitman's work, and avoiding most of it himself.

In addition to Dr. Whitman's pitching in to help with the daily chores of the expedition, he made a lifelong friend of Bridger when he cut a Blackfoot arrowhead out of his back, where it had been painfully lodged for several years. When Whitman expressed surprise that the wound had never grown infected, Bridger sardonically replied: "Meat don't spoil in the Rockies."[23] When the group reached the annual trappers' rendezvous at Green River (in what is today Wyoming), Reverend Parker had concluded from the trapping Indians' favorable response to his rendition of the hymn "Watchman, Tell Us of the Night," that they were ready to be evangelized. Whitman, on his part, concluded that if the traders' wagons could make it through that unbroken wilderness so could wagons of pioneer families wishing to go to Oregon. So while Parker went on to Oregon, to teach the Indians the Lord's Prayer and the Ten Commandments, Whitman headed back east to recruit Christian settlers—and marry his fiancée, a devout and beautiful young lady named Narcissa.

After the wedding, Whitman attempted to sign up a number of families for his expedition in the spring. He succeeded in recruiting a grand total of three people: a carpenter named William Gray, and an ordained minister and his wife, Henry and Eliza Spaulding. Reverend Spaulding, jealous that the mission board had not put him in charge of the expedition (and that Whitman had bested him for the hand of the fair Narcissa), picked one quarrel after another with Whitman, until Narcissa would write to her father: "The man who came with us is one who never ought to have come. My dear husband has suffered more from him in consequence of his wicked jealousy, and his great pique towards me, than can be known in this world."[24]

Whitman planned to join their two wagons to the annual rendezvous caravan, this one led by Broken Hand Fitzpatrick. But they were delayed leaving Independence and had to push long into the nights to catch up, which they finally did. Narcissa's spirit remained unbroken as she took to the trail like a veteran, milking four cows and baking bread in the embers of the campfire. From the fork of the Platte, she wrote her sister: "I never was so contented and happy before. Neither have I enjoyed such health for years."[25]

In the middle of June, Fitzpatrick brought the train into Fort Laramie, where, to Whitman's intense disappointment, the guide insisted that they leave their heavy farm wagon behind. To Whitman, an essential part of their mission was to demonstrate that wagons *could* make it all the way to Oregon. Now he had to content himself with driving the much lighter Dearborn wagon. Yet the going became such that even the little wagon caused them to arrive in camp long after dark—a practice that was becoming extremely dangerous as they neared hostile Indian country.

At Independence Rock, they paused long enough to carve their names alongside the others in that immortal register of American pioneers. But they stopped only briefly, for Fitzpatrick wanted to make record time—they reached the Green River rendezvous site by July 16. With the beaver trade dying, this was the next-to-last rendezvous—and the first at which the Gospel was preached. A number of these hard-bitten mountain men attended both morning and evening devotions, and the Whitmans and Spauldings passed out scores of tracts and Bibles. Narcissa exulted, "This is a cause worth living for!" and noted they could easily have distributed two mule loads of Christian literature.[26]

But now the going became harrowing indeed, and finally at Soda Springs the Whitman wagon broke its front axle. Inwardly, Narcissa, who had become pregnant, rejoiced that at last her husband would have to give up his obsession with getting the wagon through. But Marcus Whitman was not so easily defeated. Fashioning a two-wheeled cart out of the back half of the wagon, he carried on. Food grew scarce as the way grew more precipitous. For Narcissa, the nadir came at Salmon Falls on the Snake River, where her husband informed her that to lighten the load she would have to abandon her clothes trunk that contained her wedding dress. "Poor little trunk," she wrote, "I am sorry to leave thee. Thou must abide here alone."[27]

Fort Boise was a Hudson's Bay Company trading post at the junction of the Snake and the Boise Rivers, and there everyone's spirits revived—Narcissa's especially, as her husband, facing the steepest mountains yet, reluctantly agreed to give up the cart. On August 29, camping at five thousand feet, they could now see Mount Snow, silhouetted at sunset two hundred miles to the west, and knew that the Pacific lay just beyond it. The end was in sight! Three days later, they hurriedly ate their last breakfast on the trail and practically galloped the entire rest of the way down to Fort Walla Walla (in what is today Washington), and on September 1, 1836, they entered the fort, having traveled nearly four thousand miles in a little over half a year. On they pressed to Fort Vancouver, reaching it a fortnight later, and there they basked in the warmth of Dr. McLoughlin's hospitality. Now the Whitmans and the Spauldings parted company, the former going to live with the Cayuse Indians, and the latter with the Nez Perce.

So, on Narcissa's twenty-ninth birthday, March 14, 1837, the first white American was born west of the Rockies—Alice Clarissa Whitman. Her father, Marcus, had had a vision of fast wagon trains of pioneer families rolling west, and four years later it would come to pass as the first cavalcade of seventy settlers left Saint Louis and headed west, once again under the watchful eye of Broken Hand Fitzpatrick. In another two years, many trains and many guides would follow—and one of the best was Jim Bridger.

For the first few weeks in that summer of '43, as Bridger's wagon train followed the well-worn tracks of the hundreds of pioneers who had gone before, the air of a family picnic outing by and large prevailed. The days followed a predictable routine: at 4:00 A.M., as the sky in the east was beginning to lighten, the lookouts fired off their rifles to signal the end of sleep. After a hot breakfast, the pioneers packed and lined up their wagons, and the train stood ready to roll at the sound of the 7:00 bugle. Slowly, steadily, it stretched out across the prairie for the better part of a mile, with Bridger, the "pilot," riding well out in front, his eyes on the horizon. To keep the dust down, they herded cattle and spare horses behind, and the wagons were divided into four platoons, which shifted places in line throughout the day so that none would be subjected to the choking dust at the end of the train for too long. At midday, Bridger would select a site for the "nooning"—a brief lunch stop, with oxen and mules still in yoke and harness. Then the bugle sounded, and the wagons rolled, with bone-weary women and children sleeping in them, while the men walked beside teams that were so tired that it sometimes seemed as if the oxen were dozing as they moved.[28]

For their evening campsite, Bridger would usually pick the first watering place that they came to after 4:00. Another fifteen to eighteen miles would lie behind them, and as the days stretched into weeks, they could plainly see their progress on even the crudest of maps. Wives made sure that whatever they would be cooking in the evening was easily accessible, and each child had his or her list of specific responsibilities, from making certain that the squeaking wheel received the grease, to watering the livestock. Young men rode out ahead of the train in search of the buffalo that roamed the plains and seldom came back empty-handed.

Attachments formed quickly en route, for such a shared journey rapidly brought people closer together, whether they were children playing, married couples dreaming, or single men and women ready and waiting to fall in love. With the sky so big, the stars so close, and the moon so round, and danger present but not ominous, one could hardly find a setting more conducive to romance.

No sooner had the train come to a halt, than Bridger insisted that the drivers draw the wagons into a hollow square, even before they cared for livestock or started the cooking fires. Once the camp's perimeter was established and lookouts posted, people could relax and go on about their chores. Bridger and the other guides who had had experience in the wilderness insisted upon this, even though there had never been a single recorded instance of Indians attacking a squared wagon train. In fact, the frightening vision of whooping, bloodthirsty Indians riding bareback at great speed and firing arrows into the huddled wagons, while grim-faced pioneers returned fire, their brave wives standing by their sides and reloading their rifles, seems to have been just that: a vision dreamed up by romanticizers who had never traveled west of the Mississippi, but knew how to write a gripping narrative. According to George R. Stewart, a specialist in this era of American history, "I have been reading covered wagon records for a long time now. All I can say is that I have never found one such example."[29]

In those first few weeks of late spring and early summer, when the trail was still flat and meat plentiful and the travelers fresh, the train seemed not unlike a moving camp meeting. Children played after supper, and men and women fellowshiped around their cooking fires. The Methodists organized hymn sings and devotional services and argued the finer points of sanctification as they herded the animals, while orators declaimed on why God had destined Oregon for American settlement. There was, in historian DeVoto's words, an essential "Yankeeness" about it all—America on the move.

But before long, the hardships of the trail began to take their toll. No longer could they afford the luxury of rest days; no chance remained to recuperate or shake off the fatigue that settled in deeper and deeper.

Tempers grew short and fights broke out easily as men vented their frustration over broken axles or sick oxen or relentless dysentery. The country just before the mountains was arid, and the incessant wind drove alkali dust into pioneer eyes, till all suffered unbearably, and some even went blind.[30] But for those who could appreciate it, the scenery now became so breathtaking that it inspired many a prairie poet, to the delight of newspaper and book publishers back east, who seemed ever ready to publish anything that they were sent. And there *were* remarkable sights to behold, like Chimney Rock, which towered 500 feet in the air and measured "10,040 steps around its base."[31] Beyond it was Scott's Bluff, a natural fortress so named because fur trapper Hiram Scott had died there of mysterious causes—no one knew how exactly, but his skeleton was found propped in a sitting position among the crags. A wagon train, traveling more or less on schedule, would reach the bluff in late June. Now they were in the badlands, a landscape aptly named, for grass disappeared, and the travelers needed ropes to haul wagons up steep slopes and lower them over boulders, and all under the blazing sun. Two more days would bring them to Fort Laramie, where J. M. Shively's guidebook told its readers: "You are now 640 miles from Independence, Missouri, and it is discouraging to tell you that you have not yet traveled one third of the long road to Oregon."[32]

At the fort, they paused long enough to reshoe wheels that had thrown their iron rims and make other absolutely essential repairs, but soon got underway again. As rough as the trail had been before Fort Laramie, it was as nothing compared to what was coming next. For now, as they followed the north fork of the Platte into the foothills of the Rockies, the trail grew steeper and progress slowed even more. Now they considered eight miles' travel a good day. At Independence Rock, so named because most trains reached it around July 4, the caravan paused long enough for all who wished to carve their names in what had come to be known as the "Great Record of the Desert."

The trail now climbed steeply toward the Continental Divide, and the oxen drivers and mule skinners had to constantly encourage their animals. Back on the plains a team of six oxen had seemed extravagant, but now those who had six wished for eight, and those who had eight wished they had had the foresight or wherewithal to bring ten or a dozen. For the animals labored awfully now, straining at the yoke, and the fewer of them to do the pulling, the quicker they reached the limit of their endurance. Oxen began to go down from exhaustion, which put the remainder of a team in extremis, and suddenly, almost overnight, the journey became a nightmare. Their owners immediately butchered fallen oxen, for there was no way that they, let alone the entire train, could stop and give them a chance to recover. Grimly, the skeletons of oxen from previous trains now began to mark the side of the trail, their bones picked clean by vultures and bleached white by the broiling summer sun.

Nor did Bridger take pity on the animals and slow the pace, for they *had* to get through the Sierra Nevada Mountains before the first snow in early fall. So, on he drove his train, and on the pioneers drove their oxen, until the formerly poetic journals now became filled with numbing descriptions of animals collapsing in their yokes or thirst-crazed oxen having to be put out of their misery. A driver with a team of five, now, instead of six, and a trail that was going to get considerably steeper before they went through the pass and started down, faced some hard decisions. He could yoke only four, which meant that while one could rest, they would have to lighten the load drastically. Now alongside the trail, in addition to the carcasses of oxen and mules, appeared beloved sideboards and beautifully carved credenzas and bureaus, passed down through families for generations—priceless heirlooms that had been considered indispensable back in Independence when Bridger had urged everyone to be utterly ruthless in lightening their wagons before they started, so that they wouldn't be forced to, later. Now *everybody* walked, even pregnant women. For the alternative was to abandon the wagon. Indeed, an increasing number of wagon beds lay by the trailside—often angrily smashed, so that no one else could benefit from their misfortune.

Travelers came upon more ominous signs—the first human graves. For cholera struck many of the trains, and again no one could stop and rest or care for the sick. They rode in the wagons with large teams . . . until they died, and the death toll was steep: one out of every seventeen settlers bound for Oregon never made it. On the average, a grave was dug every eighty yards, from the Missouri to the Willamette Valley, and at popular campsites whole graveyards exist. Burials were swift and simple. With no lumber for coffins, they wrapped bodies in cloth and put them in shallow graves or under piles of rocks—too often to be dug up by wolves or scavenging Indians.[33]

Time became the enemy now. Each day brought the first snow that much closer, and Bridger and the other mountain men guiding other trains knew full well that the snow could drift thirty feet deep in the narrow mountain passes. Stragglers, caught by an early snow and hopelessly drifted in, had starved to death, their final agonies recorded in their journals discovered by the first comers the following summer. Ironically, the most famous of these unfortunates was one party in which all hands did *not* starve to death—the Donner expedition of 1846. Blinded by arrogant stupidity and plagued by misfortune, they followed Lansford Hastings's train by several weeks into an untested shortcut. Hastings' "shortcut" left the main Oregon Trail at Fort Bridger and headed directly southwest for California, thus saving some 400 miles. But Hastings had come this way only once, from west to east, and without wagons. The trail, barely wide enough for a single laden mule, proved too narrow for the wagons, with the result that they had to use the riverbed, and progress slowed to no more than a mile and a half a day. When, in the Weber River gorge, the riverbed itself proved impassable, they were left with the option of either abandoning the wagons or winching them over the adjacent bluffs. There they literally raised the wagons by windlass up the side of a rocky precipice. When Hastings's party finally reached the Humboldt River, they found themselves three weeks behind other pioneers who had left Fort Bridger at the same time but had ignored the "shortcut." At least they remained ahead of the snow—barely.

The Donner party behind them was not so fortunate. Eighty-seven men, women, and children, with twenty-three severely overloaded wagons, followed the tracks of the Hastings party a few days behind. But when they reached the impassable gorge, they decided that it really was hopeless and turned back, to attempt a new, unbroken route. That took time; it took them twenty-eight days to reach the Great Salt Lake, about fifty miles distant. Now the desert, under a relentless September sun, cost them nearly a hundred oxen, which meant that many wagons would have to be left behind. Tempers exploded; a teamster named Snyder threatened one of the leaders, James Reed, with his bullwhip, and Reed sank a knife into his chest. Expelled from the train, Reed hurried ahead, trying to catch up with the Hastings party.

Meanwhile, the rest of the Donner party came close to starvation. By October 30, the first three families reached Truckee Lake, high in the Sierras. Ahead lay Truckee Pass, the last major barrier between them and the Sacramento Valley. An inch of snow already covered the ground when they began their last climb, and it soon became impassable drifts five feet deep. They turned back. Four days later, they attempted a second assault, but more snow had fallen, clogging the pass and making wagon travel hopeless. Two men did make it to the top, but turned back, when they saw that the others were trapped. The party returned to the lake and faced the ominous truth: they could not get through until spring. The oxen and cattle, left unwatched, had wandered off and gotten lost in the snow, more of which was falling all the time now. The meat they had left would not last them through December, let alone till April. Deer and other game had disappeared—presumably going down out of the mountains to avoid the snow buildup. With the infants crying weakly, the camp began boiling hides, even those used as roofing. They did manage to kill a bear, which everyone devoured almost immediately.

Clearly they would all starve soon, if help were not forthcoming. Seventeen men and women desperately set out on snowshoes, and seven of them made it to help—but at a fearful cost. Ravenously hungry, they had eaten the flesh of those in their group who had perished. A relief expedition of Californians headed for the Truckee Pass on February 4, and two weeks later made it to the lake encampment, now almost totally buried under fifteen feet of snow. One of the Donner brothers was dead, the other dying. Those still alive were half-mad with hunger, and a lone woman greeted them: "Are you from California or Heaven?"[34] To their horror, the rescuers discovered that cannibalism had become so commonplace in the Donner camp that its inhabitants had become indifferent to it. All told, four rescue parties reached them and were able to save forty-seven of the eighty-one people who had made it to the lake. But the gruesome tragedy of what everyone now called Donner Pass would remain forever fixed in the imaginations of all who turned their wagons to the west.

Act IV of the Great Western Migration tells of another tragedy, the more tragic because it reflected on the national character of this country. The beginning of this act returns to the beginning of America—

where before white men came, red men lived—often in warfare, but also in acceptance of one another's tribal realities. Indian culture was a fragile thing—it recognized no specific territorial boundaries, no transfer of land. If a neighboring tribe encroached on the hunting grounds of a given tribe, a raid of reprisal was inevitable, and a state of war could result. Indeed, much of the tribe's life focused on survival. From childhood, young braves learned courage and the skills of hunting, tracking, and killing. In the seventeenth century, and again in the nineteenth, romantic writers who had never met a "noble savage" depicted the Indian as a creature of nature, innocent and undefiled by corrupt civilization. In reality, very little that was noble or innocent had a place in the Indian's life; while tribal personalities differed markedly, cruelty and indifference were a routine part of most Indians' lives. White men looked aghast at their methods of torture, and the enjoyment they derived out of inflicting prolonged, excruciating pain. But all that paled to in comparison to the wanton, wholesale cruelty of a different sort of which the white men demonstrated that they themselves were capable.

Westward expansion invariably meant westward expulsion of countless Indian tribes from their ancestral homes. Sometimes the Indians resisted, and sometimes they very nearly succeeded in holding their ground. In almost all instances, the whites spoke falsely, making treaties with the Indians that would guarantee them new land in perpetuity. A few years later, they would want the Indians' land after all and would concoct some technical excuse for abrogating the treaty. In the South, tribes of Indians had simply been left on land reserved for them by federal grants, but now with cotton fever running high, these reservations suddenly appeared very attractive to the whites. Thus in 1825, President Monroe presented to Congress a plan drawn up by his Secretary of War, John C. Calhoun: As a final solution to the Indian problem, it proposed the wholesale removal of all tribes to the bison territory west of the Mississippi and north of Mexico's Texas Territory. Each Indian nation would be given its own broad strip of land, many miles wide and running all the way across the plains from the Mississippi to the end of the Louisiana Territory. It was a land plentiful with buffalo (and considered uninhabitable by white men).

Congress saw this arrangement as eminently satisfactory. To have Indian tribes within state boundaries, waging war on one another, was unthinkable, and besides, the wild game they depended on for their livelihood had begun to run out. No, they definitely wanted to create new domains for the Indians' own good, whether Indians saw it that way or not. So they dispatched General William Clark to treat with the Osage and Kaw Indians for the use of the Great Plains for this purpose.[35] He encountered only one problem: the Indians did not wish to be removed. Their ancestors lay buried in the land they were on, which made it sacred to them. The Great Spirit had put them here, and here they would remain and be buried themselves.

Something had to be done, however, and quickly, or the five southern Civilized Nations, which western-rushing civilization had bypassed—the Creek, the Cherokee, the Choctaw, the Chickasaw, and the Seminoles—were doomed. For even before the removal policy received Congressional approval, whites in Georgia, Alabama, and Mississippi flagrantly violated the federal guarantees of the Indians' exclusive right to their ancestral domains. Hundreds and then thousands of land-hungry whites simply squatted on Indian land and treated it as if they owned it. White law supported them. When the Indians sought redress, they were rebuffed or routinely ignored. Georgia soon moved to make the land piracy within its borders quasilegal by declaring that Indians living in the state were subject to the state's jurisdiction. Heretofore, Indians on their own land remained subject to their own system of justice, just as if they were a foreign nation.

On the surface, requiring the Indians to obey Georgia state laws seemed reasonable enough, except that one of those laws provided that: "No Indian or descendant of any Indians, residing within the Creek or Cherokee Nation of Indians, shall be deemed a competent witness in any court in the State to which a white person may be a party. . . ."[36] In other words, no Indian's testimony could be taken against a white man, nor could any Indian's complaint be taken to court. To Georgians around the reservations that signaled open season on Cherokees and Creeks. Alabama and Mississippi immediately passed identical legislation. On top of everything else, gold was discovered on Cherokee land in Georgia; by the summer of 1830, more than three thousand white men were frantically digging for the yellow metal. Sensing trouble, the Georgia legislature promptly passed laws forbidding the meeting of any Cherokee council or court.

Whether or not the white man effected Indian removal, it became obvious that the three southern states intended to simply seize those lands guaranteed to the tribes by treaty with the United States. How would the President and Congress respond? Response from New England came in the form of outrage. Northern missionaries sent south to work with the Indians now sent impassioned and articulate reports north, and matters rapidly came to a head. The Georgia legislature moved against the missionaries, enacting a bill that would force them to accept licensing by the state and swear allegiance to it or get out. Failure to comply was punishable by four years' confinement at hard labor. Two missionaries did refuse, were duly arrested, and appealed to the Supreme Court of the United States.

The unanimous opinion was delivered by Chief Justice Marshall:

> From the commencement of our Government, Congress has passed acts to regulate trade and intercourse with the Indians, which treat them as nations, respect their rights, and manifest a firm purpose to afford that protection which treaties stipulate. All these acts . . . manifestly consider the several Indian nations as distinct political communities, having territorial boundaries, and within which their authority is exclusive . . . which is not only acknowledged but guaranteed by the United States. . . . The Acts of Georgia are repugnant to the Constitution, laws, and treaties of the United States."[37]

All eyes turned to the White House: would President Jackson now send federal troops into Georgia to get the missionaries back? The President is reported to have said: "John Marshall has made his opinion; now let him enforce it."[38] Cynical historians have pointed out that 1832 was an election year, and Jackson was up for reelection. But Jackson prided himself on being a man of principle and never hesitated to take an unpopular stand, if he deemed it the right one. Less than a year later, he would face down South Carolina in the nullification crisis, as we have seen.

Jackson had the discernment of an experienced combat officer; he knew that nullification was the right issue on which to enforce federal authority over state sovereignty. The sanctity of Indian lands was not. He saw, correctly, that while he might have forced Georgia to release the missionaries it held, the federal government could not force that state and Alabama and Mississippi to change their basic attitudes toward the Indians within their borders. Considering the atrocities the natives had already suffered, Jackson himself honestly believed that removal was in the Indians' own best interest. Their fragile culture simply could not survive alongside the debilitating effects of white society. Liquor was too cheap and too plentiful; Indians were too naive, too trusting. The outrages already perpetrated on them would only multiply. Besides, it would take an entire division to root out and keep out the white settlers who had already carved out homesteads on Indian land. The Supreme Court's decision was unenforceable. The most humane thing was to get them out of there completely, as quickly as possible, and over to where the white men would leave them alone and not covet their land. (An interesting footnote: historian Page Smith conjectures that, had JQA won a second term, he almost certainly would have moved federal troops against Georgia—and might well have precipitated the secession of the other southern states, thirty years before the country was morally or materially ready to contest that issue.)

With the state of Georgia, in effect, sanctioning the most wanton depredations against the Indians and the federal government demonstrably unwilling to act on their behalf, the last vestige of civil restraint was now received. Venal Georgians turned on their Indian neighbors with a vengeance. Men arrived with wagons loaded with whiskey, got the Indian farmers and home owners drunk and then persuaded them to sign away their property for a song. In the morning the white men arrived with the sheriff to evict the hungover braves and take over what was legally theirs. Others, anticipating the imminent removal of the Indians, simply set up housekeeping in the Indians' backyards, carving their initials on the trees and waiting for the moment when they could take over. Still others worked in cahoots with real estate agents, who would offer to represent the Indians, then sell their property at a fraction of its worth, splitting the take with their partners.

The situation was just as bad in Alabama. In desperation, the Creeks sent two chiefs to Washington in 1831 to appeal to the federal government for protection against the rapacity and exploitation of the whites.

> Murders have taken place, by both reds and whites. We have caused the red men to be brought to justice, but the whites go unpunished.... They bring spirits among us for the purpose of practicing frauds; they daily rob us of our property; they bring white officers among us, and take our property from us for debts we never contracted.... We have made many treaties with the

> United States at all times with the belief that the one making was to be the last. . . .[39]

So appalling was the treatment of the Indians that even the Montgomery *Advertiser,* in the state capital, could not remain silent:

> We do trust, for the credit of those concerned, that these blood suckers may be ferreted out, and their shameful misrepresentations exposed. . . . [The red men's property] has been taken from them—their stock killed, their farms pillaged—and by whom? By white men. . . . Such villains may go unpunished in this world, but the day of retribution will most certainly arrive. [And it did arrive, in this world, about thirty years later, as blood and tears atoned for blood and tears.][40]

Removal now gained urgency: the Indians had to be gotten out as quickly as possible, before all semblance of civilized behavior toward them collapsed. The Georgia governor fixed May of 1838 as the final month for the Cherokees to be out of the state. With bayonets fixed, soldiers went in to search out every man, woman, and child they could find. Some Cherokee, when rounded up, knelt and prayed to Christ to have mercy on them. The Cherokee chieftain William Coodey wrote to John Howard Payne:

> Multitudes were allowed no time to take anything with them, except the clothes they had on. Well-furnished houses were left a prey to plunderers. . . . The property of many has been taken and sold before their eyes for almost nothing—the sellers and buyers in many cases having combined to cheat the poor Indians. . . . Many of the Cherokees, who a few days ago were in comfortable circumstances, are now victims of abject poverty . . . this is not the description of extreme cases. It is altogether a faint representation of the work which has been perpetuated on the unoffending, unarmed, and unresisting Cherokees.[41]

Fifteen thousand Cherokee began to move west—on horseback, wagon, and foot. Chief Coodey watched the pathetic line of march, observing "my poor and unhappy countrymen, driven by brutal power from all they loved and cherished in the land of their fathers, to gratify the cravings of avarice."[42] What must have convicted all but the most callous hearts was the sight of well-educated, prosperous—and devout—Indians treated as mindless savages. These Indians, martyrs to the color of their skin, had assimilated the ways of the white man so completely that their ministers requested the march be halted on the Lord's Day and for altars to be erected and services conducted. Moreover, these Cherokee preachers never tired in their evangelical labors, holding a baptismal service at the next river crossing for the benefit of new members of their flocks. "Some whites present affirm it to have been the most solemn and impressive religious service they ever witnessed."[43]

Federal troops were assigned to escort the Cherokee, and the men did much to assist the Indians. Once removed from their environment and lacking control over their lives, they proved surprisingly helpless. Their culture taught them to live from day to day and not plan ahead. If they had no food, they went hungry, while their hunters went further afield in search of game. Nothing in their individual or collective experiences prepared them for the massive logistics problem of a two-month trek. As a result, even those who had an opportunity to prepare were improperly clad and pathetically underprovisioned—to the extent that those in charge often had to appeal to the mercy of the Christian churches in the villages they passed, or their charges would have starved or frozen to death.

Illness now began to ravage their ranks, especially the children. Lack of food, no sanitation, bad water, and bad whiskey combined with heat, trail dust, and despair, to kill thousands. One traveler from Maine, passing through western Kentucky on his way to Nashville, encountered a group of 2,000 Cherokee: "The Indians carry a downcast, dejected look, bordering upon the appearance of despair; others, a wild frantic appearance, as if about to burst the chains of nature and pounce like a tiger upon their enemies. . . ." As the last of the forlorn caravan passed by, the man from Maine "wept like childhood" when he thought that "my native countrymen had thus expelled . . . those suffering exiles. . . . I wished the President could have been there that very day in Kentucky with myself . . . full well I know that many prayers have gone up to the King of Heaven from Maine, on behalf of the Cherokees."[44]

The loss of life continued. Of the 15,000 Cherokee forcibly removed, approximately 4,000 died. No wonder the way west became known in Cherokee legend as the Trail of Tears. One Georgia volunteer, who later served as a colonel in the Confederate army, wrote many years after the event: "I fought through the Civil War and have seen men shot to pieces and slaughtered by the thousands, but the Cherokee removal was the cruelest work I ever knew."[45]

Of all the Indian nations, only the Seminoles resisted with force of arms. Under Osceola, they fought in the swamps of the Everglades, successfully countering the thrusts of the best commanders the whites had, including Winfield Scott and Zachary Taylor. Finally the whites succeeded in capturing Osceola, by pretending to parlay with him under a flag of truce. Nevertheless, many Seminoles continued their resistance and were finally allowed to remain in the Everglades (territory no white man could ever conceivably covet).

Thus ended one of the darkest episodes in our history, in a way even worse than slavery, because so many people who could have changed the federal government's policy chose to turn blind eyes to what happened. Tragically, those who formulated and carried out the policy, far from trying to liquidate the Indians, were trying their best to prevent that from happening.

Meanwhile, hundreds of wagons headed northwest where Lewis and Clark had led, and southwest through the pass Jedediah Smith had opened. Cotton plantations sprang up further and further west of the Mississippi. The biggest land of all was about to offer the greatest adventure of all—Texas!

15

"Remember the Alamo!"

A few campfires dotted the courtyard, and around each a handful of men gathered, trying to exchange the flames' warmth for the chill of the March night that had settled in close to their bones. No one spoke; they were exhausted beyond conversation, faces gaunt, eyes sunken into their sockets from ten days with little more than fitful, dream-wracked dozing as a substitute for sleep. They stared into the fire, and they listened to the same tune with its mournful, haunting trumpet solo that had played all night long, night after night—"Deguello," the song of no quarter, which went back centuries to a time when the Moors had played it for their besieged enemies whom they intended to slaughter. Santa Anna had commanded his army's bands to take turns playing that song—had any army ever had so many musicians?—so that it would be continually in the ears of the Texans who defied him inside the walls of the ancient mission. By day, he had the visual counterpart of "Deguello," a huge blood-red pennant, flown from the highest rooftop in San Antonio. But somehow, on the still night air, in the last slow hours before dawn, the sound of the trumpet became more effective, penetrating deeper to the bone than the warmth of the fires ever could.

There was no point in sleeping; one had heard that refrain so often that it lingered inside, even when one went into one of the storage rooms and closed the door. Besides, why sleep now, anyway? The Mexicans had finally gotten their cannon close enough to breach one of the walls, and while the defenders had filled the break with sandbags, little doubt remained as to what would follow. Concentrated cannon fire would quickly open the hole again. That meant they would have to put extra men on the walls on either side of the breach, to hold the attackers back. Only there weren't any extra men. There had been only 182 to begin with, and there were considerably less than that now.

No, it would be all over tomorrow, so it made little difference whether or not they slept tonight.

By the flickering firelight, some men wrote letters to their loved ones, letters they knew no one would deliver. Others simply stared into the flames, perhaps trying to find in them some explanation of why they had come. A few were Texas pioneer farmers who had enlisted in the militia which the territory had hastily raised to defend itself against the Mexicans. These volunteers served under one of that army's few regular officers, young Buck Travis, the man who decided they would make their stand at the Alamo. But most of the farmers had drifted away to their homes, their places taken by American adventurers looking for a good fight. After all, there hadn't been one since Old Hickory had given the lobsterbacks what for at the Battle of New Orleans, a generation before. Some had come in with Bowie and Crockett, legendary frontiersmen whose names alone were enough to attract mountain men and sharpshooters spoiling for action. There was even a uniformed contingent who actually looked like soldiers—the New Orleans Greys. But for the most part, they were a scruffy lot, in grease-darkened buckskins and matted hair; indeed, the only thing clean about them was the firing action of their deadly, long-barreled rifles.

The situation in the old mission—of a handful of Americans holding out against an army thirty times their number—had cast its spell. "Bowie and Crockett you say? Just like those two to get themselves into such a fix. Well, the beaver's about played out, and I've got nothing better to do; might as well go down there and get those poor, misbegotten sons out of trouble." The last thirty-two men to join the defenders, Texas settlers from Gonzales, had to fight their way inside.

The first Anglo-American homesteaders to the Territory of Texas at the invitation of the government of the new republic of Mexico, which in 1821 had won its independence from Spain. It was a liberal democracy, and in 1824 it passed a constitution remarkably similar to America's own. But the government encountered a problem with its northernmost province—the vast, largely unoccupied territory between the Sabine and the Rio Grande that lay south of the Louisiana Purchase, known as Texas. The Indians, specifically the wild and vicious Comanche, seemed to have an instinctive loathing for the mixed-race, Hispanic-Indian settlers who were now Mexican citizens. Marauding bands of Comanche took pernicious delight in razing

Mexican settlements, stealing their livestock, and whenever possible, their women and children. The cost of maintaining a large, standing army in Texas to protect its settlers was prohibitive. But now an inexpensive, felicitous alternative presented itself: open the territory to settlers from America. Vast tracts of arable, unclaimed land were suddenly made available to Americans at the nominal cost of $1.25 an acre.

Three hundred Americans colonists under the leadership of Stephen Austin first took advantage of this windfall. The Federal Colonization Law required only that the Anglo-Texans take an oath of allegiance to Mexico and swear to obey its laws. They were also expected to embrace the Roman Catholic faith, but no one pressured them in this regard, as most of the revolutionary leadership in Mexico City had no use for their church themselves. In fact, no pressure of any sort was put on the Anglo-American newcomers—they were exempted from all taxes and levies to the extent that an American land commissioner in Nacogdoches commented: "Come what may, I am convinced that [the colonization of] Texas must prosper. We pay no taxes, work no public roads, and perform no public duties of any kind."[1] Of course, the Anglo-Texans received no military protection or governmental services of any kind either, and the land allotted to them had been uninhabitable by the Mexicans, due to the Comanche problem. Still, for ten years they enjoyed a freedom of de facto self-government not seen in the New World since the founding of the first American colonies nearly a century before. This freedom, granted by a friendly, tolerant Mexican government, allowed their unique American frontier culture to develop unhindered. Two other factors combined with the Texas way of life to attract settlers by the thousands: the unheard of low cost of good crop land and a solid peace treaty that the Anglo-Texans had made with the Comanche (who had a healthy respect for these tall men who kept their word and had seemingly supernatural power when it came to marksmanship).

Alas, the pastoral movement of this symphony lasted all too briefly. For unlike young America, young Mexico did not have a strong, dynamic Christianity at its core, and perhaps the greatest lesson of history is that, without a durable Judeo-Christian faith to establish, nurture, and regenerate corporate moral standards, no democracy can last. For democracy depends upon the moral decency and selfless caring for others of its citizens, and these things spring only from a deep and vibrant religion.

Mexico's constitution of 1824 was as liberal and democratic as that of the United States. Yet the corruption at the heart of those who already held power or those maneuvering to obtain power doomed it from the start. Hispanic culture and tradition had always favored a strong, centralist government in Madrid and subsequently in Mexico City. This tradition could be traced all the way back to the *encomienda* system, in which absentee landlords in Spain owned vast tracts of Mexico. In turn, these landlords relied on a strong army presence in Mexico to protect their holdings and they supported the Catholic Church, to keep the natives pacified. Now, even though Mexico had gained its independence from Spain, and the *campesinos* (white-shirted peasant farmers) and Mexican Indians and mixed breeds far outnumbered the prominent Centralist landowners, nevertheless the latter retained a disproportionate influence in affairs of state. Without a living faith to inspire public servants and give them moral backbone, money in the right palms could work miracles of statecraft. The men with the money had a profound distrust of the starry-eyed Federalists who would entrust the government of the republic into the hands of ignorant field hands.

In the first national election of 1828 the results of the polls were overturned at musket point, and after considerable turmoil the aristocrats who led the Centralist faction gained control of the government. Almost instantly a Federalist uprising erupted, with men prepared to face muskets with machetes for the sake of the democracy their 1824 constitution guaranteed. To the Centralists, the Anglo-Texans, with their own working democracy in place, were a dangerous example to have on Mexican soil. On April 6, 1830, they passed a law that closed Texas to all further Anglo immigration and called for a military presence in the territory, to keep an eye on the Texans. Moreover, they made it clear that they intended to end the Texans' self-government and reintegrate them into the republic, under the central authority of Mexico City. The halcyon days of live-and-let-live were over.

The shortsightedness and bullheadedness of the Centralist government proved tragic—but no more so than the British government of George III, who had taken a similar attitude toward the self-governing American colonies. Texans, who had acted as loyally to Mexico in their own way as they felt anyone could ask for, now began to resent the distrust and intrusion of the new Centralist government to the south. These men of the American frontier tradition remained fiercely independent and resentful of anyone who attempted to tell them what to do. To make matters worse, a racial element now added to the resentment—on both sides. The Centralists in Mexico City regarded the Anglo-Texans as frontier riffraff, uncultured and boorish, with no appreciation of the refinements of civilization. The Texans began to express their own contempt for the little brown *mestizos* ("mixed-bloods") who now sought to impose their will on them. What made matters worse was that the Comanche apparently shared the Texans' contempt for the Mexicans, continuing to raid their settlements while leaving the Anglo-Texans alone. The Centralists accused the Texans of entering into a secret pact with the Comanche, and all *norteamericanos* of having designs on Texas.[2]

The revocation of the Constitution of 1824 accelerated a rapidly deteriorating situation. Military opportunist Antonio Lopez de Santa Anna came to power at the head of the successful Federalist uprising, but subsequently he betrayed his allies, realigned himself with the Centralists, and assumed personal command of the army. Taken by surprise, the Federalists scattered, many of them fleeing north, to Texas. Inevitably the Centralist government would dispatch a military force to Texas, to disarm the settlers there and thereby defuse a potentially explosive situation. And what was equally inevitable, anyone trying to disarm the Texans by force would light the fuse, rather than remove it. Texan settlers got together and organized a militia for self-defense, and a minor clash followed, with Texans taking a fort without a shot and then giving it back.

This action shocked most Texans, who clearly told the authorities in Mexico that they strongly disapproved of it. Yet when the Centralists demanded that they turn over the perpetrator of the clash, a young lieutenant named William Barrett Travis, along with two leaders of the Federalists known to be hiding in Texas, they balked. For as reprehensible as the Anglo-Texans may have considered Travis's action, they were familiar with the Mexican military's idea of justice: a five-minute trial followed by a firing squad. Consider, too, the case of their own Stephen Austin, arrested on specious charges and held incommunicado in a Mexico City jail without trial for a year and a half.

In the summer of 1835 Austin was released in a general amnesty, and in the face of an imminent military advance into Texas he began to campaign vigorously for American settlers to come south and join them. Enough Kentucky and Tennessee rifles would make them secure. Now no one questioned that he and his neighbors intended to Americanize Texas and keep it that way. When General Cos, Santa Anna's brother-in-law, crossed the Rio Grande with a large army bound for San Antonio, Austin, as colonel of the Texas militia, put out a general call for Texans to stand to arms: "War is our only resource. There is no other remedy. We must defend our rights, ourselves, and our country by force of arms."[3]

Our country—not Mexico, not the United States, but Texas, and specifically the land. Broad and flat and desolate, the land had nonetheless in the space of a decade and a half become inextricably combined with their very being and seemed to forge an almost mystical bond with them. Legally, it belonged to Mexico, but by everything right and holy, in their eyes, it was theirs. No one had wanted it, and they had come and worked it and made it liveable. They had become a part of that land, and since they would die someday, somewhere, it might as well be here, and if necessary, sooner rather than later.

Cos began garrisoning the towns in Texas and made San Antonio his headquarters. The first shots were fired over a cannon at Gonzales. The Mexicans demanded it; the Texans raised a flag with a picture of the cannon on it, and the words *Come and take it.*[4] The Texans now laid siege to San Antonio. A convention of Texans assembled at Washington-on-the-Brazos and declared by more than a two-to-one vote that the sole purpose of their resistance was to restore the Constitution of 1824.[5] Finally, against the wishes of Austin, their commander in chief, two senior officers led a volunteer assault on the city, taking it house by house, with Cos finally surrendering 1,105 men (more than 180 had already deserted). The Mexicans had been beaten by a force one third their size.

Enraged at this insult to his family and to Mexico's national honor, Santa Anna now took personal command of the Army of the North, swelling its ranks to 10,000 and referring to himself as "the Napoleon of the West." He marched with maximum speed on San Antonio—and caught the Texans in a wash of victory euphoria. Many of their number, thinking the war over, had gone back to their farms. Moreover, a lack of central government paralyzed Texas, for what they had called self-government really meant no government at all. Who commanded the garrison at San Antonio depended on whose orders one acknowledged: General Sam Houston had sent Colonel James Bowie; newly elected Governor Henry Smith had dispatched (now) Colonel Travis. That situation resolved itself when Bowie came down with pneumonia. The tables had turned, with the Mexicans under Santa Anna laying siege and determined to destroy every one of the 182 Americans within the walls.

The noose was fashioned but not yet drawn so tight that bands of defenders could not make forays under cover of darkness, rounding up cattle, horses, and provisions. Messengers like James Bonham could still slip over the walls on desperate missions for help—to Colonel James Fannin, who had 500 men in Goliad and refused to come to their aid, and to the Texas Council, in session at Washington-on-the-Brazos and about to declare independence. Travis wrote eloquently in these appeals, well aware that the words might have to do their work posthumously, if help was not immediately forthcoming. "We consider death preferable to disgrace," he wrote to Governor Smith, "For God's sake and the sake of our country, send us reinforcements."[6] In his final letter, written on March 3, in the knowledge that it was extremely unlikely that any help would be forthcoming, he said: "I shall have to fight the enemy on his own terms. . . . The victory will cost the enemy so dear, that it will be worse for him than defeat. I hope your honorable body will hasten reinforcements. . . . Our supply of ammunition is limited. . . . God and Texas. Victory or Death."[7]

But now Santa Anna grew impatient. For nearly two weeks, this stubborn band of Texas rebels had held up his march to the Sabine, and he lacked heavy enough cannon to properly breach their walls. But now that a hole had finally been made, he determined to get on with it. His staff officers advised him to wait two more days, until the long-expected siege guns arrived, and his brother-in-law, who had already experienced the Americans' marksmanship, cautioned that the cost would run high. But Santa Anna replied that he did not care; the nut must be cracked.[8]

As March 6, 1836 dawned, 4,000 gray-uniformed soldiers—Santa Anna's "Invincibles," the cream of the Mexican Army—advanced on the Alamo in columns of four, the long bayonets at the ends of their muskets glinting in the early morning sun. Behind them marched the bands, playing "Deguello." The Alamo, flying the flag of the Mexican Constitution of 1824, still had a few operable cannons; with these the defenders smashed some of the advancing column, then, because they were running short of gunpowder, they concentrated on their rifles. At 100 yards any soldier using a musket could not hit a man-sized target one time in ten. At the unheard of range of 300 yards, the Kentucky and Tennessee riflemen on the walls opened fire, and Mexicans began to fall. Those behind just stepped over them and kept coming. Among the first to fall were the colonels, the majors, and the captains, for the Americans had long ago learned to drop anyone wearing braid first. Still the columns came forward, and the fire into them went more furiously as the defenders snatched up their pre-loaded rifles.

At last the assault wavered and stopped, and the Mexicans fell back. A ragged cheer ran along the walls. The Americans busied themselves reloading the rifles and leaning them carefully against the walls, within easy reach. The water bucket went around and then the powder keg, which was so low that every man knew their work would be finished this day, one way or the other. Some men prayed, but in all likelihood most engaged in the humor of men who had fought well together and knew that they would soon die together. "Ben, you're a disgrace to Kentucky, wasting ammunition the way you do. You ought to line up two of them, before you shoot, like I do."

"Aye, what are you talking about? Did you not see the row of four go down in the front of my column, right after the cannon stopped?"

"Hey, you two! Stop flapping your gums, before you tucker yourselves out, and leave it to a Texan. The best shot of the day was when I caught those two lieutenants, as they passed each other, running in opposite directions. Now the wind was coming from the north, along with the shorter lieutenant. I knew I had to shoot before they crossed, but should I favor the northbound lieutenant who was faster, or the southbound little beggar with the wind behind him?"

Abruptly the Mexican bands struck up their hell tune again, and all turned back to the business at hand. Once again the columns advanced, stepping over dozens of fallen comrades. Again the fire leaped out at them. If anything, it came even faster than before, with the riflemen shooting all the extra rifles and then reloading their own weapons at the incredible rate of ten or twelve seconds a shot. Those Mexican officers still alive had never seen such weapon handling and assumed that there were a hundred men inside, doing nothing but reloading. Still the columns came forward, until they reached the walls. Now the scaling ladders went up, while those behind formed in line abreast for a musket volley. The fire from the walls reached a fever pitch, and at last the Mexicans backed away, leaving their ladders behind them and solid paths of dead. But not before raking the walls with musket fire, so close that they could not miss.

Another cheer went up, weaker than the first. The muskets had taken their toll. "Hey, Ben? Looks like they got you!"

"Well, look around you, you dumb jackass! They got just about everybody!"

"You two can't be hurt too badly, to be making so much noise. But I'll tell you, it'll take more than one of them little beggar's musket balls to put this Texan down. . . ."

There was a lull in the fighting. The Mexicans needed to rest and call up their reserves before pressing forward a third time—which, by this time, the foot soldiers in the columns felt exceedingly reluctant to do. For all their vaunted discipline—and in the eyes of military experts the world over, the exceptionally well-trained, armed, and experienced Mexican army was considered the equal of the best that Europe could field[9]—too many of them had seen the withering, sleeting fire of the defenders up close. While they did not run, their officers literally had to beat them back into formation for the final assault.

Once more, the trumpets lofted the haunting, unforgettable "Deguello," and the columns started forward. Having noted how thin the ranks of the defenders on the walls had become, Santa Anna now directed this third wave to attack all four sides of the mission simultaneously. This time when the scaling ladders went up, there was no help available to knock them down or shoot those ascending them. Too many ladders, too few Americans—one Mexican would clamber over the wall and would look up at the last sight he would ever see: the broad end of a rifle butt whistling toward his face. But behind the wielder on the wall's platform would come another Mexican, and his bayonet would take vengeance for his comrade. Soon more Mexicans than Americans stood on the walls, and they poured into the courtyard. There was no time for reloading now. The Americans, determined to take as many attackers with them as they possibly could, swung rifles and Bowie knives and tomahawks with a savagery that the Mexicans, at least a head shorter in most instances, had never seen. A circle of dead formed around each defender. But with so many more Mexicans inevitably one would have the presence of mind to load and fire his musket or get in a bayonet thrust from behind. When they stormed into the room where Jim Bowie lay bedridden, the first two each received a ball from the brace of pistols he had hidden under the blankets.

At length, they cut down the last American. As a later inscription would state: "Thermopylae had its messenger, the Alamo had none." The Mexican officers lost control of their men: the soldiers mutilated the bodies of the fallen and tossed Bowie's on bayonets in the air. When their blood lust was sated, the Mexicans withdrew. All told, the Alamo had cost the lives of 1,600 Mexican soldiers—eight for every American killed. When he pulled out of San Antonio, Santa Anna also left 500 more wounded behind.[10] As Travis had predicted, Santa Anna's victory had indeed come at a greater cost than he could afford. It had created a dual legend: of *Los Diablos Tejanos*—the blue-eyed, light-skinned six-footers who fought with the fury of the devil himself and who would haunt Mexican folklore for generations—and of a small band of heroes who fought and died for liberty and attracted thousands more just like them from every state in the Union.

Santa Anna was to be allowed one more victory (if one could call it that) before the tide began to turn. In Goliad, ninety-two miles to the southeast, stood the sum and substance of the Texas "army"—Colonel Fannin and his 500 men. To preserve that army, Fannin had twice refused Travis's plea to come to the aid of the Alamo defenders. Finally, at the personal urging of Colonel Bonham, who had risked his life to try a third time to persuade him, he had reluctantly agreed and headed his force toward San Antonio. Four miles out, a supply wagon broke down, and Fannin, according to his own report, took this as a sign that the relief of the Alamo was "not feasible"[11] and called off the rescue attempt. Obviously, Fannin's troops, added to those in the Alamo, could not have defeated Santa Anna. But together, especially with Fannin's cavalry unit, they could have held out until a relief force was mustered. Ironically, when they heard that Fannin had refused to help the Alamo, the thirty-two men garrisoned at Gonzales decided that they would go, knowing that it meant certain death.

The irony deepened when Fannin tarried in obeying Houston's order to retreat from Goliad immediately and blow up its fortress. By the time he finally made ready to move, the Mexicans had arrived. For reasons known only to himself, instead of holding out in the fortress, which was considerably stronger than the Alamo, he decided to make a run for it and take his chances out on the prairie. Soon he and his men were pinned down in a gully, away from water, and surrounded by a vastly superior force. The Americans formed a hollow square and held out all day long, but the following morning, when Mexican field guns began to spray them from all sides with grapeshot and cannister, Fannin surrendered unconditionally and appealed for clemency.[12] He fully expected to be accorded the honors of war, and foreign officers in the Mexican army who spoke English assured him and the others that they would be paroled and shipped home in a matter of days. But the Napoleon of the West had other plans. On the following Sunday (Palm Sunday, as it turned out) the able-bodied prisoners, under the impression that they were going home, were marched out of town in three columns, down three separate roads, and shot. Then the Mexicans dragged wounded prisoners out in the street and shot them; after the officers learned what had happened to their men, they received the same death, and last of all, Fannin himself was shot.

Now the avenging Texans had a dual battle cry: "Remember the Alamo!" was followed by "Remember Goliad!" But for a while it didn't look as if they would be shouting anything as Houston withdrew his vastly outnumbered army farther and farther north. Santa Anna chased hard after him, deeper and deeper into the Texas Territory, his supply lines getting more and more tenuous. Finally Houston, with his back to the San Jacinto River, allowed himself to be "trapped" by Santa Anna. By now the West's Napoleon had lost all respect for the ever-retreating general of the Texan "army," and having at last brought him to bay, he allowed his men to observe a well-earned siesta as was their custom.

The air along the San Jacinto hung hot, still, and heavy that noon of April 21, 1836. After a cooked meal, nearly all the Mexican army—officers and men alike, and Santa Anna himself—lay fast asleep in whatever shade they could find. Even the sentries (there were no out-posted pickets), leaned against trees or propped themselves up with their muskets, listening to the dull drone of cricket and grasshopper and trying to keep at least one eye at a time open.

Three-quarters of a mile away in the Texas ranks, the exact opposite was taking place. At the suggestion of postponing the fight yet another day, they became so angry that Houston practically had a mutiny on his hands. Tired of running, they wanted to fight *now,* and company by company they voted to attack immediately. Houston smiled; for the first time since they had come together, his army was one. At three o'clock in the afternoon, right in the middle of the enemy's siesta, he formed them up—the cavalry (all sixty horsemen) on the right, to keep the Mexicans from breaking across the prairie, the Texas regulars in the middle, flanked by the Twin Sisters (two cannon, gifts from Cincinnati, Ohio), with all the corps of riflemen from Kentucky, Tennessee, and the like on the left. Those on foot he formed into a single line of infantry a thousand yards wide that stretched from the river to the bayou. Shouting "Hold your fire till you make it count! Forward. . . . Texas!"[13] he drew his sword and pointed at the distant rise, behind which lay the Mexican encampment.

Forward they marched across the open plain toward the enemy's position—bearded, scruffy, buckskinned, and remembering the Alamo, with their long rifles leveled. Incredibly, they were well within rifle range before someone finally spotted them and the Mexican bugles bleated a frantic alarm. Now the Texans yelled and shifted from a walk to a trot. The Mexicans panicked; their gunners sent grapeshot whistling harmlessly over the heads of the advancing army, and only the sentries fired their muskets. The rest of the troops desperately tried to form into orderly columns, having never learned to fight as individuals, without command.

Down went Mosely Baker, and down went Houston's white charger, Saracen. But the general remained unhurt and scrambled to his feet, his sword still thrust forward. The Texans broke into a run, and their yells, forerunners of the blood-curdling cries that would issue from Confederate throats in another generation, wrought as much havoc as a concerted volley. With *Los Diablos Tejanos* practically upon them, the Mexicans remembered the stories they had heard about the superhuman giants who had fought inside the Alamo, and they began to think more about preserving their skins than preserving discipline.

At twenty yards, practically point-blank range, the Texans opened fire. The Mexicans' barricades were swept clear. The Texans stormed over them, and their gray-uniformed adversaries had no time to reload, no time to regroup. Once again, it became tomahawk, rifle butt, and Bowie knife versus bayonet, only this time the odds favored the Mexicans by only two to one, instead of thirty to one, and the Texans knew they were going to win. "Remember the Alamo!" came the shout again and again as they waded into the midst of the Mexicans. Houston had his second horse shot out from under him, but this time his ankle caught a musket ball and his boot filled with blood. Still he pressed on. The Mexicans now broke and fled for their lives—only they had no place to go. Those who ventured out on the prairie were cut down by cavalry; those headed for the bayou either drowned or found themselves stacked up against their comrades. Calmly, the Texans dropped to one knee and began firing into that mass, and re-loading, and firing again.

The "battle," lasted only a few minutes. The aftermath lasted until sunset, when Colonel Juan Almonte surrendered the remaining Mexican troops to save their lives, Cos and Santa Anna having disappeared. Littering the field were 630 Mexican bodies; 200 of the 600 surviving prisoners had wounds. Texan losses amounted to 2 men killed in action, and another 24, including Houston, wounded.[14]

Late in the afternoon of the following day, one of the Texan patrols came across "a bedraggled little figure" in a blue cotton dress, a leather cap, and red felt slippers. Since this was such an oddity, they brought him into camp for questioning—and were stunned when Mexican prisoners, catching sight of him, doffed their caps and murmured, "*El Presidente*!" They had found the Napoleon of the West, and when the Texans brought him before Houston, the latter promptly dictated the terms of an armistice: Santa Anna was to order Mexican forces out of Texas at once, "passing to the other side of the Rio Grande."[15] The flag with the lone star on it flew supreme over the Republic of Texas and would never again be lowered until the Stars and Stripes took its place.

Good news traveled fast, and in those days it seemed to have its own telegraph. When the news of Texas's astounding victory and the destruction of the Mexican Army of the North reached Washington, suddenly everyone called for the recognition of the new republic. Nor should it stop there, politicians cried; the Lone Star should remain alone no longer, but take its rightful place with the others in the field of blue. But at the height of the clamor, one voice suddenly spoke out against the tide—a voice that had become a cry in the wilderness, but that still carried more weight in Congress than any other. John Quincy Adams rose on the floor and denounced the Texas revolution, conjecturing that its whole purpose was the "re-establishment of slavery in territory where it had already been abolished through Mexican law."[16] JQA's startling denunciation had the effect of reducing the question of Texas's annexation to another slavery debate. He soon found himself the rallying point of abolitionists who now claimed that the entire uprising had been plotted and fomented by proslavery forces in order to bring another slave state into the Union. A number of modern historians have tried to make this case.

But available documentation reveals that no more than 3,000 slaves and slavers existed in the Republic of Texas—less than a tenth of the Anglo-American population there. Sam Houston was no more a tool of the slavery interests than Andrew Jackson was. To them, slavery appeared as an economic not an ideological problem, and it concerned them only when it threatened the Union. That they would think alike was no surprise, for they had much in common. Both men traced their heritage to Tennessee. Houston had fought under Jackson in the War of 1812, served in Congress for four years, and was then elected Governor. But their greatest similarity lay in the vision they shared for America—a Union that would stretch from sea to sea. While both saw Texas as eventually part of that Union, they had no more use for northern abolitionists than southern nullifiers; both threatened the greater Union.

JQA's fiery speech had permanently shattered the rose-colored glasses of those north and south of the Sabine who would see Texas annexed. From now on, the Texas question would be fought out on the slavery battlefield—which made it such a hot potato politically that even recognition of the new republic was deferred until after the 1836 presidential election. Once they had elected Jackson's protégé, Martin Van Buren, it became be safe to reintroduce the issue. But Van Buren hardly received the mandate that he and his mentor expected; in fact, his margin of victory was so narrow that his supporters urged him to downplay the recognition of Texas, resolutions for which had languished in the Senate and House for months. But a strong, well-financed and articulate Texas lobby now hinted that if recognition were not soon forthcoming, they might have to look for help elsewhere (meaning Great Britain). They persisted in their efforts, and finally, on February 26, 1837, the House passed a version, confident that it would die in the Senate. It didn't: through some fancy political footwork, it got attached as a rider to another bill and squeaked through as the result of a tie vote.

On March 3, less than twenty-four hours before he would leave office, President Jackson put his signature to the bill, pleased that his last official act was another blaze on the trail that ran to the western sea.

That night, he invited the Texan agents to the White House to celebrate, and at the stroke of midnight, he raised his glass: "Gentlemen, the Republic of Texas."[17]

In 1838 one of America's most widely read editorialists, John L. O'Sullivan, summed up the general optimism then prevalent concerning America:

> The far-reaching, the boundless future will be the era of American greatness. In its magnificent domain of space and time, the nation of many nations is destined to manifest to mankind the obedience of divine principles; to establish on earth the noblest temple ever dedicated to the worship of the Most High—the Sacred and the True. Its floor shall be a hemisphere, its roof the firmament of the star-studded heavens, and its congregation an Union of many Republics, comprising hundreds of happy millions, calling, owning no man master, but governed by God's natural and moral law of equality, the law of brotherhood, of "peace and good will amongst men."[18]

"Destined to manifest"—for the first time those two words were yoked together, but the concept of Manifest Destiny would soon appear in sermons and newspapers throughout the land, capturing the imagination of every visionary, expansionist, and romantic intoxicated with the heady brew of America's potential. There was nothing really new about the core of this idea. Two centuries earlier, the Pilgrims and Puritans had believed that God intended America as a type of Israel for their age, a land where He had called a newly chosen people to settle and provide a living example of the life to which He had called all men. America was to be a "city set on a hill," they said, and a light to the rest of the world. Their children carried this idea of God's call even further: America was to be an asylum for the oppressed and a spiritual generator that would power the spread of Christianity and democracy all over the globe.

But the earlier settlers' views differed dramatically in one respect: their attitude upon perceiving such awesome, God-given responsibility had reflected the most abject humility. Because of their commitment to sobering self-examination and repentance, they had harbored no illusions about their fallen natures and had accepted that it was their privilege to spend the rest of their lives cooperating with God as He conformed them more to the image of His Son. They had known that they remained unworthy of such a calling and that only by the sheer grace and mercy of God would they ever fulfill His desire for them.

At the same time, they believed that if enough people chose to live for Christ, instead of for self, there could arise a different society on earth—one dedicated to providing true liberty and justice for everyone. They believed that if God's Word was at the heart of that society's life, the Kingdom of God could begin to be formed on earth before, and in a sense in preparation for, Christ's return. But that could only happen where and when enough men and women who were called by His name (Christians), would humble themselves (voluntarily) and pray and seek His face (first, and above all other faces), and turn from their wicked ways (which they had to first acknowledge and then repent of).

That had been the vision of those Early Comers—that God did indeed have a plan for America, and that He intended to use them to show the way to the rest of the world. That vision had initially given birth to the concept of Manifest Destiny. But how different was the attitude of their nineteenth-century descendants! Any notion of the need for ongoing repentance and the complementary humility that so characterized the first Christians who embraced the vision slipped away. When America had finally won her independence against seemingly insurmountable odds, most Americans echoed their first President in giving the Almighty all the praise and glory for their safe deliverance. But after the War of 1812, scarcely one in ten turned back to thank the Lord for prospering their cause. Most seemed convinced that they had done it themselves. In song and story, they boasted of the stunning outcome of the Battle of New Orleans, which permanently established America in the first rank of world powers; from now on, she need fear no nation on earth. As for democracy, God's chosen form of government for those called by His name—where on earth did it work better?

No wonder the Almighty was shedding His grace on America! Or that the promise of this "New Israel" seemed to extend from sea to shining sea—it deserved no less. As O'Sullivan would later write, it was "the right of our manifest destiny to overspread and possess the whole of the continent which Providence has given us for the development of the great experiment of liberty and federated self-government entrusted to us."[19] He and the other expansionists did not mean merely the territories of Texas, California, and Oregon; they meant all of Mexico and Canada, too.

Manifest Destiny thinking had begun several decades before the phrase was coined. Indeed, even before the Revolutionary War, young Timothy Dwight would write in his poem, "America":

> O land supremely blest! To thee 'tis given
> To taste the choicest joys of bounteous heaven;
> Thy rising glory shall expand its rays,
> And lands and times unknown rehearse thine endless praise . . .
> Hail land of light and joy! Thy power shall grow
> Far as the seas which round thy regions flow. . .
> Then, then an heavenly kingdom shall descend,
> And Light and Glory through the world extend.[20]

After the Revolutionary War, America's mission and destiny became more apparent, even on Britain's side of the ocean. Speaking of their recent colonial adversaries, the great English preacher Richard Price exclaimed: "It will be true of them, as it was of the people of the Jews, that in them all the families of the earth shall be blessed. . . . Perhaps, there never existed a people on whose wisdom and virtue more depended; or to whom a station of more importance in the plan of Providence has been assigned."[21]

By 1837, millennial thinking had coalesced to the point where the Reverend Horace Bushnell would write:

> There are too many prophetic signs admonishing us, that Almighty Providence is pre-engaged to make this a truly great nation, not to be cheered by them, and go forth, seeking out the principles of national advancement. This western world had not been preserved unknown through so many ages, for any purpose less sublime, than to be opened, at a certain stage of history, and become the theatre wherein better principles might have their action and free development.[22]

In Europe, opinion toward America underwent similar revision. Prussian historian Frederick von Raumer would write: "The poetry of the Americans lies not in the past but in the future. We Europeans go back in sentiment through the twilight of ages that lose themselves in night; the Americans go forward through the morning dawn to day! Their great, undoubted historical past lies near them; their *fathers* did great things, not their *great-great-grandfathers!*"[23]

But perhaps this sense of America's mission and destiny was best summed up by Herman Melville, in *White-Jacket,* the novel he wrote just prior to *Moby Dick:*

> Escaped from the house of bondage, Israel of old did not follow after the ways of the Egyptians. To her was given an express dispensation; to her were given new things under the sun. And we Americans are the peculiar, chosen people—the Israel of our time; we bear the ark of the liberties of the world. . . . God has predestined, mankind expects, great things from our race; and great things we feel in our souls. The rest of the nations must soon be in our rear. We are the pioneers of the world, the advance guard sent on through the wilderness of untried things, to break a new path in the New World that is ours. In our youth is our strength; in our inexperience, our wisdom. . . .[24]

The biggest difference between the self-styled prophets of the New Israel and those of the original chosen people was that the Old Testament prophets invariably included an *if: If* God's people repent, humble themselves, and obey Him, then will He will forgive them and bless their land. But *if* they do not obey His commandments, then will His judgment come upon them. Very few nineteenth-century visionaries speaking of America's Manifest Destiny mentioned the negative alternative. Lyman Beecher, however, was one:

> If this nation is, in the providence of God, destined to lead the way in the moral and political emancipation of the world, it is time she understood her high calling, and were harnessed for the work. For mighty causes, like floods from distant mountains, are rushing with accumulating power to their consummation of good or evil, and soon our character and destiny will be stereotyped forever."[25]

If, however, America should fail in its calling . . . if, for example, the nation should break up, as was the case with the original Israel, if the "great experiment of self-government" which was part of the preparation for the Millennium, should collapse, "the descent of desolation will correspond with the past elevation." In this, we hear Beecher echoed by Albert Maury, who in 1847, after predicting that America would become "a beacon and a land-mark on the cliffs of time to the nations of the earth," declared:

> But if we should become corrupt and unprincipled, if passion should dominate over reason, faction be paramount to patriotism, liberty degenerate into licentiousness. . . . no horoscope will be needed to forecast our destinies. Ours, and not ours only, but bound up indissolubly with them, the fortunes of free institutions all the world over, will suffer disastrous shipwreck; and borne on time's unebbing tide, will finally be lost in that great ocean of the past, where already in numbers numberless, "the graves of buried empires heave like passing waves."[26]

America's destiny would be decided in Congress, by the elected Senators and Representatives of the United States. Addressing them for the last time as President on March 4, 1837, Andrew Jackson challenged them:

> You have the highest of human trusts committed to your care. Providence has showered on this favored land blessings without number, and has chosen you as the guardians of freedom, to preserve it for the benefit of the human race. May He who holds in His hands the destinies of nations, make you worthy of the favors He has bestowed, and enable you, with pure hearts and hands and sleepless vigilance, to guard and defend to the end of time the great charge He has committed to your keeping.[27]

That last speech solemnly reminded them who had commissioned them and what He expected. All present felt sobered by it. But there was one thing which He had never intended to be a part of the City on the Hill, and until it was faced and resolved, there could be no fulfillment of destiny, manifest or otherwise. For 3 million souls were still held in bondage.

16

Sounding Forth the Trumpet

The morning of August 22, 1831, dawned quietly in the Virginia Tidewater Country. The mists rose off the water, songbirds greeted the sun, and crickets chirped in the fields. The crops were laid, and in another month the heavy work of harvesting would begin. Taking advantage of the hiatus, many farmers had hitched up their teams and taken their families south to the camp meetings in North Carolina, to refresh their souls and renew acquaintances. All told, few whites remained home, and in this pause in the tempo of the field work, one black man looked at the sky for a sign—and found one. A strange, bluish cast covered the sun, and Nat Turner saw this as the signal from God he had been waiting for. Carefully he ran his thumb over the edge of his razor-sharp field knife and smiled.

Born in 1800, Nat had been a precocious child, and his first owners noting his intelligence, taught him to read and write and submitted him to intensive religious instruction. But times had gotten hard in the 1820s, and conditions forced the Turners to sell Nat. During the following bleak and barren decade, the young black's religious ardor turned to quiet madness. He heard voices now, telling him what to do, and he adopted the ways of a lay preacher, developing a powerful charisma. Fasting and meditating in the woods, he frequently beheld such visions as "white spirits and black spirits engaged in battle . . . and blood flowing in streams."[1]

In 1831, he was sold again, to the Travis family in Southampton County, west of Norfolk, and here he prepared to put his plan into action, enlisting the aid of seven other blacks whom he felt he could trust. It was a simple plan: they would fulfill his vision by slaughtering every white in the county. Other blacks would rise en masse to their aid, and together they would march to Jerusalem, the county seat, with its armory. From there, it was only thirty miles to the Dismal Swamp, where whites would be hard pressed to find them and where blacks from all over the South would join them. (Some would say later that he had been influenced by the published appeal to insurrection of the ex-slave David Walker, many copies of which had been sent into the South by antislavery activists, but Nat Turner had dreamed of streams of blood long before *Walker's Appeal.*)

Turner summoned his men, and as the morning sun began to burn off the mist they silently padded into the Travis household, where the master and his family lay fast asleep. Out came the sharp knives, and the slaves slit the Travises' throats before they could awaken. The streams of blood had begun, and the self-styled instrument of "God's vengeance" led his band on to the adjacent plantation. Here, they went to the slave quarters first, and although some slaves joined them, many, out of fear or loyalty, refused. Turner and his followers visited the big house, and again the use to which they put their weapons turned white linen bedsheets bright red. Another plantation was struck, and another, until they came to Dr. Blount's house. This gouty old gentleman rallied his slaves, and together they fought off the raiders and raised the alarm.

By the end of the second day, Turner's force, now numbering about seventy, had murdered fifty-five men, women, and children and rejoiced that the long-overdue day of judgment had come at long last to their oppressors. With each success, Nat grew more confident that his plan would succeed. But it was an obvious plan, and any white man in the county knew exactly where they were headed and why. A few miles outside Jerusalem four crack companies of state militia suddenly confronted the slaves. In the fight that followed, discipline became nonexistent in the black ranks; they soon broke and fled for their lives.

Now the whites experienced a blood frenzy, chasing the blacks into the swamp and gunning them down indiscriminately. Still, Turner eluded them and managed to avoid capture for two months, during which time all Virginia trembled as wild rumors of one Turner-led insurrection followed upon the heels of another. Indeed, throughout the South, men and women shuddered at unidentified sounds in the night, for the thing that they had feared above all else had come to pass. In every southern state, legislation was immediately passed, clamping more stringent controls on the black population. It became a crime to teach a Negro to read or write, to allow him freedom of unauthorized assembly, even to let him have his own, unsupervised preachers. The United States mail could not be used for the dissemination of incendiary pamphlets like *Walker's Appeal* and that new abolitionist paper out of Boston, the *Liberator*. This, of course, would eventually entail the censoring of the mails, a grievous breach of the First Amendment, but the physical safety of their loved ones lay at stake.

Before Nat Turner's revolt, there had been only two other incidents: an abortive uprising planned by Gabriel Prosser in 1800 (he had been betrayed by two of his co-conspirators before he could take action), and Denmark Vesey's, a generation later, in Charleston, which other slaves also thwarted. Those had been enough: with the black population actually outnumbering the white in three states and equal to it in four others, the possibility of a massed servile insurrection became so real that it kept a sizable portion of the white population in a state of perpetual fear. Like a low-grade infection, people seldom spoke of it, but it remained below the surface. As John Randolph confided to one of his fellow Congressmen, "I speak from facts, when I say that the night bell never tolls for fire in Richmond, that the mother does not hug the infant more closely to her bosom. I have been witness to some of the alarms in the capital of Virginia."[2]

Up North, the media reacted with shock and sympathy. An editorial in the New York *American,* while maintaining its hatred of the institution of slavery, nevertheless declared that in the areas where slavery existed through no fault of the present generation of owners, "We would go to the utmost length to sustain the rights and safety of those whom circumstances have placed in the relation of masters."[3] That was typical of the response in the North, where heretofore the antislavery movement had always conducted its business with decorum, mindful of the sensibilities of their southern cousins, whom they hoped to persuade. Indeed, the Fredericksburg *Arena* informed its Virginia readership that the northern newspaper comments were "entirely unobjectionable." Of course, one notable exception existed: the fanatical *Liberator,* the first issue of which was brought out by William Lloyd Garrison at the beginning of 1831.

From volume 1, number 1, the radical Garrison, who demanded immediate emancipation—not the gradual emancipation that most antislavery societies, northern and southern, advocated—served notice that he had no use for moderation.

> Tell a man whose house is on fire, to give a moderate alarm; tell him to moderately rescue his wife from the hands of the ravisher; tell the mother to gradually extricate her babe from the

> fire into which it has fallen; but urge me not to use moderation in a cause like the present! I am in earnest. I will not equivocate—I will not excuse—I will not retreat a single inch—AND I WILL BE HEARD. The apathy of the people is enough to make every statue leap from its pedestal and to hasten the resurrection of the dead.[4]

People would later accuse Garrison of being responsible for influencing Nat Turner, and in truth the previous month's *Liberator* had contained a poem urging "Africa" to "strike for God and vengeance now."[5] Yet is seems highly unlikely that Turner ever saw the paper, whose paid subscriptions numbered less than sixty at the time of the rebellion. But southern editors did see it, as it was the custom in those days for newspapers to exchange copies with more than a hundred papers. In this way, editors throughout the South became immediately aware of what Garrison said—and responded in rage (thereby building the reputation of Garrison, who was practically unknown in the North, even after several years of campaigning on behalf of abolition).

Meanwhile, white patrols scoured the byroads, interrogating witnesses and generally reflecting the mounting apprehension of their white countrymen. The unthinkable had happened—and if the slaves ever reacted in concert, what had happened in Haiti would seem mild in comparison. . . . But at last they apprehended Turner, and Virginia breathed a collective sigh of relief. His swift trial resulted in a sentence of death by hanging, and the aftermath was as bizarre and horrible as the entire episode: presumably to avoid his remains being stolen and revered as a martyr's relics, his body was turned over to doctors who melted it down into grease.[6]

Like the heaving of an underwater earthquake, the Nat Turner rebellion brought about a sudden, great change in the attitude of Virginia and the entire South. Until this time, slavery had been regarded as a social evil, definitely unpleasant and the cause of profound moral conflict for sensitive people. As late as 1827, the great majority of the antislavery societies in the United States existed in slaveholding states, and the four abolitionist papers founded before Garrison's were all in the South.[7] But slavery remained so essential to the region's economy and so inextricably entwined into the southern way of life that little serious thought had been given to its termination. An Englishman named Basil Hall had traveled extensively in the South in the late

1820s. He found the southern planters who were his hosts quite ready to admit "that slavery is an evil in itself and eminently evil in its consequences," but to eradicate it seemed "so completely beyond the reach of any human exertions" that he had decided that the abolition of slavery was the "most profitless of all possible subjects of discussion.[8]

In the beginning, the Founding Fathers, so many of them Virginians, had agreed with Washington and Jefferson that it was deleterious to both races, and must go—eventually. As we saw in the opening chapter, at the Constitutional Convention in 1787, they prepared to specify a date upon which it would be halted, except that Georgia and South Carolina would have no part in putting any limit to it. For the sake of uniting the states of America, the convention set aside the slavery issue. Get the Union first, and Congress would deal with slavery later, they promised the northern states. Only they never did, and South Carolina and Georgia even successfully forestalled the prohibition of the loathsome importation of slaves for an additional twenty years. Ironically, Virginia opposed them in this, and they were only able to push the legislation through with the help of some New England delegates, who reflected the interests of merchant constituents making enormous profits from the slave trade.[9]

For the nearly two hundred years that the colonies and now states had been in existence, Virginia had provided much of the key leadership in America, a fact of which she was justly proud. Indeed, for thirty-two of the nation's first thirty-six years, a procession of her sons was in the White House, and for nearly that long, another held the position of Chief Justice of the Supreme Court. So now in an increasing era of sectionalization, South looked to Virginia—the Old Dominion with its genteel refined ways so similar to those of the English aristocracy—to show the way, especially in the matter of culture and the pursuits of the intellect. Even in the philosophical approach to slavery, no one expressed the southern attitude better than the man who penned the Declaration of Independence. But Jefferson was of another era, of a time when planters had inherited sufficient wealth or had brought enough with them from their ancestral estates to seriously consider manumitting their slaves as a gesture of egalitarianism.

Unfortunately, by 1831, such a gesture had become financially inexpedient for nearly all planters. Tobacco used up so much land so quickly, and with the landowners still smarting from the depression of 1819 a dozen years later, it simply didn't make sense to part with the principal wealth of a poor plantation—especially at a time when the price of slaves was going up so rapidly with the cotton explosion throughout the Deep South. Even so a sharp division developed among Virginians on the subject of slavery—a division that followed the spine of the Blue Ridge Mountains. For the planters of the Tidewater, where the slave population had mushroomed (in 1790, whites exceeded blacks by 25,000; now they were outnumbered by 81,000), emancipation would mean economic disaster. Those in the Piedmont foothills would be similarly, albeit less drastically, affected. But in the Shenandoah Valley and to the west, most Virginians did not own slaves but were yeomen accustomed to doing their own work, like their northern neighbors. Here, antislavery sentiment ran the highest, and Jefferson's democratic views remained very much in evidence.

Such a division in thought, with the whole slavery question brought to a boil by the Turner Rebellion, promised a lively debate when the House of Delegates reconvened in December. Nor would Virginians alone follow the proceedings; the entire nation would watch. Virginia had so often led the way in the past; would she do so now? Was the slavery question finally about to be settled? Some of the most eloquent men in America would present their case, pro and con. Journalists packed the gallery and those onlookers without press affiliation felt fortunate to find a seat as the legislators of this 200-year-old body filed in. There was Thomas Marshall, eldest son of the Chief Justice, and Thomas Jefferson Randolph, favorite grandson of the third President. There was Governor Floyd's nephew, James McDowell, and coming in with him, another nephew, William B. Preston, whose father had served as Governor. And here was William Roane of Hanover, Patrick Henry's grandson. The First Families of Virginia were well represented, and most of their handsome young men spoke for antislavery. The balance between pro and anti forces was about sixty each, with a dozen more delegates straddling the fence.

To northerners' dismay, the antislavery position presupposed that virtually no one advocated emancipation without deportation. The prospect of tens of thousands of unemployed blacks suddenly turned loose on the Virginia countryside with no visible means of support, save to steal necessities, was too appalling to receive serious consideration. If that madman Garrison had his way, the delegates could well imagine, they'd be given the vote, as well, and everyone in this room would be black. No, the only decent thing to do was to ship them back to Africa, where they came from, to the colony of Liberia, which had been secured by the American Colonization Society for that very purpose. Of course, you could send them up north, but the Yankees had already made it clear that they didn't want any more free Negroes in their own towns and had passed restrictive legislation accordingly. Africa was the final solution, even if it did cost $80 to send a slave back.

By the way, slaveholders asked, who would pay for their deportation? Or reimburse the slaveholder $200 each, the worth of the average slave? They didn't hear any northerners volunteering. Usually they heard it was their problem. But just to deport all the slaves in Virginia would cost $100 million; if you sold every piece of land, every dwelling and every stick of furniture in the Old Dominion, you might come up with that much, but then how would you cover the cost of reimbursing the owners? Not even Jefferson's concept of gradual emancipation seemed to hold the answer, although his grandson now put it forth:

> The children of all female slaves, who may be born in this state on or after the 4th of July, 1840, shall become the property of the commonwealth, the males at the age of twenty-one years, and the females at the age of eighteen, if detained by their owners within the limits of Virginia, until they shall respectively arrive at the ages aforesaid, to be hired out until the net sum arising therefrom shall be sufficient to defray the expense of their removal beyond the limits of the United States.[10]

That certainly sounded feasible. Just one gnawing concern remained, which Garrison and his ilk quickly pointed out: they had based the whole colonization movement on the presumption that the Negro was biologically and intellectually inferior, incapable of being sufficiently educated and elevated to take an equal place in society. If Garrison was right, then the American Colonization Society was nothing more than a giant sop to guilty consciences and a convenient political escape hatch. If the truth be told, in the first twenty years of existence it had deported fewer than five thousand blacks—less than one quarter of one percent of the slaves in America. To those who would congratulate themselves on their humanitarianism in espousing such a scheme, one might well ask how humanitarian it was to take someone born and raised in America (as his parents had been before him), tear him away from his family and friends, and ship him across the ocean to a land he had never heard of, where no one had made provision for him, and dump him there to fend for himself?

Some of the finest sons of Virginia nonetheless toiled to unravel this dilemma. George Williams, from beyond the Alleghenies, responded to the claim of John Brown of Petersburg that slaves didn't want their freedom: "The poorest tattered negro who tills the planter's field under his task-master, and labors to produce those fruits which he may never call his own, feels within him that spark which emanates from the Deity—the innate longing for liberty—and hears in the inmost recesses of his soul, the secret whisperings of nature, that tell him he should be free. . . . God never made a slave—slavery is the work of man alone." And James McDowell was on his feet right after him: "The idea that he was born to be free will survive it all. It is allied to his hope of immortality—it is the ethereal part of his nature which oppression cannot reach. It is a torch lit up in his soul by the hand of the Deity and never meant to be extinguished by the hand of man."[11]

Now Thomas Marshall, who had perhaps ten thousand 1832 dollars invested in slaves, arose to condemn slavery:

> Because it is ruinous to the whites—retards improvement—roots out an industrious population—banishes the yeomanry of the country—deprives the spinner, the weaver, the smith, the shoemaker, the carpenter, of employment and support. . . . The master has no capital but what is invested in human flesh; the father, instead of being richer for his sons, is at a loss to provide for them. . . . Labor of every species is disreputable, because performed mostly by slaves.[12]

More than a few of his listeners had not thought of that before: slavery effectively did away with the entire middle class of society, leaving only the very rich, who would not labor, and the very poor, who could not avoid it. Even the rich—what did they have to pass on to their children? Only a plantation that could not function without slaves and whose only disposable assets were those same slaves. It provided food for thought.

But the antislavery side by no means had the only orators. Alexander Knox of Mecklenburg County stood, and for the first time in the seven-week-long debate presented slavery as a positive good that benefited both races: "I cannot force my mind, even by calling to its aid humanity, religion or philanthropy, to the conclusion that slavery, as it exists in Virginia, is an evil. But, Sir, on the contrary, I consider it susceptible of demonstration that it is to this very cause that we may trace the high and elevated character which she has heretofore sustained."[13]

There was an audible gasp from the gallery. Not even the staunchest proslavery spokesman had dared to claim that the institution was beneficial! But now with the ground broken, others quickly followed suit—a new way of thinking had surfaced in the South. James Gholson of Brunswick County said:

> I will not discuss the abstract question of the right of slavery, but I will say that the slaves of Virginia are as happy a laboring class as exists upon the habitable globe. . . . In health, but reasonable labor is required of them; in sickness, they are nursed and attended to. In times of plenty, they live in waste; in times of scarcity, they do not want. They are content today and have no care or anxiety for tomorrow. Cruel treatment of them is discountenanced by society. . . . Among what laboring class will you find more happiness and less misery? Not among the serfs and laboring poor of Europe! No, sir! Nor among the servants to the North of us.[14]

John T. Brown refused to let the present generation shoulder the blame for slavery.

> Whether it be a blessing or a curse, the moment has never yet been, when it was possible for us to free ourselves from it. This is enough to satisfy my conscience. . . . [slavery] was forced upon us by a train of events that could not be controlled. . . . In what code of ethics, human or divine, is it written that slavery is an offense of so odious a character that no circumstance can palliate it—no necessity excuse it? Whence is derived the authority for saying it is a sin, so very foul and monstrous, that Virginia is bound to pluck it from her bosom, though her life's blood should gush after it? . . . The Saviour of mankind did not condemn it. . . . He came into the world to reprove sin, and He did reprove it, in all the diversified forms in which it appeared before Him. Yet He rebuked not slavery. . . . Again, Sir, I contend that the happiness of the slave does not call for his emancipation. His condition is better than that of four-fifths of the human family. . . . He is not free, but that is a blessing only in name to a

> large majority of the human race. Man must be civilized, his mind enlightened, and his feelings refined, before he is fitted for the enjoyment of liberty.[15]

Here murmurs of "Nay, nay!" from delegates and gallery alike interrupted Brown. Yet he continued—and his argument that would become the touchstone of the emerging southern attitude toward slavery.

> The greater part of mankind must, in the nature of things, be poor and ignorant, toiling anxiously for their daily bread. All cannot be raised to the top of the scale, and the Negro, of all others, is the least susceptible of elevation. . . . And yet it is certain that whatever evils may flow from slavery, it would now be a far greater evil to abolish it.

The Negro was happy in his lot, happier than most men; he could not handle freedom if they handed it to him; slavery might be evil, but it was *not* a sin. . . .

And yet others were prepared to prove that it most definitely *was* sin. Thomas Randolph rebutted: "The gentleman has appealed to the Christian religion in justification of slavery. I would ask him upon what part does he rely? What part of those pure doctrines does he avert to sustain his position? Is it that which teaches charity, justice and good will to all? Or is it that which teaches that ye do unto others as ye would they should do unto you?"[16] Just as Knox's assertion that slavery was good for both races set one precedent, Randolph's assertion that it was not just a social evil, but sin, set another. For if it *was* sin, and could be so demonstrated in God's Word, then the believing Christian, regardless of his heritage or any other consideration, had no alternative but to foreswear it immediately.

The North initially reacted to the Virginia slavery debates with amazement. Antislavery proponents felt stunned and overjoyed to at last hear southern representatives speaking out against slavery and doing so as eloquently as any of their own could have done. Many rejoiced at what they took to be a new wave of reform that had finally reached south of the Mason-Dixon line, just as wave after wave of reform swept over the North in the wake of the great revivals (to the point where poet James Russell Lowell wryly observed that everyone in the North was apparently bent on reforming something or someone). In the South, newspaper editors were relieved to have the whole question out in the open at last, after years of discreetly and abstractly temporizing about the evils of slavery. Perhaps now they could accomplish something definite.

But nothing happened. For, in truth, the proslavery attitude in the South had already hardened well before the debates began. In 1824, the Ohio legislature adopted resolutions proposing a plan of gradual emancipation, colonization of freed blacks outside the boundaries of the United States, and federal compensation to slaveholders "upon the principle that the evil of slavery is a national one, and that the people and the states of this Union ought mutually to participate in the duties and burdens of removing it."[17] Eight northern states promptly endorsed Ohio's plan, and Senator Rufus King of New York proposed to raise the necessary money it would take through the sale of public lands. It was a generous offer, and hardly the first time that northerners of good conscience declared that slavery was a national, not a regional, calamity. But the Upper South reacted negatively and the Deep South with hostility and threats. The South Carolina senate vowed it would not permit slave property "to be meddled with or tampered with" by outsiders, and Georgia's Governor denounced the "combination of fanatics" who sought to destroy "everything valuable in the Southern country." He urged the Georgia legislature "to step forth, and having exhausted the argument, to stand by your arms."[18]

With this the unspoken but pervasive attitude in the South, no wonder the Virginia antislavery proposals that triggered the debate were overwhelmingly defeated. And as winter receded into memory, so did the Turner Rebellion and the urgency it had provoked. Virginia's concern turned once again to the debilitating tariffs imposed to protect northern manufacturers, and fear of splitting the state kept idealistic editorialists from pursuing the cause. When ordinary people saw that nothing whatever came of the debates, they assumed slavery had proven to be ineradicable and resigned themselves to its permanent presence. The South's antislavery societies withered and died. One heard no further open antislavery talk in the South. As for the slaveholders themselves, for the most part, they felt less inclined to manumit their property than ever, for with an increase in the demand for slaves in the Deep South, the price of a prime slave daily reached new highs.

What, then, did the debates accomplish? Looking back years later, Congressman Roger Pryor would sum it up: "From that day, the slaveholder stood on surer and more solid ground. From that day, his conscience being clear, and his judgment convinced, he renounced the expedients of apology and extenuation, and planted himself on the impregnable basis of reason and right."[19]

An attempt to provide academic documentation for that basis appeared in an extraordinary essay published soon after the debates by a young professor at William and Mary College, Thomas Roderick Dew. Professor Dew had taken all the proslavery arguments and expanded on them, presenting the South with a book that would conclusively answer every question leveled at her by critics within or without. It became a best-seller, with thousands reporting that they converted to this new way of thinking as soon as they read it. Significantly, it was published in response to those Virginians who still had doubts about slavery—long before northern abolitionists would be blamed for all the state's ills. Dew stated his basic thesis in his introduction: "Every plan of emancipation and deportation which we can possibly conceive, is totally impracticable." And instead of merely condoning slavery, he extolled it as "perhaps the principal means for impelling forward the civilization of mankind."[20]

The astonishing popularity of Dew's book emboldened other proslavery advocates, who went even further as the South shifted its stance from defensive justification to propounding slavery as a positive good. Their arguments included several assumptions (that were, however, not granted by northern Christians who were beginning to speak out and that today none save the most rabid racists would grant them): blacks were racially inferior—stunted in their emotional and intellectual capacity to the point where they were "perpetual children"; they were placed on earth by God to serve white men; they had no redeemable social value, being inherently lazy, shiftless, thievish, and incapable of caring for themselves. If one granted these presuppositions, it became the slaveholder's solemn responsibility before God and to society to look after his slaves.

Nor were they at all reluctant to bring God into their presentations; on the contrary, they quoted Scripture to demonstrate that slavery had been acceptable in Moses' time, and that Christ and His Apostles said or did nothing to discourage the system. All the patriarchs had bond servants, Abraham with more than 300, and Isaac with "a great store" (Genesis 26:14). As God Himself gave His Commandments (Exodus 20), in the tenth He adjured His people not to covet their neighbor's manservants or maidservants. The sixth verse of the next chapter tells the master to bore a hole in the ear of his servant, to mark him, although Leviticus 25:43 admonishes masters to rule over their servants not "with rigour" but in fear of God. The chapter goes on to say that the master must buy his bond servants from the heathen round about them. "And ye shall take them as an inheritance for your children after you, to inherit them for a possession" (Leviticus 25:46).

What did the New Testament have to say? In his first letter to the believers at Corinth, Paul wrote: "Let every man abide in the same calling wherein he was called. Art thou called being a servant [slave]? Care not for it. . ." (1 Corinthians 7:20, 21). And in his first letter to Timothy, he expanded: "Let as many servants [or slaves] as are under the yoke count their own masters worthy of all honour, that the name of God and his doctrine be not blasphemed" (1 Timothy 6:1). Similarly, Peter wrote: "Servants [or slaves], be subject to your masters with all fear; not only to the good and gentle, but also to the froward. . . . For what glory is it, if, when ye be buffeted for your faults, ye shall take it patiently? but if, when ye do well, and suffer for it, ye take it patiently, this is acceptable with God" (1 Peter 2:18, 20).

To the "positive good" advocates, this last verse indicated that "buffeting" was a natural part of a slave's life. One of them, Chancellor William Harper of the supreme court of South Carolina asked: "Is pain not to be inflicted on the child, when it is the only means by which he can be effectually instructed to provide for his own future happiness?"[21] What gives the master the right to decide when pain shall be inflicted? Harper goes on:

> It belongs to the being of superior faculties to judge of the relations which shall subsist between himself and inferior animals, and the use he shall make of them. . . . On the very same foundation, with the difference only of circumstance and degree, rests the right of the civilized and cultivated man, over the savage and ignorant. It is the order of nature and of God, that the being of superior faculties and knowledge, and therefore of superior power, should control and dispose of those who are inferior. . . . If there are sordid, servile, and laborious offices to be performed, is it not better that there should be sordid, servile, and laborious beings to perform them?[22]

This assumption of natural superiority was now openly acknowledged throughout the South with astonishing speed, for it coincided with convictions already widely held. Those who had spoken out against slavery in the past now fell silent and never again would well-meaning or conscience-stricken slaveholders publicly call for an end to slavery. Some historians have wondered how the vast majority of white southerners, many of them poor dirt farmers, could have so totally espoused the selfish beliefs and goals of their few slaveholding neighbors. Part of the answer, as we have seen, lay in the fundamental difference in the founding of Jamestown and Plymouth. Another part was that the widespread presence of slavery in the South subtly reinforced class distinctions: it did not matter how poor or bad off a white man was or how miserable his lot in life; he was still better off than the "niggers" around him. And as long as he could compare himself to them and occasionally vent his frustration on them, he remained more or less content with his station and willingly took leadership from his aristocratic neighbors.

Indeed, many considered themselves every bit as highborn as those who still had money. In the words of contemporary historian Richard Boyer, the southern gentry considered their virtues:

> Not so much the result of effort as of blood, as decisive in a man as in a racehorse. Blood would tell, and high worth was inevitable through that straight descent so many planters claimed from the Norman nobility which had conquered England, from the cavaliers who had opposed the regicide Cromwell before fleeing to Virginia. From there, the aristocrats had replenished the earth so effectively that men claiming the bluest of blood were likely to be found at any crossroads widening in Arkansas, at any log cabin plantation in the wilderness of Alabama. . . .[23]

Harper proceeded to make an elaborate case for the good that slavery did for the white aristocracy, freeing them from manual labor, indeed, from labor of any kind. This freedom gave them ample time to steep themselves in culture and the arts, including the fine art of politics, and to follow the nobler pursuits of the mind, especially the classics. How many of them actually studied long and hard enough to be able to read the classics in the original Latin and Greek is moot. But whether they actually did or not, the point is, they sincerely believed that this was how they would prefer to spend their time. Their slaves made it possible, freeing them from the encumbrances of everyday life, that they might "realize their full intellectual potential." Thus did

Harper and others extol "the southern way of life" for producing the finest and most cultured intellects the world had ever known.

Of course, not all the leisure time was spent in improving their aristocracy's minds. There were other noble pastimes, equally enriching, that were vastly more fun. . . .

The herald trumpet sounded, and all eyes turned to the far end of the tourney field, where a knight in full armor cantered in, the August sun reflecting off his helmet with its blue plumage. He wheeled his horse and brought it to a standstill, his jousting lance vertical, the sun flashing on the carefully worked, blue and white insignia on his shield. As the knight waited, the official crier announced him with great ceremony: "Brian de Bois-Guilbert." A smattering of polite gloved applause followed. The trumpet sounded again, and another knight entered the near end of the field. This one wore a black tunic over his armor, and the rest of his accoutrements were black and silver—save for a rose-colored silk scarf attached to his lance just below the point. "Wilfred," the crier exclaimed, pausing for effect, "of Ivanhoe!" A cheer burst forth from the viewing stands together with much applause, for this knight was clearly the gallery's favorite. "Go it, Johnny boy!" shouted one of the lords, forgetting for a moment to stay in character. The knight dipped his lance to a stunning, raven-haired young woman in a rose colored gown, who demurely acknowledged his salute.

Once again the herald trumpet sounded, and at the far end of the field the blue knight closed his visor, lowered his lance to the horizontal, and spurred his mount to a full gallop. On he came, his steed's hoofs pounding the turf as he took careful aim over the point of the lance at his target—not the breastplate under the black tunic, but a tilting pole with a brass ring on top of it. For this was neither Camelot nor the court of King John; it was White Sulphur Springs, Virginia, in the year 1845. The correspondent from the Richmond *Enquirer* described it as "the richest scene I ever saw enacted on any theatre. It far surpassed any tournament we ever had."[24] Nor did this passion for re-creating the Age of Chivalry exist exclusively in the hearts of sons and daughters of the Old Dominion—Maryland, Louisiana, and the Carolinas had many similar pageants.

The southern aristocracy was in the thrall of the romantic novels and poetry of Sir Walter Scott, Sir Edward Bulwer-Lytton, Thomas Carlyle, and Lord Byron—as if they could, by sheer strength of will, force the collective fantasy to become reality. Elsewhere in the world, the novelists like Dickens who championed social reform became all the rage; for the winds of change swept across Europe, just as they did the North. Smokestacks rose in cities, and urbanized populations eagerly anticipated the future that the Industrial Revolution was ushering in. For today held so much more than yesterday that no one could calculate what tomorrow might bring. Yet as much as many Northerners looked forward to tomorrow, many Southerners yearned for yesterday. With the inevitability of soil depletion, with many of the original families' personal fortunes dwindling, and with the northern majority in Congress swelling as immigrants shunned slavery, today inevitably diminished in the glow of yesterday and tomorrow seemed more of a threat than a promise. With more and more acreage turned over to cotton, slavery became more entrenched than ever—at a time when the rest of the civilized world had come to regard it as an abomination.

Smarting under the blanket condemnation of a growing percentage of the North's inhabitants and with nowhere to turn for international acceptance, the South turned inward—and back—to another place and time that held honor, courage, loyalty, chivalry, ancestry, and hospitality in the same reverence as the South held them. Medieval Scotland filled that bill, and the plantation owner saw striking similarities between himself with his "loyal" slaves and the Scottish laird with his serfs. Each had sole responsibility for the well-being of those around them, dispensing justice and wisdom as called for. In times of crisis, the small farmers around the planter looked to him for leadership, much as clansmen gathered round their chieftain, "standing to their captain" at the sound of the tocsin. Other parallels existed: the proud Scots had been forced by the economic vicissitudes of their age into an increasingly humiliating minority position by the Englishmen with whom they shared the island of Great Britain. Fiercely loyal to their friends and implacable, relentless avengers to their foes, man for man the Scots were the best warriors on earth (which was how many southern white men saw themselves). No wonder, then, that Scott's *Ivanhoe,* published in America in 1827, should so capture the collective southern imagination. When viewed through the soft candlelight of southern memory and Scott's romantic dreams, the two worlds fitted together almost seamlessly.

Some modern-day historians have seen this collective plunge into fantasy as an escape mechanism,[25] triggered by either the boredom of a rural routine devoid of change, challenge, and goals or by a universal, suppressed guilt complex and sense of shame. For in their "secret hearts," southerners knew they ran counter to the prevailing moral notions of their age. Whatever the reasons, in an unspoken, perhaps unconscious, mutual pact, entered into by all strata of white society in the South, they sought solace in the past. Though meat was rarely served now in many of the paneled dining rooms, and the "house niggers" were getting increasingly uppity, appearances must be kept up. So the Magnolia Ball would go on as scheduled, even if it meant quietly selling the north field's last remaining creek parcel. Once again, the circular driveway would fill with a line of gleaming carriages, waiting to discharge their precious cargoes of silk, taffeta, and crinoline. Under the tall white columns liveried blacks would hold torches to light the guests' way, their flames casting huge, leaping shadows on the freshly whitewashed main facade. Just inside the foyer, violins wafted the arrivals inside to three-quarter time, and a brimming punch bowl stood ready to slake the thirst of the merry dancers. The best Magnolia Ball ever would soon take its place among the big house's store of treasured memories. . . .

Thus did the South embrace chivalry, to the extent that it profoundly influenced every aspect of their way of life. Medieval place names abounded, buildings were constructed in neoclassic style, and southern men aspired to become, not successful businessmen like their northern cousins, but romantic knights, especially in the eyes of their ladies. Southern women were expected to play the game with the same intensity and commitment as their menfolk. (*Everyone* had to play, or the whole illusion would collapse.) Gradually, for the very small percentage of slaveholders who owned plantations, the fantasy of the gracious, chivalrous, mellow southern way of life came into being and became almost a religious belief—that depended on the faith of the entire congregation to sustain it.

Southern womanhood emerged as the finest flower of this way of life, though retaining the responsibilities of having to run the plantation house, while their men busied themselves with hunting or entertaining guests or occasionally studying the classics after the model of Thomas Jefferson, improving their minds by reviewing the achievements of the higher civilizations of antiquity. In fact, a number of southern women, forced to cope with hard reality on a daily basis, found that they were actually very good at managing things, and a few ran plantations as large and complex as factories (which in a sense, they were).

Other southern women so immersed themselves in the role assigned to them that they actually believed they were indeed the fragile specimens that their men considered them to be—porcelain figurines on the mantelpiece. For those willing to keep up the pretense, undeniable rewards followed: southern womanhood became elevated to so lofty a pedestal that one twentieth-century historian, Rollin Osterweis, dubbed it nothing less than "gyneolotry":

> She was the South's palladium, this Southern woman—the shield-bearing Athena, gleaming whitely in the clouds, the standard for all its rallying, the mystic symbol of its nationality in the face of the foe. She was the lily-pure maid of Astolat and the hunting goddess of the Boeotian hill. Merely to mention her was to send strong men into tears, or shouts. . . . At the last, I verily believe, the ranks of the Confederacy went rolling into battle in the misty conviction that it was wholly for her that they fought.[26]

Southern gentlemen stood ready to defend the honor of southern womanhood—with their lives, if necessary. For in the South, dueling continued long after it had been condemned by the Church and abolished by law, and a man had better have the heart to stand and face sword or pistol under the oaks. As violent as Andrew Jackson's early life was, it was not unusual; the code of honor and chivalry formed a crucial part of the southern way of life. A perceived slight to a man's honor demanded a challenge for satisfaction, and many a young swain would discover to his chagrin that life wasn't all gambling and drinking and hunting and riding. For them "death before dishonor" was no outmoded credo; it became the cardinal rule of the game, and its ritual was as intricately choreographed as the most elegant formal dance.

While a woman received considerable ego gratification in having two men fight over her honor, being Athena, gleaming whitely in the clouds, or the lily-pure maid of Astolat, did have its drawbacks: it pretty much precluded open and honest relationships between men and women, where both parties expressed their needs to one another and shared their mutual hopes and concerns. Southern women were expected to play the role of delicate flowers (except, of course, when it came to dealing with the stressful demands of running the big house and entertaining; there, they could act as tough and resourceful as master sergeants, as long as it didn't show). Far from daunted by this schizophrenic existence, southern women, for the most part, became surprisingly adept at running things without appearing to do so and letting their husbands think that *they* made the decisions.

Out of this chivalrous view of women grew a strange dichotomy. In medieval tradition, the men saw their women as almost untouchable, the epitome of pure, delicate femininity. With such an unrealistic view of women, adultery became a problem of major proportions among many slaveholders; because a white woman could not mention it, let alone confront it, many such women became tight lipped and bitter. But most wives chose to overlook such indiscretions—and the children who resulted from them.

All the more reason to play the game of "Then" for all it was worth, and Scott provided a hardy brew. The players imbibed heavily, even adopting his language idioms as their own. Scott had his characters refer to lowlanders as "Southrons," and southerners immediately began referring to themselves in this fashion. Indeed, such was the extent of Scott's influence that Mark Twain, commenting on what he called "the Sir Walter disease," observed: "He did measureless harm, more real and lasting than any other individual that ever wrote. . . . [he] had so large a hand in making Southern character as it existed before the [Civil] War, that he is in great measure responsible for the war."[27] Like many of Twain's judgments, that is a bit extreme, but it indicates how wide and deep the romantic influence became among gentry who had taken to referring to themselves as "the Chivalry" and "the quality."

Why was the South so predisposed to immerse itself in a shared fantasy? At bottom, it resulted from a desperate struggle to escape the reality of slavery—an ugly, no-end-to-the-tunnel reality. Many southerners privately acknowledged the dark side of slavery in their diaries, even as they publically acclaimed the virtues of their way of life and the slavery which made it possible.

Was there truly no way out? Collective, committed, concerted

Christian endeavor *might* have provided a way, for it seems that by the time of the Virginia debates, the Nineveh point—the point at which a whole people might repent and go the other way—had not yet been reached. But short of admitting one's wrongs before God and man and praying for the grace to reverse course, the natural way to escape reality requires one to enter into unreality; and the more appealing the fantasy, the more effort the escapist puts into it. So the carriages arrived, and the violins played, and the handsome young men of the Chivalry, perhaps the most gallant on earth, bowed to their ladies, and trusted that their hearts would be ready when the day came that they would face the ultimate test, whether at twenty paces or leading a cavalry charge. . . .

What of the North? By the third decade of the nineteenth century, North and South were progressively becoming two separate nations, sharing little more than the same language and borders. The South had convinced itself that God Himself intended them to rule over the blacks, benevolently of course, but totally. But supposing (as more and more northerners insisted), He had *not* intended them to be a master race? Then their fervent embracing of Dew, Harper, and other proponents was more easily understood: it emanated from guilt. If God, by His Spirit, through circumstance or the lips of others, sought to convict a Christian of wrongful behavior, that Christian had two choices: he could accept God's conviction, repent of his sin, and determine to "go and sin no more." Or he could refuse the conviction. Should he do the latter, he must then, for his own psychological equilibrium, convince himself that God had not tried to convict him, but that He entirely approved of his actions, and that anyone who said otherwise was totally wrong. Indeed, anyone who did not agree with him had obviously joined the devil's camp. One hardly feels surprise, therefore, to see Harper declare: "I believe our slaves are the happiest three millions of human beings on whom the sun shines. Into their Eden is coming Satan in the guise of an abolitionist."[28]

The antislavery movement had its roots in the Second Great Awakening and the subsequent reforms that swept the country. Its societies remained, for the most part, genteel in manner and decorum, deploring the existence of the institution, praying for God to do something about it, and discreetly appealing to the southern population to prayerfully reconsider their position. Their watchwords had included "moderation," "temperance," and "gradualism,"[29] and they supported the scheme to ship freed slaves to colonies outside the United States. In everything they said or wrote, they took great care to neither offend nor antagonize the slaveholders—with the result that they wound up achieving exactly the opposite of what they desired. They so downplayed the institution's evils and the slaveholder's responsibility that they inadvertently encouraged a do-nothing attitude on the part of those whose consciences they hoped to prick and made it more difficult than ever to arouse public concern. Not surprisingly, by 1831 these antislavery societies, devoid of any thrust of impetus, began to gradually disappear.

But a handful of reformers, totally frustrated at the overcaution of their colleagues, decided to take matters into their own hands. The first was a New Jersey Quaker named Benjamin Lundy, who castigated apathetic northerners for refusing to join their antislavery efforts, which "are viewed in the light of encroachment on the established order of society . . . and thus our usefulness is checked, and our endeavors to lay before the public the train of evils attendant on a state of slavery is retarded."[30] For fifteen years, Lundy toiled alone in the vineyard until, in 1827, he met a twenty-two-year-old lad named William Lloyd Garrison. Lundy persuaded Garrison to join him in a newspaper venture, and eventually the *Liberator* had been born.

Garrison became increasingly radical. Determined to pull no punches, he painted slaveholders as despicable criminals; he was for emancipation *now*. Moreover, he wrote against any remuneration to slaveholders, for that would be making crime profitable, and he dubbed the African colonization plan a blatantly racist scheme to avoid the problem of making room for the Negro in a white man's society. Gone was any semblance of tact or diplomacy; Garrison had no time for what to him seemed hypocrisy. The South had perpetrated an obscenity, and it fouled the entire land with its stench. You didn't treat Satan's bloody-handed henchmen like gentlemen!

As Garrison and like-minded associates redoubled their efforts to incite insurrection in the South, encouraging any slaves who could read to rise up and kill their masters, the South responded in kind. The state legislature of Mississippi passed a law offering a reward of $5,000 for the arrest and conviction of any person "who shall utter, publish or circulate within the limits of that State, the *Liberator,* or any other circular, pamphlet, letter, or address of a seditious character."[31] The more southerners recoiled in horror and fury at his accusations, the more northerners attended his speaking engagements—important people, who could influence others. Amos Bronson Alcott of Boston was one, and his daughter Louisa May Alcott, and her relative Samuel May, the only Unitarian minister in Connecticut, and their friends Theodore Parker and Nathaniel Hawthorne. Years later, May would describe his meeting with Garrison in terms usually reserved for an individual's meeting Christ: "That night my soul was baptized in his spirit, and ever since I have been a disciple and fellow-laborer of William Lloyd Garrison."[32]

Abruptly, the fortunes of the northern antislavery societies reversed themselves. In 1835, some 500 such societies existed, and in that year alone, 328 new societies were formed. Three years later, 1,350 societies belonged to the national organization, with a membership of around a quarter of a million people.[33] Clearly, radical abolitionism accomplished what temperance, moderation, and gradualism had never done. But it cost them heavily, for it began to polarize the complacent mainstream, and initially the majority were decidedly antiabolitionist. Garrison and other speakers were frequently mobbed and their presses and headquarters destroyed; ultimately, in 1837, the Reverend Elijah P. Lovejoy, a prominent antislavery editor and one of the founders of the Illinois antislavery society, was slain while trying to prevent the destruction of his fourth newspaper press.

Standing in the shadow of death, in the courtroom of Alton, Illinois, Lovejoy confronted the antiabolitionists who had railed against him:

> You have courts and judges and juries; they find nothing against me. And now you come together for the purpose of driving out a confessedly innocent man, for no cause but that he dares to think and speak his conscience as his God dictates. . . . You may hang me up as the mob hung up the individuals at Vicksburg. You may burn me at the stake, as they did McIntosh at St. Louis. . . . I shall not flee away from Alton. Should I attempt it, I would feel that the angel of the Lord with his flaming sword was pursuing me wherever I went . . . the contest has

> commenced here, and here it must be finished . . . The deepest of all disgrace would be, at a time like this, to deny my Master by forsaking His cause. . . . If I fall, my grave shall be made in Alton."[34]

He moved many of his opponents to tears with these words. But four days later a mob that included a number of those same men who had wept shot him down. His death achieved more than all his editorials; it finally began to swing northern sentiment in favor of abolitionism.

No other single event of that era had such a galvanizing effect. When the news of Lovejoy's death reached Boston, men openly wept in the streets. As Senator Henry Wilson of Massachusetts would write: "Nothing had so clearly indicated to antislavery men the nature of the conflict in which they were engaged, the desperate character of the foe with which they were grappling. . . . They saw that the conflict was not to be the bloodless encounter of ideas."[35] Sarah Grimké wrote to a friend that she had little hope that an end to "the evil of slavery will be brought about by peaceful means. The blood spilled at Alton will be the seed of future discord."[36]

Meanwhile, Garrison, possessing the zeal and focus of all successful reformers but not a large measure of self-righteousness, became increasingly strident in his attacks. Nor did he direct his wrath exclusively to slaveholders; now anyone or anything in disagreement with him received a withering blast. In 1845, having already called upon his followers to regard every law that condoned slavery as "null and void," he now attacked the Constitution itself for the same reason, calling it a "covenant with death and an agreement with hell"[37] and urging abolitionists to campaign for the North to secede from the diseased South. Challenged by southern critics who produced Scriptures which apparently condoned slavery, Garrison exclaimed that if the Bible sanctioned slavery, then it opposed the "self-evident truth that 'all men are created equal' " and therefore "the Bible is a self-evident falsehood" which should be considered an "enemy . . . of the progress of the human race, in liberty, justice, and goodness."[38]

That finished Garrison with the committed Christians, and the more radical he became, fewer and fewer abolitionist leaders were prepared to go along with him. One who did not was Theodore Dwight Weld, who came to be regarded as the spiritual leader of abolitionism, even as Garrison grabbed the headlines. Still a young man when he was converted under the preaching of Charles Finney, Weld had promptly joined Finney's "band of holy men," bent on winning the world for Christ. He had come to the attention of English abolitionist Charles Stuart, who had won him to the cause of abolitionism and taken him on as a protégé, sending him to Lyman Beecher's Lane Seminary, in Ohio. There Weld had led the antislavery movement on campus—and had his first brush with the establishment. In 1834, three years before the murder of Lovejoy, abolitionism remained suspect; it was still regarded as fanatical. As Weld organized antislavery debates the powers at Lane gathered against him. The debates gained nationwide attention, and as a result, the seminary's antislavery society was disbanded and the student body forbidden to discuss slavery, even casually or in private.

Practically the entire student body, led by Weld, left Lane and went to work for the antislavery cause. But not without a parting salvo:

> Sirs, you have mistaken the cause, the age, and the men, if you think to intimidate by threats, or to silence by clamor, or shame by sneers, or put down by authority, or discourage by opposition, or appall by danger, those who have put their hands to this work. . . . Slavery, with its robbery of body and soul from birth to death, its exactions of toil unrecompensed, its sunderings of kindred, its frantic orgies of lust, its intellect leveled with dust, its baptisms of blood, and its legacy of damning horrors to the eternity of the spirit—Slavery in this land of liberty and light . . . its days are numbered . . . the nation is shaking off its slumbers, to sleep no more.[39]

Weld and many of the others completed their ministerial training at another Ohio seminary, Oberlin, where Weld's spiritual father, Finney, joined the faculty as head of theology. Though many of the Lane rebels would go on to carve distinguished careers in public service, Weld became in several ways unique. In the relentless honesty of his self-examination, he was a throwback to the Puritans of an earlier age. Writing to Angelina Grimké (whom he would one day marry), he described himself as "an untamed spirit, wild as the winds . . . proud as Lucifer . . . too proud to be ambitious, too proud to betray emotions, too proud ever for an instant to lose my self-possession whatever the peril . . . too proud ever to wince, when the hot iron enters my soul and passes through it,"[40] and went on to berate himself for being impatient, foul-tempered, selfish, indolent, and willful. Honest with himself, Weld could thus speak forcefully with a humble spirit. And his willingness to see and acknowledge his own shortcomings gave him uncommon insight into the motivations of others—and the lengths of hypocrisy to which they would go to avoid seeing the truth about themselves.

Weld put the emphasis on the religious nature of the struggle against slavery, insisting that slavery was a *sin:*

> God has committed to every moral agent the privilege, the right, and the responsibility of personal ownership. This is God's plan. Slavery annihilates it, and surrenders to avarice, passion, and lust, all that makes life a blessing. It crushes the body, tramples into the dust the upward tendencies of the intellect, breaks the heart, and kills the soul.[41]

Rebutting the southern argument that slaves did not need legal protection, because decent men would always treat them decently, Weld laid bare the insidious corrosion that slavery worked on the character of the slaveholder: "Arbitrary power is to the mind what alcohol is to the body; it intoxicates. It is perhaps the strongest human passion; and the more absolute the power, the stronger the desire for it; and the more it is desired, the more its exercise is enjoyed. . . . The fact that a person intensely desires power over others *without restraint,* shows the absolute necessity of that restraint."[42]

Now the Abolitionists weighed in with *their* Scriptures, beginning and ending with the Golden Rule, in Matthew 7:12, "Therefore all things whatsoever ye would that men should do to you, do ye even so to them. . . ." Their challenge to slaveholders: would one of them voluntarily take the place of one of their slaves for a single day? How, too, would slaveholders answer Exodus 21:16, "And he that stealeth a man, and selleth him, or if he be found in his hand, he shall surely be put to death"? Or Proverbs 22:22, 23, "Rob not the poor . . . for the Lord will plead their cause, and spoil the soul of those that spoiled them"? And Jeremiah 22:13, "Woe unto him that buildeth his house by unrighteousness, and his chambers by wrong; that useth his neighbour's service without wages, and giveth him not for his work"? And in the New Testament, James 5:4, "Behold, the hire of the labourers who have reaped down your fields, which is of you kept back by fraud, crieth: and the cries of them which have reaped are entered into the ears of the Lord of sabbaoth."

Christians from all the northern states now united with Weld in denouncing slavery as sin, "always, everywhere, and only sin." As

Weld's branch of abolitionism became transformed into a holy crusade, his spiritual mentor Finney asked him:

> Is it not true, at least do you not fear it is, that we are in our present course going fast into a civil war? Will not our present movements in abolition result in that? Shall we not, ere long, be obliged to take refuge in a military despotism? Have you no fear of this? If not, why have you not? Nothing is more manifest to me than that the present movements will result in this, unless your mode of abolitionizing the country will be greatly modified. . . . the absorbing abolitionism has drunk up the spirit of some of our most efficient moral men and is fast doing so to the rest, and many of our abolition brethren seem satisfied with nothing less than this. This I have been trying to resist from the beginning, as I have all along foreseen that, should that take place, the church and the world, ecclesiastical and state leaders, will become embroiled in one common infernal squabble that will roll a wave of blood over the land.[43]

Finney failed to see that increasingly it appeared that nothing short of war would expunge slavery—and that nothing short of abolitionism (Weld's version, not Garrison's) would cast the struggle in its ultimate terms: a spiritual battle, the outcome of which would decide whether America could ever fulfill her divine calling.

One day Julia Ward Howe would write the words: "He has sounded forth the trumpet that shall never call retreat." Yet even as the herald trumpet was sounding on the tourney fields of the Chivalry, in the North the notes of that other, distant trumpet were beginning to be heard.

Epilogue
1837

The flag snapping in the breeze over the dome of the white marbled Capitol Building displayed twenty-six stars in the summer of 1837. Exactly half a century had passed since the Constitutional Convention in Philadelphia established the United States as a democratic republic under law. The Founding Fathers had left the stage, and America now lay in the hands of their successors. While few possessed the extraordinary stature of their predecessors, more than a few exerted able and effective leadership.

The nation's western migration had now reached to the Pacific, but America's good could not yet be crowned with brotherhood. For despite all her intellectual and physical achievements in this half century, spiritually America stayed in a holding pattern. As long as slavery existed within her borders, she could not fulfill God's call upon her—to be a people in covenant with Him and with one another and a light to the world. Those tiny seeds of darkness that Satan had tucked into the soil had grown into weeds that were fast becoming a jungle. Whenever men thought of the future of America, their thoughts invariably revolved around slavery, the hidden reality behind every national issue. No peaceful solution appeared on the horizon, for the South was rapidly convincing itself that, far from being the moral sin that Weld and others claimed, owning slaves was a positive good. Gradually, thanks to the efforts of the abolitionists, both moderate and rabid, a massive shift occurred in the hearts of northerners, who were less and less willing to tolerate slavery's excesses and horrors. As each exchange on the floor of the Senate and the House grew increasingly bitter, as northern and southern editorialists alike cried out for secession, thinking men despaired, while unthinking men buried their heads in the sand and hoped that it would all go away. What would the next three decades hold? A glimpse of four people in 1837—an author, a statesman, a fanatic, and a servant-leader, each of whom would play a key role in the coming years—gives some idea.

In 1837 Harriet Beecher, who was cut from the same Puritan bolt as her father Lyman, had been married to Calvin Stowe for a year. A few month before, she had seen mobs in Cincinnati wreck the press of James Birney, printer of the antislavery newspaper the *Philanthropist,* and pull down the houses of respectable free blacks. Two years later, in 1839, her husband and her brother, Henry Ward Beecher would rescue her free black maid from illegal capture by those who would sell her into slavery. The next year, mobs would attack the black quarters in town with a cannon, murdering men, raping women, and in the confusion kidnapping children, to sell them. From her hilltop home, Harriet would see the fires and hear the cries. It was not surprising that she developed impassioned views on slavery. A gifted writer whose descriptive sketches were much in demand by newspaper editors of her day, she would receive a note from her sister-in-law: "Now, Hattie, if I could use a pen as you can, I would write something that would make this whole nation feel what an accursed thing slavery is."

Her son later recalled her response when she read that letter to the family: she rose up from her chair, crushing the letter in her hand, and with an expression on her face that stamped itself on his mind, said, "I *will* write something. I will, if I live."[1]

But the abolitionists were making deep inroads, and to lead her defense, the South looked to the man who had assumed Thomas Jefferson's mantle—Senator John C. Calhoun. Born of Scotch-Irish Presbyterian stock in the upland country of South Carolina, Calhoun was once a staunch Unionist with little use for the luxuries of the planter class that ruled the coastlands—until he fell in love with one of their daughters. Not only did he marry into the aristocracy, he adopted their viewpoint as his own and fashioned it into a political philosophy. In 1837 he took the Senate floor to deliver the most crucial address of his career. Nearly twenty years had passed since he had conceded the equality of men to be a just and noble ideal, but one impossible to obtain in the South. Now he, too, had reexamined the institution of slavery in the South and found it not evil, but good in itself. He held it "an inevitable law of society that one portion of the community depended upon the labor of another portion, over which it must unavoidably exercise control." To abolish slavery—even to talk of abolishing slavery—was to set the two races at each other's throats.[2]

All eyes turned to him. "If my attachment to the Union were less, I might . . . keep silent," he began. "They who imagine the [abolitionist] spirit abroad in the North will die away of itself . . . have formed a very inadequate concept of its real character. . . . Already it has taken possession of the pulpit . . . the schools . . . the press." He listed the facts: 1,500 abolitionist societies with an average of 100 members each, and one more new society joining their ranks every day. Yet they were told, "if we would keep . . . cool and patient, and hear ourselves and our constituents attacked as robbers and murderers . . . without moving hand or tongue, all would be well.

"We are reposing on a volcano!" Calhoun shouted. The present generation of northerners would be succeeded by those taught to hate the people and institutions "of nearly one half of this Union, with a hatred more deadly than one hostile nation ever entertained towards another." Gone would be "every sympathy between the two great sections" and their remembrance of shared dangers and common glory. The abolitionists were "imbuing the rising generation at the North with the belief that . . . the institutions of the Southern States were sinful and immoral, and that it was doing God service to abolish them, even if it should involve the destruction of half the inhabitants of this Union."

He ridiculed the assertion that "slavery is sinful, notwithstanding the authority of the Bible to the contrary," and the spirit of abolitionism reminded him of the Spanish Inquisition, that "blind, fanatical zeal . . . that made one man believe he was responsible for the sins of his neighbor, that two centuries ago convulsed the Christian world" and "tied the victims that it could not convert to the stake."

He paused and appeared to look into the future. "It is easy to see the end," he resumed sadly. "We must become two people. . . . Abolition and Union cannot co-exist. As the friend of the Union, I . . . proclaim it."[3] The South's final solution to the abolitionist crisis: secession.

But some saw the progress too slow, and even Garrison's venomous, raging diatribes seemed too mild. For some, deeds spoke louder than words, and the sword was mightier than the pen. The most pivotal event in 1837, indeed in the past two decades, was the murder of the antislavery editor Elijah Lovejoy. Throughout the North, abolitionists held protest meetings, and while those in Boston and New York attracted the most attention, what happened at a meeting in the little college town of Hudson, Ohio, might have proved the most significant.

Lovejoy's brother Owen dramatically described the editor's last days and his courageous final speech. Most of the listeners wept, but in the back of the church, a lean, sunken-cheeked man stared stonily at the ceiling above the speaker. When the speaker finished, he stood up in the back of the church, and raising his right hand as if taking a oath, he solemnly declared: "Here, before God, in the presence of these witnesses, I consecrate my life to the destruction of slavery."[4] Those were the first public words ever spoken on slavery by John Brown. There would not be many others.

Brown had failed at practically every venture he had set his hand to, and the most recent unquestionably became the most bitter. At the time when land speculation had reached fever pitch in America, plans were announced for an east-west canal that would pass right through Franklin, Ohio, six miles from Hudson, and would draw power from the nearby Cuyahoga River. Land values in Franklin skyrocketed, and John Brown borrowed money and bought land. But with the crash of 1837, all work on the canal ceased, mighty Akron diverted the waters of the Cuyahoga to its own use, and suddenly land in Franklin dropped to a twentieth of its earlier value. Along with so many others, Brown was forced into bankruptcy. With a large family to feed and owing money on all sides, he resorted to desperate measures. He embezzled money, confident he could return it with other borrowed funds, before anyone discovered the loss. When he couldn't, he made a clean breast of it, vowing to repay every cent. Charges were not pressed; too many others faced similar circumstances.

But perhaps the failure and the ignominy, along with his jealousy of others who seemed to have come through the crisis unscathed, gnawed at Brown. Whether he subconsciously identified with the slaves, projecting his plight into theirs, only God could know. This much is certain: two years after he had made his vow in the Hudson church, he was sitting with his wife and three sons around the fire in the kitchen hearth. According to his son John, "He asked who of us were willing to make common cause with him, in doing all in our power to 'break the jaws of the wicked, and pluck the spoil out of his teeth.' "

Brown turned his deep-set gray eyes on first one member of the family and then another. "Are you, Mary?" His wife nodded. "John?" His eldest son murmured assent, as did Jason and Owen, when their turns came. Then, "He kneeled in prayer, and all did the same. This position in prayer impressed me greatly, as it was the first time I had ever known him to assume it. After prayer, he asked us to raise our right hands, and he then administered to us an oath . . . in substance, it bound us to secrecy and devotion to the purpose in fighting slavery, by force and arms, to the extend of our ability."[5] This was the man who would one day see himself as the sword of God's vengeance.

Still, the majority of northern communities remained opposed to the abolitionists' radical tactics and extremist language. On March 3, 1837, the Illinois Assembly passed a resolution that began: "Resolved . . . that we highly disapprove of the formation of abolition societies, and of the doctrines promulgated by them." One tall, angular, young assemblyman, with a shock of hair down on his forehead, refused to vote for the resolution—a country lawyer named Abraham Lincoln felt that no expression on the slavery question should remain unaccompanied by a statement that it was an evil.[6]

Lincoln, who had just turned twenty-eight, had begun to come to grips with his own position on slavery. A man of principle, he could not deny the right to own slaves as property which the Constitution specifically granted. However, in a letter to his close friend, slaveholder Joshua Speed, he reveals his personal feelings:

> I also acknowledge your rights and my obligations, under the Constitution, in regard to your slaves. I confess I hate to see the poor creatures hunted down and caught and carried back to their stripes and unrewarded toils; I bite my lip and keep quiet. In 1841, you and I had together a tedious low-water trip on a steamboat from Louisville to St. Louis. You may remember, as I well do, that from Louisville to the mouth of the Ohio, there were on board ten or a dozen slaves shackled together with irons. That sight was a continual torment to me; I see something like it every time I touch the Ohio, or any other slave border. It is hardly fair for you to assume that I have no interest in a thing which has, and continually exercises, the power of making me miserable.[7]

Twenty more years passed before the Springfield lawyer stood on the marble terrace of the Capitol and raised his right hand to receive the oath of office as the sixteenth President—and in so doing, signaled the time of harvest and the fiery eradication of the weed that had so blotted out the sky that it had turned day into night.

In 1837, some Christians wondered how much longer God would continue to shed His grace on America and were predicting a time of supreme trial, in which the refiner's fire would burn away the dross. Few anticipated a nationwide day of judgment, when God's wrath would fall on the North, as well as the South. For the blame for the condition of the country lay as much with the North, as with the South. Northern Methodist and Baptist and Presbyterian leaders could have risked denominational schism (which came later anyway) and stood firm in their condemnation of slavery. Congress could have regarded slavery as a national, rather than a southern, calamity. Yankee congressmen could have stood against the pressure of slave traders among their constituents and abolished that lucrative trade. New York financiers could have eschewed the immense profits they were reaping in the southern cotton market. The Jackson administration and all northern idealists could have ameliorated the atrocious treatment that the Indians received. The list of missed northern opportunities went on endlessly. The responsibility was nationwide.

The purging of slavery from the land could have taken place through nationwide repentance and revival. England had already shown the way. Through the untiring efforts and prayers of evangelical Christians led by Parliamentarian William Wilberforce, slavery had been outlawed throughout the British Empire in 1833. In America the social impact of the Gospel had already been proven, in the success of the Temperance Movement, the explosive rise of charitable institutions, and the radical changes that revival brought in the life of such cities as Rochester.

Yet sadly enough, when it came to dealing with the greatest social evil of the age, the groundswells of local revival did not produce the necessary tidal wave of change. The revivals failed to touch the vital nerve of slavery. In spite of the many voices calling for its abolition —some compassionately pleading and others self-righteously demanding—no national repentance took place. The prophets went unheeded; they remained voices crying in the wilderness. The opportunity slipped by.

Today prophetic voices can again be heard, warning of personal and social evils, which if left unrepented of, will bring a fresh judgment of God upon our beloved land. The national curse of abortion can claim responsibility for the annual killing of 1.5 million unborn babies. The breakdown of marital and family relationships is catastrophic, and reckless promiscuity has resulted in an epidmic of incurable diseases that we had scarcely even heard of eight years ago. One wonders how long we can continue to presume on the divine favor earned for this land by the faithful, obedient Christians among our forefathers.

Revival—many Christians today hope and pray for the direct intervention of God by His Holy Spirit, a miraculous solution to a seemingly hopeless situation. Only we have already *had* an outpouring of the Holy Spirit that was supposed to accomplish that. In the late sixties and early seventies, the Charismatic Renewal, and Jesus movement brought thousands upon thousands of nominal Christians and agnostics to Christ. New multitudes raised hands in praise of God, but the renewal was in the main individually and vertically oriented. Where was the horizontal commitment to change society that traditionally followed in the wake of revivals? Where was the concern for the poor and needy about which Scripture speaks so clearly?

Surely, lately some encouraging signs have appeared on our horizon—black and white evangelicals and charismatics working together with other Protestants and Catholics to combat abortion and a genuine nationwide yearning to recover the moral and spiritual values that once formed the bedrock of our society. Most Christians seem to agree that we need national revival now—another Great Awakening. But the price will be high.

For the key to revival has always been repentance. Before God will pour out His Spirit on all flesh, an individual and corporate turning away from sin and self, to God, must occur. No other way—no cheap grace, no putting the country ahead of God, none of the "we're God's Chosen People, and we know that He will see us through, no matter what" kind of thinking that too many Christians like to comfort themselves with these days will suffice. Repentance is the missing ingredient in much of modern American Christianity. Yet its pivotal role in national revival is clearly revealed in Holy Scripture in such passages as the much quoted 2 Chronicles 7:14: "If my people, which are called by my name, shall humble themselves, and pray, and seek my face, and turn from their wicked ways; then I will hear from heaven, and will forgive their sin, and will heal their land." Those of us already committed to Christ are being challenged not only to face our personal needs for growth and change and take them to God in prayer, but most important of all, He is calling for us to repent of our wicked ways. No matter how much we might prefer to see ourselves as freed from sin, we still have wicked ways. We still often live for our own personal comfort or success, ignoring the needs of the poor or hurting around us. We are still self-righteous, still get jealous or vindictive, we still lust after other people's approval.

Repentance involves heartfelt change; and change—the lifelong process of being conformed to the image of God's Son—involves pain. Unlike Dwight or Asbury, JQA or Jackson, most of us today are unwilling to go through much emotional or spiritual pain. We can wear out our knees praying for revival, but if we are not willing to go through the pain of repentance, the Great Awakening we seek will not come.

But there *can* be a victorious conclusion. We have forgotten that true repentance is also tremendously freeing, cleansing, and uplifting! And that repentance on the part of a few can spread throughout a family, a church—or a whole society. The salt *can* regain its savor!

Once again, America stands, like Nineveh, at the crossroads of mercy and judgment. If we Christians will hear and heed in time, God's plan for America will yet be fulfilled. And He will crown her good with brotherhood, from sea to shining sea!

Notes

Chapter 1: 1787

1. Page Smith, *The Shaping of America* (New York: McGraw-Hill Book Co., 1980), 3:53.
2. Ibid., 38.
3. Ibid., 24.
4. Boyd, Julian P., ed., *The Papers of Thomas Jefferson* (Princeton, N.J.: Princeton University Press, 1955), 11:93.
5. Norman Cousins, *In God We Trust* (New York: Harper & Bros., 1958), 42.
6. Smith, *Shaping,* xvi.
7. Ibid., xvii.
8. Ibid., 86.
9. John Winthrop, *The Winthrop Papers* (Boston: Massachusetts Historical Soc., 1931), 2:292–295.
10. George F. Willison, *Behold Virginia.* (New York: Harcourt, Brace & Co., 1952), 3, 10.
11. Edmund S. Morgan, *American Slavery—American Freedom* (New York: W. W. Norton & Co., 1975), 63.
12. George Bancroft, *Bancroft's History of the United States,* 3d ed. (Boston: Charles C. Little & James Brown, 1838), 1:133.
13. Catherine Drinker Bowen, *Miracle at Philadelphia* (Boston: Little, Brown & Co., 1966), 92.
14. Henry Adams, *The United States in 1800* (Ithaca, N.Y.: Cornell University Press, 1960), 1.
15. Smith, *Shaping,* 84.
16. Edward Everett Hale, *Memories of a Hundred Years* (New York: Macmillan, 1902), 95. This quote from Gouverneur Morris was given to Hale by ninety-one-year-old Josiah Quincy during the Civil War.
17. Smith, *Shaping,* 57.
18. Bowen, *Miracle,* 202.
19. Al Masters, "George Washington's Forgotten People," *American History Illustrated* 19, no. 10 (Feb. 1985): 18–19.

20. Smith, *Shaping,* 90.
21. Bowen, *Miracle,* 203.
22. This quote and the one following are from ibid., 203.
23. James Madison, *Notes of Debates in the Federal Convention of 1787* (New York: W. W. Norton & Co., 1966), 411.

Chapter 2: Heading West

1. Stewart H. Holbrook, *The Yankee Exodus* (New York: Macmillan, 1950), 17.
2. Chard Powers Smith, *Yankees and God* (New York: Hermitage House, 1954), 301.
3. Holbrook, *Yankee Exodus,* 36.
4. Ibid., 26.
5. Ibid.
6. Rev. William Speer, *The Great Revival of 1800* (Philadelphia: Presbyterian Board of Publication, 1872), 12.
7. Rev. Benjamin Mortimer, unpublished diary, 150–152.
8. Henry Adams, *The United States in 1800* (Ithaca, N.Y.: Cornell University Press, 1960), 24.
9. Ibid., 97.
10. Ibid., 95.
11. Ibid., 23.
12. Ibid., 97.
13. Ibid., 97–98.
14. Donald G. Mathews, *Religion in the Old South* ed. Martin E. Marty, Chicago History of American Religion (Chicago: University of Chicago Press, 1977), 41, 76.
15. Adams, *United States,* 127.
16. Speer, *Great Revival,* 13–14.
17. Bernard A. Weisberger, *They Gathered at the River* (Boston: Little, Brown & Co., 1958), 3.

Chapter 3: Like a Mighty River

1. Arthur K. Moore, *Frontier Mind: A Cultural Analysis of the Kentucky Frontiersman* (Lexington: University Press of Kentucky, 1957), 71.
2. Ibid., 17.
3. Ibid., 24.
4. Henry Adams, *The United States in 1800* (Ithaca, N.Y.: Cornell University Press, 1960), 30–31.
5. Ibid., 31.
6. Terry D. Bilhartz, ed., *Francis Asbury's America* (Grand Rapids, Mich.: Francis Asbury Press, 1984), 99.

7. This quote and the following one are from Moore, *Frontier Mind,* 66–67.

8. Ibid., 67.

9. Ibid., 56.

10. Louis B. Wright, *Life on the American Frontier* (New York: G. P. Putnam's Sons, 1971), 51, 62.

11. Moore, *Frontier Mind,* 84–87.

12. Timothy Flint, *Biographical Memoir of Daniel Boone,* ed. James K. Folsom (New Haven: College and University Press, 1967), 158.

13. Thomas Baldwin, *Narrative of the Massacre, by the Savages, of the Wife and Children of Thomas Baldwin* (New York: Martin & Perry Pubs., 1836), 4.

14. Flint, *Daniel Boone,* 159–160.

15. Ibid., 165–169.

16. Adams, *United States,* 39.

17. Moore, *Frontier Mind,* 87.

18. Ibid.

19. Warren A. Candler, *Great Revivals and the Great Republic* (Nashville, Tenn.: Publishing House of the M. E. Church, South, 1904), 172–173.

20. Ibid., 174.

21. Bernard A. Weisberger, *They Gathered at the River* (Boston: Little, Brown & Co., 1958), 23–24.

22. Catherine C. Cleveland, *The Great Revival in the West, 1797-1805* (Chicago: University of Chicago Press, 1916), 40.

23. Charles A. Johnson, *The Frontier Camp Meeting* (Dallas: Southern Methodist University Press, 1955), 33–34.

24. Weisberger, *They Gathered,* 24.

25. Johnson, *Frontier Camp Meeting,* 35.

26. Ibid.

27. Weisberger, *They Gathered,* 25.

28. Candler, *Great Revivals,* 178–179.

29. Rev. William Speer, *The Great Revival of 1800* (Philadelphia: Presbyterian Board of Publication, 1872), 40.

30. Luther A. Weigle, *American Idealism* (New Haven: Yale University Press, 1928), 152.

31. Ibid.

32. Johnson, *Frontier Camp Meeting,* 54.

33. Ibid., 57.

34. Ibid., 59.

35. Ibid., 61.

36. Ibid., 64.

37. Ibid., 64–65. *Also* Ross Phares, *Bible in Pocket, Gun in Hand* (Garden City, N.Y.: Doubleday, 1964), 80.

38. Missionary Society of Connecticut, *The Connecticut Evangelical Magazine* (March 1802).

Chapter 4: "On The Stretch For God"

1. Catherine C. Cleveland, *The Great Revival in the West, 1797–1805* (Chicago: University of Chicago Press, 1916), 26.
2. Ibid., 28.
3. Donald E. Byrne, Jr., *No Foot of Land: Folklore of American Methodist Itinerants,* ATLA Monograph Series, no. 6. (Metuchen, N.J.: Scarecrow Press, 1975), 132.
4. Ibid.
5. Ibid., 284.
6. Ross Phares, *Bible in Pocket, Gun in Hand* (Garden City, N.Y.: Doubleday, 1964), 34–35.
7. Ibid., 155.
8. Peter Cartwright, *The Autobiography of Peter Cartwright* (New York: Carlton & Porter, 1856), 164.
9. Elmer T. Clark, ed., *The Journals and Letters of Francis Asbury* (Nashville, Tenn.: Abingdon Press, 1958), 1:561.
10. L. D. Rudolph, *Francis Asbury* (Nashville, Tenn.: Abingdon Press, 1966), 82.
11. Ibid., 221–222.
12. Ibid., 72–73.
13. Clark, *Journals and Letters,* 2:124–125.
14. Clark, *Journals and Letters,* 1:512.
15. Ibid., 534.
16. Ibid.
17. Ibid., 368.
18. Ibid., 422–423.
19. Ibid., 116.
20. Rudolph, *Francis Asbury,* 154–155.
21. Clark, *Journals and Letters,* 2:474.
22. Rudolph, *Francis Asbury,* 107.
23. Ibid., 143.
24. Ibid., 145.
25. Clark, *Journals and Letters,* 1:162, 115.
26. Ibid., 422.
27. Clark, *Journals and Letters,* 2:417.
28. Rudolph, *Francis Asbury,* 178–179.
29. Ibid., 180.
30. Clark, *Journals and Letters,* 2:311.
31. Ibid., 151.
32. Ibid., 80.
33. Ibid., 149.
34. Ibid., 794.
35. "Francis Asbury," *Encyclopaedia Britannica,* 1970, 2:560.
36. Cartwright, *Autobiography,* 9.

37. Keith J. Hardeman, *The Spiritual Awakeners: American Revivalists from Solomon Stoddard to D. L. Moody* (Chicago: Moody Press, 1983), 142.
38. Cartwright, *Autobiography,* 36.
39. Ibid., 38.
40. Ibid., 43.
41. Hardeman, *Spiritual Awakeners,* 144.
42. Phares, *Bible in Pocket,* 63.
43. Ibid., 147.
44. Frank Grenville Beardsley, *A History of American Revivals* 3d ed. (New York: American Tract Society, 1912), 199–200.
45. Ibid., 203.
46. Cartwright, *Autobiography,* 94.
47. Ibid., 7.
48. Ibid., 94.
49. Ibid., 120.
50. Ibid., 94.

Chapter 5: Needles of Light

1. Chard Powers Smith, *Yankees and God* (New York: Hermitage House, 1954), 289–290.
2. Charles Roy Keller, *The Second Great Awakening in Connecticut* (New Haven: Yale University Press, 1942), 24.
3. Stephen E. Berk, *Calvinism Versus Democracy* (Hamden, Conn.: Archon Books, 1974), p. 68.
4. Milton Rugoff, *The Beechers* (New York: Harper & Row, 1981), 70.
5. Lyman Beecher, *The Autobiography of Lyman Beecher,* edited by Barbara M. Cross (Cambridge: Harvard University Press, 1961), 1:xxi.
6. "Deism," *Encyclopaedia Britannica,* 1970, 7:181–183.
7. Keith J. Hardeman, *The Spiritual Awakeners: American Revivalists from Solomon Stoddard to D. L. Moody* (Chicago: Moody Press, 1983), 110.
8. Ibid., 115.
9. This quote and the following two quotes are from ibid., 113.
10. *See* "A Letter From the President of the United States," *Guideposts,* May 1975.
11. Hardeman, *Spiritual Awakeners,* 112.
12. Keller, *Second Great Awakening,* 14.
13. Rugoff, *Beechers,* 8.
14. Hardeman, *Spiritual Awakeners,* 115.
15. Keller, *Second Great Awakening,* 1.
16. Ibid., 38.
17. Hardeman, *Spiritual Awakeners,* 118.
18. *A Brief Account of the Late Revivals of Religion in a Number of Towns in the New England States* (Boston: Manning & Loring, 1797).
19. Hardeman, *Spiritual Awakeners,* 115–116.

20. Timothy Dwight's sermon of September 9, 1797.

21. Timothy Dwight's sermon of July 23, 1812.

22. This quote and the following one are from Timothy Dwight's sermon of January 7, 1801.

23. Timothy Dwight's sermon of September 9, 1797.

24. This quote and the following two quotes are from Berk, *Calvinism,* 94, 105.

25. Rev. William Speer, *The Great Revival of 1800* (Philadelphia Presbyterian Board of Publication, 1872), 85.

As the revival spread beyond the confines of Yale College one of its most important converts was a New Haven resident by the name of Noah Webster. Giving his life to Christ in 1807, he would write: "In my view, the Christian religion is the most important and one of the first things in which all children, under a free government, ought to be instructed. . . . No truth is more evident to my mind than that the Christian religion must be the basis of any government intended to secure the rights and privileges of a free people."

Webster himself contributed greatly to the impact of Christianity on the United States with the publication in 1828 of the first American dictionary, a colossal twenty-six year project that used biblical word definitions and frequent Scripture references. (*See Noah Webster's First Edition of an American Dictionary of the English Language* [San Francisco, Calif.: Foundation for American Christian Education, 1980], 12.)

26. Keller, *Second Great Awakening,* 42.

27. Frank Grenville Beardsley, *A History of American Revivals* (New York: American Tract Society, 1912), 89.

28. Timothy Dwight's sermon of July 23, 1812.

29. Keller, *Second Great Awakening,* 15–16.

30. James Ward Smith and A. Leland Jamison, eds., *The Shaping of American Religion,* Religion in American Life (Princeton, N.J.: Princeton University Press, 1961), 1:357.

31. Beecher, *Autobiography,* 1:xx.

32. "Unitarianism," *Encyclopaedia Britannica,* 1970, 22:553.

33. Thomas Jefferson, *Writings of Thomas Jefferson,* Andrew A. Lipscomb, ed. (Washington, D.C.: Thomas Jefferson Memorial Association, 1903), 15: 391–392.

34. *Time,* Bicentennial Issue, 14.

35. Cousins, Norman, *In God We Trust* (New York: Harper & Bros., 1958), 149.

36. Jefferson, *Writings,* 385.

37. Ibid., 430.

38. Marie Caskey, *Chariot of Fire* (New Haven: Yale University Press, 1978), 5.

39. Beecher, *Autobiography,* 1:27.

40. Rugoff, *Beechers,* 10.

41. Beecher, *Autobiography,* 1:242.
42. Ibid., 46.
43. Bernard A. Weisberger, *They Gathered at the River:* (Boston: Little, Brown & Co., 1958), 72–73.
44. Beecher, *Autobiography,* 1:105.
45. Rugoff, *Beechers,* 20–21 and ibid., 109.
46. Beecher, *Autobiography,* 1:146.
47. Keller, *Second Great Awakening,* 149.
48. Beecher, *Autobiography,* 1:184.
49. Beecher, *Autobiography,* 2:85.
50. Ibid., 81–82.
51. Ibid., 51.
52. Ibid., 52.
53. Ibid., 54–55.
54. Ibid., 125–126.
55. Rugoff, *Beechers,* 78.
56. Keller, *Second Great Awakening,* 111.
57. George M. Stephenson, *The Puritan Heritage* (New York: Macmillan, 1952), 154–157.
58. Luther A. Weigle, *American Idealism,* The Pageant of America (New Haven: Yale University Press, 1928), 143.
59. Keller, *Second Great Awakening,* 83–84.
60. John F. Schermerhorn, and Samuel J. Mills, *A Correct View of that Part of the United States Which Lies West of the Allegany Mountains With Regard to Religion and Morals* (Hartford: Peter B. Gleason & Co., 1814), 4–6.
61. Ibid., 30.
62. Keller, *Second Great Awakening,* 112.

Chapter 6: "Don't Give Up the Ship!"

1. Neil H. Swanson, *The Perilous Fight* (New York: Farrar & Rinehart, 1945), 156.
2. Page Smith, *The Shaping of America* (New York: McGraw-Hill Book Co., 1980), 3:563.
3. Kate Caffrey, *The Twilight's Last Gleaming* (New York: Stein & Day, 1977), 110–112.
4. Ibid., 112 and forward.
5. Timothy Dwight's sermon of July 23, 1812.
6. George H. Taylor, *The Causes of the War of 1812.* Edited by Bradford Perkins (New York: Holt, Rinehart & Winston), 79–80.
7. Caffrey, *Twilight's Last Gleaming,* 147.
8. Allan Lloyd, *The Scorching of Washington: The War of 1812* (Newton Abbot: David & Charles, 1974), 73–74.
9. Ibid., 79. The exact figures of troops and boats vary with different histo-

rians. James Truslow Adams: in *The March of Democracy, A History of the United States* (New York: Charles Scribner's Sons, 1965), 2:87, says Van Rensselaer had 4,000 troops, and that not over 1,000 would attack with him across the Niagara River. Harry L. Coles, in *The War of 1812* (Chicago: University of Chicago Press, 1965), 62–64, writes that Van Rensselaer had over 6,000 and took only 12 of 30 boats available.

10. Ibid., 81.

11. Glenn Tucker, *Poltroons and Patriots: A Popular Account of the War of 1812* (Indianapolis: Bobbs-Merrill Co., 1954), 1:228–233.

12. Ibid., 320.

13. Ibid., 321.

14. Smith, *Shaping,* 608–609.

15. This quote and the one following are from Tucker, *Poltroons and Patriots,* 331–332.

16. Smith, *Shaping,* 620.

17. Tucker, *Poltroons and Patriots,* 337.

18. Ibid., 338–339.

Chapter 7: The Dawn's Early Light

1. Neil H. Swanson, *The Perilous Fight* (New York: Farrar & Rinehart, 1945), 156.

2. Page Smith, *The Shaping of America* (New York: McGraw-Hill Book Co., 1980), 623–624.

3. Ibid., 628.

4. Walter Lord, *The Dawn's Early Light* (New York: W. W. Norton & Co., 1972), 126–127.

5. Allan Lloyd, *The Scorching of Washington: The War of 1812* (Newton Abbot: David & Charles, 1974), 172.

6. Adam Wallace, *The Parson of the Islands: A Biography of the Late Rev. Joshua Thomas . . .* (Philadelphia: Methodist Home Journal, 1872), 144–146.

7. Lord, *Dawn's Early Light*, 262.

8. Swanson, *Perilous Fight,* 417–428.

9. Ibid., 442–443.

10. Lord, *Dawn's Early Light,* 281.

11. Wallace, *The Parson of the Islands*, 148–149.

12. This quote and the following are from Swanson, *Perilous Fight,* 502–503.

13. Lloyd, *Scorching of Washington,* 179–183.

14. Kate Caffrey, *The Twilight's Last Gleaming* (New York: Stein & Day, 1977), 256–257.

15. Burke Davis, *Old Hickory: A Life of Andrew Jackson* (New York: Dial Press, 1977), 123.

16. Ibid., 7.

17. Ibid., 8–9.

18. Ibid., 11.
19. Ibid., 97.
20. Ibid., 124.
21. Ibid., 129.
22. Ibid., 136.
23. Lord, *Dawn's Early Light,* 334.
24. Davis, *Old Hickory,* 140.
25. Ibid., 141.
26. Lord, *Dawn's Early Light,* 342.
27. Ibid., 343.
28. Caffrey, *Twilight's Last Gleaming,* 290.
29. Davis, *Old Hickory,* 150.

Chapter 8: The Last Puritan

1. Gouverneur Morris, *Diary and Letters of Gouverneur Morris,* ed. Anne Cary Morris (New York: Charles Scribner's Sons, 1888), 394.
2. Albert J. Beveridge, *The Life of John Marshall* (Boston: Houghton Mifflin, 1919), 3:1–8.
3. James Monroe, *The Writings of James Monroe,* ed. Stanislaus Murray Hamilton (New York: G. P. Putnam's Sons, 1902), 6:6–14.
4. Burke Davis, *Old Hickory: A Life of Andrew Jackson* (New York: Dial Press, 1977), 159.
5. Page Smith, *The Shaping of America* (New York: McGraw-Hill Book Co.) 3:660.
6. Monroe, *Writings,* 5:342.
7. This quote and the preceding one are from Andrew Jackson, *Correspondence of Andrew Jackson,* ed. John Spencer Bassett (Washington, D.C.: Carnegie Institution of Washington, 1927), 2:327, 339.
8. Ibid., 329.
9. Ibid., 346.
10. Davis, *Old Hickory,* 163.
11. This quote and the one following are from ibid., 164.
12. George Dangerfield, *The Era of Good Feelings* (New York: Harcourt, Brace & World, 1952), 136.
13. John Quincy Adams, *The Diary of John Quincy Adams,* ed. Allan Nevins (New York: Longmans, Green & Co., 1928), 199.
14. Dangerfield, *Era of Good Feelings,* 7.
15. Adams, *Diary,* 103.
16. Dangerfield, *Era of Good Feelings,* 7.
17. Ibid., 133.
18. Ibid., 125.
19. Ibid., 133.
20. Ibid., 136.

21. Davis, *Old Hickory,* 181.
22. John Quincy Adams, *Writings of John Quincy Adams,* ed. Worthington Chauncey Ford (New York: Macmillan, 1915), 5:329.
23. Ibid., 362.
24. Ibid., 431–433.
25. Adams, *Writings of John Quincy Adams,* 6:135–136.
26. Ibid., 384.
27. Adams, *Diary,* 199–200.
28. Bennett Champ Clark, *John Quincy Adams: "Old Man Eloquent"* (Boston: Little, Brown & Co., 1932), 148–149.
29. Ibid., 160.
30. Adams, *Diary,* 303.
31. Clark, *John Quincy Adams,* 164–165.
32. Davis, *Old Hickory,* 172.

Chapter 9: Chief Justice

1. Saul K. Padover, ed., *The Complete Jefferson* (Freeport, N.Y. Books for Libraries Press, 1943), 11.
2. Thomas Jefferson, *Writings of Thomas Jefferson,* ed. Andrew A. Lipscomb (Washington, D.C.: Thomas Jefferson Memorial Association, 1903), 17:387, 18:xvii.
3. Albert J. Beveridge, *The Life of John Marshall* (Boston: Houghton Mifflin, 1919), 3:11.
4. Ibid.
5. Ibid., 1:118.
6. Ibid., 115.
7. Ibid., 127.
8. Ibid., 244.
9. Justice Story, *An Address on Chief Justice Marshall* (Rochester, N.Y.: The Lawyers Co-operative Publishing Co., 1900), 47.
10. Thomas Jefferson, *The Works of Thomas Jefferson,* ed. Paul Leicester Ford (New York: G. P. Putnam's Sons, 1905), 11:140.
11. Jefferson, *Writings,* 10:302.
12. Beveridge, *Life of Marshall,* 3:82.
13. Ibid., 85.
14. Ibid., 89.
15. Ibid., 281–282.
16. Ibid., 139.
17. Page Smith, *The Shaping of America* (New York: McGraw-Hill Book Co., 1980), 3:482.
18. Ibid., 495.
19. Beveridge, *Life of Marshall,* 3:157.
20. Ibid., 158.
21. Ibid., 218–219.

22. Story, *Address,* 47.

23. Albert J. Beveridge, *The Life of John Marshall* (Boston: Houghton Mifflin, 1919), 4:83.

24. Ibid., 80–81, 62.

25. Story, *Address,* 40–41.

26. Beveridge, *Life of Marshall,* 4:70–71.

In his stalwart defense of the Christian faith, Marshall was following in the footsteps of the first Chief Justice of the United States, John Jay. In 1777, as Chief Justice of the Supreme Court of New York, Jay declared: "Providence has given to our people the choice of their rulers, and it is the duty, as well as the privilege and interest, of a Christian nation to select and prefer Christians for their rulers."

For the five years prior to his death in 1827, Jay was the president of the American Bible Society, and on his deathbed, when asked if he had any further words of counsel for his children, he replied: "They have the Book." (From B. F. Morris, *The Christian Life and Character of the Civil Institutions of the United States.* [Philadelphia: George W. Childs, 1864], 153–154.)

27. Smith, *Shaping,* 673–675.

28. George Dangerfield, *The Era of Good Feelings* (New York: Harcourt, Brace & World, 1952), 186.

29. Ibid., 184.

30. Smith, *Shaping,* 672.

31. Beveridge, *Life of Marshall,* 4:176.

32. Dangerfield, *Good Feelings,* 186.

33. Ibid., 175–179.

34. Beveridge, *Life of Marshall,* 4:201.

35. Smith, *Shaping,* 675.

36. Beveridge, *Life of Marshall,* 4:248–249.

37. Ibid., 265.

38. Ibid., 272.

39. Jefferson, *Writings,* 15:46.

40. Beveridge, *Life of Marshall,* 4:283.

41. Ibid., 285.

42. Ibid., 291.

43. Ibid., 295–296.

44. Dangerfield, *Good Feelings,* 171.

45. Beveridge, *Life of Marshall,* 4:309.

46. Ibid., 293.

47. Ibid., 346.

48. Ibid., 350–352.

49. Ibid., 353.

50. Ibid., 356.

51. Ibid., 368–369.

52. Ibid., 358–359.

53. Ibid., 360.

54. Ibid., 362.
55. Ibid., 363–364.
56. Ibid., 364.
57. Ibid., 365–366.
58. Story, *Address,* 46.

Chapter 10: A House Dividing

1. Glover Moore, *The Missouri Controversy 1819-1821* (Lexington: University Press of Kentucky, 1953), 62.
2. Ibid., 93.
3. John Quincy Adams, *The Diary of John Quincy Adams,* ed. Allan Nevins (New York: Longmans, Green & Co., 1928), 228–229.
4. Robert Liston, *Slavery in America: The History of Slavery,* Of Black American Series (New York: McGraw-Hill Book Co., 1970), 70.
5. Moore, *Missouri Controversy,* 35.
6. Smith, *Shaping,* 447.
7. Moore, *Missouri Controversy,* 49.
8. Ibid., 50.
9. Ibid., 50–51.
10. Ibid., 49.
11. Liston, *Slavery in America,* 41.
12. Ibid., 42.
13. Arthur Young Lloyd, *The Slavery Controversy 1831-1860* (Chapel Hill: University of North Carolina Press, 1939), 9–10.
14. Liston, *Slavery in America,* 42–43.
15. Ibid., 42.
16. George Dangerfield, *The Era of Good Feelings* (New York: Harcourt, Brace & World, 1952), 210.
17. Lloyd, *Slavery Controversy, 8.*
18. Liston, *Slavery in America,* 35.
19. Ibid., 35–36.
20. Ibid., 38.
21. Rollin G. Osterweis, *Romanticism and Nationalism in the Old South* (New Haven: Yale University Press, 1949), 11.
22. Henry Savage, Jr., *Seeds of Time* (New York: Henry Holt & Co., 1959) 50.
23. Liston, *Slavery in America,* 44–45, 58–59.
24. Ulrich Bonnell Phillips, *Life and Labor in the Old South* (Boston: Little, Brown & Co., 1929), 96.
25. Savage, *Seeds,* 95.

Chapter 11: "A Fire Bell in the Night"

1. John W. Blassingame, *The Slave Community: Plantation Life in the Antebellum South* (New York: Oxford University Press, 1979), 187.
2. Harvey Wish, ed., *Slavery in the South* (New York: Farrar, Straus & Co., 1964), 43.
3. *Interesting Memoirs and Documents Relating to American Slavery . . . Complete Emancipation* (Miami: Mnemosyne Pub., 1967), 84.
4. Ibid., 84–85.
5. Wish, *Slavery in the South,* 41–42.
6. Ibid., 43.
7. Robert Liston, *Slavery in America: The History of Slavery,* Of Black America Series (New York: McGraw-Hill Book Co., 1970), 98.
8. American Anti-Slavery Society, Executive Committee. *Slavery and the Internal Slave Trade* (London: Thomas Ward & Co., 1841), 87.
9. Ibid., 86.
10. Ibid., 85–86.
11. American Anti-Slavery Society, *American Slavery As It Is* (New York: American Anti-Slavery Society, 1839), 53–54.
12. *Interesting Memoirs and Documents,* 139.
13. American Anti-Slavery Society, *Slavery and the Internal Slave Trade,* 106–119.
14. *Interesting Memoirs and Documents,* 143.
15. American Anti-Slavery Society, *American Slavery,* 143.
16. Ibid., 147–148.
17. Ibid., 148.
18. Ulrich Bonnell Phillips, *Life and Labor in the Old South* (Boston: Little, Brown & Co., 1929), 212.
19. Thomas H. Jones, *The Experience of Thomas H. Jones Who Was a Slave* (Worcester: Henry J. Howland, 1857), 8.
20. George Dangerfield, *The Era of Good Feelings* (New York: Harcourt, Brace & World, 1952), 213.
21. Wish, *Slavery,* 25–26.
22. American Anti-Slavery Society, *American Slavery,* 57.
23. Albert J. Raboteau, *Slave Religion: The "Invisible Institution" in the Antebellum South* (New York: Oxford University Press, 1978), 102.
24. Ibid.
25. Blassingame, *Slave Community,* 192–193.
26. Ibid., 302–303.
27. Jones, *Experience,* 22–27.
28. *Interesting Memoirs and Documents,* 144–145.
29. American Anti-Slavery Society, *American Slavery* 70.
30. *Interesting Memoirs and Documents,* 94.
31. Richard O. Boyer, *The Legend of John Brown* (New York: Alfred A. Knopf, 1973), 57.
32. Thomas Jefferson, *Writings of Thomas Jefferson,* ed. Andrew A. Lip-

scomb (Washington, D.C.: Thomas Jefferson Memorial Association, 1903), 2:227.

33. Ibid., 225–226.

34. C. Vann Woodward, ed. *Mary Chesnut's Civil War* (New Haven: Yale University Press, 1981), 29.

35. Liston, *Slavery in America,* 89.

36. Robert E. Riegel, *Young America* (Westport, Conn.: Greenwood Press, 1973), 108–109.

37. Dangerfield, *Good Feelings,* 214–216.

38. Page Smith, *The Shaping of America* (New York: McGraw-Hill Book Co., 1980), 439.

39. Ibid., 439–440.

40. American Anti-Slavery Society, *American Slavery,* 141–142.

41. Raboteau, *Slave Religion,* 292.

42. Liston, *Slavery in America,* 43–46.

43. Blassingame, *Slave Community,* 78.

44. John Q. Anderson, ed. *Brokenburn: The Journal of Kate Stone* (Baton Rouge: Louisiana State University Press, 1972), 7–8.

45. Blassingame, *Slave Community,* 79–80.

46. Anne C. Loveland, *Southern Evangelicals and the Social Order 1800–1860* (Indianapolis: Bobbs-Merrill Co., 1967), 186–187.

47. Glover Moore, *The Missouri Controversy 1819–1821* (Lexington: University Press of Kentucky, 1953), 92.

48. John Quincy Adams, *The Diary of John Quincy Adams,* ed. Allan Nevins (New York: Longmans, Green & Co., 1928), 229.

49. Moore, *Missouri Controversy,* 93.

50. Ibid., 100.

51. Charles Francis Adams, ed., *The Works of John Adams* (Boston: Little, Brown & Co., 1854), 9:420.

52. Smith, *Shaping,* 692.

53. Jefferson, *Writings,* 15:249.

54. Ibid., 604.

Chapter 12: Old Hickory

1. Page Smith, *The Nation Comes of Age* (New York: McGraw-Hill Book Co., 1981), 4:17.

2. Margaret Bayard Smith, *The First Forty Years of Washington Society* (New York: Charles Scribner's Sons, 1906), 291.

3. Ibid., 295–296.

4. Robert V. Remini, *The Revolutionary Age of Andrew Jackson* (New York: Harper & Row, 1976), 21.

5. Burke Davis, *Old Hickory: A Life of Andrew Jackson* (New York: Dial Press, 1977), 47.

6. David Lindsey, *Andrew Jackson and John C. Calhoun,* Shapers of His-

tory Series, ed. Kenneth C. Colegrove (Woodbury, N.Y.: Barron's Educational Series, 1973), 18–19

7. Robert V. Remini, *Andrew Jackson and the Course of American Freedom* (New York: Harper & Row, 1981), 2:1–3.

8. Andrew Jackson, *Correspondence of Andrew Jackson,* ed. John Spencer Bassett (Washington, D.C.: Carnegie Institution of Washington, 1927), 3:218.

9. Paul I. Wellman, *The House Divides* (Garden City, N.Y.: Doubleday & Co., 1966), 168–169.

10. Remini, *Revolutionary Age,* 10–11.

11. The reported election returns vary, depending on which historian is consulted. The numbers quoted in the text are from Remini, *Revolutionary,* 2:83. Burke Davis, in *Old Hickory,* p. 208, gives Jackson 155,800 votes; Adams 105,300; Clay 46,500, and Crawford, 44,200.

12. Remini, *Andrew Jackson,* 2:93–94.

13. Ibid., 84.

14. Ibid., 99.

15. Jackson, *Correspondence,* 3:402.

16. Davis, *Old Hickory,* 223.

17. Ibid., 226.

18. Richard O. Boyer, *The Legend of John Brown* (New York: Alfred A. Knopf, 1973), 50.

19. Davis, *Old Hickory,* 230.

20. Smith, *Nation* 4:7.

21. Ibid., 34–35.

22. Walker Lewis, ed. *Speak for Yourself, Daniel: A Life of Webster in His Own Words* (Boston: Houghton Mifflin Co., 1969), 190–191.

23. Ibid., 191.

24. Ibid., 196.

25. Ibid., 189.

26. This quote and the following four quotes are from ibid., 199–205.

27. Ibid., 205.

28. Smith, *Nation,* 39.

29. Marquis James, *Andrew Jackson: Portrait of a President* (Indianapolis: Bobbs-Merrill Co., 1937), 306.

30. Lindsay, *Jackson and Calhoun,* 151.

31. Smith, *Nation,* 65.

32. Ibid., 66 and Lindsay, *Jackson and Calhoun,* 160.

33. Smith, *Nation,* 70.

34. Davis, *Old Hickory,* 323.

35. Smith, *Nation,* 72.

Chapter 13: New Wine, New Wineskins

1. Charles Grandison Finney, *An Autobiography* (Westwood, N.J.: Fleming H. Revell Co., 1908), 9.

2. Ibid., 12.
3. Ibid., 13.
4. Ibid., 14.
5. This quote and the preceding quotes are from ibid., 13–23.
6. Frank Grenville Beardsley, *A History of American Revivals,* 3d ed. (New York: American Tract Society, 1912), 123.
7. Finney, *Autobiography,* 45–46.
8. Ibid., 54.
9. Ibid., 55.
10. Bernard A. Weisberger, *They Gathered at the River* (Boston: Little, Brown & Co., 1958), 96–97.
11. Beardsley, *American Revivals,* 125.
12. Finney, *Autobiography,* 65.
13. Ibid., 71–72.
14. Ibid., 77.
15. Charles Grandison Finney, *Lectures on Revivals of Religion,* ed. William G. McLoughlin (Cambridge: Harvard University Press, 1960), 196–197.
16. Beardsley, *American Revivals,* 135.
17. Benjamin P. Thomas, *Theodore Weld: Crusader for Freedom* (New Brunswick, N.J.: Rutgers University Press, 1950), 15.
18. Finney, *Autobiography,* 186.
19. Finney, *Lectures,* 294–297.
20. Beardsley, *American Revivals,* 142.
21. Weisberger, *They Gathered,* 120.
22. Charles C. Cole, Jr., *The Social Ideas of the Northern Evangelists 1826–1860* (New York: Octagon Books, 1966), 70.
23. Timothy L. Smith, *Revivalism and Social Reform in Mid-Nineteenth-Century America* (New York: Abingdon Press, 1957), 9, 62.
24. Cole, *Social Ideas,* 13–14.
25. Ibid., 92.
26. Perry Miller, *The Life of the Mind in America from the Revolution to the Civil War* (New York: Harcourt, Brace & World, 1966), 1:6.
27. Ibid., 22.
28. Cole, *Social Ideas,* 77.
29. Miller, *Life of the Mind,* 10.
30. Finney, *Lectures,* 297.
31. Miller, *Life of the Mind,* 69.
32. Ibid., 71–72.
33. Ibid., 36.

Chapter 14: "From Sea to Shining Sea"

1. This quote and the following two quotes are from Huston Horn, *The Pioneers,* The Old West (Alexandria, Va.: Time-Life Books, 1974), 24.

2. Ralph Andrist, *To the Pacific with Lewis and Clark,* American Heritage Junior Library (New York: American Heritage Pub. Co., 1967), 18.

3. Thomas Jefferson, *Writings of Thomas Jefferson,* ed. Andrew A. Lipsomb (Washington, D.C.: Thomas Jefferson Memorial Association, 1903), 18:150.

4. Meriwether Lewis, *The Lewis and Clark Expedition,* 1814 ed. (New York: J. P. Lippincott Co., 1961), 1:73.

5. Page Smith, *The Shaping of America,* (New York: McGraw-Hill Book Co., 1980), 3:521.

6. Ralph Henry Gabriel, ed., *The Pageant of America: A Pictorial History of the United States* (New Haven: Yale University Press, 1927), 2:167.

7. Ibid., 169.

8. Andrist, *Lewis and Clark,* 93.

9. Bernard DeVoto, *The Year of Decision 1846* (Boston: Houghton Mifflin Co., 1942), 60.

10. Ray Allen Billington, *The Far Western Frontier 1830–1860* (New York: Harper & Bros., 1956), 48.

11. Ibid., 46.

12. Dale L. Morgan, *Jedediah Smith and the Opening of the West* (Indianapolis: Bobbs-Merrill Co., 1953), 108.

13. Billington, *Western Frontier,* 55.

14. Morgan, *Jedediah Smith,* 310–311.

15. Stephen W. Sears, "Trail Blazer of the Far West," *American Heritage* (June 1963), 63.

16. Page Smith, *The Nation Comes of Age* (New York: McGraw-Hill Book Co., 1981), 4:350.

17. Morgan, *Jedediah Smith,* 196.

18. Horn, *Pioneers,* 43, 46.

19. Ibid., 46.

20. Ibid., 49.

21. Ibid.

22. Billington, *Western Frontier,* 80.

23. Horn, *Pioneers,* 54.

24. Ibid., 58.

25. Bernard DeVoto, *Across the Wide Missouri* (Boston: Houghton Mifflin Co., 1947), 257.

26. Horn, *Pioneers,* 58.

27. Ibid., 61.

28. Billington, *Western Frontier,* 101–102.

29. George R. Stewart, "The Prairie Schooner Got Them There," *American Heritage* (February 1962), 101.

30. DeVoto, *Year of Decision,* 159–164.

31. Horn, *Pioneers,* 99.

32. Ibid.

33. Ibid., 97–98, 105.

34. Ibid., 117.
35. Gabriel, *Pageant of America,* 2:204.
36. Smith, *op. cit.,* 4:84.
37. Ibid., 86–87.
38. Ibid., 87.
39. Ibid., 93.
40. Ibid., 95–96.
41. Ibid., 101–102.
42. Ibid., 100.
43. Ibid., 99.
44. Ibid., 100.
45. Ibid., 101.

Chapter 15: "Remember the Alamo!"

1. T. R. Fehrenback, *Lone Star: A History of Texas and the Texans* (New York: Macmillan, 1968), 166.
2. Seymour V. Connor and Odie B. Faulk, *North America Divided: The Mexican War 1846–1848* (New York: Oxford University Press, 1971), 7–10.
3. Fehrenback, *Lone Star,* 189.
4. Ibid., 192.
5. Connor and Faulk, *North America,* 12.
6. Fehrenback, *Lone Star,* 190.
7. Ibid., 211.
8. Ibid., 212.
9. Connor and Faulk, *North America,* 28.
10. Fehrenback, *Lone Star,* 214–215.
11. Ibid., 221.
12. Ibid., 226.
13. Ibid., 231.
14. Ibid., 233.
15. Paul I. Wellman, *The House Divides: The Age of Jackson and Lincoln . . . the Civil War* (Garden City, N.Y.: Doubleday, 1966) 161–163.
16. Fehrenback, *Lone Star,* 248.
17. Ibid., 251.
18. Albert K. Weinberg, *Manifest Destiny: A Study of Nationalistic Expansionism in American History* (Baltimore: Johns Hopkins Press, 1935), 107.
19. Ibid., 145.
20. Ernest Lee Tuveson, *Redeemer Nation: The Idea of America's Millennial Role* (Chicago: University of Chicago Press, 1968), 104–106.
21. Ibid., 158.
22. Ibid., 154.
23. Ibid., 156.
24. Herman Melville, *White-Jacket* (Evanston, Ill.: Northwestern University Press, 1970), 150–151.

25. This quote and the following one are from Lyman Beecher, *Plea for the West* (Cincinnati: Truman & Smith, 1835), 11.

26. Rush Welter, *The Mind of America 1820–1860* (New York: Columbia University Press, 1975), 52–53.

27. *Annals of America,* (Chicago: Encyclopaedia Britannica, 1968), 6:310.

Chapter 16: Sounding Forth the Trumpet

1. Harvey Wish ed., "Confessions of Nat Turner," *Slavery in the South* (New York: Farrar, Straus & Co., 1964), 8–10.

2. Kenneth M. Stampp, *The Imperiled Union: Essays on the Background of the Civil War* (New York: Oxford University Press, 1980), 243.

3. Joseph Clarke Robert, *The Road From Monticello: A Study of the Virginia Slavery Debate of 1832* (Durham, N.C.: Duke University Press, 1941), 7.

4. Louis Ruchames, *The Abolitionists: A Collection of Their Writings* (New York: G. P. Putnam's Sons, 1963), 31.

5. Robert, *Road From Monticello,* 6.

6. William Styron, "Nat Turner," *Encyclopaedia Britannica,* 1970, 22:413.

7. Arthur Young Lloyd, *The Slavery Controversy 1831–1860* (Chapel Hill: University of North Carolina Press, 1939), 20.

8. Ibid., 23.

9. Ibid., 28.

10. Robert, *Road From Monticello, 19.*

11. Ibid., 94, 21.

12. Ibid., 78–79.

13. Ibid., 25.

14. Ibid., 67.

15. Ibid., 90.

16. Ibid., 97.

17. Stampp, *Imperiled Union,* 229.

18. Ibid., 229–230.

19. Robert, *Road From Monticello,* 55.

20. Chancellor Harper, Governor Hammond, Dr. Simms, and Professor Dew, Professor Dew's essay, *The Pro-Slavery Argument; Several Essays on the Subject,* (New York: Negro University Press, 1852), 293, 325.

21. Ibid., Chancellor Harper's essay, 13.

22. Ibid., Chancellor Harper's essay, 14, 51.

23. Richard O. Boyer, *The Legend of John Brown* (New York: Alfred A. Knopf, 1973), 53.

24. Rollin G. Osterweis, *Romanticism and Nationalism in the Old South* (New Haven: Yale University Press, 1949), 5.

25. Ibid., 14.

26. Ibid., 89.

27. Ibid., 50.

28. Harper, *Pro-Slavery Argument,* 133.
29. Ruchames, *The Abolitionists,* 14.
30. Ibid.
31. Page Smith, *The Nation Comes of Age* (New York: McGraw-Hill Book Co., 1981), 4:119.
32. Ruchames, *The Abolitionists,* 17.
33. Ibid., 20.
34. Rev. Edward Beecher, *Narrative of Riots at Alton* (Alton, Ill.: George Holton, 1838), 89–91.
35. Boyer, *John Brown,* 312.
36. Ibid.
37. Arthur Lloyd, *Slavery Controversy,* 65.
38. Ibid., 191.
39. Gilbert H. Barnes, and Dwight L. Dumond, eds., *Letters of Theodore Dwight Weld Angelina Grimké Weld, and Sarah Grimké 1822–1844,* American Historical Association Series (New York: D. Appleton-Century Co., 1934), 1:146.
40. Ibid., 2:576–577.
41. Ibid., 1:120.
42. Dwight L. Dumond, *Antislavery Origins of the Civil War in the United States* (Ann Arbor: University of Michigan Press, 1959), 41–42.
43. Barnes and Dumond, *Letters,* 1:318–319.

Epilogue: *1837*

1. Charles H. Foster, *The Rungless Ladder: Harriet Beecher Stowe and New England Puritanism* (Durham, N.C.: Duke University Press, 1954), 28–29.
2. Charles M. Wiltse, *John C. Calhoun: Nullifier, 1829–1839* (Indianapolis: Bobbs-Merrill Co., 1949), 365–366.
3. Margaret L. Coit, *John C. Calhoun: American Portrait* (Boston: Houghton Mifflin Co., 1970), 311–312.
4. Richard O. Boyer, *The Legend of John Brown* (New York: Alfred A. Knopf, 1973), 314.
5. Ibid., 332–333.
6. Ida M. Tarbell, *The Life of Abraham Lincoln* (New York: Macmillan, 1923), 1:142–144.
7. Abraham Lincoln, *The Collected Works of Abraham Lincoln,* ed. Roy P. Basler (New Brunswick, N.J.: Rutgers University Press, 1953), 2:320.

Bibliography

Aaron, Daniel, ed. *America in Crisis: Fourteen Crucial Episodes in American History.* Hamden, Conn.: Archon Books, 1971.

Abbott, Shirley. "Southern Women and the Indispensable Myth." *American Heritage* 34, no. 1 (December 1982).

Adams, Charles Francis, ed. *The Works of John Adams.* Boston: Little, Brown & Co., 1854.

Adams, Ephraim Douglass. *The Power of Ideals in American History.* New Haven: Yale University Press, 1913.

Adams, Henry. *The United States in 1800.* Ithaca, N.Y.: Cornell University Press, Great Seal Books, 1960.

Adams, John Quincy. *The Diary of John Quincy Adams.* Edited by Allan Nevins. New York: Longmans, Green & Co., 1928.

———. *Writings of John Quincy Adams.* Edited by Worthington Chauncey Ford. Vols. 5 and 6. New York: Macmillan, 1915, 1916.

American Anti-Slavery Society. *American Slavery As It Is: Testimony of a Thousand Witnesses.* New York: American Anti-Slavery Society, 1839.

American Anti-Slavery Society, Executive Committee. *Slavery and the Internal Slave Trade in the United States of North America.* London: Thomas Ward & Co., 1841.

Anderson, John Q., ed. *Brokenburn: The Journal of Kate Stone.* Baton Rouge: Louisiana State University Press, 1972.

Andrist, Ralph. *To the Pacific with Lewis and Clark.* American Heritage Junior Library. New York: American Heritage Pub. Co., 1967.

Annals of America. Vol. 6. Chicago: Encyclopaedia Britannica, 1968.

Bacon, Leonard Woolsey. *A History of American Christianity.* New York: Christian Literature Co., 1907.

Bailey, Thomas A. *Probing America's Past: A Critical Examination of Major Myths and Misconceptions.* Vol. 1. Lexington, Mass.: D. C. Heath & Co., 1973.

Baldwin, Thomas. *Narrative of the Massacre, by the Savages, of the Wife and Children of Thomas Baldwin. . . .* New York: Martin & Perry Pubs., 1836.

Bancroft, George. *Bancroft's History of the United States.* 3d ed. Vol. 1. Boston: Charles C. Little & James Brown, 1838.

Barnes, Gilbert Hobbs. *The Antislavery Impulse 1830–1844.* American Historical Association Series. Gloucester, Mass.: Peter Smith, 1957.

Barnes, Gilbert H. and Dwight L. Dumond, eds. *Letters of Theodore Dwight Weld, Angelina Grimké Weld, and Sarah Grimké 1822–1844.* American Historical Association Series. Vols 1 and 2. New York: D. Appleton-Century Co., 1934.

Bates, Ernest Sutherland. *American Faith.* New York: W. W. Norton & Co., 1940.

Beardsley, Frank Grenville. *A History of American Revivals.* 3d ed. New York: American Tract Society, 1912.

Beecher, Rev. Edward. *Narrative of Riots at Alton: In Connection with the Death of Rev. Elijah P. Lovejoy.* Alton, Ill.: George Holton, 1838.

Beecher, Lyman. *The Autobiography of Lyman Beecher.* Edited by Barbara M. Cross. Vols. 1 and 2. Cambridge: Harvard University Press, Belknap Press, 1961.

———. *Plea for the West.* Cincinnati: Truman & Smith, 1835.

Bemis, Samuel Flagg. *John Quincy Adams and the Union.* New York: Alfred A. Knopf, 1956.

Berk, Stephen E. *Calvinism Versus Democracy.* Hamden, Conn.: Archon Books, 1974.

Beveridge, Albert J. *The Life of John Marshall.* Vols. 1–4. Boston: Houghton Mifflin Co., 1916–1919.

Bidwell, General John. *Echoes of the Past About California.* Edited by Milo Milton Quaife. Lakeside Classics. Chicago: R. R. Donnelley & Co., 1928.

Bidwell, John. *A Journey to California, 1841: The Journal of John Bidwell.* Berkeley, Calif.: Friends of the Bancroft Library, 1964.

Bilhartz, Terry D., ed. *Francis Asbury's America: An Album of Early American Methodism.* Grand Rapids, Mich.: Francis Asbury Press, 1984.

Billington, Ray Allen. *The Far Western Frontier 1830–1860.* New York: Harper & Bros., 1956.

Black Hawk. *Black Hawk, An Autobiography.* Edited by Donald Jackson. Urbana: University of Illinois Press, 1955.

Blassingame, John W. *The Slave Community: Plantation Life in the Antebellum South.* New York: Oxford University Press, 1979.

Bode, Carl, ed. *American Life in the 1840s.* Garden City, N.Y.: Doubleday, Anchor Books, 1967.

Bodo, John R. *The Protestant Clergy and Public Issues 1812–1848,* Princeton, N.J.: Princeton University Press, 1954.

Bowen, Catherine Drinker. *Miracle at Philadelphia: The Story of the Constitutional Convention, May to September 1787.* Boston: Little, Brown & Co., Atlantic Monthly Press Book, 1966.

Boyd, Julian P., ed. *The Papers of Thomas Jefferson.* Princeton, N.J.: Princeton University Press, 1955.

Boyer, Richard O. *The Legend of John Brown.* New York: Alfred A. Knopf, 1973.

A Brief Account of the Late Revivals of Religion in a Number of Towns in the New England States. Boston: Manning & Loring, 1797.

Bugg, James L., Jr., and Peter C. Stewart. *Jacksonian Democracy.* 2d ed. Hinsdale, Ill.: Dryden Press, 1976.

Byrne, Donald E., Jr. *No Foot of Land: Folklore of American Methodist Itinerants.* ATLA Monograph Series, no. 6. Metuchen, N.J.: Scarecrow Press and American Theological Library Assoc., 1975.

Caffrey, Kate. *The Twilight's Last Gleaming: Britain vs. America 1812–1815.* New York: Stein & Day, 1977.

Candler, Warren A. *Great Revivals and the Great Republic.* Nashville, Tenn.: Publishing House of the M. E. Church, South, 1904.

Cappon, Lester J., ed. *The Adams-Jefferson Letters, 1812–1826,* Vol. 2. Chapel Hill: University of North Carolina Press, 1959.

Carson, Kit. *Kit Carson's Autobiography.* Edited by Milo Milton Quaife. Lakeside Classics. Chicago: R. R. Donnelley & Sons Co., 1935.

Cartwright, Peter. *The Autobiography of Peter Cartwright.* New York: Carlton & Porter, 1856.

Carwardine, Richard. *Trans-atlantic Revivalism: Popular Evangelicalism in Britain and America, 1790-1865.* Westport, Conn.: Greenwood Press, 1978.

Caskey, Marie. *Chariot of Fire: Religion and the Beecher Family.* New Haven: Yale University Press, 1978.

Catton, William and Bruce. *Two Roads to Sumter.* New York: McGraw-Hill Book Co., Inc., 1963.

Cave, Alfred A. *Jacksonian Democracy and the Historians.* University of Florida Monographs. Westport, Conn. Greenwood Press, 1964.

Chevalier, Michel. *Society, Manners, and Politics in the United States: Letters on North America.* Edited by John William Ward. Garden City, N.Y.: Doubleday, 1961.

Clark, Bennett Champ. *John Quincy Adams: "Old Man Eloquent."* Boston: Little, Brown, & Co., 1932.

Clark, Elmer T., ed. *The Journals and Letters of Francis Asbury,* Vols. 1–3. Nashville, Tenn.: Abingdon Press, 1958.

Clark, Thomas D. *Frontier America: The Story of the Westward Movement.* New York: Charles Scribner's Sons, 1959.

———. *The Rampaging Frontier: Manners and Humors of Pioneer Days in the South and the Middle West.* Indianapolis: Bobbs-Merrill Co., 1939.

Clebsch, William A. *From Sacred to Profane America: The Role of Religion in American History.* New York: Harper & Row, 1968.

Cleveland, Catharine C. *The Great Revival in the West, 1797-1805.* Chicago: University of Chicago Press, 1916.

Coit, Margaret L. *John C. Calhoun: American Portrait.* Boston: Houghton Mifflin Co., 1970.

Cole, Charles C., Jr. *The Social Ideas of the Northern Evangelists 1826-1860.* New York: Octagon Books, 1966.

The Connecticut Evangelical Magazine 2, 4, and 5 (July 1801–June 1802, July 1803–June 1805).

Conner, Seymour V. and Odie B. Faulk. *North America Divided; The Mexican War 1846-1848.* New York: Oxford University Press, 1971.

Cornelison, Isaac A., *The Relation of Religion to Civil Government in the United States of America.* New York: Da Capo Press, 1970.

Cousins, Norman. *In God We Trust.* New York: Harper & Bros., 1958.

Cowley and Daniel P. Mannix. "Middle Passage." *American Heritage* 13, no. 2 (February 1962).

Craven, Avery. *The Repressible Conflict 1830-1861.* Baton Rouge: Louisiana State University Press, 1939.

Current, Richard N. *Daniel Webster and the Rise of National Conservatism.* Edited by Oscar Handlin. Boston: Little, Brown & Co., 1955.

Curtis, James C. *Andrew Jackson and the Search for Vindication.* Edited by Oscar Handlin. Boston: Little, Brown & Co., 1976.

Dana, Richard Henry. *Two Years Before the Mast: Twenty-four Years After.* Boston: Houghton Mifflin Co., 1911.

Dangerfield, George. *The Era of Good Feelings.* New York: Harcourt, Brace and World, 1952.

Davis, Burke. *Old Hickory: A Life of Andrew Jackson.* New York: Dial Press, 1977.

de Tocqueville, Alexis. *Democracy in America.* Edited by J. P. Mayer and Max Lerner. Translated by George Lawrence. New York: Harper & Row, 1966.

DeVoto, Bernard. *Across the Wide Missouri.* Boston: Houghton Mifflin Co., 1947.

———. *The Year of Decision 1846.* Boston: Houghton Mifflin Co., 1942–1943.

Dodd, William E. *Statesmen of the Old South: From Radicalism to Conservative Revolt.* New York: Macmillan, 1911.

Douglass, Frederick. *My Bondage and My Freedom.* New York: Miller, Orton, & Mulligan, 1855.

Dumond, Dwight Lowell. *Antislavery Origins of the Civil War in the United States.* Ann Arbor, Mich.: University of Michigan Press, 1959.

Dwight, Timothy. "The Nature and Danger of Infidel Philosophy." Address to the Baccalaureate Candidates, Yale College, September 9, 1797. George Bunce, Publisher.

———. "The Duty of Americans at the Present Crisis." Preached July 4, 1798. New Haven: Thomas & Samuel Green, 1798.

———. "A Discourse on Some Events of the Last Century." Delivered at the Brick Church, New Haven, January 7, 1801. New Haven: Ezra Reed, 1801.

———. "Discourse on the Public Fast." Delivered at the Chapel of Yale College, July 23, 1812. New York: J. Seymour, 1812.

———. "Discourse in Two Parts." Delivered at the Yale College Chapel, August 20, 1812. New York: J. Seymour, 1812.

Eaton, Clement. *The Civilization of the Old South: Writings of Clement Eaton.* Edited by Albert D. Kirwan. Lexington: University Press of Kentucky, 1968.

Elsbree, Oliver Wendell. *The Rise of the Missionary Spirit in America 1790–1815.* Williamsport, Penn.: Williamsport Printing & Binding Co., 1928.

Fehrenbacher, Don E. *The South and Three Sectional Crises.* Baton Rouge: Louisiana State University Press, 1980.

Fehrenback, T. R. *Lone Star: A History of Texas and the Texans.* New York: Macmillan, 1968.

Filler, Louis. *The Crusade Against Slavery 1830–1860.* The New American Nation Series. New York: Harper & Bros., 1960.

Finney, Charles G. *An Autobiography.* Westwood, N.J.: Fleming H. Revell Co., 1908.

Finney, Charles Grandison. *Lectures on Revivals of Religion.* Edited by William G. McLoughlin. Cambridge: Harvard University Press, Belknap Press, 1960.

Flint, Timothy. *Biographical Memoir of Daniel Boone.* Edited by James K. Folsom. New Haven: College and University Press, 1967.

Foster, Charles H. *The Rungless Ladder: Harriet Beecher Stowe and New England Puritanism.* Durham, N.C.: Duke University Press, 1954.

Gabriel, Ralph Henry, ed. *The Pageant of America: A Pictorial History of the United States.* Vols. 2, 3, and 8. New Haven: Yale University Press, 1925–1929.

Garrity, John A. "Marbury v. Madison: The Case of the 'Missing' Commissions." *American Heritage* 14, no. 4 (June 1963).

Gaustad, Edwin Scott, ed. *Religious Issues in American History.* New York: Harper & Row, 1817.

Genovese, Eugene D. *The Political Economy of Slavery: Studies in the Economy & Society of the Slave South.* New York: Pantheon Books, 1965.

Green, Ashbel. "A Report to the Trustees of the College of New Jersey Relative to a Revival of Religion in Winter and Spring of 1815." New Haven, 1815.

Gribbin, William. *The Churches Militant: The War of 1812 and American Religion.* New Haven: Yale University Press, 1973.

Gruver, Rebecca Brooks. *American Nationalism 1783–1830: A Self-Portrait.* New York: G. P. Putnam's Sons, 1970.

Hale, Edward Everett. *Memories of a Hundred Years.* Vol 1. New York: Macmillan, 1902.

Hardeman, Keith J. *The Spiritual Awakeners: American Revivalists from Solomon Stoddard to D. L. Moody.* Chicago: Moody Press, 1983.

Harper, Chancellor, Governor Hammond, Dr. Simms, and Professor Dew. *The Pro-Slavery Argument: Several Essays on the Subject.* New York: Negro University Press, 1852.

Harris, John. "Old Ironsides: Her Birth, Heroes and Victories." *Boston Globe* (October 16, 1977).

Hart, Albert Bushnell, ed. *National Expansion 1783–1845, Vol. 3.* American History Told by Contemporaries. New York: Macmillan, 1901.

Harvey, Peter. *Reminiscences and Anecdotes of Daniel Webster.* Boston: Little, Brown, & Co., 1890.

Heimert, Alan. *Religion and the American Mind from the Great Awakening to the Revolution.* Cambridge: Harvard University Press, 1966.

Holbrook, Stewart H. *The Yankee Exodus: An Account of Migration from New England.* New York: Macmillan, 1950.

Hone, Philip. *The Diary of Philip Hone 1828–1851.* Vols. 1 and 2. Edited by Bayard Tuckerman. New York: Dodd, Mead & Co., 1889.

Horn, Huston, *The Pioneers.* The Old West. Alexandria, Va.: Time-Life Books, 1974.

Horsman, Reginald. *The Causes of the War of 1812.* Philadelphia: University of Pennsylvania Press, 1962.

Hudson, Winthrop S., ed. *Nationalism and Religion in America: Concepts of American Identity and Mission.* New York: Harper & Row, 1970.

Interesting Memoirs and Documents Relating to American Slavery . . . Complete Emancipation. Miami, Florida: Mnemosyne Pub., 1969.

Jackson, Andrew. *Correspondence of Andrew Jackson.* Edited by John Spencer Bassett. Washington, D.C.: Carnegie Institution of Washington, 1927.

James, Marquis. *Andrew Jackson: Portrait of a President.* Indianapolis: Bobbs-Merrill Co., 1937.

———. *The Raven: A Biography of Sam Houston.* New York: Paperback Library, 1962.

Jefferson, Thomas. *The Works of Thomas Jefferson.* Edited by Paul Leicester Ford. New York: G. P. Putnam's Sons, 1905.

———. *Writings of Thomas Jefferson.* Edited by Andrew A. Lipscomb. Washington, D.C.: Thomas Jefferson Memorial Association, 1903.

Jewett, Robert. *The Captain America Complex: The Dilemma of Zealous Nationalism.* Philadelphia: Westminster Press, 1973.

Johnson, Charles A. *The Frontier Camp Meeting: Religion's Harvestime.* Dallas: Southern Methodist University Press, 1955.

Jones, Katherine M. *The Plantation South.* Indianapolis: Bobbs-Merrill Co., 1957.

Jones, Thomas H. *The Experience of Thomas H. Jones Who Was a Slave . . . Written by a Friend as Given to Him by Brother Jones.* Worcester: Henry J. Howland, 1857.

Josephy, Alvin M., Jr., ed. *The American Heritage History of the Great West.* New York: American Heritage Pub. Co., 1965.

Journals of Two Cruises Aboard the American Privateer Yankee by a Wanderer. New York: Macmillan, 1967.

Keller, Charles Roy. *The Second Great Awakening in Connecticut.* New Haven: Yale University Press, 1942.

Kistler, Rev. Charles E. *This Nation Under God.* Boston: Richard G. Badger, 1924.

Lathrop, John. "Patriotism and Religion." A sermon preached on April 25, 1799, on the National Fast Day. Boston: John Russell, 1799.

Letters of an English Traveller to His Friend in England on the "Revivals of Religion" in America. Boston: Bowles & Dearborn, 1828.

Lewis, Meriwether. *The Lewis and Clark Expedition,* 1814 ed. Vol. 1. New York: J. P. Lippincott Co., 1961.

Lewis, Walker, ed. *Speak for Yourself, Daniel: A Life of Webster in His Own Words.* Boston: Houghton Mifflin Co., 1969.

Lincoln, Abraham, *The Collected Works of Abraham Lincoln.* Vol. 2, Edited by Roy P. Basler. New Brunswick, N.J.: Rutgers University Press, 1953.

Lindsey, David. *Andrew Jackson & John C. Calhoun.* Shapers of History Series. Edited by Kenneth C. Colegrove. Woodbury, N.Y.: Barron's Educational Series, 1973.

Liston, Robert. *Slavery in America: The History of Slavery.* Of Black America Series. New York: McGraw-Hill Book Co., 1970.

Lloyd, Allan. *The Scorching of Washington: The War of 1812.* Newton Abbot: David & Charles, 1974.

Lloyd, Arthur Young. *The Slavery Controversy 1831–1860.* Chapel Hill: University of North Carolina Press, 1939.

Lord, Walter. *The Dawn's Early Light.* New York: W. W. Norton & Co., 1972.

Loth, David. *Chief Justice: John Marshall and the Growth of the Republic.* New York: W. W. Norton & Co., 1949.

Loveland, Anne C. *Southern Evangelicals and the Social Order 1800–1860.* Baton Rouge: Louisiana State University Press, 1980.

Lynd, Staughton. *Class Conflict, Slavery, and the United States Constitution.* Indianapolis; Bobbs-Merrill Co., 1967.

McCaskey, Marie. *Chariot of Fire: Religion and the Beecher Family.* New Haven: Yale University Press, 1978.

McLoughlin, William G., Jr. *Modern Revivalism: Charles Grandison Finney to Billy Graham.* New York: Ronald Press Co., 1959.

McLoughlin, William G. *Revivals, Awakenings, and Reform: An Essay on Religion and Social Change in America 1607–1977.* Edited by Martin E. Marty. Chicago History of American Religion. Chicago: University of Chicago Press, 1978.

McNemar, Richard. *The Kentucky Revival.* New York: Edward O. Jenkins, 1846.

Madison, James. *Notes of Debates in the Federal Convention of 1787.* New York: W. W. Norton & Co., 1966.

Marshall, Peter, and David Manuel. *The Light and the Glory.* Old Tappan, N.J.: Fleming H. Revell Co., 1977.

Masters, Al. "George Washington's Forgotten People." *American History Illustrated* 19, no. 10 (February 1985).

Mathews, Donald G. *Religion in the Old South.* Edited by Martin E. Marty. Chicago History of American Religion. Chicago: University of Chicago Press, 1977.

Mead, Sidney E. *The Lively Experiment: The Shape of Christianity in America.* New York: Harper & Row, 1963.

Melville, Herman. *White-Jacket.* Evanston, Ill.: Northwestern University Press, 1970.

Merk, Frederick. *Manifest Destiny and Mission in American History: A Reinterpretation.* New York: Alfred A. Knopf, 1963.

Merrill, Pastor Daniel. "Balaam Disappointed." Thanksgiving sermon at Nottingham-West, Concord, Mass., April 13, 1815. Concord: Isaac Hill, 1816.

Miller, John Chester. *The Wolf by the Ears: Thomas Jefferson and Slavery.* New York: Macmillan, Free Press, 1977.

Miller, Perry. *The Life of the Mind in America from the Revolution to the Civil War.* Books 1–3. New York: Harcourt, Brace & World, 1966.

Monroe, James. *Writings of James Monroe.* Vol. 4. Edited by Stanislaus Murray Hamilton. New York: G. P. Putnam's Sons, 1902.

———. *The Writings of James Monroe.* Edited by Stanislaus Murray Hamilton. New York: AMS Press, 1969.

Moore, Arthur K. *Frontier Mind: A Cultural Analysis of the Kentucky Frontiersman.* Lexington: University Press of Kentucky, 1957.

Moore, Glover. *The Missouri Controversy 1819–1821.* Lexington: University Press of Kentucky, 1953.

Morgan, Dale L. *Jedediah Smith and the Opening of the West.* Indianapolis: Bobbs-Merrill Co., 1953.

Morgan, Edmund S. *American Slavery—American Freedom.* New York: W. W. Norton & Co., 1975.

Morison, Samuel Eliot, Frederick Merk, and Frank Freidel. *Dissent in Three American Wars.* Cambridge, Mass.: Harvard University Press, 1970.

Morris, Gouverneur. *Diary and Letters of Gouverneur Morris.* Vol. 2. Edited by Anne Cary Morris. New York: Charles Scribner's Sons, 1888.

Morse, Jedidah. "A Sermon Delivered at Charlestown" on July 23, 1812. Samuel Etheridge, Jr., 1812.

Mortimer, Rev. Benjamin. Diary of the Rev. Benjamin Mortimer dated April 1798, courtesy of Mrs. Frank W. Renwick of Scottsdale, Arizona.

Mulder, John M., and John F. Wilson, eds. *Religion in American History: Interpretive Essays.* Englewood Cliffs, N.J.: Prentice-Hall, 1978.

Nagel, Paul C. *Descent From Glory: Four Generations of the John Adams Family.* New York: Oxford University Press, 1983.

———. *This Sacred Trust: American Nationality 1798–1898.* New York: Oxford University Press, 1971.

Nichols, Roy F. *Religion and American Democracy.* Baton Rouge: Louisiana State University Press, 1959.

Nock, Albert Jay. *Jefferson.* American Century Series. New York: Hill & Wang, 1960.

Nye, Russel Blaine. *Society and Culture in America 1830–1860.* New York: Harper & Row, 1974.

Ogg, Frederic Austin. *Builders of the Republic.* New Haven: Yale University Press, 1927.

Olmsted, Frederick Law. *The Cotton Kingdom: A Traveller's Observations on Cotton and Slavery in the American Slave States.* Edited by Arthur M. Schlesinger. New York: Alfred A. Knopf, 1953.

Osterweis, Rollin G. *Romanticism and Nationalism in the Old South.* New Haven: Yale University Press, 1949.

Padover, Saul K., ed. *The Complete Jefferson.* Freeport, N.Y.: Books for Libraries Press, 1943.

Padover, Saul K. *Jefferson.* New York: New American Library, Mentor, 1959.

Parish, Elijah. "A Protest Against the War." A discourse delivered at Byfield. Newburyport: A. W. Allen, 1812.

Parkman, Francis. *The Oregon Trail.* Garden City, N.Y.: Doubleday, 1946.

Perkins, Bradford, ed. *The Causes of the War of 1812: National Honor or National Interest?* American Problem Studies. New York: Holt, Rinehart & Winston, 1962.

Phares, Ross. *Bible in Pocket, Gun in Hand: The Story of Frontier Religion.* Garden City, N.Y.: Doubleday, 1964.

Phillips, Ulrich Bonnell. *The Course of the South to Secession.* Edited by E. Merton Coulter. New York: D. Appleton-Century Co., 1939.

———. *Life and Labor in the Old South.* Boston: Little, Brown & Co., 1929.

Plumer, William, Jr. *The Missouri Compromises and Presidential Politics 1820–1825.* Edited by Everett Sommerville Brown. New York: Da Capo Press, 1970.

Potter, David M. *The South and the Sectional Conflict.* Baton Rouge: Louisiana State University Press, 1968.

Pratt, Julius W. *Expansionists of 1812.* New York: Macmillan, 1925.

Raboteau, Albert J. *Slave Religion: The "Invisible Institution" in the Antebellum South.* New York: Oxford University Press, 1978.

Remini, Robert V. *Andrew Jackson and the Course of American Freedom, 1822–1832.* Vol. 2. New York: Harper & Row, 1981.

———. *The Revolutionary Age of Andrew Jackson.* New York: Harper & Row, 1976.

Riegel, Robert E. *Young America.* Westport, Conn.: Greenwood Press, 1973.

Robert, Joseph Clarke. *The Road From Monticello: A Study of The Virginia Slavery Debate of 1832.* Durham, N.C.: Duke University Press, 1941.

Rozwenc, Edwin C., ed. *Ideology and Power in the Age of Jackson.* New York: New York University Press, 1964.

———. *The Meaning of Jacksonian Democracy.* Problems in American Civilization. Boston: D. C. Heath & Co., 1963.

Ruchames, Louis, *The Abolitionists: A Collection of Their Writings.* New York: G. P. Putnam's Sons, 1963.

Rudolph, L. D. *Francis Asbury.* Nashville: Abingdon Press, 1966.

Rugoff, Milton. *The Beechers: An American Family in the Nineteenth Century.* New York: Harper & Row, 1981.

Savage, Henry, Jr. *Seeds of Time.* New York: Henry Holt & Co., 1959.

Schermerhorn, John F., and Samuel J. Mills. *A Correct View of that Part of the United States Which Lies West of the Allegany Mountains With Regard to Religion and Morals.* Hartford: Peter B. Gleason & Co., 1814.

Sears, Stephen W. "Trail Blazer of the Far West" *American Heritage* 14, no. 4 (June 1963).

Sellers, Charles, ed. *Andrew Jackson, Nullification, and the State-Rights Tradition.* Chicago: Rand-McNally & Co., 1963.

Seward, William H. "The Life and Public Services of John Quincy Adams with the Eulogy . . . Auburn." Harry Miller & Co., 1851.

Silverman, Kenneth. *Timothy Dwight.* New York: Twayne Publishers, 1969.

Sisson, Daniel. *The American Revolution of 1800.* New York: Alfred A. Knopf, 1974.

Slave Narratives: A Folk History of Slavery in the U.S. From Interviews with Former Slaves. Vol. 14. Washington, D.C.: Federal Writers Project, 1941.

Smith, Chard Powers. *Yankees and God.* New York: Hermitage House, 1954.

Smith, James Ward, and A. Leland Jamison, eds. *The Shaping of American Religion.* Vol. 1. Religion in American Life. Princeton, N.J.: Princeton University Press, 1961.

———. *Religious Perspectives in American Culture.* Vol. 2. Religion in American Life. Princeton, N.J.: Princeton University Press, 1961.

Smith, Margaret Bayard. *The First Forty Years of Washington Society.* New York: Charles Scribner's Sons, 1906.

Smith, Page. *The Shaping of America.* Vol. 3. New York: McGraw-Hill Book Co., 1980.

———. *The Nation Comes of Age.* Vol. 4. New York: McGraw-Hill Book Co., 1981.

Smith, Timothy L. *Revivalism and Social Reform in Mid-Nineteenth-Century America.* New York: Abingdon Press, 1957.

Speer, Rev. William. *The Great Revival of 1800.* Philadelphia: Presbyterian Board of Publication, 1872.

The Spirit of the Pilgrims, Vols. 3 and 4. Boston: Peirce & Parker, 1830, 1831.

Stampp, Kenneth M. *The Causes of the Civil War.* Englewood Cliffs, N.J.: Prentice-Hall, 1959.

———. *The Imperiled Union: Essays on the Background of the Civil War.* New York: Oxford University Press, 1980.

Stephenson, George M. *The Puritan Heritage.* New York: Macmillan, 1952.

Stewart, George R. *The California Trail: An Epic with Many Heroes.* The American Trails Series. Edited by A. B. Guthrie, Jr. New York: McGraw-Hill Book Co., 1971.

———. "The Prairie Schooner Got Them There." *American Heritage* 13, no. 2 (February 1962).

Story, Justice. *An Address on Chief Justice Marshall.* Rochester, N.Y.: The Lawyers Co-operative Publishing Company, 1900.

Sullivan, Maurice S. *The Travels of Jedediah Smith.* Santa Ana, Calif.: Fine Arts Press, 1934.

The Suppressed Book About Slavery. New York: Arno Press and the New York Times, 1968.

Swanson, Neil H. *The Perilous Fight.* New York: Farrar and Rinehart, 1945.

Sweet, William Warren. *Religion in the Development of American Culture 1765–1840.* New York: Charles Scribner's Sons, 1952.

———. *Revivalism in America: Its Origin, Growth and Decline.* New York: Charles Scribner's Sons, 1944.

Tarbell, Ida M. *The Life of Abraham Lincoln.* Vols. 1 and 2. New York: Macmillan, 1923.

Taylor, William R. *Cavalier and Yankee: The Old South and American National Character.* New York: George Braziller, 1961.

Tefft, Rev. B. F. *Webster and His Master-Pieces.* Vols. 1 and 2. Buffalo: Miller, Orton & Mulligan, 1854.

Thomas, Benjamin P. *Theodore Weld: Crusader for Freedom.* New Brunswick, N.J.: Rutgers University Press, 1950.

Time, Bicentennial Issue #2. "The New Nation," "September 26, 1789" 107, No. 21.

Tucker, Glenn. *Poltroons and Patriots: A Popular Account of the War of 1812.* Vols. 1 and 2. Indianapolis: Bobbs-Merrill Co., 1954.

Tuveson, Ernest Lee. *Redeemer Nation: The Idea of America's Millennial Role.* Chicago: University of Chicago Press, 1968.

Van Deusen, Glyndon G. *The Life of Henry Clay.* Boston: Little, Brown & Co., 1937.

———. *The Rise and Decline of Jacksonian Democracy.* Anvil Series. Gen. ed. Louis L. Snyder. Huntington, N.Y.: Robert E. Krieger Pub. Co., 1970.

Wallace, Adam. *The Parson of the Islands: A Biography of the Late Rev. Joshua Thomas. . . .* Philadelphia: Methodist Home Journal, 1872.

Wayland, Francis. "The Duties of an American Citizen." Two Discourses Delivered in the First Baptist Meeting House in Boston, on Thursday, April 7, 1825. Boston: James Loring, 1825.

———. *The Moral Law of Accumulation.* 2d. ed. Boston: Gould, Kendall & Lincoln, 1837.

Weigle, Luther A. *American Idealism.* The Pageant of America. New Haven: Yale University Press, 1928.

Weinberg, Albert K. *Manifest Destiny: A Study of Nationalistic Expansionism in American History.* Baltimore: Johns Hopkins Press, 1935.

Weinstein, Allen, and Frank Otto Gatell, eds. *American Negro Slavery: A Modern Reader.* New York: Oxford University Press, 1968.

Weisberger, Bernard A. *They Gathered at the River: The Story of the Great Revivalists and Their Impact Upon Religion in America.* Boston: Little, Brown, & Co., 1958.

Wellman, Paul I. *The House Divides: The Age of Jackson and Lincoln . . . the Civil War.* Garden City, N.Y.: Doubleday, 1966.

Welter, Rush. *The Mind of America 1820–1860.* New York: Columbia University Press, 1975.

Willison, George F. *Behold Virginia.* New York: Harcourt, Brace & Co., 1952.

Wiltse, Charles M. *John C. Calhoun: Nullifier, 1829–1839.* Indianapolis: Bobbs-Merrill Co., 1949.

———. *John C. Calhoun: Sectionalist, 1840–1850.* New York: Russell & Russell, 1951.

Winthrop, John. *The Winthrop Papers: 1623–1630,* Vol. 2. Boston: Massachusetts Historical Society, 1931.

Wish, Harvey, ed. *Slavery in the South: First-hand Accounts of the Ante-Bellum American Southland. . . .* New York: Farrar, Straus & Co., 1964.

Wood, Gordon S., ed. *The Rising Glory of America, 1760–1820.* New York: George Braziller, 1971.

Woodward, C. Vann, ed. *Mary Chesnut's Civil War.* New Haven and London: Yale University Press, 1981.

Wright, Louis B. *Life on the American Frontier.* Capricorn Books. New York: G. P. Putnam's Sons, 1971.

Index

Dana read Mar-Apr, 2009